IMAGES OF THE HUMAN

D1367371

IMAGES OF THE HUMAN

THE PHILOSOPHY OF THE HUMAN PERSON
IN A RELIGIOUS CONTEXT

Edited by

Hunter Brown
Dennis L. Hudecki
Leonard A. Kennedy
John J. Snyder

Loyola
Press
Chicago

CONTRIBUTORS

Sister Prudence Allen, R.S.M., Ph.D.
Concordia University, Montreal

Hunter Brown, Ph.D.
King's College, University of Western Ontario

Desmond J. FitzGerald, Ph.D.
University of San Francisco

John J. Haldane, Ph.D.
St. Andrews, University of Scotland

R. E. Houser, Ph.D.
University of St. Thomas, Houston

Dennis L. Hudecki, Ph.D.
Brescia College, University of Western Ontario

Deal W. Hudson, Ph.D.
Fordham University

Reverend Leonard A. Kennedy, C.S.B., Ph.D.
St. Peter's Seminary, University of Western Ontario

Janine D. Langan, Licence ès Lettres Modernes
St. Michael's College, University of Toronto

John D. Morgan, Ph.D.
King's College, University of Western Ontario

Reverend Michael T. Ryan, Ph.D.
St. Peter's Seminary, University of Western Ontario

John J. Snyder, Ph.D.
King's College, University of Western Ontario

Celia Wolf-Devine, Ph.D.
Stonehill College, North Easton, Massachusetts

© 1995 Leonard A. Kennedy
All rights reserved
Printed in the United States of America
∞

Loyola Press
3441 North Ashland Avenue
Chicago, Illinois 60657

Cover design by Diana Rigas.
Interior design by Diana Rigas and Jill Mark Salyards.
Cover and interior illustrations by John MacDonald.

Library of Congress Cataloging-in-Publication Data
Images of the human : the philosophy of the human person
    in a religious context / edited by Leonard A. Kennedy . . .
[et al.].
        p.   cm.
    Includes bibliographical references and index.
    ISBN 0-8294-0826-6 (alk. paper)
    1. Man 2. Philosophical anthropology. 3. Agent
(Philosophy) 4. Man (Christian theology) I. Kennedy,
Leonard A.
    BD450.I4596 1995
    128—dc20   95-8782
                                                        CIP

The use of selections from copyrighted material has been graciously granted by the following publishers and copyright proprietors.

Aquinas, Thomas, *Summa Theologiae*, translated by the Fathers of the English Dominican Province, and published by Burns, Oates, and Washbourne Ltd., Westminster, 1911, 1913, reprinted with the permission of Burns and Oates Ltd.

Aristotle, *De Anima* [On Soul], translated by J. A. Smith, and published by Oxford University Press, 1931, revised by R. E. Houser.

Augustine, *On the Trinity*, translated by A. W. Haddan, Edinburgh, 1873; *The Confessions*, translated by J. G. Pilkington, Edinburgh, 1882; *The City of God*, translated by M. Dods and J. J. Smith, Edinburgh, 1881. With improvements in the translations by L. A. Kennedy.

Becker, Ernest, *The Denial of Death*, copyright 1973 by The Free Press, with permission of The Free Press, a member of Paramount Publishing.

de Beauvoir, Simone, *The Second Sex*, translated by H. M. Parshley, copyright 1952, and renewed 1980 by Alfred A. Knopf, Inc., with permission of the publisher; *Memoirs of a Dutiful Daughter*, translated by James Kirkup, copyright 1958 by Librairie Gallimard, with permission of HarperCollins Publishers; *Les écrits de Simone de Beauvoir*, by Claude Francis and Fernande Gontier, copyright 1979 by Editions Gallimard, with permission of Editions Gallimard.

Descartes, René, *Discourse on Method*, translated by E. S. Haldane and G. R. T. Ross, Cambridge University Press, 1912, corrected in 1934, with permission of Cambridge University Press.

Freud, Sigmund, *Civilization and Its Discontents*, translated by James Strachey, with the permission of W. W. Norton & Company, Inc. Copyright 1961 by James Strachey, renewed 1989 by Alix Strachey.

Hume, David, *A Treatise of Human Nature*, 1739, edited by L. A. Selby-Bigge, London, 1888, 1896. With modernization by L. A. Kennedy.

James, William, *Principles of Psychology*, 1890, and *Psychology: Briefer Course*, 1892.

Kierkegaard, Søren, *Concluding Unscientific Postscript to the Philosophical Fragments*, copyright 1941 and renewed; [*Fear and Trembling* and] *The Sickness unto Death*, copyright 1954 and renewed; *Philosophical Fragments, or a Fragment of Philosophy*, copyright 1962 and renewed; *Either/Or*, copyright 1959 and renewed—all with permission of Princeton University Press. *The Journals of Kierkegaard*, 1959, with permission of Alfred A. Knopf, Inc.

Marx, Karl, *The Communist Manifesto,* translated by S. Moore, London 1888; *Karl Marx: Selected Writings,* translated and edited by D. McLellen, Oxford University Press, 1977, with permission of the publisher, Oxford University Press.

Nietzsche, Friedrich, *The Will to Power,* translated by Walter Kaufmann, copyright 1967 by Walter Kaufmann, with permission of Random House, Inc.

Plato, *Phaedo,* translated by B. Jowett, 1892, as abridged and revised by R. E. Houser.

Sartre, Jean-Paul, *Existentialism,* Philosophical Library, 1957, with permission of Philosophical Library.

Skinner, B. F., *Beyond Freedom and Dignity,* copyright 1971 by B. F. Skinner, with permission of Alfred A. Knopf, Inc. *Science and Human Behavior,* copyright 1953, 1981, by B. F. Skinner, and *Walden Two,* copyright 1948, 1976, by B. F. Skinner— both with the permission of Macmillan College Publishing Company.

Stein, Edith, "Problems of Women's Education," in *Essays on Woman,* translated by Freda Mary Oben, Ph.D., copyright 1987, Washington Province of the Discalced Carmelites, Inc. ICS Publications, 2131 Lincoln Road N.E., Washington, D.C. 20002 U.S.A, from *The Collected Works of Edith Stein.*

Unamuno, Miguel de, *The Tragic Sense of Life,* translated by J. E. C. Flitch, London, 1921.

Wittgenstein, Ludwig, *Philosophical Investigations,* New York, 1953, and *Remarks on the Philosophy of Psychology,* Oxford, 1980—both with the permission of Basil Blackwood, Ltd.

TABLE OF CONTENTS

Preface   xvii

1. **Plato: The Human Person as Spirit**   1
   Introduction and commentary by R. E. HOUSER
     Introduction   3
     Selected Text   9
       Phaedo
     Commentary   29

2. **Aristotle: The Human Person as a Besouled Body**   49
   Introduction and commentary by R. E. HOUSER
     Introduction   51
     Selected Text   55
       De Anima [On Soul]
     Commentary   69

3. **Saint Augustine: The Human Person as
   Relational and Volitional**   89
   Introduction and commentary
   by LEONARD A. KENNEDY

Introduction 91
Selected Texts 95
  On the Trinity
  The Confessions
  The City of God
Commentary 107

4. **Saint Thomas Aquinas: The Human Person
as Embodied Spirit** **119**
Introduction and commentary
by LEONARD A. KENNEDY
  Introduction 121
  Selected Text 125
    Summa Theologiae
  Commentary 135

5. **René Descartes: The Human Person as a Dualism** **147**
Introduction and commentary
by DESMOND J. FITZGERALD
  Introduction 149
  Selected Text 155
    Discourse on Method
  Commentary 167

6. **David Hume: The Human Person as a Construct** **183**
Introduction and commentary by HUNTER BROWN
  Introduction 185
  Selected Text 191
    A Treatise of Human Nature
  Commentary 203

7. **Søren Kierkegaard: The Human Person
as a Collision of Opposites** **213**
Introduction and commentary
by DENNIS L. HUDECKI
  Introduction 215
  Selected Texts 221
    The Journals of Kierkegaard
    *Concluding Unscientific Postscript to the
      Philosophical Fragments*
    The Sickness unto Death
    Either/Or

*Philosophical Fragments, or a Fragment of
Philosophy*
Commentary   235

8. Karl Marx: The Human Person as Worker   **251**
Introduction and commentary
by MICHAEL T. RYAN
   Introduction   253
   Selected Texts   257
      On the Jewish Question
      Grundrisse
      The German Ideology
      Capital
      *Toward a Critique of Hegel's Philosophy of
         Right: Introduction*
      The Communist Manifesto
   Commentary   277

9. William James: The Human Person as Elusive **295**
Introduction and commentary by HUNTER BROWN
   Introduction   297
   Selected Texts   305
      Principles of Psychology
      Psychology: Briefer Course
   Commentary   319

**10. Friedrich Nietzsche: The Human Person
   as Will to Power**   **331**
Introduction and commentary by JOHN J. SNYDER
   Introduction   333
   Selected Text   337
      The Will to Power
   Commentary   351

11. Sigmund Freud: The Human Person as Sexual **367**
Introduction and commentary
by DEAL W. HUDSON
   Introduction   369
   Selected Text   375
      Civilization and Its Discontents
   Commentary   385

**12. Edith Stein: The Human Person
as Male and Female**   397
Introduction and commentary
by PRUDENCE ALLEN
   Introduction   399
   Selected Text   405
     Essays on Woman
   Commentary   419

**13. Ludwig Wittgenstein: The Human Person
as Linguistic Animal**   433
Introduction and commentary
by JOHN J. HALDANE
   Introduction   435
   Selected Texts   443
     Philosophical Investigations
     Remarks on the Philosophy of Psychology
   Commentary   457

14. B. F. Skinner: The Human Person as Necessitated   467
Introduction and commentary
by CELIA WOLF-DEVINE
   Introduction   469
   Selected Texts   473
     Beyond Freedom and Dignity
     Science and Human Behavior
     Walden Two
   Commentary   489

15. Jean-Paul Sartre: The Human Person as Freedom   505
Introduction and commentary
by LEONARD A. KENNEDY
   Introduction   507
   Selected Text   511
     Existentialism
   Commentary   523

**16. Simone de Beauvoir: The Human Person
as Co-existent**   **535**
Introduction and commentary
by JANINE D. LANGAN
    Introduction   537
    Selected Texts   545
      The Second Sex
      Memoirs of a Dutiful Daughter
      Les écrits de Simone de Beauvoir
    Commentary   561

**17. Miguel de Unamuno and Ernest Becker:
The Human Person as Mortal**   **577**
Introduction and commentary
by JOHN D. MORGAN
    Introduction   579
    Selected Texts
      Unamuno, Selected Text   583
       The Tragic Sense of Life
      Becker, Selected Text   587
       The Denial of Death
    Commentary   597

PREFACE

The philosophy of the human person is important because human beings live in accordance with their understanding of themselves. Those approaching this philosophy already have an implicit understanding of themselves. But, since life is so important, they should make this understanding explicit. To achieve this explication, a knowledge of what some of the world's most significant writers have said about the human person can be of great help, especially if readers have a guide in this search. The poet Alexander Pope said, "the proper study of mankind is man," indicating that it is most natural, and indeed necessary, for us to know as much as possible about ourselves.

This book is the collective effort of thirteen professors who have spent many years teaching college-level course involving the philosophy of the human person. We have prepared an approach to this philosophy that represents generous selections from the significant writers we have referred to but that also introduces these selections to the reader, analyzes them, and evaluates them philosophically.

To give an idea of some of the many conflicting views about the human person, this book considers philosophers who say that there is no human soul, that there is a soul but that it is not immortal, and that there is a soul but that it is immortal; those who say that we are truly free when our freedom is limited, that we are truly free when our freedom is unlimited, and that we have no freedom at all; and those who say that the most important human concern is economics, that it is sex, and that it is God. Indeed, the selections have been chosen to give a great variety of complementary and even contradictory teaching about the human person, so that the reader is forced to face them and to decide about them.

To limit our consideration to philosophy alone, however, would be a mistake. If we limit our understanding of the human person to what we can learn from the empirical sciences, such as psychology or sociology, we deprive ourselves of the deeper insights provided by philosophy. Similarly, if we limit our understanding of the human person to what we can learn from philosophy, we deprive ourselves of the further help of revealed religion. This book therefore, while remaining philosophical, calls attention to the relationship between what the philosophers say and what religion teaches, particularly the Judeo-Christian religion. Other books in the philosophy of the human person do not make this relationship explicit.

In choosing authors for inclusion in this book we have selected those who have had an acknowledged impact on the understanding of human nature and who, at least in the text we have selected from them, are relatively easy to read. We have also chosen selections that deal with a large number of different aspects of our topic.

Even readers approaching the study of these authors for the first time will benefit from reading what the authors themselves have written. An introduction or a commentary can be helpful in pinpointing difficulties and dealing with them, but this is not enough. One wants, when possible, to have a firsthand knowledge of what is being discussed.

We direct our lives according to the image we have of ourselves. We have chosen "Images of the Human" as the title of this book in order to emphasize how important our self-image is. And, since the philosophical and religious component of our self-image is its most significant component, we urge the reader to enter into dialogue with some of the most influential image-makers of all time.

These men and women are presented here in a chronological order, but the reader is invited to browse at random.

It might be pointed out that a study of the philosophy of human nature can be an excellent introduction to philosophy in general because, in studying the human, it is necessary to bring everything else into consideration. We are, as Alexander Pope indicates, the focus of all our study. In dealing with the human person we must deal with knowledge, the soul, the will, freedom, immortality, God, the purpose of life, and gender and sexuality.

The editors would like to pay special thanks to Jeremy Langford, Managing Editor of Loyola Press, for his many suggestions for improving the organization and readability of this book.

The Editors

1

PLATO

· · ·

THE HUMAN PERSON AS SPIRIT
Introduction and Commentary by R. E. Houser

INTRODUCTION

■ ■ ■

Plato and Philosophy

The word *philosophy* is a compound the Greeks created from *phil-* (love) and *sophia* (wisdom). The Athenian statesman Pericles (495–429 B.C.) used it in a general sense to describe the Athenians in his famous funeral oration: "We love beauty, but without extravagance; and we love wisdom, but without becoming soft" (Thucydides, *Peloponnesian War* 2.40). But the first Greek intellectuals, including the poets Homer (ca. 850 B.C.) and Hesiod (ca. 750 B.C.), the early scientist Thales (ca. 600 B.C.), and the first real philosopher Parmenides (ca. 485 B.C.), were called sages *(sophoi)*. Their approach to life and thought was aristocratic. The rise of the political democracy in the fifth century B.C. produced new teachers, who called themselves Sophists. The Sophists invented rhetoric and sought a wisdom useful for democratic politics. The Sophist Gorgias was the first to use *philosophers* to designate a special group—Sophists committed to teaching the truth. Foremost among them was Socrates (470–400 B.C.), who was called a philosopher first by the rhetorician Isocrates (436–338 B.C.) and then by Plato (429–347 B.C.). Unfortunately, these two disagreed over Socrates' definition of wisdom. Isocrates thought philosophy should follow "the common opinions of the Greeks" (*Antidosis* 84); Plato said it should rise above opinions to a goal of true and certain knowledge.

■ ■ ■

Plato's Works

Socrates never recorded his thoughts in writing. To pass on the inspiration he had received from Socrates, Plato composed Socratic dramas, called dialogues, whose characters were real Greeks (not the mythic characters of Greek tragedy) who had actually conversed with Socrates, and whose hero was Socrates himself. During 390 B.C., Plato wrote short dialogues usually showing the search for, but not the achievement of, some ethical concept related to wisdom. The most important of these dialogues are set around Socrates' trial: *Euthyphro* (about piety); *Apology* (Socrates' speech in his own defense); and *Crito* (about justice). Other early dialogues include *Charmides* (about self-control), *Lysis* (about friendship), *Laches* (about courage), and *Ion* (about art).

After visiting Sicily in 387 B.C., Plato founded a school in Athens to rival the one Isocrates had started. Plato called his school the Academy, and it lasted until A.D. 529. In one group of dialogues, which fall under the category known as his middle dialogues, Plato undercut Isocrates by having Socrates attack Sophists and their students: in the *Protagoras, Cratylus, Meno, Euthydemus, Gorgias, Menexenus,* and *Phaedrus.* The Athenians, such as Pericles, who followed the Sophists had built a city of possessions, not of moral excellence: "With no regard for self-control or justice they stuffed our state with harbors and docks and walls and tribute money and all such nonsense" (*Gorgias* 519a). In the other middle dialogues, widely acknowledged to be his masterpieces, Plato showed Socrates "turning the souls" of his followers toward true reality, and uncovering genuine wisdom: *Phaedo; Symposium,* a drinking party at which the guests offer speeches in praise of love; and *Republic,* about a truly just, utopian city-state. All three cover the broad range of Plato's philosophy, and Socrates attempts to induce in his companions an organized vision of the whole of reality that he, the fully wise philosopher, has.

Plato never lost the political inspiration for his work; consequently, his last book, *Laws*, is devoted to founding a city that could actually exist. But his other later dialogues, all written for advanced students in his school, are detailed and argumentative treatments of the principles in various areas of philosophical research: *Timaeus* (the origin and nature of the physical universe), *Parmenides* (being), *Philebus* (pleasure), *Theatetus* (knowledge), and *Sophist* and *Statesman* (politics).

■ ■ ■

Phaedo

Phaedo, the dialogue chosen for study here, deals with the immortality of the human soul. At the beginning, Echecrates, from the remote village of Phlius, wonders why Socrates was not immediately executed after his trial. It turns out that Athens was holding a religious commemoration in honor of Theseus's mythical trip to Crete, during which time no one could be executed. Theseus had gone to rescue seven Athenian youths and seven maidens from the Minotaur, who lived in the depths of the labyrinth (an underground maze), and to whom the fourteen were to be sacrificed. Guided by the thread Ariadne had given him, Theseus had gone in, slain the monster, and led everyone out. The myth serves as a metaphor for the dialogue. After Socrates' wife Xanthippe is unceremoniously led away, fourteen of Socrates' followers are left in the cell, not counting Phaedo, who is like Ariadne in offering us the thread of the dialogue. Socrates is like Theseus; death is like the Minotaur; and the twists and turns of the long argument in the dialogue are like the labyrinth. We must follow the dialogue in order to slay our own fear of death by coming to understand the immortality of the soul.

One way in which the *Phaedo* is labyrinthine concerns the way questions about the soul arise. It is not a systematic treatise. Socrates starts with what is uppermost in the minds of everyone, the immortality of his own soul. All present simply assume humans have souls. But there is good reason for such an assumption: inanimate things like rocks act differently from animate things. A dog moves across the marketplace to sniff out Socrates; but for a rock to move, Socrates must pick it up and throw it. There must be something in the dog, or in Socrates, that is the internal source causing life activities. The Greek word for this internal source is *psyche* (from which comes *psychology*), and in Latin *anima* (from which comes *animate*). Soul in this sense is an internal principle of life activity. While its nature is not obvious, the inference to its existence is as natural as that from visible smoke to unseen fire, an inference proceeding from effect (visible life activities) to cause (soul). Roses, centipedes, and humans all have some internal principle of life, even if it is purely physical. The initial issue in the dialogue is whether the *kind* of internal principle humans do have lives on after death.

The *Phaedo* is also labyrinthine in the way its arguments are developed. Like the labyrinth's tunnels, the paths of argument cross and recross. Socrates has been putting Aesop's fables into verse, and Plato arranges the dialogue according to the structure of a Greek lyric poem. Such poems have three parts: strophe, followed by an opposing antistrophe, and ending with an epode. The *Phaedo* follows this basic structure (see the commentary for points of detail in each section):

I. Strophe: Into the Labyrinth of Arguments
  A. The Theseus myth (57a–63b)
    B. Socrates' Speech (63b–69e)
      C. Cebes' Wonder (69e–70b)
        D. Argument from Opposites (70b–72e)
          E. Recollection Argument (72e–77a)
            F. Indestructibility Argument (77a–80d)
              G/G'. Transition: Reincarnation
                    Myth (80d–84b)
II. Antistrophe: Out of the Labyrinth of Arguments
    (working in reverse order)
              F'. Simmias' Harmony
                    Counterargument (84c–86e)
            E'. Cebes' Weaver Counterargument
                    (86e–88c)
          D'. Socrates Replies to Simmias (88c–95a)

C'. Socrates' Wonder (95a–102a)
B'. Socrates Replies to Cebes (102b–107c)
A'. Cosmic Myth (107c–115a)
III. Epode: The Death of Socrates' Body (115a–118b)

■ ■ ■

What to Look For in the Selection

General Questions

1. Each section of the dialogue is designed to lead your mind to the overall conclusion that the soul is immortal. But different parts of the dialogue try to reach this conclusion in different ways. For each section, ask yourself: *How* is this section leading to the overall conclusion? Is Plato appealing to me through poetry and myth, or through rhetoric (effective speechmaking), or through philosophical argument?
2. For each section, ask yourself: Are the points made in this section (1) leading to the conclusion that the soul is immortal, (2) presenting a *difficulty* getting in the way, or (3) offering a way to *solve* such a difficulty?
3. Each section in the strophe (Part I) is designed to lead to the next section while simultaneously pointing to the corresponding part of the antistrophe (e.g., B leads to C, but also points forward to B'). Ask yourself how each section fits this pattern.
4. Likewise, each section of the antistrophe (Part II) is designed to flow out of the preceding section of the antistrophe while simultaneously resolving some problem in the corresponding section of the strophe (e.g., C' flows from D' and resolves a problem in C). Ask yourself how each section does this.

Specific Questions

For section C: Explain what is involved in Cebes' wonder. Is it necessary for philosophy to start in wonder?

For D: Is the argument from opposites deductive or inductive?

For E: Why does Socrates think it necessary to hold the initially implausible theory that learning is recollecting?

For F: What sorts of things are subject to destruction?

For F': To what conclusion about the soul's immortality does Simmias' analogy with harmony and lyre lead?

For E': After making sure you understand Cebes' analogy, ask yourself whose analogy offers a stronger argument: Simmias' or Cebes'?

For D': Where does Socrates think Simmias' analogy breaks down?

For C': In this section, Socrates distinguishes between different kinds of explanations. Which kind does he accept, which kind does he reject? To answer this question, focus on the reasons why Socrates is sitting in prison.

For B': Socrates offers his own analogies in this section. Be sure you can explain how they work. Do they answer Cebes?

SELECTION FROM PLATO

■ ■ ■

Phaedo

A. The Theseus Myth (57a–60b)

ECHECRATES: Were you yourself, Phaedo, in the prison with
   Socrates on the day when he drank the poison?

PHAEDO: Yes.

E: I would like to hear about his death. We could not understand why, after he was condemned, he was put to death,
   not at that time, but long afterwards.

P: An accident. The stern of the ship which the Athenians send
   to Delos had been crowned on the day before he was tried.
   It was the ship in which, by Athenian tradition, Theseus
   went to Crete when he took with him the fourteen youths,
   and saved them and himself. The whole period of the voyage is a holy season, when the city is not allowed to be pol-
   luted by public executions.

E: How did he die?

P: I could hardly believe I was present at the death of a friend,
   and so did not pity him, he died so fearlessly, and his words
   were so noble and gracious that to me he appeared blessed.

I shall start at the beginning, and try to repeat the entire conversation. On entering we found Socrates released from his chains, and Xanthippe [the wife of Socrates], whom you know, sitting by him, and holding his child in her arms. When she saw us she uttered a cry and said, as women will: "Socrates, this is the last time you will converse with your friends, or they with you." Socrates turned to Crito and said: "Crito, let someone take her home."

B. Socrates' Speech (60b–69e)

SOCRATES: I am quite ready to admit that I ought to be grieved at death, if I were not persuaded in the first place that I am going to other gods who are wise and good (of which I am as certain as I can be of any such matters), and (though I am not sure of this) to men departed, better than those whom I leave behind; and therefore I do not grieve as I might have done, for I have good hope that there is yet something remaining for the dead, and, as has been said of old, some far better thing for the good than for the evil. And how this is, I shall try to explain. I think the true philosopher is likely to be misunderstood by other men; they do not perceive that he is always pursuing death and dying; and if this be so, and he has had the desire of death all his life long, why when his time comes should he fear what he has always been pursuing? Is not death the separation of soul and body? And to be dead is the completion of this, when the soul exists in itself and is released from the body, and the body is released from the soul. And when real philosophers consider all these things, they will be led to say something like this: "Have we not found a path of thought which seems to bring us and our argument to the conclusion that, while we are in the body, and while the soul is infected with the evils of the body, our desire will not be satisfied? That is, our desire for the truth. For the body is a source of endless trouble to us by reason of the mere requirement of food; and is liable also to diseases which overtake and impede us in the search after true being. It fills us full of loves and desires and fears and fancies of all kinds, and endless foolery, and, in fact, as men say, takes away the power of thinking at all. From where come wars and fights and factions? Where else but from the body and the desires of the body? But if this be true, there is great reason to hope that, going where I go, when I come to the end of my journey, I shall attain what has been the pursuit of my life. And so I go on my way rejoicing, and not only I, but every other man who believes that his mind has been made ready and that he is in a way purified."

C. Cebes' Wonder (69e–70a)

CEBES: I agree, Socrates, with most of what you say. But about the soul, men are apt to be incredulous; they fear that when it has left the body its place may be nowhere, and that on the very day of death it may perish and come to an end, immediately on its release from the body, dispersed like smoke or air.

D. The First Argument: From Opposite (70b–72e)

SOC: Suppose we consider the question whether the souls of men after death are or are not in the world below. There comes to mind an ancient doctrine saying they go from here into the other world and, returning here, are born again from the dead. Now if it is true that the living come from the dead, then our souls must exist in the other world for, if not, how could they have been born again? And let us consider the whole question, not in relation to man only, but in relation to animals generally, and plants, and everything which comes to be, and the proof will be easier. Are not all things which have opposites generated out of their opposites? I mean such things as good and evil, just and unjust, and there are innumerable other opposites which are so generated. And I want to show that in all opposites there is necessarily a similar change. Is there not an opposite of life, as sleep is the opposite of waking?

C: True.

SOC: What is it?

C: Death.

Soc: Then the living, whether things or persons, Cebes, are generated from the dead?

C: Clearly.

Soc: Then the inference is that our souls exist in the world below?

C: True.

Soc: That these admissions were not unfair, Cebes, may be shown as follows. If generation were in a straight line only, and there were no compensation or circle in nature, no turn or return of elements into their opposites, then you know that all things would at last have the same form and pass into the same state, and there would be no more generation of them.

E. The Second Argument:
Knowledge is Recollection (72e–77b)

C: Your favorite doctrine, Socrates, that knowledge is simply recollection, if true, also necessarily implies a previous time in which we learned that which we now recollect. But this would be impossible unless our soul had been in some place before it existed in the form of man; here then is another proof of the soul's immortality.

SIMMIAS: But tell me, Cebes, what arguments are urged in favor of this doctrine of recollection?

C: One excellent proof is afforded by questions. If you put a question to someone in the right way, he will give a true answer of himself, but how could he do this unless there were intellectual knowledge and right reason already in him?

Soc: If you are still skeptical, Simmias, you may agree when you look at the matter another way. Recollection is most commonly a process of recovering what has been already forgotten through time and inattention.

SIM: True.

Soc: And may you not remember a man from seeing the picture of a house or a lyre? And from the picture of Simmias, you may be led to remember Cebes?

SIM: True.

Soc: Or you may also be led to recollect Simmias himself? And in all these cases, the recollection may be derived from things like or unlike? And when the recollection is derived from like things, then another consideration is sure to come up, whether or not the likeness in any degree falls short of what is recollected?

Sim: Very true.

Soc: And shall we go a step further, and say that there is such a thing as equality, not of one piece of wood or stone with another, but, over and above this, that there is equality itself?

Sim: By Zeus, yes indeed.

Soc: And do we know the nature of this very thing?

Sim: Certainly.

Soc: From where do we get knowledge of this? Is it not from seeing equalities in pieces of wood and stones, and gathering from them the equality which is different from them? You will acknowledge that there is a difference? Or look at it another way: do not the same pieces of wood or stone appear at one time equal, at another time unequal?

Sim: Certainly.

Soc: But are real equals always equal? Or is the idea of equality the same as that of inequality?

Sim: Impossible.

Soc: Then these (so-called) equals are not the same as the idea of equality?

Sim: Clearly not.

Soc: And yet from these equals, although they differ from the idea of equality, you conceived and attained that idea?

Sim: True.

Soc: Which might be like, or might be unlike them?

Sim: Yes.

Soc: But that makes no difference. Whenever from seeing one thing you conceived another, whether like or unlike, there must surely have been an act of recollection?

Sim: Very true.

Soc: But what would you say of equal portions of wood and stone, or other material equals? And what is the impression produced by them? Are they equals in the same sense in which absolute equality is equal? Or do they fall short of this perfect equality in a measure?

SIM: Yes, in a very great measure too.

SOC: And must we not allow that, when I or anyone, looking at any object, observes that the thing which he sees aims at being some other thing, but falls short of, and cannot be, that other thing, and is inferior, he who makes this observation must have had a previous knowledge of that to which the other, though similar, was inferior.

SIM: Certainly.

SOC: And has not this been our own case in the matter of equals and of absolute equality?

SIM: Precisely.

SOC: Then we must have known equality previous to the time when we first saw the material equals, and reflected that all these apparent equals strive to attain absolute equality, but fall short of it?

SIM: Very true.

SOC: Then before we began to see or hear or perceive in any way, we must have had knowledge of absolute equality, or we could not have referred to that standard the equals which are derived from the senses? For to that they all aspire, and of that they fall short.

SIM: No other conclusion can be drawn from the previous statements.

SOC: And did we not see and hear and have the use of our other senses as soon as we were born?

SIM: Certainly.

SOC: Then we must have acquired the knowledge of equality at some previous time?

SIM: Yes.

SOC: Before we were born, I suppose?

SIM: True.

SOC: And if we acquired this knowledge before we were born, and were born having the use of it, then we also knew before we were born, and at the instant of birth, not only the equal or the greater or the less, but all other ideas; for we are not speaking only of equality, but of beauty, goodness, justice, holiness, and of everything which we stamp with the name of "essence" in the dialectical process, both when we ask and when we answer questions. Of all this we may certainly affirm that we acquired the knowledge before birth?

SIM: We may.

SOC: But if the knowledge which we acquired before birth was lost by us at birth, and if afterwards by the use of the senses we recovered what we previously knew, will not the process which we call learning be a recovering of the knowledge which is natural to us, and may not this rightly be termed "recollection"?

SIM: Very true.

SOC: Then may we not say that if, as we are always repeating, there is an absolute beauty and goodness, and an absolute essence of all things, and if to this essence, which is now discovered to have existed in our former state, we refer all our sensations, and with this compare them, finding these ideas to be pre-existent and our inborn possession, then our souls must have had a prior existence, but, if not, there would be no force in the argument? There is the same proof that these ideas must have existed before we were born as that our souls existed before we were born; and if not the ideas, then not the souls.

F. The Third Argument: The Soul Has No Parts (77b–80b)

C: About half of what was required has been proven: that our souls existed before we were born. That the soul exists after death as well as before birth is the other half of which the proof is still wanting, and has to be supplied.

SOC: But that proof has already been given, if you put the two arguments together. Still I suspect that you and Simmias would be glad to probe the argument further. Like children, you are haunted with a fear that when the soul leaves the body, the wind may really blow it away and scatter it, especially if a man should happen to die in a great storm and not when the sky is calm. Must we not ask ourselves what that is which, as we imagine, is liable to be scattered, and about which we fear, and what that is about which we have no fear? And then we may proceed further to enquire whether that which suffers dispersion is or is not of the nature of soul. Our hopes and fears as to our own souls will turn upon the answers to these questions.

C: Very true.

SOC: Now a compound may be supposed to be naturally capable both of being composed and also of being taken apart; but that which is not compounded, and only that, must be, if anything, incorruptible. Reflect, then, that the soul is very like the divine and immortal and intellectual and uniform and incorruptible and unchangeable, while the body is very like the human and mortal and unintellectual and multiform and corruptible and changeable. Can this be denied?

C: It cannot.

G and G'. The Reincarnation Myth (80c–84c)

SOC: That soul, I say, itself invisible, departs to the invisible world, to the divine and immortal and intellectual. Arriving there, it is secure of happiness and released from the error and folly of humans, their fears and passions and all other human ills, and forever dwells, as they say of the initiated, in company with the gods. But the souls of the evil are compelled to wander about in payment of the penalty of their former evil ways of life. They continue to wander until, through the craving after the corporeal which never leaves them, they are imprisoned in another body. And they may be supposed to find their prisons in the same natures which they have had in their former lives.

C: What natures do you mean?

SOC: Those who have followed after gluttony and wantonness and drunkenness, and have had no thought of avoiding them, would pass into asses and animals of that sort. What do you think?

C: Quite likely.

SOC: And those who have chosen the portion of injustice and tyranny and violence will pass into wolves or hawks.

F'. The First Counterargument:
Simmias and Harmony (84c–86e)

When Socrates had finished speaking, for a considerable time there was silence; he appeared to be meditating, as most of us were, on what had been said; only Cebes and Simmias spoke a few words to one another. And Socrates observing them asked what they thought of the argument, and whether there was anything wanting. "For," he said, "there are many points still open to suspicion and attack, if anyone were disposed to sift the matter thoroughly."

SIM: Very good, Socrates, I shall tell you my difficulty, and Cebes his. Suppose a person were to use the same argument about harmony and the lyre. Might he not say that harmony is a thing invisible, incorporeal, perfect, divine, existing in the lyre which is harmonized, but that the lyre and the strings are material, composite, earthy, and mortal? The thought, Socrates, must have occurred to your own mind that such is our conception of the soul. And that when the body is in a manner strung and held together by the elements of hot and cold, wet and dry, then the soul is the harmony or due proportionate mixture of them. If so, whenever the strings of the body are unduly loosened or overstrained through disease or other injury, then the soul, though most divine, like other harmonies of music or of works of art, of course perishes at once, although the material remains of the body may last for a considerable time, until they are either decayed or burnt. And if anyone maintains that the soul, being the harmony of the elements of the body, is the first to perish in that which is called death, how shall we answer him?

Socrates looked fixedly at us as his manner was, and said with a smile: "Simmias has reason on his side. But perhaps before we answer him, we had better also hear Cebes."

E'. The Second Counterargument: Cebes' Weaver (87a–88c)

C: I will ask you to consider whether the objection which I, like Simmias, express in an image, has any weight. The analogy which I will adduce is that of an old weaver, who dies, and after his death someone says: "He is not dead, he must be alive. See, there is the coat which he wove and wore." And he proceeds to ask someone who is incredulous whether a man lasts longer, or the coat which he wears. But that is a mistake. The truth is that the weaver, having woven many coats, outlived several of them, but was outlived by the last. Now the relation of the body to the soul may be expressed in a similar way; and anyone may fairly say likewise that the soul is lasting, and the body weak and shortlived in comparison. But whenever the soul perishes, it has on its last garment, and this survives. When the soul is dead, the body shows its native weakness, quickly decomposes, and passes away. Even granting that there is a natural strength in the soul which will hold out and be born many times, nonetheless, we may be still inclined to think that it will weary in the labors of successive births, and at last succumb in one of its deaths and perish utterly.

D'. Socrates to Simmias (88c–95a)

All of us, as we afterwards remarked to one another, were depressed at hearing what they said. When we had been so firmly convinced before, now to have our faith shaken seemed to introduce confusion and uncertainty.

Soc: Let us now take care to avoid a danger.

P: Of what?

Soc: Lest we become misologists. No worse can happen to man than this. For as there are misanthropists, or haters of men, so there are misologists, or haters of arguments. Let us be careful of admitting into our souls the notion that there is no soundness in any arguments at all. Rather say that we have not yet attained soundness in ourselves, and that we must struggle like men to gain health of mind, you and all the others looking at your future life, and I at death. Now, Simmias, do you imagine that a harmony or any other composition can be in a state other than that of the elements out of which it is compounded?

Sim: Certainly not.

Soc: Or do or suffer anything other than they do or suffer?

Sim: No.

Soc: Then a harmony does not, properly speaking, *lead* the parts or elements which make up the harmony, but only *follows* them.

Sim: Yes.

Soc: For harmony cannot possibly have any motion or sound or other quality which is opposed to its parts.

Sim: That would be impossible.

Soc: And is the soul in agreement with the affections of the body? Or is it at variance with them? For example, when the body is hot and thirsty, does not the soul incline us against drinking? And, when the body is hungry, against eating? And this is only one instance out of ten thousand of the opposition of the soul to the things of the body.

Sim: Very true.

Soc: But we have already acknowledged that the soul, being a harmony, can never utter a note at variance with the tensions and relaxations and vibrations and other affections of the strings out of which it is composed; it can only follow, it cannot lead them? Then, my friend, we can never be right in saying that the soul is a harmony.

C'. Socrates' Wonder (95a–100b)

Socrates paused awhile, and seemed absorbed in reflection. At last he said: "You are raising a tremendous question, Cebes, involving the whole nature of generation and destruction, about which, if you like, I shall give you my own experience; and if anything which I say is likely to avail towards the solution of your difficulty, you may make use of it. When I was young, Cebes, I had a prodigious desire to know that part of wisdom called natural science. To know the causes of things, and why a thing is and comes to be or is destroyed, appeared to me a lofty profession. I was always concerned with questions like these: is the blood the element with which we think, or air, or fire? Or perhaps nothing of the kind, but the brain may be the source of the perceptions of hearing and sight and smell, and memory and opinion may come from them, and science may be based on memory and opinion when they have become stable. At last I concluded I was utterly incapable of these enquiries. I was so fascinated by them my eyes grew blind to things which I seemed to myself, and to others, to know quite well. I forgot what I had before thought obvious, as that humans grow from eating and drinking, for when, by the digestion of food, flesh is added to flesh and bone to bone, and whenever there is an aggregation of like elements, the lesser bulk becomes larger and the small man big. By Zeus, I am far from imagining I know the cause of any of them. I cannot satisfy myself that, when one is added to one, the one to which the addition is made becomes two, or that the two units added together make two by reason of the addition. I wonder that, when separated from each other, each was one and not two, and now, when brought together, the mere juxtaposition and meeting is the cause of their becoming two. Nor am I persuaded that division of one is the cause making two. Then a different cause would produce the same effect. In the first instance addition and juxtaposition was the cause, but here separation and taking away are the cause. I am no longer persuaded that I understand why one or anything else is generated or destroyed or even is, but I have in my mind some confused notion of a new method, and can never admit the other. Then I heard someone reading, as he said, from a book of Anaxagoras, that mind is the disposer and cause of all. I was delighted with this cause, which appeared good to me. I thought: if mind is the cause of all, mind will dispose all for the best. If anyone wants to know the cause of generation or destruction or being, he must find out what state of being or doing or suffering is best for that thing. Therefore, one had only to consider the best about this or other things and then one would also know the worse, since the same knowledge comprehended both. What expectations I had formed, and how grievously was I disappointed! As I proceeded, I found him altogether forsaking mind as a principle of order, and he had recourse to air and ether and water and other strange things. I might compare him to a person who began by maintaining that mind is the cause of all Socrates' actions, but who, when he attempted to explain the causes of my actions in detail, went on to show that I sit here because my body is made up of bones and muscles. And the bones, he would say, are hard and have joints which divide them, and the muscles are elastic. And he would assign ten thousand other causes of the same sort, forgetting to mention the true cause, which is, that the Athenians have thought it better to condemn me, and accordingly I have thought it best to remain here and undergo my sentence. For I am inclined to think these muscles and bones of mine would have gone off long ago to Megara or Boeotia, by the Dog, if they had been moved only by their own idea of what was best, and if I had not chosen the better and nobler part, instead of playing truant and running away, of enduring any punishment which the state inflicts. There is surely a strange confusion of causes and conditions in all this. It may be said, indeed, that without bones and muscles and other parts of the body I cannot execute my purposes. But to say that I do as I do because of them, and that this is the way in which mind acts, and not from the choice of the best, is a very careless and idle way of speaking. I wonder that they cannot distinguish the cause from the condition, which the many, feeling about in the dark, are always mistaking and misnaming. Of the obligatory and containing power of the good they think nothing. And yet this is the principle which I would gladly learn, if anyone would teach me. But as I have failed to learn from myself or another the nature of the best, shall I show you the second best mode of enquiring into the cause?"

C: I wish that above all else.

SOC: I thought that as I had failed in the contemplation of things, I ought to take care to avoid what happens to people observing and gazing on the sun during an eclipse. Some ruin their eyes unless they take the precaution of only looking at the image reflected in the water, or some similar medium. So in my own case, I was afraid that my soul might be blinded altogether if I looked at things with my eyes or tried to apprehend them by the senses. And I thought that I had better have recourse to arguments and seek there the truth of things. I dare say the simile is not perfect, for I am very far from admitting that he who contemplates things through the medium of arguments sees them through an image, any more than he who considers them in action and operation. However, this was the method I adopted: I first assumed some principle which I judged the strongest, and then I affirmed as true whatever seemed to agree with this, whether relating to the cause or to anything else. And what disagreed with this I regarded as untrue. But I should like to explain my meaning more clearly, as I do not think that you as yet understand me.

C: No, not very well.

B'. Socrates to Cebes (100b–107b)

SOC: There is nothing new in what I am about to tell you, but only what I have been everywhere repeating in the previous discussion and other places. I want to show you the nature of that cause which has occupied my thoughts. I must go back to those things talked of so much, and assume that there exists a "beautiful" itself through itself, and a "good," and a "great," and all the others. Grant me this and I hope to be able to show you the nature of the cause, and to prove the immortality of the soul.

C: You may proceed at once with the proof, for I grant you this.

SOC: Well, I should like to know whether you agree with me in the next step; for I cannot help thinking, if there is anything beautiful other than beauty itself, that it can be beautiful because of nothing else than because it partakes of that beauty, and I should say the same of everything. Do you agree in this notion of the cause?

C: Yes.

SOC: I know nothing and can understand nothing of the other causes, the sophistic ones. And if someone says to me that the bloom of color, or shape, or any such thing is a cause of beauty, I leave all that, which is only confusing to me, and simply and singly and perhaps foolishly hold that nothing makes a thing beautiful but the presence and participation of beauty, in whatever way or manner obtained. As to the manner I am uncertain, but I stoutly contend that by beauty all beautiful things become beautiful. This appears to me the safest answer I can give, to myself or another, and I cling to this, in the persuasion that this principle will never be overthrown, and that to myself or to any one who asks the question, I may safely reply that by beauty beautiful things become beautiful. Do you agree?

C: I do.

Soc: And that by greatness great things become great and greater greater, and by smallness small things become small?

C: True.

Soc: Again, would you not be cautious of affirming that the addition of one to one, or the division of one, is the cause of two? And you would loudly say you know of no way in which anything comes to be except by participation in its own proper nature; and consequently, as far as you know, the only cause of two is participation in "twoness." And if anyone assails you there, you would not mind him, or answer him, until you had seen whether the consequences which follow agree with one another or not. And when you are further required to give an account of this hypothesis, you would go on to assume a higher hypothesis, and a higher, until you found a resting-place in the best of the higher. But you will not confuse hypothesis and consequence, like argumentative "counter-arguers," at least if you want to discover something of real beings. They give not one argument, nor even a thought, to this, their wisdom making them well pleased with themselves, however great the jumble of their ideas. But you, if you are a philosopher, will certainly do as I say.

"What you say is most true," said Simmias and Cebes, both speaking at once.

Soc: I speak as I do because I want you to agree with me in thinking both that greatness itself will never be great and also small, and that greatness in us will never admit the small or be overcome by it. Instead, one of two things will happen: either the great will fly or retire before its opposite, the small, or be destroyed by its approach. Nor can any other opposite which remains the same ever be or become its own opposite, but either goes away or is destroyed in the change.

C: I agree wholeheartedly.

Soc: Yet again let me ask you to consider the question from another point of view, and see whether you agree with me. There is a thing you call heat, and another called cold?

C: Certainly.

Soc: But are they the same as fire and snow?

C: Not at all.

Soc: Heat is different from fire, and cold is not the same as snow?

C: Yes.

Soc: And yet you will admit that when snow is under the influence of heat, they will not remain snow and heat, but at the advance of heat the snow will either retreat or be destroyed?

C: True.

Soc: I will try with another example: the odd number is always called by the name of odd?

C: True.

Soc: But is this the only thing which is called odd? Are there not other things which have their own name, and yet are called odd, because, although not the same as oddness, they are never without oddness? Then mark the point at which I am aiming: not only do essential opposites exclude one another, but also concrete things which, although not in themselves opposed, contain opposites. These, I say, likewise reject what is opposed to what is contained in them, and when it approaches them they either perish or withdraw. For example, will not the number three perish or undergo anything rather than be made an even number, while remaining three?

C: Very true.

Soc: Perhaps you may be able to arrive at the general conclusion not only that opposites will not receive opposites, but also that nothing which brings the opposite will admit the opposite of what it brings, in that to which it is brought. And now let us begin again. Tell me, what is it whose presence will render the body alive?

C: The soul.

Soc: To whatever the soul possesses, to that it comes bearing life?

C: Certainly.

Soc: And is there any opposite of life?

C: Death.

Soc: The soul, as has been acknowledged, will never receive the opposite of what it brings.

C: Impossible.

Soc: And what do we call that principle which does not admit of death?

C: The immortal.

Soc: Then the soul is immortal?

C: Yes.

Soc: And may we say that this has been proven?

C: Yes, abundantly proven, Socrates.

Soc: If the immortal is also imperishable, the soul when attacked by death cannot perish; for the preceding argument shows that the soul will not admit of death, or ever be dead, any more than three or the odd number will admit of the even; or fire, or the heat in the fire, of the cold. But if not, some other proof of the soul's imperishableness will have to be given.

C: No other proof is needed; for if the immortal, being eternal, is liable to perish, then nothing is imperishable.

Soc: Yes, and yet all men will agree that the god and the form of life itself and anything else immortal will never perish.

C: Yes, all men, by Zeus, and what is more, the gods, I think.

Soc: Seeing then that the immortal is indestructible, must not the soul, if immortal, also be imperishable?

C: Most certainly.

Soc: Then when death attacks a man, the mortal portion may be supposed to die, but the immortal retires at the approach of death and is preserved safe and indestructible?

C: So it seems.

Soc: So above all, Cebes, the soul is immortal and imperishable, and our souls will remain in being in Hades.

C: I have nothing else to say about that Socrates, but if Simmias or anyone else has any further objection to make, let him speak out.

Sim: I have nothing more to say, nor can I see any reason for doubt after what has been said. But I still feel uncertain in my own mind, when I think of the greatness of our subject and the feebleness of man.

Soc: Well said. And first hypotheses, even when they are convincing to us, should be carefully examined. And when they are satisfactorily ascertained, then you may, I think, follow the course of the argument, as far as a man can. And if it be clear, there will be no need for further enquiry.

A'. The Cosmic Myth (107b–115a)

Soc: But then, my friends, if the soul is really immortal, what care should be taken of it, not only in respect of the portion of time called life, but of eternity. And the danger of neglecting it from this point of view does indeed appear to be awesome. For after death, as they say, the guardian spirit of each individual, to whom he belonged in life, leads him to a certain place in which the dead are gathered together, and after judgment has been given they pass into the world below, following the guide who is appointed to conduct them from this world to the other. And when they have there received their due and remained their time, another guide brings them back again after many revolutions of ages.

Socrates' Death (115b–118)

When he had done speaking, Crito said: "And have you any commands for us, Socrates, anything to say about your children, or any other matter in which we can serve you?"

Soc: Nothing in particular, Crito; only, as I have always told you, take care of yourselves.

C: We will do our best. And how shall we bury you?

Soc: In any way you like; but you must get hold of me, and take care that I do not run away from you.

When he had taken a bath his children were brought to him (he had two young sons and an older one); and the women of his family also came, and he talked to them and gave them a few directions in the presence of Crito. Then he dismissed them and returned to us. Now the hour of sunset was near, for a good deal of time had passed while he was within. Crito made a sign to the servant, who was standing by; and he went out, and having been absent for some time, returned with the jailer carrying the cup of poison.

Socrates said: "You, my good friend, who are experienced in these matters, shall give me directions how I am to proceed."

The man answered: "You have only to walk about until your legs are heavy, and then to lie down, and the poison will act." At the same time he handed the cup to Socrates, who in the easiest and gentlest manner, without the least fear or change of color or feature, looking right at the man, Echecrates, as his manner was, took the cup and said: "What do you say about making a libation out of this cup to some god? May I, or not?" He answered: "We only prepare, Socrates, just so much as we think enough."

"I understand," he said, "but I may and must ask the gods to prosper my journey from this to the other world, even so, and so be it according to my prayer." Then, raising the cup to his lips, quite readily and cheerfully he drank off the poison. Up to then most of us had been able to control our sorrow; but when we saw him drinking and saw too that he had finished the drink, we could no longer forbear, and in spite of myself my own tears were flowing fast, so that I covered my face and wept, not for him, but at the thought of my own calamity in having to part from such a friend. Nor was I the first; for Crito, when he found himself unable to restrain his tears, had got up, and I followed; and, at that moment, Apollodorus, who had been weeping all the time, broke out in a loud and passionate cry which made cowards of us all. Socrates alone retained his calmness: "What is this strange outcry? I sent away the women mainly in order that they might not misbehave in this way, for I have been told that a man should die in peace. Be quiet then, and have patience." When we heard his words we were ashamed, and restrained our tears; and he walked about until, as he said, his legs began to fail, and then he lay on his back, according to the directions, and now and then the man who gave him the poison looked at his feet and legs; and after a while he pressed his foot hard, and asked him if he could feel; and he said, no. And then his leg, and so upwards and upwards, and showed us that he was cold and stiff. And he felt them himself, and said: "When the poison reaches the heart, that will be the end." He was beginning to grow cold about the groin, when he uncovered his face, for he had covered it up, and said (they were his last words): "Crito, I owe a cock to Asclepius; will you remember to pay the debt?" "The debt shall be paid," said Crito. "Is there anything else?" There was no answer to this question, but in a minute or two a movement was heard, and the attendants uncovered him. His eyes were set, and Crito closed his eyes and mouth. Such was the end, Echecrates, of our friend; concerning whom

Chapter 1

I may truly say that of all the men of his time whom I have
known, he was the best and wisest and most just.

Extracted from *Phaedo*, translated by B. Jowett, 1892, as abridged and
revised by R. E. Houser.

COMMENTARY

■ ■ ■

Analysis of the Selection

A. The Theseus Myth

Plato uses the myth of Theseus to introduce his overriding theme: the immortality of the soul. Theseus rescued the fourteen youths and maidens from physical death. Socrates will try to rescue his fourteen followers from believing that physical death also means the death of the soul. They will be rescued from this error only by becoming convinced of the immortality of their own souls. So the opening points beyond itself.

At the level of poetry, the more convincing story is the one that offers a larger vision. Homer's *Iliad* is finer for involving gods and nature, in addition to Greeks and Trojans. Consequently, as the *Phaedo* progresses, Socrates the storyteller moves from a comparison with one mythical character— Theseus (A)—to a second story encompassing all reincarnated souls (G and G'), and ends with a picture placing souls within the whole cosmos (A'). His myths become progressively more convincing because they are set on a wider stage.

But poetry can go only so far; it must be supplemented by other ways of thinking. As a result, Socrates moves from poetry to giving a speech (as Sophists do) to arguing philosophically. Plato so carefully weaves together all three that it is virtually impossible to separate fully philosophy from the other two. The real argument is in the cumulative effect on the three persons who constitute Plato's main audience: the potential philosophers Cebes and Simmias, and the reader. The reader of a dialogue must link together all the modes of discourse and all the arguments, as the reader of a poem finds its meaning in the whole. Plato requires such active reading because this is how he teaches us to become philosophers like Socrates.

B. Socrates' Speech

Socrates likens this speech to his defense before the Athenians. He attempts to persuade this jury by using assertions about the philosopher's way of life and death. He offers his theses as truth (and never denies them), but also as a test.

Because Socrates views philosophy as "practice for death," he begins by defining death as the "separation of soul from body," understood to mean that after death the soul and body exist apart from each other. From this definition he deduces the following theses: The philosopher learns to despise the pleasures of the body, and as a result become a wiser and better person. The soul grasps knowledge of the natures of things through pure reasoning. Thus the philosopher's soul seeks to be "by itself," and death offers the positive attainment of knowledge. Morally, philosophy purifies the soul, which attains the four cardinal virtues: wisdom, courage, moderation, and justice.

We become aware of two problems in Socrates' speech, however, because he so clearly distinguishes principle (or premise) from a conclusion deduced from a principle. First, everything rests on his definition of death. Even if true, the definition simply assumes that the soul and body exist separately from each other. Without proving this separation, however, the definition alone is not a useful basis for deduction, and the speech is therefore unconvincing. This problem engenders Cebes' wonder (C). Second, deductive reasoning serves as a good method of proving conclusions if a strong enough principle can be found. But only later (at C') will Socrates reveal those stronger principles. The sophistic deduction here at B is valuable because it foreshadows Socrates' philosophical deduction at B'. This speech serves to pull us into the dialogue's reasoning, without being completely convincing on its own.

C. Cebes' Wonder

Most of those in the room silently receive Socrates' theses as the master's final opinions. But what exists as the last word at the level of sophistry is only the first word for philosophy. Cebes breaks the silence, wondering about the soul, because people think that it "is dispersed like breath or smoke" at death. In this way, Plato works into the very structure of the dialogue the proper method for philosophy. Opinions like those Socrates has just presented evoke wonder and a precise question in Cebes, who needs to be persuaded. "Persuasion" is achieved through argument and counterargument, repeated, not indefinitely, but until certain truth is found. But how do we know when we have arrived at such truth? The structure of the dialogue reveals the answer: Cebes' wonder (C) points forward to the wonder that revealed the true causes of reality to Socrates (C'). Philosophical truth, therefore, can be attained when the discussion gives us insight into first principles, and the initial question is answered through them. This then is the order of philosophy: opinion, wonder, question, argument, counterargument, first principles, certain truth.

D. Argument from Opposites

Life is the opposite of death. This stark fact leads Socrates to uncover some general truths about how nature works, and these truths provide the basis for a deductive argument about the soul: Natural change is a transition from one opposite to another, for example, from smaller to larger, from weaker to stronger. Second, the process of change is different from the two opposed states. The process of growing larger is different from being small and being large. Third, this process must work in a circular way; otherwise, nature would come to a halt. Sleeping and waking, for example, follow each other. From these premises, Socrates concludes that the human soul must be immortal by arguing from the process all recognize, dying, to the opposite process, it could be called enlivening, understood as uniting the soul to a body. To complete the circle, the soul must exist on both sides of bodily death, even "in the underworld."

Cebes gives a sophist's reply, "It seems likely," which is a sign that something is amiss. First, the analysis of change is incomplete. The subject of change is a third factor, distinct from opposing properties and processes. In many changes the same subject is found on both sides of the transformation, as when Socrates grew larger in becoming an adult. But sometimes the subject disappears altogether, as when Socrates dies. The argument simply assumes all changes are of the first type, because the subject of the dying process is not yet clear. This problem leads to a discussion of recollection (E), which will clarify the subject by focusing on an obviously psychic activity, knowledge.

Second, imprecision about the subject of change amounts to imprecision about the subject of the argument. The argument ought to be about the soul. If so, Socrates envisions a soul oscillating between life and death. But a dead soul looks like a contradiction in terms, if the soul is truly the cause of life. When the soul is "dead," of course, it is really the body that is dead. The body clearly can exist in both states. But if the body, not the soul, is its subject, the argument has slipped completely from sight. It is not just deficient, it is nonexistent, as Socrates' soul may shortly be. The argument has become a dilemma. If the body is its subject, the argument works, but proves nothing about the soul; if the soul is the subject, the argument simply does not work. The discussion needs to be clear about the causal relation between body and soul. This points ahead to D'.

E. Recollection Argument

Cebes reminds Socrates of his doctrine that learning is actually a process of remembering ideas we already possess. If humans are born with the concepts they use, the soul possessing them previously existed, making immortality a side effect of Socrates' theory of knowledge. But this theory is not obviously true; it needs proof.

Socrates' proof-strategy consists in finding something we readily accept, everyday remembering, and proceeds backward, analyzing it by examining the presuppositions of such remembering. This analysis reveals an analogy between remembering and learning. Socrates takes us on an inner journey from nature to our cognitive processes, to the mind, and finally to what the mind knows, Plato's famous *forms*.

When we see Simmias' cloak, we remember Simmias himself. Everyday remembering involves *(a)* present sensing, which is passive; *(b)* active remembering; *(c)* past sensing, which gives the content of what we remember; *(d)* the thing previously sensed; and *(e)* myself who unite past and present in the act of remembering. Socrates uses these aspects of remembering to argue that intellectual learning has analogous features.

Remembering may seem to be a purely sensory activity, but it is not. We express our remembrances in universal language. So *(a)* intellectual knowledge has the very same starting point as remembering—sensory experience. But *(b)* knowledge involves making active intellectual judgments about our sensory experiences. Just as remembering involved reference to a standard (the previous experience we remember) so *(c)* intellectual judgments require a standard. Judging that two sticks (or stones) are equal to each other requires us to use the concept of equality, "the equal itself."

Socrates picks "the equal" to show that universal concepts are an absolute prerequisite for all mental life. Equality is a kind of unity. Now, knowledge is formed in propositions, which unite a predicate with a subject. The verbal sign of this unity is the copula *is*. Without such a unity one could never make any mental judgment. Are such concepts nothing more than other words for experiences? The "itself" in the phrase "the equal itself" underscores how different "the equal" and "the equal itself" are. The concept of equality is pure in a way that equal sticks never can be, because it is our understanding of the very nature of equality, alone and by itself. Equality never changes and is the foundation for necessary and universal truths, such as one of the axioms of arithmetic: when equals are added to equals the results are equal.

At this point, Socrates appears to have hit a dead end in the labyrinth. Intellectual concepts are so primordial that it seems impossible to draw them "from" sensation, yet Socrates says they come from it. But could we not have obtained intellectual concepts from a kind of prior experience, as we obtained the basis for remembering through a prior sensation? This experience would be purely intellectual. If so, I would get concepts "from" sensation only in the limited sense that a particular experience would trigger my intellectual memory of the concepts I already have, which are appropriate for judging that experience, in a way analogous to that by which a sensation can trigger my memory of a prior sense experience.

The real payoff from the analogy, however, lies in its two final features. First, *(d)* there must exist some reality that provided me with my concepts. All humans are open to the same truths because they obtain them from the same things. These must possess the perfection, permanence, necessity, and unity found in my concepts, since concepts are but their mirrors. Socrates calls them *forms*. Finally, *(e)* just as in everyday remembering, the "I" had to encompass present and past sensations, intellectual remembering further expands the range of the "I" to unite all my intellectual concepts with each other, as well as with my sense experiences and everyday recollections. This "I" is the soul. Since I cannot have received and forgotten concepts at the same time, my soul must have preexisted.

Socrates' argument, therefore, uncovers five features of intellectual knowledge corresponding to the five features of everyday remembering: *(a)* present sensation, about which we make *(b)* intellectual judgments, which presuppose *(c)* possession of intellectual concepts, derived from *(d)* the forms illuminating *(e)* the soul prior to the present life.

Two criticisms of this theory of recollection lead the dialogue forward. Simmias notes that the preexistence of the soul does not guarantee its postexistence, so they immediately proceed to F. And a deeper problem points ahead to E': suppose concepts are logically prior to sense, and the forms are the true causes of knowledge. Socrates' way out of the dilemma is to say the soul preexists. But this is not the only possible solution. One might equally well say knowledge comes to the soul by illumination during this life, rather than in a prior existence.

F. Indestructibility Argument

Even adding the first two arguments together, as Socrates playfully suggests, is unconvincing. Perhaps a third argument will charm away the bogeyman of death. Socrates now focuses on how the soul might be destroyed, looking at destructibility as such first, and then at the soul.

Things subject to destruction all have one thing in common: they are made up of parts. Consequently, destroying something means taking its parts apart. Destructibility and being made up of separable parts imply each other. This opens the way for an argument about the soul. If it does not have the kind of parts subject to such separation, then it will follow logically from the definition of destructibility that the soul is indestructible. The argument, therefore, turns on whether the soul has parts, and Socrates offers two comparisons to try to convince Cebes that it does not.

The first comparison states that the soul seems unlike the things that obviously are destructible, such as physical objects. There is part of us that is quite like destructible things, but this part is our body, not our soul. Socrates notes several features of destructible things, like the human body. The body is "mortal" because we know it dies; "multiform" because its parts are different from each other; "unintelligible" because it is an individual thing; and "soluble" because it falls apart. The reason for each of these qualities is that, as a physical object, the body is "never consistently the same." In short, the body is "human." The soul, however, is the invisible ruler over the visible body. Should not the soul then have characteristics that are the opposite of the body's? This negative comparison is the first way Socrates leads us to the intuition that the soul lacks parts.

Drawing positive conclusions from negative comparisons, however, is risky. So Socrates offers a second comparison, a positive one. He likens the soul to the forms. This approach requires Socrates to clarify what the forms are like. The "equal itself" and the "beautiful itself" are "immortal" because they always exist, even if individual equal and beautiful objects begin and cease to exist. Beauty itself is "intelligible" because it is the abiding nature common to all individual beautiful things. Forms are "uniform" because each has one specific content—beauty, for example, is not equality. And the forms are "indissoluble" because they have no separable parts—beauty itself does not have one part that is beautiful, another that is ugly. The reason for all this is that each form is "always the same as itself." The forms, in short, are "divine," each of these points contrasting forms with things that participate in them, such as the human body. The basis for the contrast is unity. A form is in two ways more fully one than what participates in it. Internally, it is always the same as itself; consequently, it never changes, has no parts, and is eternal. Externally, it causes whatever unity two participants might enjoy; beauty itself unifies two beautiful objects in beauty.

Given the two comparisons, where does the soul fit? The soul is not exactly the same as either the forms above or physical objects below it. But Socrates says it is more "like" the forms. He argues from a contrast between soul and body. As invisible master of the body, the soul is the source of unity and personal identity for a human. This makes the soul more fully one than the body, as a form is more fully one than its participants. The body changes over the course of one's life, but it is still "one's" life. So whatever unity over time is found in the body must be caused by something else—the soul—as the unity in participants is caused by a form. But the soul also must be *internally* unified, the same as itself, as a form is. Otherwise, it couldn't be the one master over the body, and the source of personal identity and responsibility. But if the soul is one in these ways, it, like a form, should not have parts, and should be indestructible and immortal, as are they.

Socrates gives an ambiguous summary: the soul is "altogether indissoluble, or nearly so." The last phrase does clarify the conclusion. The soul is only *near* the full reality of the forms. This puts it on the horizon, as it were, between the fully unified forms above and the multiple participants below. Each soul is eternal like the forms, but is a distinct individual within a species, like participants. Curiosity about what will happen to this horizon-being leads to the next selection (G/G'). But "nearly so" is also deflating. We doubt whether the argument really succeeds. It has been based on two comparisons, soul to body, and form to participants. Both relations are extrinsic to the very nature of the soul itself. What is lacking here is an answer to the question "What is that nature?" This deficiency foreshadows the discussions in F' and E', which will at long last focus the dialogue on the central question: What is the *nature* of the soul?

G and G'. Transition: Reincarnation Myth

Socrates presents a poetic vision of reincarnated souls. The picture of "inferior men" becoming asses and wolves is not appealing, even less so "moderate men" becoming bees and ants. But the story need not be literally true to be helpful.

The off-putting message forces us to recognize the difference between literary truth (the moral contained within the story) and literal truth. As with the fables of Aesop, the moral is what is important.

The myth has two philosophical morals. If the soul is immortal, it must exist in some definite state after death, either separated from a body or united with one. And, in addition, there must be some rationale for the state the soul attains; and Socrates thinks it only just that the soul's state depend on the kind of life one has led. Virtue should be rewarded and vice punished, if the cosmos really is organized under the forms of the good and the beautiful.

Finally, the mixed signals this vision presents are a climax to the first half of the dialogue and initiate the counterarguments of the second half.

F'. Simmias' Harmony Counterargument

Though swayed by Socrates, Simmias and Cebes are not yet convinced. Their perplexity and love of truth are genuine. Therefore, each takes up a premise from the incorruptibility argument, offers a counterargument admitting that premise but denying Socrates' conclusion, and sums up the matter in a telling image. Simmias accepts the soul's invisibility. He likens the relation of body and soul to that of lyre and harmony. The harmony that comes from the instrument cannot be directly perceived. Harmony is a real yet not directly perceptible quality of the instrument, making it like the imperceptible yet real soul. But the difficulty for immortality is that when the lyre is destroyed, so too is its harmony, which has no existence apart from the instrument. Neither should the soul survive the body.

Simmias' analogy is not merely a critique of Socrates: it drives the discussion to a deeper level by illustrating one view of the very nature of the soul. Whether harmony means the "attunement" of the lyre, a physical property *in* the strings, or "melodiousness," which results *from* properly playing the strings, harmony is clearly a function of the physical makeup of the lyre. By analogy, the soul would be a property or function of the body. This conception of the soul is materialist because, if Simmias' analogy holds, the principle of life and thought would be merely a part or aspect of our physical bodies.

E'. Cebes' Weaver Counterargument

Cebes concentrates on the soul as master of the body. The soul is stronger and more perfect, that is, more complete, than the body. And he even grants that it sometimes survives death. The soul is like a weaver who produces many cloaks during a long life. No one would dispute that the weaver is better than his products and outlives most of them. But, as the last cloak survives the weaver, the soul's mastery over the body is no guarantee of immortality.

Cebes's analogy presents a second view of the very nature of the soul. It is an entity in its own right. Only in this way can it control the body and order it to act against its physical inclinations, as the weaver forces the cloth out of its natural shape in making a cloak. Such an invisible master must be an immaterial entity. Immateriality and causal priority over the body, however, do not by themselves ensure immortality. Cebes sees the soul as immaterial but also mortal.

These counterarguments are "depressing." Phaedo recollects that upon hearing them, Socrates "turned us around" by offering yet a third view: the soul as a fully spiritual, and consequently immortal, being. These three views can be called materialist, immaterialist, and spiritualist. A properly philosophical treatment must consider all fundamental options. Plato sums them up in three images: Simmias' harmony, Cebes' weaver, and the living image of Socrates himself, a prisoner awaiting release from the prison of the body. The rest of the argument is designed to show how the first two doctrines about the soul are wrong, and only Socrates' is correct.

D'. Socrates Replies to Simmias

Sensitive to the psychology of dashed hopes, Socrates notes that the counterarguments of Simmias and Cebes could lead to misology (hatred of argument), as wrongful behavior can lead to misanthropy (hatred of human beings). But both reactions would be wrong. The worst misanthropists are those who mouth the platitudes of concern; the worst misologists are trained arguers. Faced with the power of arguments to overturn each other, sophists despair of ever finding truth. But Socrates tries to engender hope of attaining truth. It depends on insight into human nature. While none of Socrates' points ensures immortality by itself, each leads to that conclusion by turning us toward the form of "humanity," for our hope lies there. In argument, as elsewhere, appearance differs from reality. The arguments of the first half of the dialogue looked as if they could stand on their own, but they were constantly undercut; those of the second half look merely critical, but they build to a positive outcome.

Socrates begins with the central issue, causality. Simmias' lyre is clearly the cause of harmony, not the reverse. This is the reason why destroying the lyre destroys the harmony. But the body is under the control of the soul. The cause of physical action is mental decision; the cause of life in the body is the soul itself. Soul is cause, harmony effect. Since Simmias has reversed cause and effect, Socrates rejects the analogy. But he is not critical merely of this one example. Any account that reverses the causality between body and soul is wrong, and wrongheaded. This is how Socrates offers the wider insight that any materialist view of human nature, since it reduces the soul and psychic processes to effects of the body, must be wrong. The truth depends on getting cause and effect the right way round. Consequently, Socrates turns to the issue of causality in C'.

C'. Socrates' Wonder

This section appears to be an aside, but in reality it is the most important part of the *Phaedo*. To understand how the soul is a cause requires understanding causality itself. The most basic principle of Socrates' argument is the doctrine of causality he presents here. There are two issues: What are the true causes? And how do we know them? Socrates begins his explanation by turning autobiographical. When younger and less wise, he followed the method of the sages who investigated nature, and used their kinds of causes. This constituted his "first voyage" toward the causes.

On this unsuccessful journey, Socrates faced directly into the winds of nature, seeking to know the causes for the generation, destruction, and being of each thing. Direct inspection led him to conclude that all knowledge comes from sense through generalization. Through the unifying of many sensations, memories and opinions arise; then these develop into knowledge when they "become stable." He found two kinds of causes: "I thought *before* that it was obvious to anybody that men grow through *eating* and *drinking,* for *food* adds flesh to flesh and bones to bones." Food is matter out of which new physical bulk is constituted. Eating and drinking are activities that effectuate such changes. On his first voyage, therefore, Socrates used an experiential method to uncover material and efficient causes. All this seems eminently reasonable, even commonsensical; but it is wrong.

Socrates mentions two problems. The naturalists' method led to contradictions. In mathematics, for example, how is *two* generated? Sometimes *"because* of the *addition* of one to the other"; at other times *"division* is the *cause* of its becoming two." This is perplexing: one effect, two opposite causes. Using himself as an example, Socrates shows that the material and efficient factors only *contribute* to his sitting in the cell. The true causes are that, "after the Athenians decided it was *better* to condemn me, for this reason it seemed *best* to me to sit here." Notions of good produce actions in a new way, by indicating the goal. In human action, a goal is an unchanging end. But it still stamps actions—which do change—with a certain character, because the actions are directed toward the goal. Walking to the city square becomes good when it helps Socrates realize his goal of philosophizing. Without itself changing, the goal imparts its *own* character on actions directed toward it, making them good.

These examples help Socrates to draw conclusions about causality. One must separate the factors responsible for things happening into two different sorts: necessary conditions and true causes. Material factors (like the food we eat), and agency (like the activity of eating), are necessary conditions but not true causes. Everyone who has tried to bulk up or slim down knows that actually eating and having the right food are required, but are not the true causes of gaining or losing weight. These factors are subordinate to the true cause, keeping your mind on your goal. The goal-oriented character of human actions illuminates the nature of the true causes and first principles—the forms. Just as a goal is an unchanging end that imparts its own character on the means to it, making them good or bad based on its own goodness or badness, so a form is unchanging, but imparts its own formal character to the changing things that participate in it. The form, like a goal in human decision-making, acts as both final cause, drawing participants to act, and formal cause, bestowing its own nature on them.

Socrates can draw his conclusions because he has taken a "second" more successful "voyage" to the causes. This time he looks only indirectly at reality, and so avoids being blinded by inspecting arguments in the same way as the sophists would. Unlike them, he uses arguments to draw insightful, certain knowledge about the causes. This voyage constitutes half of his own philosophical method, which he describes as "one I have mixed together." The mixture has two parts: the second voyage *to* the causes, and rational deductions *from* them, such as Socrates will use at B'. Such deductions accomplish two things at once. They draw conclusions from principles. But, since deductions are only as good as their principles, they also offer the best opportunity yet for insight into those principles. Since Socrates' method is a mix of deduction from the forms as first principles and insight into the forms as true causes, the *Phaedo* exhibits all four ways of thinking identified in the *Republic:* the recollection argument had started with everyday remembering, an example of "image thinking," or associating one experience or idea with another. Analogies such as Simmias and Cebes have offered trade on such associations. They are also instances of the generalizing from particulars that characterizes "belief," as was the inductive method of the naturalists. Socratic deduction is "reasoning." While these three ways of thinking are not equal, their ultimate value lies beyond themselves, and beyond argument altogether, in "noetic insight" into the natures, that is, the forms, of things.

No argument or combination of arguments can substitute for such insight. This is why Socrates never simply presents arguments for the forms. In the end, no argument will be completely convincing, and those who pin their hopes on argument alone become sophists. But Socrates has drawn attention to three sets of reasons that can lead the mind up to this insight, and uncover three different features of the forms. *(a)* The recollection argument uncovered the forms as true causes of knowledge, a conclusion independent of the pre-existence of the soul. Socrates' example of choosing to stay in prison and be executed uncovers *(b)* the forms as final causes that are ends engendering activities, and *(c)* the forms as formal causes, imparting their own perfected natures to imperfect participants. The particular arguments of the dialogue are designed to prepare us for these insights that go beyond the scope of the arguments themselves.

If the soul is truly a cause, should it not be like the true causes? Reflection on the forms should open up insight into the soul as well. Like the forms, the soul is not an efficient or material cause, but acts in the final and formal orders. As final cause, or end for the body, it should be unchanging and immortal, like the forms. This clarifies in causal terms how the soul lies on the horizon between the eternal forms above it, and individual physical objects, like our bodies, trapped in time beneath it. As formal cause, the soul bestows its own life on the body. The consequences of this function Socrates takes up next in B'.

B'. Socrates Replies to Cebes

Socrates looks at the logic of the life bestowed by the soul on the body. Being alive is clearly opposed to being dead. Socrates uses some examples to draw the consequences for the soul. Heat and cold are opposed to each other. Fire is always hot, snow always cold. Fire is not susceptible to both hot and cold, as water is, because the very nature of fire requires that it be hot. This kind of relation is that between something and a property that flows from its nature. The same is true of the number 3 and being odd. Consequently, though snow is not directly opposed to hot, it is opposed *through* its necessary property of being cold. The question at issue, then, is whether living is a necessary property of the soul, making it impossible for the soul to die.

Answering this question involves three terms, however, not just two: soul, body, life. So Socrates expands his examples. Fire is always hot and is the proximate cause of heat in a physical body. So too a fever is the cause of sickness in a human body. Both are analogous to the individual soul. Fever causes sickness in its subject, the human body, as the soul causes life in that body. This makes sickness a necessary property of fever, and is the reason why a fever is opposed to health. Socrates draws the analogous inferences about the soul: it also possesses life as its own property, and thereby is opposed to death.

Socrates has shown that the soul in its own nature is undying or im-mortal. This conclusion, however, is not as strong as might first appear. Fever is un-healthy, but does not live on when health is regained: the fever "dies." Consequently, it is not yet clear whether the soul is opposed to death as an individual snowflake, which is destroyed by melting, is opposed to heat, or as the number 3, which is forever and indestructibly odd, is opposed to even. For this reason, Socrates states his conclusion hypothetically: if the immortal is also indestructible, then the soul will live on.

This conclusion is disappointing if we are looking for the argument to fully prove immortality. But it does complete Socrates' clarification of the nature of the soul: soul as formal cause of life in the body is incompatible with death. Beyond that, Socrates appeals to that insight about immortality toward which all the arguments in the dialogue lead, but which none fully attain, because argument is no substitute for insight. The soul lives eternally because it is like "the god" and "the form of life itself," which Simmias and Cebes readily agree are both immortal and indestructible. Socrates has come round to the divine forms, where he started. The soul is "like" the forms in causality, so it should also be like them in eternality. Cebes responds by saying that he cannot doubt the argument. Simmias has some misgivings that Socrates says require further examination of the "first hypotheses," not because Socrates lacks insight into them, but because Simmias does.

A'. Cosmic Myth

The extension of this myth is designed to make it more convincing than the myths of Theseus and of reincarnation; it covers the whole cosmos. If the human soul is an intermediate reality, a true myth would make the human habitat an in-between place. And so the story goes. Though we think of ourselves as living on the surface of the earth, in reality we live in a kind of middle earth. Death will free the pious to move up to the surface, and philosophers will go further, living unconnected to the earth, "altogether without a body." Socrates recognizes that no one "with insight" will believe this tale literally. Reading the myth rightly involves taking a risk, because there is always an interpretive step from what the story says to what it means. But the risk is a "fine" one, analogous to stepping from argument to insight. This risk makes stories and arguments similar. The last step in both is the always risky one of personal insight. Since Socrates cannot take that step for us, he ends the argumentative portion of the dialogue by offering us this opportunity.

■ ■ ■

The Death of Socrates' Body

Greek heroes were excellent in word and deed. Socrates has exhibited his excellence in words. Now he shows that wisdom produces excellence in deeds. Like the warrior-hero Achilles,

44

Socrates the philosopher-hero overcomes death. Achilles had to stifle real fear of evil death. Socrates, however, tells Crito he owes a cock to Asclepius, the god of healing, not for any past favor, but for the present one. Wisdom has eliminated fear through understanding that death is not an evil, but a healing. So Socrates has surpassed Achilles. Socrates' courage is born of understanding, Achilles' had come from emotion. This is Plato's final lesson, and his last test for us, the would-be philosophers.

■ ■ ■

Summary

Socrates' arguments for the immortality of the human soul are as follows: (1) that life comes from death just as death comes from life (Sec. D), (2) that we must have had a previous life because learning is remembering (Sec. E), (3) that the soul has no parts and therefore cannot be destroyed (Sec. F). These arguments show that the question of immortality leads to the deeper issue of the very nature of the soul.

The counterarguments uncover two erroneous views of the nature of the soul: (a) Simmias' view that the soul is the harmony of the body, a form of materialism (Sec. F'); and (b) Cebes' view that the soul, while immaterial, is mortal (Sec. E').

Socrates leads us to the truth that (c) the soul is an immortal spiritual reality by replying to (a) and (b). Simmias' argument has cause and effect backward (Sec. D'). Cebes' argument misunderstands the true causes. The true causes are the eternal forms (Sec. C'). The truth about the soul is that life is a property of the human soul making it immortal (Sec. B'). The nature of the human soul is that it exists on the horizon between the eternal forms above it and individual physical bodies below it (Sec. A'). This truth is achieved through insight. Arguments merely lead the mind to truth; they can never guarantee we will acquire the truth.

■ ■ ■

Philosophical and Religious Critique

While Plato's achievements in the *Phaedo* are as multifaceted as the dialogue itself, four stand out. First, Plato focuses the philosophical study of humans on the soul, not the body. He concludes that the human *is* the soul. Second, Plato shows that the issue uppermost in our minds—immortality for Socrates—can be resolved only by looking to its universal cause, the very nature of soul as an *individual spirit*. Third, immortality should be thought of as a characteristic inevitably following upon that nature, but not identical with the nature itself; it is a property due to the causal relation between soul and body. The soul is an *unchanging end* for the body—the body is for the sake of the soul, not the reverse. And the soul causes the *perfection of life* in the body. Fourth, Plato reflects on how he uses reason to draw these conclusions. Arguments show the relationship between eternal but abstract forms and particular but mortal participants. But the *mental insight* that the soul is "on the horizon," a particular but eternal spirit, each mind must attain on its own. Insight surpasses story, speech, and argument.

Since the dialogue imbues the reader with the critical spirit of Socrates, Plato's conclusion should itself be critiqued.

Indeed, it looks as if Plato has proven too much. Based on its nature, all soul is immortal. But soul is present in plants and animals as well as humans. It looks as if Plato must say that individual souls of all three types are spiritual and live forever. This would make the reincarnation myth literally true. This problem has given rise to very different solutions among Plato's followers.

Aristotle (384–322 B.C.) agreed that Plato was right to focus on the nature of the soul, but concluded that a proper understanding of its nature does not require immortality. So he will solve the problem by saying that humans and their souls are more like plants and animals than like the gods. The Platonic argument for immortality will not work for even one kind of soul.

Plotinus (A.D. 205–270) will draw the opposite conclusion. Plato's insight is true. But this does not prove that any individual soul is immortal, it only shows that soul as such, in its very nature, is immortal. There is immortality, but it is not personal. This is because when we distinguish soul in its own nature from the soul in some individual, we are not merely distinguishing two ways of *thinking* about soul, but two different ways in which soul actually *exists*. The two ways are (1) existing in its own nature as one, unchanging, immortal, "cosmic" soul, and (2) existing in a multitude of individual, changing, and mortal living things—including humans. There is no immortality for *them*, even while there is for *it*.

Finally, Thomas Aquinas, though he never even read the *Phaedo* directly, will concentrate on Plato's argument at B' and develop yet a third conclusion. Aquinas will connect Plato's numerical example of 3 and oddness with Aquinas's own basic principles to conclude that the human soul, as the subsistent cause of being for the whole person, is personally immortal, though this is not true of the souls of other living creatures. Humans, not just their souls, will be the horizon-beings.

All three philosophers will take up Plato's doctrine of the soul in a Socratic spirit, just as Plato had wanted. And this, more than anything else, is his eternal legacy to philosophy.

■ ■ ■

Further Reading

G. M. A. Grube, *Plato's Thought*, 2nd ed. (Indianapolis, Ind., 1980).
R. Kraut, ed., *The Cambridge Companion to Plato* (Cambridge, UK, 1992).

2

ARISTOTLE

■ ■ ■

THE HUMAN PERSON
AS A BESOULED BODY

Introduction and Commentary by R. E. Houser

INTRODUCTION

■ ■ ■

Aristotle's Life and Works

Aristotle was the student of Plato. Born in Stagira in 384/3 B.C., he came to Athens in 367, liked what he saw in Plato's school, and stayed for twenty years. But the most important lesson he learned made him part company with his teacher. Plato had understood wisdom to be the all-encompassing wisdom of the philosopher king. But who has ever met such a person? To preserve the reality of wisdom, Aristotle fractured it into pieces. Each of these he called a science (we might say a discipline), the autonomy of which comes from its own limited subject matter and its own principles used to uncover conclusions. When Aristotle returned to Athens after tutoring Alexander the Great of Macedon (343–336 B.C.), he organized a new school, called the Lyceum, according to these disciplines. The lectures from his courses became the treatises we have today. He died in 322 B.C.

To determine what are the parts of wisdom, Aristotle followed the example of Socrates, who had talked with craftsmen, politicians, and poets. Each group represents one of the three areas of human activity: production of goods and services, practical action affecting others, and theoretical life.

51

Productivity demands technique (or art), but not science. Science, however, is found in practical and theoretical spheres. There are three practical sciences. Ethics concerns the individual; economics (from the word for house) concerns the family; and politics concerns the community. *Nicomachean Ethics* is devoted to the first, *Politics* to the third. From the practical perspective, politics is the master science. There are also three areas of theoretical science: the physical sciences, mathematics, and metaphysics. Aristotle's bent toward nature uncovered a host of physical sciences, and made him beyond question the first great scientist. *Physics* treats the basic principles of the natural world, which are applied in treatises on astronomy, geology, and biology. *On Soul* fits into the last group. *Metaphysics* contains the highest theoretical science and is devoted to the first principles of reality. Aristotle calls this discipline theology because it studies the divine.

Each of Aristotle's sciences is demonstrative. The need for proof led Aristotle to perhaps his most important invention: logic. Logical thinking had been employed by previous thinkers, but never studied systematically in its own right. Aristotle studied it in this way, inventing the art of logic. He understood himself to have done for logic, in the theoretical sphere, what the Sophists had already done for rhetoric in the practical sphere. Logic opens up the possibility of actually attaining at least part of the wisdom for which philosophy strives. Such knowledge will be certain, because it is rational, universal, necessary, and causal.

Aristotle thought the right approach to a subject represented half the battle, because, as he says, "a small mistake in the beginning is multiplied later a thousandfold" (*On the Heavens* 1.5.271b8–13). For example, by focusing on immortality, Plato had approached the soul the wrong way round, and made mistakes. The right approach, according to Aristotle, is to start with the whole human being, not one of the parts, and then, through analysis, proceed from the whole to its parts. Thus, Aristotle did not have a separate treatise on the immortality of the soul, or even on the *human* soul itself. His treatise is entitled *On Soul*, and is part of his study of nature. The treatise is structured accordingly:

I. Background
   (a) The importance of soul as the basic principle of animate life (bk. 1, chap. 1)
   (b) Previous thinkers on soul (1.2–5)
II. General definition of soul
   The nature of soul defined broadly enough to include all animate beings (2.1–2)
III. Specific types of soul as principles of different types of animate beings
   (a) Soul as a principle of growth, nutrition, and reproduction: plant life (2.3–4)
   (b) Soul as a principle of sensory cognition: animal life (2.5–3.2)
   (c) Soul as a principle of intellectual cognition: intellectual life
      (1) Acquiring knowledge: the theoretical use of the intellect (3.3–6)
      (2) Using knowledge: the practical use of the intellect (3.7–12)

■ ■ ■

What to Look For in the Selection

1. Aristotle offers a "scientific" (his term for philosophical) explanation of the soul. Philosophical knowledge is causal knowledge. Be on the lookout for how Aristotle uses his philosophical principles—the categories, causes, and predicables—in analyzing the human person and the soul.

2. Aristotle, like Socrates, loved examples and analogies because he thought we learn by comparing what we don't fully understand with what we already know. Be sure to note the following examples and analogies, making sure you understand how Aristotle uses them to make his philosophical points: the axe and the eye at 2.1; color, movement, and the son of Diares at 2.5; the wax, signet ring, and lyre at 2.12; the scraped tablet (or clean slate) at 3.4; light at 3.5.

3. At 1.1 Aristotle introduces the subject by indicating the questions he wants to answer about the soul. Write

down Aristotle's questions in your own terms. Then add any other questions you think Aristotle had left out but which you would like answered.

4. At 2.1 Aristotle gives a definition of the nature of the soul. Find that definition and try to explain it in your own terms.

5. Does Aristotle's view of the soul at 2.1 lead to the conclusion that the soul is mortal or immortal?

6. What is the difference between the three kinds of objects we sense, as Aristotle describes them in 2.6: "special" objects, "common sensibles," and "incidental objects" of sensation?

7. After reading 2.12, try to (*a*) identify each of the four causes of sensation; and (*b*) explain the relation between a sense power and a sense organ.

8. After reading 3.4–5, try to identify each of the four causes of intellectual knowing.

9. Is the passive power involved in intellectual knowing, which Aristotle takes up at 3.4, part of the body or distinct from it?

10. What is the relation between the passive power of knowing explained in 3.4 and the active power of knowing explained in 3.5?

11. How are sense knowing and intellectual knowing related to each other, according to Aristotle?

12. Compare the conclusions about the nature of the soul that Aristotle draws from analyzing it in terms of the causes with the conclusions he draws about the soul from his analysis of intellectual knowledge. Are these conclusions consistent with each other?

11. Compare the picture of the human soul you get from Aristotle with Plato's ideas on the subject. Where do they agree and where do they part company?

SELECTION FROM ARISTOTLE

■ ■ ■

De Anima [On Soul]

Book 1, Chapter 1

(402a) Holding as we do that, while knowledge of any kind is a thing to be honored and prized, one kind of it may, either by reason of its greater exactness or of a higher dignity and greater wonderfulness in its subjects, be more honorable and precious than another, on both accounts we should naturally be led to place in the front rank the study of soul. The knowledge of soul admittedly contributes greatly to the advance of truth in general, and, above all, to our understanding of nature, for soul is in some sense the principle of animal life. Our aim is to grasp and understand, first its essential nature, and secondly its properties.

First, no doubt, it is necessary to determine in which of the categories soul lies, what it is. Is it an individual entity, a substance, or is it a quality or a quantity, or some other of the remaining kinds of predicates which we have distinguished? Further, does soul belong to the class of potential existents, or is it not rather an actuality? Our answer to this question is of the greatest importance.

(402b) We must consider also whether soul is divisible or is without parts, and whether it is everywhere homogeneous or not; and if not homogeneous, whether its various forms are different specifically or generically: up to the present time those who have discussed and investigated soul seem to have confined themselves to the human soul.

(403a) A further problem presented by the affections of soul is this: are they all affections of the complex of body and soul, or is there any one among them peculiar to the soul by itself? To determine this is indispensable but difficult. If we consider the majority of them, there seems to be no case in which the soul can act or be acted upon without involving the body; for example, anger, courage, appetite, and sensation generally. Thinking seems the most probable exception; but if this too proves to be a form of imagination or to be impossible without imagination, it too requires a body as a condition of its existence. If there is any way of acting or being acted upon proper to soul, soul will be capable of separate existence; if there is none, its separate existence is impossible.

Book 1, Chapter 2

(403b) For our study of soul it is necessary, while formulating the problems of which in our further advance we are to find the solutions, to call into council the views of those of our predecessors who have declared any opinion on this subject, in order that we may profit by whatever is sound in their suggestions and avoid their errors.

The starting-point of our inquiry is an exposition of those characteristics which have chiefly been held to belong to soul in its very nature. Two characteristic marks have above all others been recognized as distinguishing that which has soul in it from that which has not: movement and sensation. It may be said that these two are what our predecessors have fixed upon as characteristic of soul.

Book 2, Chapter 1

(412a) Let the foregoing suffice as our account of the views concerning the soul which have been handed on by our predecessors; let us now pass over them and make as it were a completely fresh start, endeavouring to give a precise answer to the question "What is soul?", that is, to formulate the most general possible definition of it.

We are in the habit of recognizing, as one determinate kind of what is, substance; and that in several senses: in the sense of matter, and in the sense of form or essence, and thirdly in the sense of that which is compounded of both. Now, matter is potentiality, form actuality; of the latter there are two grades related to one another as, for example, knowledge to the exercise of knowledge.

Among substances are by general consent reckoned bodies; and especially natural bodies, for they are the principles of all other bodies. Of natural bodies some have life in them, others do not; by life we mean self-nutrition and growth (with its correlative, decay). It follows that every natural body which has life in it is a substance in the sense of a composite.

But since it is also a body of such and such a kind, that is, having life, the body cannot be soul; the body is the subject or matter, not what is attributed to it. Hence the soul must be a substance in the sense of the form of a natural body having life potentially within it. But substance (in the sense of form) is actuality, and thus soul is the actuality of a body as above characterized. Now the word *actuality* has two senses corresponding respectively to the possession of knowledge and the actual exercise of knowledge. It is obvious that the soul is actuality in the first sense, that is, that of knowledge as possessed, for both sleeping and waking presuppose the existence of soul, and of these waking corresponds to actual knowing, sleeping to knowledge possessed but not employed; and, in the history of the individual, knowledge comes before its employment or exercise.

That is why the soul is the first grade of actuality of a natural body having life potentially in it. The body so described is a body which is organic [which has different organs].

(412b) The parts of plants in spite of their extreme simplicity are "organs." For example, the leaf serves to shelter the pericarp, the pericarp to shelter the fruit, while the roots of plants are analogous to the mouth of animals, both serving for the absorption of food. If, then, we have to give a general formula applicable to all kinds of soul, we must describe it as the first grade of actuality of a natural organic body. That is why we can wholly dismiss as unnecessary the question whether the soul and the body are one: it is as meaningless as to ask whether the wax and the shape given to it by the stamp are one, or generally the matter of a thing and that of which it is the matter. Unity has many senses (as many as "is" has), but the most proper and fundamental sense of both is the relation of an actuality to that of which it is the actuality.

We have now given an answer to the question "What is soul?"—an answer which applies to it universally. It is substance in the sense which corresponds to the definitive formula of a thing's essence. This means that it is "the essential whatness" of a body of the character just assigned. Suppose that what is literally an "organ" [an instrument], like an axe, were a natural body; its "essential whatness" would have been its essence, and so its soul; if this disappeared from it, it would have ceased to be an axe, except in name. As it is, it is just an axe; it lacks the character which is required to make its whatness or formulable essence a soul; for that, it would have had to be a natural body of a particular kind, that is, one having in itself the power of setting itself in movement and stopping itself. Next, apply this doctrine in the case of the "parts" of the living body. Suppose that the eye were an animal—sight would have been its soul, for sight is the substance or essence of the eye which corresponds to the formula [the definition of the eye], the eye being merely the matter of seeing. When seeing is removed the eye is no longer an eye, except in name— it is no more a real eye than the eye of a statue or of a painted figure. We must now extend our consideration from the "parts" to the whole living body; for what the particular sense is to the bodily part which is its organ, that the whole faculty of sense is to the whole sensitive body as such.

We must not understand by that which is "potentially capable of living" what has lost the soul it had, but only what still retains it; but seeds and fruits are bodies which possess the qualification. Consequently, while waking is actuality in the sense corresponding to the cutting and the seeing (413a), the soul is actuality in the sense corresponding to the power in the tool and the power of sight; the body corresponds to what exists in potentiality; as the pupil plus the power of sight constitutes the eye, so the soul plus the body constitutes the animal.

From this it indubitably follows that the soul is inseparable from its body, or at any rate that certain parts of it are (if it has parts)—for the actuality of some of them is nothing but the actualities of their bodily parts. Yet some may be separable because they are not the actualities of any body at all. Further, we have no light on the problem whether the soul may not be the actuality of its body in the sense in which the sailor is the actuality of the ship.

This must suffice as our sketch or outline determination of the nature of soul.

Book 2, Chapter 2

We resume our inquiry from a fresh starting-point by calling attention to the fact that what has soul in it differs from what has not in that the former displays life. Now this word [life] has more than one manifestation, and provided any one alone of these is found in a thing we say that that thing is living. Life, that is, may mean thinking or perception or local movement and rest, or movement in the sense of nutrition, decay, and growth.

This power of self-nutrition can be isolated from the other powers mentioned, but not they from it—in mortal beings at least. The fact is obvious in plants; for it is the only power of soul they possess.

This is the originative power, the possession of which leads (413b) us to speak of things as *living* at all, but it is the possession of sensation that leads us for the first time to speak of living things as animals; for even those beings which possess no power of local movement but do possess the power of sensation we call animals and not merely living things.

The primary form of sense is touch, which belongs to all animals. Just as the power of self-nutrition can be isolated from touch and sensation generally, so touch can be isolated from all other forms of sense. Soul is the source of these phenomena and is characterized by them, that is, by the powers of self-nutrition, sensation, thinking, and motivity.

Book 2, Chapter 4

It is necessary for the student of these forms of soul first to find a definition of each, expressive of what it is, and then to investigate its derivative properties. But if we are to express what each is, that is, what the thinking power is, or the perceptive, or the nutritive, we must go farther back and first give an account of thinking or perceiving, for in the order of investigation the question of what an agent does precedes the question of what enables it to do what it does. If this is correct, we must on the same ground go yet another step farther back and have some clear view of the objects of each; thus we must start with these objects, for example, with food, with what is perceptible, or with what is intelligible.

The soul is the cause or principle of the living body. The terms *cause* and *principle* have many senses. But the soul is the cause of its body alike in all three senses which we explicitly recognize. It is the principle or origin of movement, it is the end, it is the essence of the whole living body.

That it is the last, is clear; for in everything the essence is identical with the ground of its being, and here, in the case of living things, their being is to live, and of their being and living the soul in them is the cause or principle. Further, the actuality of whatever is potential is identical with its formulable essence.

Nutrition and reproduction are due to one and the same power of soul.

Book 2, Chapter 5

Having made these distinctions let us now speak of sensation in the widest sense. Sensation depends, as we have said, on a process of movement or affection from without, for it is held to be some sort of change of quality.

Book 2, Chapter 6

In dealing with each of the senses we shall have first to speak of the objects which are perceptible by each. The term "object of sense" covers three kinds of objects, two kinds of which are, in our language, directly perceptible, while the remaining one is only incidentally perceptible. Of the first two kinds one consists of what is perceptible by a single sense, the other of what is perceptible by any and all the senses. I call by the name of special object of this or that sense that which cannot be perceived by any other sense than that one and in respect of which no error is possible; in this sense color is the special object of sight, sound of hearing, flavor of taste. Touch, indeed, discriminates more than one set of different qualities.

"Common sensibles" are movement, rest, number, figure, magnitude; these are not peculiar to any one sense, but are common to all. There are at any rate certain kinds of movement which are perceptible both by touch and by sight.

We speak of an incidental object of sense where, for example, the white object which we see is the son of Diares; here because "being the son of Diares" is incidental to the directly visible white thing, we speak of the son of Diares as being incidentally perceived or seen by us. Because this is only incidentally an object of sense, it in no way as such affects the senses.

Book 2, Chapter 7

The object of sight is the visible. Whatever is visible is color, and color is what lies upon what is in its own nature visible. Every color has in it the power to set in movement what is actually transparent; that power constitutes its very nature. That is why it is not visible except with the help of light; it is only in light that the color of a thing is seen.

The following experiment makes the necessity of a medium clear. If what has color is placed in immediate contact with the eye, it cannot be seen. Color sets in movement not the sense organ but what is transparent, for example the air, and that, extending continuously from the object to the organ, sets the latter in movement.

The same account holds also of sound and smell; if the object of either of these senses is in immediate contact with the organ no sensation is produced. In both cases the object sets in movement only what lies between, and this in turn sets the organ in movement: if what sounds or smells is brought into immediate contact with the organ, no sensation will be produced. The same, in spite of all appearances, applies also to touch and taste.

Book 2, Chapter 10

The species of flavor are, as in the case of color, (a) simple, that is, the two contraries, the sweet and the bitter, (b) secondary, that is, (i) on the side of the sweet, the succulent, (ii) on the side of the bitter, the saline; (iii) between these come the pungent, the harsh, the astringent, and the acid; these pretty well exhaust the varieties of flavor.

Book 2, Chapter 12

The following results applying to any and every sense may now be formulated.

By a "sense" is meant what has the power of receiving into itself the sensible forms of things without the matter. This must be conceived of as taking place in the way in which a piece of wax takes on the impress of a signet-ring without the iron or gold; we say that what produces the impression is a signet of bronze or gold, but its particular metallic constitution makes no difference: in a similar way the sense is affected by what is colored or flavored or sounding, but it is indifferent to what in each case the substance is; what alone matters is what quality it has, that is, in what ratio its constituents are combined.

By "an organ of sense" is meant that in which ultimately such a power is seated.

The sense and its organ are the same in fact, but their essence is not the same. What perceives is, of course, a spatial magnitude, but we must not admit that either the having the power to perceive or the sense itself is a magnitude; what they are is a certain ratio or power in a magnitude. This enables us to explain why objects of sense which possess one of two opposite sensible qualities in a degree largely in excess of the other opposite destroy the organs of sense; if the movement set up by an object is too strong for the organ, the equipoise of contrary qualities in the organ, which just *is* its sensory power, is disturbed; it is precisely as concord and tone are destroyed by too violently twanging the strings of a lyre.

Book 3, Chapter 2

(426b) Each sense then is relative to its particular group of sensible qualities: it is found in a sense-organ as such and discriminates among the differences which exist within that group; for example, sight discriminates white from black; taste, sweet from bitter; and so in all cases. Since we also discriminate white from sweet, and indeed each sensible quality from every other, with what do we perceive that they are different? It must be by sense; for what is before us is sensible objects. Hence it is also obvious that the flesh cannot be the ultimate sense-organ: if it were, the discriminating power could not do its work without immediate contact with the object.

Therefore discrimination between white and sweet cannot be effected by two agencies which remain separate; both the qualities discriminated must be present to something that is one and single. On any other supposition, even if I perceived sweet and you perceived white, the difference between them would be apparent. What says that two things are different must be one; for sweet is different from white. Therefore, what asserts this difference must be self-identical, and as what asserts, so also what thinks or perceives.

Book 3, Chapter 3

There are two distinctive peculiarities by reference to which we characterize the soul—local movement and thinking, discriminating, perceiving. Thinking, both speculative and practical, is regarded as akin to a form of perceiving; for in the one as well as the other the soul discriminates and is cognizant of something which is. Indeed the ancients go so far as to identify thinking and perceiving. They all look upon thinking as a bodily process like perceiving, and hold that like is known as well as perceived by like. That perceiving and practical thinking are not identical is obvious; for the former is universal in the animal world, the latter is found in only a small division of it. Further, speculative thinking is also distinct from perceiving—I mean that in which we find rightness and wrongness—rightness in prudence, knowledge, true opinion, wrongness in their opposites; for perception of the special objects of sense is always free from error, and is found in all animals, while it is possible to think falsely as well as truly, and thought is found only where there is discourse of reason as well as sensibility. For imagination is different from either perceiving or discursive thinking, though it is not found without sensation, or judgment without it. That this activity is not the same kind of thinking as judgment is obvious. For imagining lies within our own power whenever we wish (e.g., we can call up a picture, as in the practice of helping memory by the use of mental images), but in forming opinions we are not free: we cannot escape the alternative of falsehood or truth.

Book 3, Chapter 4

(429a) Turning now to the part of the soul with which the soul knows and thinks (whether this is separable from the others in definition only, or spatially as well) we have to inquire what differentiates this part, and how thinking can take place.

If thinking is like perceiving, it must be either a process in which the soul is acted upon by what is capable of being thought, or a process different from but analogous to that. The thinking part of the soul must therefore be, while impassible, capable of receiving the form of an object; that is, must be potentially identical in character with its object without being the object. Mind must be related to what is thinkable as sense is to what is sensible.

Therefore, since everything is a possible object of thought, mind in order, as Anaxagoras says, to dominate, that is, to know, must be pure from all admixture; for the co-presence of what is alien to its nature is a hindrance and a block: it follows that it too, like the sensitive part, can have no nature of its own, other than that of having a certain capacity. Thus that in the soul which is called mind (by mind I mean that whereby the soul thinks and judges) is, before it thinks, not actually any real thing. For this reason it cannot reasonably be regarded as blended with the body: if so, it would acquire some quality, e.g., warmth or cold, or even have an organ like the sensitive faculty: as it is, it has none.

Observation of the sense-organs and their employment reveals a distinction between the impassibility of the sensitive and that of the intellective faculty. After strong stimulation of a sense we are less able to exercise it than (429b) before, as e.g. in the case of a loud sound we cannot hear easily immediately after, or in the case of a bright color or a powerful odor we cannot see or smell; but in the case of mind thought about an object that is highly intelligible renders it more and not less able afterwards to think objects that are less intelligible: the reason is that, while the faculty of sensation is dependent upon the body, mind is separable from it.

Once the mind has become each set of its possible objects, as a man of science has, when this phrase is used of one who is actually a man of science (this happens when he is now able to exercise the power on his own initiative), its condition is still one of potentiality, but in a different sense from the potentiality which preceded the acquisition of knowledge by learning or discovery: the mind too is then able to think itself.

Since we can distinguish between a spatial magnitude and what it is to be such, and between water and what it is to be water, and so in many other cases (though not in all; for in certain cases the thing and its form are identical), flesh and what it is to be flesh are discriminated either by different faculties or by the same faculty in two different states; for flesh necessarily involves matter and is like what is snub-nosed, a this in a this. Now it is by means of the sensitive faculty that we discriminate the hot and the cold, i.e., the factors which combined in a certain ratio constitute flesh: the essential character of flesh is apprehended by something different either wholly separate from the sensitive faculty or related to it as a bent line to the same line when it has been straightened out.

Again in the case of abstract objects what is straight is analogous to what is snub-nosed; for it necessarily implies a continuum as its matter. Its constitutive essence is different, if we may distinguish between straightness and what is straight: let us take it to be two-ness. It must be apprehended, therefore, by a different power or by the same power in a different state. To sum up, in so far as the realities it knows are capable of being separated from their matter, so it is also with the powers of mind.

A problem might be suggested: if thinking is a passive affection, then if mind is simple and impassible and has nothing in common with anything else, as Anaxagoras says, how can it come to think at all? For interaction between two factors is held to require a precedent community of nature between the factors.

Have we not already disposed of the difficulty about interaction involving a common element, when we said that mind is in a sense potentially whatever is thinkable, though actually it is nothing until it has thought? (430a) What it thinks must be in it just as characters may be said to be on a writing-tablet on which as yet nothing actually stands written: this is exactly what happens with mind.

Book 3, Chapter 5

Since in every class of things, as in nature as a whole, we find two factors involved, a matter which is potentially all the particulars included in the class, and a cause which is productive in the sense that it makes them all (the latter standing to the former as, for example, an art to its material), these distinct elements must likewise be found in the case of soul.

And in fact mind as we have just described it is what it is by virtue of becoming all things, while there is another which is what it is by virtue of making all things: this is a sort of positive state like light; for in a sense light makes potential colors into actual colors.

Mind in this sense of it is separate, impassible, unmixed, since it is in its essential nature activity (for always the active is superior to the passive factor, the originating force to the matter which it forms).

Actual knowledge is identical with its object. In the individual, potential knowledge is in time prior to actual knowledge, but in general it is not prior even in time. Mind is not at one time knowing and at another not. When mind is set free from its present conditions it appears as just what it is and nothing more. This alone is immortal and eternal (we do not, however, remember its former activity because, while mind in this sense is impassible, mind as passive is destructible), and without it nothing thinks.

Book 3, Chapter 8

(431b) Let us now summarize our results about soul, and repeat that the soul is in a way all existing things; for existing things are either sensible or thinkable, and knowledge is in a way what is knowable, and sensation is in a way what is sensible.

Within the soul the faculties of knowledge and sensation are potentially these objects, the one what is knowable, the other what is sensible. They must be either the things themselves or their forms. The former alternative is of course impossible: it is not the stone which is present in the soul but its form.

(432a) Since according to common agreement there is nothing outside and separate in existence from sensible spatial magnitudes, the objects of thought are in the sensible forms, that is, both the abstract objects and all the states and affections of sensible things. Hence no one can learn or understand anything in the absence of sense, and when the mind is actively aware of anything it is necessarily aware of it along with an image; for images are like sensuous contents except in that they contain no matter.

Extracted from *De Anima* [On Soul], translated by J. A. Smith, 1931, and revised by R. E. Houser.

COMMENTARY

■ ■ ■

The Principles of "Scientific" Knowledge of Human Nature (1.1–2)

Aristotle's treatment of soul is scientific: he describes the facts and explains the reasons for them. Description requires concepts that accurately reflect the natures of things. Though things are individuals, they share natures in common. The concepts we use follow those natures and are universal. A thorough description of anything requires a multitude of concepts: Socrates is at once human, animal, living, the son of a stonecutter and husband to Xanthippe, short, snub-nosed, courageous, and walking in the public square. Aristotle recognized these differences and concluded that there are ten most general descriptive concepts, his *categories*. The first category he called *ousia* (being-ness) because it answers the question What is a thing in its fundamental nature? Since a thing's nature "stands under" all other features, this category is called *substance*. Aristotle's world is made up of individual substances—a man, a dog, a tree. Each substance has a nature that causes it to exist in its own right and is an active principle, a source, for other, nonsubstantial features. These nonsubstantial features depend on substance; Aristotle called nonsubstantial features *accidents.*

Quantity (e.g., "short") answers the question How much? *Quality* answers the question What kind of thing? Qualities range from sense qualities (color, odor, sound, and shape, e.g., "snub-nosed") to character traits ("courageous") to basic powers ("ability to walk"). Next come *relations* ("husband"). The question *When* sets something in its temporal relation, while the question *Where* describes it in terms of its spatial environment. *Positioning* is the configuration of the parts of the thing at the place where it is ("sitting down"). *Habit* describes the thing in terms of its most immediate environment, such as clothing. In addition to these static categories, Aristotle rounded out his list by adding two dynamic ones: *action* and its correlative, *passion* (or being acted on). When Socrates draws geometrical figures in the sand (action), the sand is drawn upon (being acted on).

This list is not the last word in developing knowledge. Categories by themselves are neither true nor false. Consequently, Aristotle sharply distinguished developing concepts from making intellectual judgments that produce statements. "Socrates" and "snub-nosed" are just concepts, but "Socrates is snub-nosed" is a statement, and it is true because it corresponds with reality.

While the number of possible statements is unlimited, the *way* the subjects and predicates of propositions can be related to each other is definitely limited. The predicate of a proposition either uncovers some property of the very nature of the subject or it does not. And if not, the predicate refers to something either causally dependent on the nature of the subject or not causally related to the subject at all, but caused by something else. Consider the following examples of various types of relations: (*a*) "Socrates is human," (*b*) "Socrates is able to laugh," and (*c*) "Socrates is pale." The predicates each describe something different: (*a*) describes the essence of Socrates, (*b*) describes a property, and (*c*) describes an accident. Because the essence can be described in more general terms (as a genus), or quite precisely (as a species), or in terms of what is most distinctive about a thing (its difference), Aristotle divided essential predicates into three, and came up with five *predicables: genus, species, difference, property, accident.*

The predicables show that each science has three parts: a determinate subject, objects of enquiry, and principles guiding investigation. The task of the scientific knower is to separate off the accidents of that subject from its essence and properties. Because they come and go, there can be no universal and necessary knowledge of accidents. So the task of a science is to uncover the essence and properties of its subject. But this can be done only if the essence and properties are fully understood, not just descriptively, but causally. In the course of uncovering the essence of the soul, Aristotle drew an analogy based on causal analysis of an axe. A cause is a factor responsible for some effect. There is more than one such factor for the axe. It is composed of wood and metal; arranged with a long handle attached to a flat, sharp, heavy blade; designed by an axe-maker; used by someone who wants to chop wood. Aristotle recognizes the same four types of responsible factors as Plato does. But Aristotle holds that all four are genuine causes because each in its own way produces the effect. Generalizing from such examples, Aristotle concludes that there are four different types of causes. The "axe-maker" is an *efficient cause* or agent. The purpose or reason for making the axe, "for chopping wood," first exists in the mind of the axe-maker and then becomes part of the very reality of the axe itself. Aristotle called this purpose the end or *final cause*, not in the sense of the thing's destruction, but as the fulfillment to which it is oriented. Since acorns just naturally grow into oak trees, Aristotle recognized natural final causes as well as the volitional final causes found in human artifacts. "Wood and bronze" are the *matter* out of which the axe is made. Now the most obvious features of all matter are size, shape, density, and other structural and qualitative characteristics. With his eye on change, however, Aristotle noted that all matter has the capacity to become a limited number of things. Since capacity is not achievement, the last cause is the actual "axe-shape" the materials take. Because only the shape produces a real axe, Aristotle adopts Plato's term and calls this the *form*. Both matter and form are intrinsic causes of the reality of the axe.

Matter and form are the basis for different features of things. "Wood and bronze" are the axe, but only potentially; they are the basis for its destructibility; and they make one axe different from another. Upon matter, therefore, is built potentiality, destructibility, and individuality. Form is the cause of opposite characteristics: actuality, permanence, and common nature. Individual things have all six characteristics, but they are due to two distinct intrinsic causes.

What exists in its own integrity is the axe. Its matter and form exist only as "parts" of the axe; so they are principles rather than things in their own right. Aristotle generalized to conclude that all human artifacts are composites of form and matter, and that things in nature are too.

The changes that characterize the world we live in are of two different types. If the blade of an axe is separated from its handle, the axe ceases to be an axe even though nothing fundamental has happened to the substances of wood and bronze. On the other hand, if the handle is burned, the axe undergoes a fundamental change because the fire has altered the very substance of the handle. The first is an accidental change, the second a substantial change, since the very nature of the thing changes. In both cases change requires some matter receiving a new form. It follows that there must be two types of form and two corresponding types of matter. In accidental change, the matter is some substance, which receives a new accidental form. Substantial change, on the other hand, affects the very substance itself. Such change presupposes that the substance itself is also made up of two parts: a substantial form and prime matter. All things subject to change, therefore, have a composition in two senses: (1) a composition of a substantial core and accidental forms, and (2) a composition within the substantial core, of substantial form activating prime matter.

Aristotle's philosophical principles—categories, causes, predicables—allowed him to offer very precise explanations of human nature and the human soul. As independently existing beings, humans are substances constituted by four causes: parents as efficient cause, happiness as final cause, body as matter, and soul as substantial form. The property that distinguishes human activities from those of other animals is that humans direct themselves with an intellectual knowledge special to them. These were Aristotle's basic conclusions. But truly philosophical knowledge requires that these conclusions be proven. Aristotle took two quite different approaches to developing such philosophical understanding: looking at the soul in light of the four causes, and looking at the human soul in light of its distinctive property—intellectual knowledge.

■ ■ ■

The Soul as Related to the Four Causes (2.1–2)

Aristotle devoted his causal treatment of the soul to resolving the primary problem he found in Plato: what is the relation between soul and body? His desire for precision led him to the formal and material causes, without neglecting completely the other two.

Final cause plays a predominant role in human morality. As rational creatures, we have many goals, but they cluster together: Socrates goes through the door in order to get into the street to go to the agora to philosophize. He wants all four things at the same time, because one is for the sake of the other. Such chains of final causes cannot go on indefinitely, for the simple reason that we cannot act on coordinated desires unless they work together. They stop at the desire for happiness, making it quite different from other goals. Happiness is an ultimate end, never a means to something else. And while all other ends are volitional because they presuppose the desire for happiness, the desire for happiness is natural. Without this desire as a necessary, ultimate, natural end, Socrates could never act. So the desire for happiness is a cause, not an effect, of human nature itself.

In the realm of efficient cause, there is an analogy between producing artifacts and producing people. There must be an efficient cause in each case. Axe-makers produce axes; parents produce people. But the cases are not identical. Producing an axe depends completely on the conscious intention of the axe-maker, and the second he changes his mind the production of the axe ceases. Parents, however, can become parents even against their wishes. This difference is due to a difference in final causality. Axe-making has no natural end, only a volitional end decided upon by the axe-maker. Sexual activity, however, has a natural end, in addition to whatever volitional ends the parents have in mind. But where the analogy between producing axes and people holds strictly is in the fact that the efficient cause is always extrinsic to the effect and produces its results by introducing a new form into matter.

Clarifying the kind of cause the parents are exposed precisely what was wrong with Plato's view of the soul-body relation. For Plato the soul was a separate entity possessing life in its own nature and bestowing it on the body. Aristotle realized that this description fit his idea of an *efficient* cause. But if Socrates' soul is the efficient cause of the life in his body, his soul would be the same kind of cause of his body as were his parents of him. This would require that Socrates' soul be just as separate from his body as his parents were from him. Plato effectively split Socrates in two; and while Plato was hesitant to draw this consequence, Aristotle's more precise causal analysis forced the issue. There is only one way out. Aristotle abandoned Plato's way of thinking of the soul as an efficient cause of the life in the body by reconceiving the soul as a formal cause of the body. This new way of thinking about the soul will not hazard the unity of the person.

Division based on the predicables is ideal for a formal analysis that does not compromise a unity of being. Difference can be used to divide a genus into subordinate species and show that, while species signifies one nature, it has two logical "parts"—genus and difference. Aristotle obtained "living thing" by dividing substance. It is divided first into substances that are physical bodies and those that are not (like God). Then bodies are divided into natural bodies (e.g., wood) and nonnatural bodies (e.g., an axe). Finally natural bodies are divided into living bodies (e.g., trees) or nonliving bodies (like a stone). Thus, the species "living thing" is constituted by two logical parts: the genus "natural body" and the difference "having a internal source of activity."

Two things are striking about Aristotle's notion of "parts." First, the parts do not exist on their own, but are merely aspects or features of the species "living thing." Second, the genus "natural body" is related to the difference as potency to act, since physicality incorporates an openness to life but does not require it. These two features of the logical species find parallels in the individual living substance. Such a substance is composed of two principles, matter and form, related as potency to act. Because it is potency, the part of the individual corresponding to the genus "natural body" must be the matter of the individual thing: "The body is the subject or matter, not what is attributed to it." Likewise, because it is act, the cause of life in the individual, the soul, must be the other real part—the form.

And this comparison holds true generally: genus is like matter, and difference is like form. Consequently, the logical composition of species reveals the real composition, in individual living things, of two principles—matter (the body) and form (the soul). This makes soul not a substance in the full sense of the word, but substance in the sense of a principle that is an act of the body. Soul thus enlivens the body without being a separate thing efficiently causing that life.

In order to further clarify what the soul is, Aristotle explained what kind of *act* it is. The soul activates the body by making it live, but living is carried on at a variety of levels— from the life of the mind to simple digestion. Aristotle draws a comparison between living as such and one particular life-activity: knowing. Having a mind gives one the capacity to know, but produces no actual knowledge. Within the sphere of actual knowledge, there is a difference between simply possessing knowledge (e.g., of carpentry) and actually using it. Since the second is built on the first, Aristotle called the exercise of knowledge second act, which is separate from the mere possession of it, or first act. Knowing, therefore, involves three factors—mind, possessing knowledge, and using knowledge—related as potency, first act, and second act. Now all further life activities are built on the soul, the basic animating principle. Therefore soul cannot be second act. On the other hand, since soul produces actual life, it is not mere potency. Consequently, soul must be analogous to "possessing knowledge," the first level of actuality. Soul's presence in the body forms the basis for all further activities of life. In this way Aristotle sharply distinguished soul, as primary animating principle, from all physical organs (like the brain, heart, or lungs) that also help cause life. Such organs must already be made to be alive before they contribute to bodily life, so they are not, and cannot be, the primary cause of life.

Comparing the soul with other life-principles led Aristotle to his final comparison, between the whole living thing and one of its parts—the eye. The eye has three distinct features related to each other in terms of potency and act: physical organ, power of sight, act of seeing. These are, respectively: potency, first level of actuality, second act. But this means that there is a parallel between part and whole. The human is composed of body, soul, and further activities built on them, also related as potency, first act, and second act. But here a crucial difficulty arises: Could the power of sight be separated from the organ of the eye and exist on its own? The answer is no. Aristotle then drew the analogous conclusion about soul: "From this it indubitably follows that the soul is inseparable from its body." Aristotle's matter-form analysis of living things, therefore, removes the prospects for personal human immortality. The human soul, understood as "form of the body," can no more exist in separation from that body than can the power of sight exist separately from the eye, or the axe's shape apart from the axe itself. Death is the end of the composite, and therefore the end of the soul. The logic of Aristotle's precise causal analysis distanced him from Plato. A human is an individual, composite substance, activated by a soul that, though it is an immaterial substantial form, cannot survive the death of the body.

■ ■ ■

The Human Soul and Knowledge

Aristotle's analysis thus far has not focused on what is unique about humans—their minds. But the most precise knowledge about humans should incorporate what distinguishes them from other animals. Consequently, Aristotle turns to that distinctive feature—intellectual knowledge—to understand the *human* soul. Intellectual knowledge is both like and unlike sense knowledge, which we share with the other animals. The best way to understand how sensation and intellection are related is to look at sensation first, then see how intellectual knowledge differs from sensation. This is just the order Aristotle followed in the rest of *On Soul*. Since the causes have worked so well when used to understand the nature of the soul, Aristotle applies them to analyze both sensation and intellection. The conclusions drawn about these acts of knowing Aristotle then will use to draw further conclusions about the nature of the knower, and the knower's soul.

■ ■ ■

Sensory Cognition (2.4–3.2)

Sensing and knowing involve change. Aristotle had succeeded in discovering four causes of real, physical changes. For example, when we heat water in a pan, water is the matter, heat is the new actuality (or form), the fire under the pan is the efficient cause, and wanting hot water for coffee might be our end. Aristotle is not surprised to find that each of the five external senses—sight, hearing, taste, smell, touch—has four significant features, corresponding to the four causes.

Each sense requires a distinct physical organ that is its subject or matter. This correlation is clear because when an organ is damaged so is the corresponding type of sensation.

Each organ has a structure appropriate to the range of stimuli it receives. It has a particular orientation (or purpose), called its natural final cause, which dictates this structure.

While the senses all have a common purpose—to perceive the qualities embodied in an individual thing—each sense is designed to perceive a different feature of the thing. Aristotle calls features perceived by only one sense the "proper objects of sensation": colors, sounds, tastes, smells, tactile qualities. In addition, some qualities (like shape) and quantities (like size) can be perceived by more than one sense. Aristotle calls these the "common objects" of sensation. But these two are only a small portion of the entire range of features that physical things actually possess. These objects of sensation are limited to the accidental categories: "The sense is affected by what is colored or flavored or sounding, but it is indifferent to what in each case the *substance* is; what alone matters to [sense] is what quality it has." Since the features we become aware of in sensation are caused by accidental forms in things, these "objects" function as the formal cause in sensation.

The efficient cause of sensation is more complicated because the objects we sense do not come in direct contact with our sense organs, unlike the fire, which directly transfers heat to the pan of water. All five senses require a medium, such as air or water. Flooding a darkened room with light changes the air in the room, making it actually transparent and a suitable medium for transporting the color from the object sensed to our eye. Consequently, there are actually two efficient causes of seeing, one immediate (or proximate) to the eye, the other remote. "Every color has in it the power to set in movement what is actually transparent," thus making the sensed object an efficient cause of sensation, but only *remotely* so, since the object directly affects only the medium—air. Fire is an efficient cause of light, and light is an efficient cause of the transparency it introduces into air. So Aristotle concludes that the medium is the *proximate* efficient cause producing the changes in the eye that constitute seeing.

Aristotle thus uncovered four causes of sensation: The sense organ is the matter, perceiving is the end, the objects of sensation are the form, and the medium is the proximate agent. These causes help us understand the very nature of sensation, which Aristotle summed up by using an example of Plato's: sensation is like a piece of wax receiving the impress of a gold signet ring. The ring has a distinctive mark it impresses into the wax to identify an official document, even though the ring itself never leaves, for example, Alexander's hand. The ring example does carry a disanalogy. There is no medium between ring and wax, because the ring itself is the only efficient cause. But the analogy illuminates the nature of sensation in three ways.

First, nothing happens to the ring when it is used to make an impression in the wax. In fact, were the ring affected in any way, it would no longer be useful as a signet. Thus, the signet is similar to the objects of sensation (which are unaffected when perceived) but different from the causes of most other real changes (in which the cause is itself affected by the process of change; for example, when a batter hits a ball).

Second, the ring functions by having a shape or form (perhaps "A" for Alexander) that it imparts to the wax. Thus, the process the wax undergoes is one of receiving the "form" in the ring. Analogously, the basic nature of sensation is simply "receiving the sensible forms without the matter." In addition, the very "A" in the ring is what gets transferred to the wax.

Were the "A" in the wax not the "A" of the ring, again the signet would be useless. Analogously, the very forms in sense objects are received in our sense powers. And Aristotle does not hesitate to draw the logical conclusion: they are received accurately. As long as object, medium, and sense are in their normal state, each sense is unerring about its special objects. Matter and form together, therefore, explain the essence of sensation, and the accuracy of our senses is due to form.

The third significant feature of the signet example is a function of matter: the "A" is transferred from one material to another. While remaining the same "A," it does not exist in the same state in gold as it does in wax. Analogously, the sensible forms received in sensation do not exist in the same condition as they do in the object and in perception. In real changes the new form produces a new real characteristic, in perception it produces *an awareness* of that real characteristic. The difference is due to matter and manifests itself in several ways.

Sensation requires an organ. The physical makeup of each sense organ is as different from the physical constitution of each sense object as wax is from gold. But simply having an organ is not enough. The organ must be in a state of "equipoise," a middle ground between "contrary qualities." Such a state allows the organ to use its full range of receptivity, while overstimulation destroys sensation; for example, twanging the strings of a lyre too hard destroys its harmony.

Aristotle used the lyre example to describe sensation for the very reason Plato had rejected it as a description of the soul-body relation, because the lyre is the cause and the harmony is the effect. The example shows two things. First, the dependence of harmony on the condition of the strings describes quite precisely the dependence of the sense organ's power of sensation on the physical condition of the organ itself. Second, while sensation requires an organ in which the power to sense resides, the organ and corresponding sense are not absolutely identical: "The sense and its organ are the same in reality, but their essence is not the same." The power to sense is like harmony that arises from proper arrangement of the physical parts of the lyre, but is not identical with the lyre itself. Within the material cause of sensation, therefore, there are two parts: the sense power proper and the organ of sense. And, as we have already seen, the two are related to each other as first act to potency, as in form to matter.

Distinguishing organ from power raises a question whether the "reception of form" is reception into the organ or into the sense power, or a combination of both. Aristotle's criticism of the materialist philosophers before him was that all they could admit were physical changes in the organs. These play a necessary but merely instrumental role for perception itself. Sensation is accomplished, not when the sensible forms are received in the organs of sense, but when the *sense power* receives "*into itself* the sensible forms of things without the matter." In other words, the sensible forms come to exist in the sense power in a way different from the way they exist in the sense object itself. Aristotle did not go into detail in describing this new mode of existence. But he did make clear that while sensation is accomplished through physical changes in the organ, it is not reducible to such changes. The existence of form in matter produces real characteristics; its existence in the sense power produces perception of real characteristics.

Finally, the combination of organ and power explains how individual objects can be sensed without sensation being utterly subjective. Sensation can be accurate and objective because sensation is receiving the form of the object without the matter. But since matter is what causes individuality, why do we sense an individual rather than a universal, when we receive its form? Aristotle answers that my sense power exists in an organ, an individual physical thing. The matter of my sense organ, not the matter of the sensed object, is what causes the individuality of my perceptions. The conditions of materiality, which cause individuality, are never completely left behind in sensation.

Aristotle's conclusions about sensation, therefore, were closely tied to his principles. Sensation is impossible unless real things are composed of form and matter. In the perceiver, sensation requires two combinations. The perceiver must be composed of body and soul, related as matter and form, because within the sense organ itself there is a composition of the sense organ and its correlative sense power, related as potency and act. Sensory cognition, therefore, both clarifies the nature of the soul as substantial form and opens up a study of intellection.

■ ■ ■

Intellectual Cognition (3.3–8)

Understanding is a higher form of cognition than sensing because it is characterized by universality, necessity, and certainty. Although both cognition and sensing are basically passive, the difference involves the kind of information received. Thus, to explain knowing and the knower, Aristotle follows the same approach as before by using the causes as principles and by adapting images from Plato.

The first image Aristotle uses focuses on receptivity. The mind is like a "scraped tablet" upon which nothing is yet written, but which can receive writing. The tablet itself is like matter. Learning is like writing on the tablet and requires a stylus (a writing instrument), which is an efficient cause. The words written are the content of our mental life. Because an agent introduces a form into matter, the words on the tablet are like a formal cause and are the object of intellectual knowledge, as sense objects were the formal cause of sensation. Finally, the writing on the tablet and intellection in the mind have the same purpose: understanding. This analogy shows that intellection is an activity involving all four causal factors.

The most marked difference between sensing and knowing is the formal cause. Sensation has for its objects singular things while understanding has as its object universals. This difference stems from what is left out of the object of sensation. The senses directly pick up only accidents, substance being perceived only "incidentally." Now this may be enough to say that through our senses we can know *that* a substance is there, but is not enough to tell us *what* the nature of any individual substance is. Consequently, to understand the substance of one individual we have to turn to the accidental features of other, similar things. Seeing the patterns in their accidents allows us to infer conclusions about their substantial natures, which we then reapply to the original individual. The limitations of the objects of sense, therefore, require the intellect to have universals as its object.

The formal cause (or object) of knowledge has an immediate impact on its final cause. Since universals are the object of the understanding, the goal of understanding must be to uncover what is unchanging about things—their essences.

Consequently, it is more important to know substance than peripheral features, properties than accidents, and unchangeable than changeable things.

Especially significant for human nature is the impact of the object of intellection on the tablet—the material cause. Aristotle does not simply *assume* the existence of mind. Rather, he starts with the reality of thought as a receptive process, applies the causes to thought, and concludes that there must exist a "material" cause for thought. This is mind in its receptive aspect, called the "material" or "passive" intellect. According to analogies with both natural change and sensation, this mind must be a part of the individual person, a power in one's soul, as the wood is part of the individual axe. The analogy with matter, however, might seem to indicate that mind is physical. As a result, Aristotle spent considerable effort studying the nature of the passive intellect as a spiritual reality: "While the faculty of sensation is dependent on the body, mind is separate from it." Aristotle offers two arguments for his conclusion.

The first argument comes from comparison with the sense organs. Overstimulation, such as looking into a bright light, is a problem for the senses because perception is accomplished *through* a physical organ. But "thought about an object that is highly intelligible renders [mind] more and not less" able to understand. Because the physicality of the senses causes sensitivity to overstimulation, the opposite reaction of the mind indicates that understanding cannot be an activity of a physical organ, and that the mental "organ" cannot be a physical thing.

Aristotle's second argument focuses on the objects of cognition. They are so universal in extension that there is absolutely nothing the mind cannot think about, and at least possibly understand. Each sense, on the other hand, has a limited range of receptivity. Since the physical structure of the organ is the *cause* of limitation, the mind's unlimited range of receptivity must indicate that no physical organ is involved. Any physical organ, by reason of its very physicality, would limit the mind's range. Consequently, sense and intellect are similar because both "have no nature of [their] own, other than that of having a certain capacity." But the difference in their ranges requires that the senses be physical powers, while the intellect "cannot reasonably be regarded as blended with body." The "tablet," therefore, must be a purely spiritual tablet.

The spirituality of the tablet has important consequences for the stylus and for the process of writing letters onto the tablet.

Aristotle seems to envision the process of knowing as being like an Olympic chariot course, with two turning poles. The starting pole is the real thing known, which has a nature actually individual but potentially universal, because it is a combination of form (causing its nature) and matter (making it individual). The other pole is the mind, which develops universal concepts that can be reapplied to individual things on the return course. The trip from starting pole to turning pole is the process of seeing Socrates with his snub nose and abstracting or "lifting off" "what it is to be snub-nosed" (or any other universal concept) from Socrates and other individuals. *Abstraction* is a process of dematerialization or separating the essences or forms of things from their matter: "To sum up, in so far as the realities [mind] knows are capable of being *separated from their matter,* so it is also with the powers of the mind." The second leg of the trip involves reapplying the universal concept to Socrates to make the judgment "Socrates is snub-nosed." What makes the whole trip possible is that form can exist both in conjunction with matter (in the thing) and fully separated from matter (in the mind), as the winning chariot can complete both turns of the course.

The openness of form to two ways of existing has significant consequences. First, abstraction cannot be a physical process: it must be a spiritual activity. Second, the mental existence of form must be a purely spiritual existence, because any hint of materiality would particularize the universal essence we know and reduce knowing to perceiving. But the mind receiving this form must be as spiritual as the form received. This is Aristotle's final argument for the spirituality of the passive intellect. Third, abstraction requires an efficient cause, which Aristotle called the *"agent intellect."*

The efficient cause in the "scraped tablet" image is the stylus. But it cannot explain understanding, because the stylus carves letters directly into the tablet whereas the content of our mental life comes through the medium of our sense experience. Thus, Aristotle turns to another Platonic image, one which does include a medium—sight. The medium of sight is air activated by light to become transparent and produce sight. Light acts as an efficient cause: "For in a sense light makes potential colors into actual colors." If sensation is like the air, since it is a necessary medium for understanding, the agent intellect "is a sort of positive state like light." It activates the medium of understanding (sensation) as light activitates the medium of sight (air). Just as seeing involves a transition from potential to actual seeing due to the influence of light on the objects seen, so understanding involves a transition from potential to actual knowing due to the influence of the agent intellect on the objects of knowledge. It produces universal ideas out of the content of our sense experiences through the abstraction process.

From its function follows the little that Aristotle said about the nature of the agent intellect. First, it is like the passive intellect in being a spiritual reality. Second, since "it is in its essential nature activity," it is superior to the passive intellect by being "separate," as are all efficient causes from the matter they affect. Clearly the agent intellect must be separate from the passive intellect, as light is a completely different thing from the human perceiver, and from the object perceived. Following the analogy with light, the agent intellect should also be a reality completely separate from the human knower and from what is known. Thus, the agent intellect *"alone* is immortal and eternal," because it is a spiritual reality separate from me, while "mind as passive is destructible," because the passive intellect is part of my individual soul, the form of my body, and not immortal, as we have seen.

Aristotle's causal analysis of knowing allowed him to add to his understanding of the human person as a substance composed of soul and body related as form and matter. Since intellectual knowledge begins in sensation, the human soul must have nutritive and sensory powers, not just intellectual powers. Intellectual knowledge requires a mind (the passive intellect), also a power in the individual soul. Finally, individual human knowers require the aid of an outside agent intellect to develop knowledge. But as marvelous as this share of divinity is, individual humans are doomed to mortality, theirs a life "of but a day."

■ ■ ■

Summary

Aristotle tried to make the study of the human person and the human soul demonstrative by using his philosophical principles—substance and accident, the causes, and the predicables—to try to develop sounder conclusions than his teacher Plato. Aristotle developed his argument in two stages.

He first tried to define the soul. Like every other living thing, a human is an individual substance, composed of matter (the body) and form (the soul). This definition preserves the unity of the human person Plato had split apart. Because the soul is a substantial form, not an individual substance existing in its own right, the human soul is not immortal.

The second and more detailed stage of Aristotle's argument was to use his principles to understand sensation and intellectual knowledge, as a means of drawing conclusions about the person who senses and knows. He concluded that sensing is receiving the object's sensible forms without their matter, and therefore requires a sense power joined to a physical sense organ. Sense power and organ are related as act and potency, thus corroborating Aristotle's view that the human soul and body are similarly related, as form to matter. Intellectual knowledge is also receptive. But the wide range of human knowledge requires that the passive intellect be fully spiritual, not at all material, while it is also a power existing in my individual soul. Since intelligible objects are universals, there must also be an efficient cause transforming the content of our sensations into universal concepts through abstraction. This cause is the agent intellect, which seems to be a spiritual being completely separate from our individual souls.

■ ■ ■

Philosophical and Religious Critique

Aristotle's insights into human nature were not immediately influential. After his death, more materialistic schools of philosophers arose: Stoics, Epicureans, Skeptics. The history of Aristotle's influence on subsequent thought is a history of rediscovery. The first, ancient revival culminated in Plotinus

(A.D. 270), the last great pagan thinker, who incorporated all the truth of "both Plato and Aristotle," according to his biographer Porphyry. The second revival occurred, in the tenth century, among Muslim and Jewish intellectuals living within the medieval Islamic Empire. When Aristotle's works were translated into Latin and incorporated into the curriculum of the newly founded universities in medieval Europe in the thirteenth century, the third revival began. The most recent revival began among German historians in the nineteenth century, determined to rescue the genuine Aristotle from the medieval one modern science had thrown out.

For the Muslims, Jews, and Christians who have been his strongest disciples, the precision of thought that made him *the* Philosopher also proved a weakness. Problems are created by Aristotle taking the two different lines of approach to human nature we have seen.

The *causal approach* helps resolve the fundamental Platonic problem of the unity of human nature. Aristotle saved unity by relating soul and body as two correlative principles, form and matter. But in the eyes of later theists the price to be paid for his view, sacrificing personal immortality, is too high.

The *approach based on intellect* yields quite different results. Human knowledge requires that the intellect be a spiritual reality. But three problems arise.

First, if the passive intellect is a spiritual reality in fact, was not Plato right to say it exists on its own? Aristotle's argument, based on the exhaustive range of what humans can think about, seems to warrant a stronger conclusion than the one he draws. If the passive intellect, a part of my individual soul, is truly spiritual, as Aristotle has said, does it not also exist on its own? But if so, is not Aristotle's approach based on intellect really a retreat back to Plato's view which split the mind apart from the body?

Second, can a spiritual being die? Plato had thought this impossible. Aristotle resolved this dilemma by splitting the intellect in two. The mind that is a part of me dies when I die. But how can this be, if the passive mind is truly spiritual? On the other hand, the mind that is immortal seems not to be a part of me at all. How does this help the prospects for *personal* immortality?

Third, how is Aristotle's "immortal and eternal" agent intellect related to the immortal and eternal God? Here two options present themselves: Muslim and Jewish philosophers and Saint Augustine chose to keep the agent intellect a spiritual being separate from the human soul, some identifying it with one of the angels, others with God himself. The other option is to place the agent intellect within the individual human soul, as Saint Thomas Aquinas did. Both options are essentially attempts to find a middle ground between Plato and Aristotle. Yet Plato and Aristotle thought their views to be irreconcilable. For religious motivations, however, their theistic followers tried to reconcile them, especially in three problem areas: (1) How can the human soul be both the form of the body, giving it life, and a spiritual substance existing in its own right? (2) How is personal immortality possible? (3) Is human knowledge illumination from a higher source or purely an activity of my own personal reason? Whatever the answers, the precision of later thinkers is due in great part to the lasting influence of Aristotle on human thought.

■ ■ ■

Further Reading

J. Barnes, *Aristotle* (Oxford, 1992).

E. Hartman, *Substance, Body, and Soul: Aristotelian Investigations* (Princeton, 1977).

3

SAINT AUGUSTINE

...

THE HUMAN PERSON AS
RELATIONAL AND VOLITIONAL
Introduction and Commentary by Leonard A. Kennedy

INTRODUCTION

■ ■ ■

Augustine's Life and Works

Saint Augustine was born at Tagaste, in Numidia, Northern Africa, in A.D. 354. His mother, Saint Monica, was a Christian but his father, Patricius, was a pagan. Augustine's baptism was delayed until he was in his thirties, though he was reared as a Christian. When he was seventeen Augustine went to Carthage for higher education. Though he was a good student, he continued to practice the evil habits he had already begun. He took a mistress, and soon had a son, Adeodatus. He lost what Christian faith he had, and when he finished his education he became a Manichee—a disciple of Mani (b. A.D. 216), who taught a mixture of Christian and pagan thought. Augustine followed this faith for nine years while he was teaching in Tagaste and Carthage. His Manicheeism was then replaced by his personal mixture of several Greek and Roman philosophies.

In 383 Augustine went to Rome to teach, and in 384 he moved to Milan, then the capital of the Empire. Here he fell under the influence of the bishop of Milan (Saint Ambrose), the teachings of the Platonists, and the letters of Saint Paul. He lost his skepticism and was convinced that he should become a Christian. But his will was unable to take the step; he could not give up his mistress. It was only because God gave him the strength (miraculously, it seems) that he was able to make the decision to leave his past life behind and start afresh. He and his son and some of his friends were then baptized.

Augustine decided to return to Africa in 387, but his mother, who had accompanied him to Italy, died at Ostia, the port of Rome, on the return journey. Augustine then remained in Rome for another year before returning to Africa; his son died soon after his arrival there. Augustine then entered a monastery. Later he became a priest in the town of Hippo, and in 395 was made its bishop.

As the bishop of Hippo, Augustine spent the next thirty-five years preaching, leading a religious community, and writing. His literary output is enormous, but his most famous works are *The Confessions* (composed 397–401), *On the Trinity* (399–422), and *The City of God* (413–427). He died at Hippo in 430.

Augustine was involved in all the theological controversies of his day, and was recognized as the great spokesperson of the Catholic Church. His influence, enormous in his own day, has been even greater since his death. He has been read in every century, and is still read in our own. If we were to name the founders of the Middle Ages we would choose Saint Benedict (480–547) in religious life, Pope Saint Gregory the Great (540–604) in church administration and development, and Saint Augustine in theology.

■ ■ ■

What to Look For in the Selections

What we wish to consider in Augustine's teaching is but a very small part of his work. It is, however, among the most important matters he dealt with. The selections chosen from *On the Trinity*, *The Confessions*, and *The City of God* show us that to be a person involves being related to many other persons; that each person builds his or her own personhood or personality by freely chosen actions relating to other persons, including God; that it is a person's will that has both the power and the responsibility to mold the personality; and that a half-hearted or divided will cannot produce a good person.

As you read the selections, ask yourself whether the following statements are true. Letters preceding each statement correspond with the letters assigned to each of the text selections that follow.

> A. Being a person means having multiple relationships with other persons.
> B. Having multiple relationships is what distinguishes a person from an individual.
> C. Our will is responsible for developing these relationships.
> D–F. We are therefore responsible for who we are.
> G–K. The moral life is a struggle.
> L. Humans are truly free only if their freedom is limited.
> M, N. The will, not what it wills, causes evil.
> O. What is most truly ourselves is our will.

SELECTIONS FROM SAINT AUGUSTINE

■ ■ ■

On the Trinity

A. Book 5, Chapter 5

Wherefore nothing in Him is said in respect to accident, since nothing is accidental to Him, and yet all that is said is not said according to substance. For, in created and changeable things, that which is not said according to substance must, by necessary alternative, be said according to accident. For all things are accidents in them which can be either lost or diminished, whether magnitudes or qualities; and so also is that which is said in relation to something, as friendships, relationships, services, likenesses, equalities, and anything else of the kind; so also positions and conditions, places and times, acts and passions. But in God nothing is said to be according to accident because in Him nothing is changeable; and yet everything that is said is not said according to substance. For it is said in relation to something, as the Father in relation to the

Son, and the Son in relation to the Father, which is not accidental because the one is always Father, and the other is always Son. . . . Because the Father is not called the Father except in that He has a Son, and the Son is not called Son except in that He has a Father, these things are not said according to substance, because each of them is not so called in relation to Himself, but the terms are used reciprocally and in relation each to the other; nor yet according to accident, because both the being called the Father, and the being called the Son, are eternal and unchangeable in regard to them. Wherefore, although to be the Father and to be the Son is different, yet their substance is not different, because they are so called, not according to substance, but according to relation, which relation, however, is not an accident, because it is not changeable.

B. Book 10, Chapter 5

Why therefore is it enjoined upon [the soul] that it should know itself? I suppose, in order that it may consider itself, and live according to its own nature; that is, seek to be regulated according to its own nature, that is, under Him to whom it ought to be subject, and above those things to which it is to be preferred; under Him by whom it ought to be ruled, above those things which it ought to rule. For it does many things through vicious desire, as though in forgetfulness of itself. For it sees some things, intrinsically excellent, in that more excellent nature which is God; and, whereas it ought to remain steadfast that it may enjoy them, it is turned away from Him by wishing to appropriate those things to itself, and not to be like to Him by His gift, but to be what He is by its own doing, and it begins to move and slip gradually down into less and less, which it thinks to be more and more; for neither is it sufficient for itself, nor is anything at all sufficient for it, if it withdraw from Him who is alone sufficient. And so, through want and distress, it becomes too intent upon its own actions and upon the unquiet delights which it obtains through them; and thus, by the desire of acquiring knowledge from those things that are without, the nature of which it knows and loves, and which it feels can be lost unless held fast with anxious care, it loses its security, and thinks of itself so much the less in proportion as it feels the more secure that it cannot lose itself. So, whereas . . . it is one thing not to know oneself, and another not to think of oneself, such is the strength of love that the mind draws in with itself those things which it has long thought of with love, and has grown into them by the close adherence of diligent study, even when it returns in some way to think of itself.

■ ■ ■

The Confessions

C. Book 2, Chapter 2

But what was it that I delighted in save to love and to be beloved? But I held it not in moderation, mind to mind, the bright path of friendship; but out of the dark concupiscence of the flesh, and the effervescence of youth, exhalations came forth which obscured and overcast my heart, so that I was unable to discern pure affection from unholy desire. Both boiled confusedly within me, and dragged away my unstable youth into the rough places of unchaste desires, and plunged me into a gulf of infamy, . . . and I was tossed to and fro, and wasted, and poured out, and boiled over in my fornications. . . .

Oh for one to have regulated my disorder, and turned to my profit the fleeting beauties of the things around me, and fixed a bound to their sweetness, so that the tides of my youth might have spent themselves upon the conjugal shore. . . .

Where was I, and how far was I exiled from the delights of Thy house, in that sixteenth year of the age of my flesh, when the madness of lust—to which human shamelessness granted full freedom, although forbidden by Thy laws—held complete sway over me, and I resigned myself entirely to it? Those about me meanwhile took no care to save me from ruin by marriage, their sole care being that I should learn to make a powerful speech and become a persuasive orator.

D. Book 2, Chapter 4

Theft is punished by Thy law, O Lord, and by the law written in men's hearts which iniquity itself cannot blot out. For what thief will suffer a thief? Even a rich thief will not suffer him who is driven to it by want. Yet I had a desire to commit robbery, and did so, compelled neither by hunger nor poverty, but through a distaste for well-doing, and a lustinesss of iniquity. For I pilfered that of which I had already sufficient, and much better. Nor did I desire to enjoy what I pilfered, but the theft and sin itself. There was a pear-tree close to our vineyard, heavily laden with fruit, which was tempting neither for its color nor its flavor. To shake and rob this, some of us wanton young fellows went, late one night, . . . and carried away great loads, not to eat ourselves but to fling to the very swine, having eaten only some of them; and to do this pleased us all the more because it was not permitted. . . . It was foul, and I loved it. I loved to perish. I loved my own error—not that for which I erred, but the error itself.

E. Book 7, Chapter 3

And I directed my attention to discern what I now heard: that free will was the cause of our doing evil, and Your righteous judgment the cause of our suffering it. . . . I knew as well that I had a will as that I had life. When, therefore, I was willing or unwilling to do anything, I was most certain that it was none but myself who was willing and unwilling, and immediately perceived that there was the cause of my sin.

F. Book 8, Chapter 5

The enemy was master of my will, which then had made a chain for me and bound me. Because of a perverse will lust was made; and lust indulged in became custom; and custom not resisted became necessity. By which links, as it were, joined together (whence I term it a "chain") did a hard bondage hold me enthralled. But that new will which had begun to develop in me, freely to worship You, and to wish to enjoy You, O God, the only sure enjoyment, was not able as yet to overcome my former wilfulness, made strong by long indulgence. Thus did my two wills, one old and the other new, one carnal, the other spiritual, contend within me, and by their discord they unstrung my soul. . . .

Nor had I now any longer my usual excuse: that as yet I hesitated to be above the world and serve you because my perception of the truth was uncertain; for now it was certain.

Thus I was sweetly burdened with the baggage of the world, as when in slumber. And the thoughts wherein I meditated upon You were like the efforts of those desiring to awake, who, still overpowered with a heavy drowsiness, are again steeped therein. And no one desires to sleep always, and in the sober judgment of everyone waking is better, yet a person generally defers to shake off drowsiness when there is a heavy lethargy in all his limbs. . . . Nor had I anything to answer You calling to me "Awake, sleeper, and rise from the dead, and Christ will give you light" (*Eph.* 5:14). And I, convicted by the truth, had nothing at all to reply to You, as you showed me on every side that what You said was true, but the drawling and drowsy words "Presently, lo, presently," "Leave me a little while." But "Presently, presently" had no present, and my "Leave me a little while" went for a long while. In vain did I delight in Your law after the inner man, when another law in my members warred against the law of my mind, and brought me into captivity to the law of sin which is in my members. For the law of sin is the violence of custom, whereby the mind is drawn and held, even against its will, deserving to be so held in that it so willingly falls into it.

G. Book 8, Chapter 7

And I beheld and loathed myself; and where to fly from myself I discovered not. . . . And if I sought to turn my gaze away from myself . . . You again brought me face to face with myself and thrust me before my own eyes so that I might discover my iniquity and hate it. I had known it, but acted as though I did not; I winked at it and forgot it. . . .

I, miserable young man, supremely miserable even in the very outset of my youth, had entreated chastity of You, and said "Grant me chastity and continence, but not yet." For I was afraid lest You should hear me soon, and soon deliver me from the disease of concupiscence, which I desired to have satisfied rather than extinguished. . . .

And to myself, what did I not say within myself? With what scourges of rebuke did I not lash my soul to make it follow me, struggling to go after You! Yet it drew back; it refused, and did not act. All its arguments were exhausted and confuted. There remained a silent trembling; and it feared, as it would death, to be restrained from the flow of that custom whereby it was wasting away even to death.

H. Book 8, Chapter 8

There was a little garden belonging to our lodging, of which we had the use, as of the whole house; for the master, our landlord, did not live there. The tempest within my breast had hurried me there, where no one might impede the fiery struggle in which I was engaged with myself, until it came to the resolution which You knew, though I didn't. But I was mad that I might be whole, and dying that I might have life, knowing what evil thing I was, but not knowing what good thing I was shortly to become. Into the garden, then, I retired. . . . We sat down at as great a distance from the house as we could. I was disquieted in spirit, being most impatient with myself that I didn't enter into Your will and covenant, O my God, which all my bones cried out to me to enter, extolling it to the skies. And we do not enter therein by ships, or chariots, or feet, no, nor by going so far as I had come from the house to that place where we were sitting. For not only to go, but to enter there, was nothing else but to will to go, but to will it resolutely and thoroughly; not to stagger and sway about this way and that, a changeable and half-wounded will, wrestling, with one part falling as another rose.

I. Book 8, Chapter 9

Whence is this monstrous thing? And why is it? The mind commands the body, and it obeys forthwith; the mind commands itself, and is resisted. The mind commands the hand to be moved, and such readiness is there that the command is scarce to be distinguished from the obedience. Yet the mind is mind, and the hand is body. The mind commands the mind to will, and yet, thought it be itself, it obeys not. Whence this monstrous thing? And why is it? I repeat: it commands itself to will, and would not give the command unless it willed; yet what it commands is not done. But it does not will entirely; therefore it does not command entirely. For it commands insofar as it wills; and the thing commanded is not done to the extent that it does not will. For the will commands that there be a will—not another, but itself. But it does not command entirely; therefore what it commands does not happen. Were it entire it would not even command it to be, because it would already be. It is, therefore, no monstrous thing partly to will, partly to be unwilling, but an infirmity of the mind, that it does not wholly rise, sustained by truth, pressed down by custom. And so there are two wills, because one of them is not entire, and the one is supplied with what the other needs.

J. Book 8, Chapter 11

Thus I was sick and tormented, accusing myself far more severely than usual, tossing and turning myself in my chain till it was fully broken. I was now held by it only a little bit, but still held. . . . I said mentally, "Lo, let it be done now, let it be done now." And, as I spoke, I all but came to a resolve. I all but did it, yet I did not do it. Yet I did not fall back to my old condition, but took up my position hard by, and drew breath. And I tried again, and came just a little short of reaching it, and then a little shorter still, and then all but touched and grasped it. And yet I did not reach it, or touch it, or grasp it, hesitating to die to death and to live to life. And the worse (to which I had been habituated) prevailed more with me than the better (which I had not tried). And, the very moment in which I was to become another man, the nearer it approached me, the greater horror it struck in me. But it did not strike me back, or turn me aside, but kept me in suspense.

The very toys of toys, and vanities of vanities, my old mistresses, still enthralled me. They shook my fleshly garment, and whispered softly, "Do you part with us? And from that moment shall we no more be with you forever? And from that moment shall not this or that be lawful for you forever?" And what did they suggest to me in the words "this or that"? . . . What impurities did they suggest! What shame! And now I far less than half heard them, not openly showing themselves and contradicting me, but muttering, as it were, behind my back, and furtively plucking me as I was departing, to make me look back upon them. Yet they did delay me, so that I hesitated to burst and shake myself free from them, and to leap over to where I was called—an unruly habit saying to me, "Do you think you can live without them?"

But now it said this very faintly; for on that side towards which I had set my face, and whither I trembled to go, did the chaste dignity of Continence appear to me, cheerful, but not dissolutely gay, honestly alluring me to come and doubt nothing, and extending her holy hands, full of a multiplicity of good examples, to receive and embrace me. . . . And I blushed beyond measure, for I still heard the muttering of those toys, and hung in suspense. And she again seemed to say, "Shut up your ears against those unclean members of yours upon the earth, that they may be mortified."

K. Book 8, Chapter 12

But when a profound reflection had, from the secret depths of my soul, drawn together and heaped up all my misery before the sight of my heart, there arose a mighty storm, accompanied by as mighty a shower of tears. . . . I flung myself down, how, I know not, under a certain fig-tree, giving free course to my tears, and the streams of my eyes gushed out. . . . I was saying these things and weeping in the most bitter contrition of my heart when, lo, I heard the voice as of a boy or girl, I know not which, coming from a neighboring house, chanting and often repeating: "Take up and read." Immediately my countenance was changed, and I began most earnestly to consider whether it was usual for children in any kind of game to sing such words; nor could I remember ever to have heard the like. So, restraining the torrent of my tears, I rose up, interpreting it no other way than as a command to me from Heaven to open a book, and to read the first chapter I should light upon. . . . So I quickly returned to the place where Alypius was sitting; for there had I put down the volume of the Apostle when I rose thence. I grasped it, opened it, and in silence read that paragraph on which my eyes first fell: "Not in rioting and drunkenness, not in chambering and wantonness, not in strife and envying; but put ye on the Lord Jesus Christ, and make no provision for the flesh, to fulfil the lusts thereof" (*Rom.* 13:13–14). No further would I read, nor did I need to, for instantly, as the sentence ended—by a light, as it were, of security infused into my heart—all the gloom of doubt vanished away.

■ ■ ■

The City of God

L. Book 11, Chapter 17

It is with reference to the nature, then, and not to the wickedness of the devil, that we are to understand these words, "This is the beginning of God's handiwork," for, without doubt, wickedness can be a flaw or vice only where the nature previously was not vitiated. Vice, too, is so contrary to nature that it cannot but damage it. And therefore departure from God would be no vice unless in a nature whose property it was to abide with God. So that even the wicked will is a strong proof of the goodness of the nature.

M. Book 12, Chapter 6

If the further question be asked, "What was the efficient cause of their evil will," there is none. For what is it which makes the will bad when it is the will itself which makes the action bad? And consequently the bad will is the cause of the bad action, but nothing is the efficient cause of the bad will. . . . For when the will abandons what is above itself, and turns to what is lower, it becomes evil—not because that is evil to which it turns, but because the turning itself is wicked. Therefore it is not an inferior thing which has made the will evil, but it is itself which has become so by wickedly and inordinately desiring an inferior thing. For if two men, alike in physical and moral constitution, see the same corporal beauty, and one of them is excited by the sight to desire an illicit enjoyment while the other steadfastly maintains a modest restraint of his will, what do we suppose brings it about that there is an evil will in the one and not in the other? What produces it in the man in whom it exists? Not the bodily beauty, for that was presented equally to the gaze of both, and yet did not produce in both an evil will. Did the flesh of the one cause the desire as he looked? But why did not the flesh of the other? Or was it the dispositon? But why not the disposition of both? For we are supposing that both were of a like temperament of body and soul. Must we, then, say that the one was tempted by a secret suggestion of an evil spirit? As if it was not by his own will that he consented to this suggestion and to any inducement whatever! This consent, then, this evil will which he presented to the evil persuasive influence—what was the cause of it, we ask? For, not to delay on such a difficulty as this, if both are tempted equally and one yields and consents to the temptation while the other remains unmoved by it, what other account can we give of the matter than this, that the one is willing, the other unwilling, to fall away from chastity? And what causes this but their own wills, in cases at least such as we are supposing, where the temperament is identical? The same beauty was equally obvious to the eyes of both, the same secret temptation pressed on both with equal violence. However minutely we examine the case, therefore, we can discern nothing which caused the will of the one to be evil. For if we say that the man himself made his will evil, what was the man himself before his will was evil but a good nature created by God, the unchangeable good?

N. Book 12, Chapter 8

And I know likewise that the will could not become evil were it unwilling to become so; and therefore its failings are justly punished, being not necessary but voluntary. For its defections are not to evil things but are themselves evil; that is to say, are not towards things that are naturally and in themselves evil, but the defection of the will is evil because it is contrary to the order of nature, and an abandonment of that which has supreme being for that which has less. For avarice is not a fault inherent in gold but in the one who inordinately loves gold to the detriment of justice, which ought to be held in incomparably higher regard than gold. Neither is lust the fault of lovely and charming objects, but of the heart that inordinately loves sensual pleasures to the neglect of temperance, which attaches us to objects more lovely in their spirituality, and more delectable by their incorruptibility. Nor yet is boasting the fault of human praise, but of the soul that is inordinately fond of the applause of men, and that makes light of the voice of conscience. Pride, too, is not the fault of him who delegates power, nor of power itself, but of the soul that is inordinately enamored of its own power, and despises the more just dominion of a higher authority. Consequently the one who inordinately loves the good which any nature possesses, even though he obtain it, himself becomes evil through this good, and wretched because deprived of a greater good.

O. Book 14, Chapter 6

But the character of the human will is of moment because, if it is wrong, these motions of the soul will be wrong; but, if it is right, they will be not merely blameless but even praiseworthy. For the will is in them all; indeed, none of them is anything else than will. For what are desire and joy but a volition of consent to the things we wish? And what are fear and sadness but a volition of aversion from the things which we do not wish? But when consent takes the form of seeking to possess the things we wish, this is called desire; and when consent takes the form of enjoying the things we wish, this is called joy. In like manner, when we turn with aversion from that which we do not wish to happen, this volition is termed fear; and when we turn away from that which has happened against our will, this act of will is called sorrow. And generally, in respect of all that we seek or shun, as one's will is attracted or repelled, so it is changed and turned into these different affections. Wherefore the one who lives according to God, and not according to man, ought to be a lover of good, and therefore a hater of evil. And since no one is evil by nature, but whoever is evil is evil by vice, he who lives according to God ought to cherish towards evil men a perfect hatred, so that he shall neither hate the man because of his vice nor love the vice because of the man, but hate the vice and love the man. For the vice being cursed, all that ought to be loved, and nothing that ought to be hated, will remain.

Extracted from *On the Trinity*, translated by A. W. Haddan (Edinburgh, 1873); *The Confessions*, translated by J. G. Pilkington (Edinburgh, 1882); and *The City of God*, translated by M. Dods and J. J. Smith (Edinburgh, 1881). A few improvements have been made in the translations for the sake of the modern reader.

COMMENTARY

■ ■ ■

Analysis of the Selections

A. Saint Augustine is the real founder of the study of the *person*. According to an eminent Augustinian scholar, P. Henry, Augustine was "the first thinker who brought into prominence and undertook an analysis of the philosophical and psychological concepts of person and personality."[1] Although Aristotle knew that human beings had an intellect and a will, his notion of person was limited. For one thing, he did not see a person as intrinsically relational, that is, almost defined as a sum of relationships to other persons. Conversely, Henry claims that Augustine, who did see the relationality of a person, was helped by his Christian faith to do so. He says: "I very much doubt that any philosophy—left to its own devices—would have developed a concept of . . . personality except it be in the . . . world . . . influenced by Christianity."[2]

Augustine worked to understand God by using the human mind as an example, but he ended up understanding the human person by using God as an example. Augustine believed that the human person, through his or her mind, is an image of God. In trying to understand God, therefore, Augustine focused his attention on the human mind. The mind exists as a threefold nature: the mind itself, its knowledge, and its love. And these are closely united to one another without being identical. In God also, according to Christian teaching, there is a threefold nature: the three Divine Persons (Father, Son, and Holy Spirit). These also are closely united to one another, but in one sense *are* identical, since each of the persons is the same God. At this point, then, the comparison between God and the human mind ceases.

To understand a little of how the three persons could be different and yet the same, Augustine had recourse to the Aristotelian teaching concerning substance and accident. Augustine did not read Aristotle's philosophy but was aware of this particular teaching because it had entered into the common philosophical patrimony. For Aristotle, everything that exists is either a substance or a quality or property of a substance, which is called an accident. Augustine understood this doctrine in his own fashion. He agreed with Aristotle that everything that exists is basically a substance, something existing in itself and not in something else. And he considered an accident to be anything superadded to a substance, something existing not in itself but in the substance; and his understanding of this concept was that an accident could not be eternal. Therefore, because God is eternal, he is a substance but has no accidents.

Augustine's conclusion caused no problem with regard to the accidents mentioned by Aristotle except for one of them: relation. Augustine saw that in the Trinity there are relations; for example, the relations of fatherhood and sonship between the Father and the Son. Augustine was forced therefore to state that, though many relations are accidents, not all of them are. He could not, of course, say that the relations in the Trinity are substantial, since the persons are all the same substance. But neither could he say that they are accidental; they are eternal and they belong to the most intimate nature of God. Augustine therefore had to say that the very notion of a divine person is a relational notion. A person then, if we take God as the highest instance of this notion, is not a substance that simply possesses intellect and will, since the divine persons have the same intellect and will. A person is a substance that, in addition to having an intellect and will, is, in its deepest reality, related to other persons.

B. Having come to such an understanding of the divine persons, Augustine had a different understanding of the human person. He saw the human person as essentially a relational being. As Henry puts it, a human being, though a substance, is "constituted as a person only insofar as he is related to other persons."[3] We have an absolute (that is, a nonrelational) aspect, since there can be no relation unless there is something that is related to something else; but it is part of our very definition that we are related to others: "Augustine teaches that the person, while being an absolute, is also and essentially a being related to others, open to others, and defined as person by this very relativity."[4]

This understanding of person has important consequences. Human beings are not meant to live in an impersonal world but in relation to other persons: "We are, it is true, little absolutes, and yet at the same time always related, correlated, and interrelated with other persons and personalities. We are not meant to live in a depersonalized world."[5]

Since other human persons are relational also, we must recognize that we are "for them" as much as they are "for us." Human beings are made for each other, for I-Thou rather than I-It relationships:

Augustine teaches us the fundamental truth that we are really persons only inasmuch as we recognize the full status of other persons as related to us; that personality is not egocentric but altruistic, that its natural movements and richness are not centripetal but centrifugal, that the more we are ourselves . . . the more we exist with and for others and are drawn to others, and others drawn to us. He teaches us that personality expresses itself in giving and receiving; in 'communicability' rather than in 'incommunicability,' in sharing rather than in possessing, in togetherness and closeness rather than in proud isolationism, whether this be intellectual, cultural, economic, or political. When we have learned these truths, then, and only then, shall we be able to build up between men, in law and in life, an I-Thou relationship transcending the I-It relationship of mere Subject and Object. We shall recognize in the 'other,' beyond all qualities and defects, beyond even his expressed needs, the unfathomable depths, of his being. . . . We shall come to see that which is . . . ours by right because he wills to share it with us and we with him.[6]

Augustine discovered, we might say, the difference between a human individual and a human person. The individual is human, it has intellect and will, but it is considered as a world in itself. If it develops relationships with other human beings it does so on its own terms, we might say. But the person is already, simply as a person, related to others. The relationships its nature calls for are not optional. It not only can count on others to help in the living of its life, but it owes the same to others.

Such an insight obviously has important consequences for personal and social ethics, but it is not the whole ethics of Augustine with which we wish to deal. We shall, instead, consider one doctrine of great importance that completes the one we have been dealing with. This doctrine has to do with what it is that constitutes the relations that should follow from our relational personality, what it is that constitutes the "personality" that completes our "person." Each of us is a person by the very fact that we are human beings. We are also different persons, of course. Yet we are all the same in that we are persons. But the person we become, the personality we produce, makes us different from what other persons become. What is involved in this becoming is located in the texts of Saint Augustine that we have selected.

C. Saint Augustine differs from most philosophers in that he describes how his life was involved in his philosophy. *The Confessions* is probably the first autobiography in the history of literature, and this account of his own life shows how Augustine was led to certain philosophical considerations that mark him again as a pioneer in philosophy. He is the first philosopher to teach certain essential truths about the human will. V. J. Bourke says: "Plato and the Stoics made certain obscure overtures toward a theory of human volition. . . .

There seems to me to be no real awareness of the importance of will in any pagan thinker of antiquity. . . . However this may be, it is clear that will as a power of self-commitment, of free choice, of turning toward or away from the good, is fully appreciated in early Christian writings and particularly in the works of St. Augustine of Hippo."[7]

Let us turn, then, to Augustine's own words in the selected passages from *The Confessions*.

We first note that Augustine recognizes both the existence of the will as distinct from the intellect and the power of this will. He knows that it can lead him to perform actions for which he can find no rational justification, actions of which his intellect disapproves. The will can build up habits of acting that overcome the intellect's better judgment. Augustine wanted to be loved by women, but he did not moderate his sexual appetite, and gradually he became unable to control his passion; he could not free himself from sexual sins despite his deepest wishes.

D. Augustine further found that not only desirable objects outside himself attracted him and overcame his self-control, but he was attracted also by evil itself. He stole pears he did not need and did not want. His will was capable of making him a rebel against morality even when he did not know why he acted as he did.

E. Augustine is also forced to admit to himself that his will is free, that the objects it desires do not force it into action, but that they must first get the permission of the will itself. And with this comes the realization that he himself is responsible for his actions.

F. Augustine is responsible not only for his actions but also for his evil habits, which are the result of his actions. It is true that he comes to wish he did not have these evil habits, but he realizes that, since he has willed each of the actions that produced them, he is responsible for the habits also. Thus he is responsible for the very chains that bind him.

Augustine then finds that he has "two wills." One of these wills wants to do what is right, while the other wants to keep on doing what the first will disapproves of. Augustine knows that earlier he was not so clear in his mind that what he was doing was wrong. But now he knows that his actions are wrong, and he cannot claim ignorance or uncertainty as a justification for going on as he is. He is like a half-awake person who thinks of doing something but is in such a daze that no action follows. He knows that God is calling on him to change his way of life, but the best he can do is to say "Presently."

G. Eventually, Augustine cannot face himself. He sees no reason why he should go on living as he has. He says "Make me pure," but immediately adds "But not yet." Augustine's reason tells him that there is not justification for his way of life, but the will is afraid to change. An intellectual conversion is not enough; what is needed is conversion of the will.

H. Augustine then admits that he does not have "two wills." What he has is one will, but a weak one. It cannot will resolutely.

I. It can command his body, and obedience is instantaneous. But, when it commands itself, there is disobedience, rebellion. The explanation is that the will does not will entirely; it has reservations; it is divided. It is like someone struggling in the water: it is held up by truth, but weighed down by habit.

J. Augustine, however, was making progress. The cords binding him were not as strong. But, as he says, even if one is held by only a single thread, one is still bound. His former mistresses were still calling to him, but their voices were getting weaker.

K. Yet still he could not make a decision to turn away from his former way of life. Finally he does so, but only, it seems, as the result of a miracle.

L. One great lesson Augustine learned is that the human will, if it is to be free, can be free only within limits. If it transgresses these limits, it loses its freedom and becomes a slave. And the limits of freedom are given by human nature. The human being is an intermediate being, between the infinite good (God) and the subhuman goods in the material world. Evil does not come from desiring evil things, because whatever God has made is good. It comes from desiring things in the wrong way, that is, choosing goods beneath us in preference to choosing the infinite good above us. Good and evil, then, are basically a matter of truth, a matter of who we are, a matter of whether a created good is greater than the Creator.

To be free is to act in accord with our nature. It is to love good things in proportion to their goodness.

M. Augustine asks what is the efficient cause of the will. He is forced to admit that there is none, other than the will itself. The will is not forced by the objects of its choice; it is free when choosing. If two men under the same general conditions see a beautiful woman, their behavior is not dictated by the object seen or by these conditions; it is dictated by the free will of each. If one gives in to lust and the other reacts chastely, the cause is the will of each. One has chosen a created object in preference to the Creator; the other has preferred the Creator.

N. The object does not cause evil, since the object itself is good. What causes evil is the will, when it chooses an inferior good in preference to a greater good, and, indeed, in preference to infinite good. There is no avarice in gold, but in the will desiring it inordinately. There is no lust in a sexually desirable object, but in the will desiring it inordinately. There is no boasting in praise, but in the will seeking it inordinately. There is no pride in power, but in the will desiring the power inordinately.

We referred earlier to the personality that is built on our person. We now see that for Augustine we build this personality ourselves, that we build it freely, and that it is a result of what we love. As the philosopher M. T. Clark says, "the person is completed by personality, and . . . a person becomes what he loves."[8]

O. For Augustine, personality is built by our free will. In a sense, for him there is nothing else to build it because our conscious self is our will. What is our desire, he asks, but our will wanting something? What is our joy but our will rejoicing in getting something? What is our fear but our will not wanting something to happen? Or our sadness but the will not wanting something that has happened? Augustine does not distinguish different faculties in the soul; the will *is* the soul.[9] Clark says: "In the last analysis the free will is the deciding factor in personality."[10]

Since person is a relational notion, personality has to do with the relationships we develop with God, with other human beings, and with material things. These relationships are the core of our personality, and, as we have seen, they should be the fulfillment of our nature. Our nature is that of rational creatures, made to choose goods in accordance with their real value, to serve God, the infinite good, and to use all other goods while keeping in mind that our use of them must be in accord with our nature as creatures made for the infinite good. When our will acts in accord with this nature of ours it is free. If, on the other hand, it seeks creatures without regard to the Creator, it becomes a slave to them, and finds itself in bondage. Our choice, then, is to be a servant of God, and in this to find our freedom, or to be a slave of habits that bind us against our will. Augustine says: "For the soul must be ruled by the superior, and rule the inferior. But God alone is superior to it, and only body is inferior to it. . . . So he knows God alone is his Lord, and he is served with the greatest freedom."[11]

Free will, then, Augustine discovered to be a paradox. Our will is free when it serves its proper master. When it wants to be absolutely its own master, when it rebels, as Augustine did when he stole the pears, it becomes a slave. True freedom, freedom in accord with truth, that is, in accord with our nature, is submission. What looks like freedom, a denial of submission, is an illusory freedom, in reality slavery. We must choose, then, between submission to God or submission to what is below us. The former is freedom, the latter is slavery. Everything depends on what we choose, and what we choose is what we love.

■ ■ ■

Summary

Saint Augustine is the philosopher of the person. It was his meditation on the Trinity that taught him that to be a person is to be a being that is relational through and through, a being the innermost nature of which is to be related to other persons. To be a person is to be "for others." And, of course, others are likewise "for us."

Saint Augustine is also the philosopher of the will and the philosopher of freedom. And what he taught about these is what he learned from his own experience and from reading Saint Paul. Yet his teaching about person, will, and freedom, though derived, at least in part, from theological considerations, is philosophical. Others can understand it and accept it without reference to the considerations that led Augustine to it.

The Greek philosophers preceding him had, at best, a limited awareness of the nature of the will. They had perhaps an implicit awareness of it, but not an explicit understanding. Some of them accepted freedom and responsibility as facts but did not have an adequate theory of them. Augustine makes clear what they were groping for.

In the words of M. T. Clark: "After reviewing the attitude toward freedom on the part of the outstanding Greek philosophers before the time of Christ, and after a close doctrinal study of the treatise of Plotinus (d. A.D. 270) on the topic of freedom, it appears to us that freedom was not adequately understood by the great non-Christian philosophers before Augustine's time. . . . Plato has scarcely done justice to the nature of free choice, while Aristotle has not recognized the role of free choice. After Aristotle there is the confusion of free choice with spontaneity by Epicurus and then the establishment of a rigorous doctrine of universal determinism by the Stoics. It would seem true then that the early Greeks, while understanding the power and the value of thought, did not understand freedom."[12]

Augustine became aware of the existence of the will, of its freedom, and of its power. He faced up courageously to the recognition and admission that he was responsible for his actions and even for the existence and power of the habits he had cultivated but later deplored.

To be a person is to be a relational being, and the task of our will is to complete our person by building our personality, that is, by developing relations. But, because our nature is a given (because we are creatures), these relations are either in accord with it or not. If they are in accord with it, they complete our nature, and its development is true. If they are not in accord with it, they twist or stunt our nature, and its development is false.

True development leads to freedom, and false development leads to slavery. If we love the infinite good, which has made us and for which we are made, our intellect rejoices in our choice; but, if we love lower goods for ourselves and not for the sake of the infinite good, our intellect constantly reminds us of our error, of our foolishnesss, and of our pitiful state.

The proper function of the will is to make us truly human, that is, to complete our nature in accord with the purpose for which it was made. This requires that the will be unified, that its love be centered on the infinite good and not divided between this love and the love of creatures. It does the will no good to issue an order unless it wholeheartedly wants what it commands.

■ ■ ■

Philosophical and Religious Critique

The Greeks no doubt found it difficult to understand the will because its function is paradoxical. In order to be free the will must be submissive, submissive to truth, to its nature, to God. It is so tempting to reject submission, to think that freedom comes from autonomy. But the type of autonomy envisaged here is contrary to truth, to human nature, and to being a creature. The reward of submission is freedom, the reward of rebellion is slavery. And this paradox, like all philosophical problems, is perennial. Each person has to solve it for himself or herself.

■ ■ ■

Notes

1. P. Henry, *St. Augustine on Personality* (New York, 1960), 1.
2. Ibid., 7.
3. Ibid., 18–19.
4. Ibid., 23.
5. Ibid., 25.
6. Ibid., 23–24.
7. M. T. Clark, *Augustine, Philosopher of Freedom* (New York, 1958), foreword.
8. Ibid., 48, 78.
9. V. J. Bourke, *Will in Western Thought* (New York, 1964), 96, n. 15.
10. Clark, *Augustine, Philosopher of Freedom*, 79.

11. St. Augustine, *On Music*, 6.5.13–14, in *The Fathers of the Church: Writings of St. Augustine* (New York, 1947), vol. 4, 338–39.
12. Clark, *Augustine, Philosopher of Freedom*, 36, 17.

■ ■ ■

Further Reading

Refer to the books by Henry, Clark, and Bourke, mentioned in the notes.

4

SAINT THOMAS AQUINAS

. . .

THE HUMAN PERSON
AS EMBODIED SPIRIT
Introduction and Commentary by Leonard A. Kennedy

INTRODUCTION

■ ■ ■

Aquinas's Life and Works

Saint Thomas Aquinas was born in 1224 or 1225 at Roccasecca, the castle of his father, Landulf of Aquino, who was a member of the lesser nobility. The castle, today a ruin, is midway between Rome and Naples. When he was five or six Thomas went to study at the neighboring monastery of Monte Cassino. At the age of fifteen he enrolled in the newly founded University of Naples. There he came into contact with a recently established religious congregation, the Dominicans, and, after five years at Naples, wanted to join them. His mother objected (his father had recently died) since she had nourished other plans for him. She had him captured by some of his brothers and kept under house arrest at Roccasecca for a year, after which she relented and let him go.

The Dominicans then (in 1245) sent Aquinas to Paris for his novitiate and further studies. From 1248 to 1252 he studied in Cologne under the Dominican Albert the Great. Then he returned to Paris to complete his theological education, becoming a Doctor of Theology in 1256. During these years

Aquinas composed his first major work, comparable in a way to a doctoral thesis: a commentary on the texts *(sententiae)* of the Fathers of the Church compiled by Peter the Lombard. He remained in Paris for three more years as professor of theology. The chief duties of such a professor were to lecture on the Bible and to hold public debates on theological topics. Scholars have identified the lectures and debates Aquinas conducted during this period. Indeed, we are fortunate in having nearly everything Aquinas ever wrote.

In 1259 Thomas returned to Italy as professor of theology in Dominican houses of study. In 1265 he opened a new house of study for Dominicans in Rome, and taught there for two years. He rejected the usual textbook of theology (Peter Lombard's *Sentences*) and began to write a new one, *A Complete Treatise on Theology (Summa Theologiae)*. All selections included here are taken from this work.

After a further year as professor at the papal court in Viterbo, Thomas returned to Paris for three years (1269–72). In addition to lecturing on the Bible and conducting public debates, he continued writing the *Summa Theologiae* and also began commentaries on many of Aristotle's works. His output was prodigious.

He returned to Italy in 1272 and continued his work at the Dominican house of studies in Naples. The two small rooms in which he worked and slept are there today. They adjoin the Dominican church, in which Thomas spent most of the night in prayer. On December 6, 1273, he had an unusual experience, certainly at least in part supernatural, and immediately ceased his theological writing. The next year he was asked to attend the Ecumenical Council at Lyon, in France, and on the way he hurt his head in an accident and died at the Cistercian monastery at Fossanova not far from where he was born. The date of his death was March 7, 1274. The room in which he died is preserved today as a museum. He was canonized in 1323.

The best account of his life and works is J. A. Weisheipl, *Friar Thomas d'Aquino* (New York, 1974). Besides the two major works already mentioned, Weisheipl lists a third, *Summa Contra Gentiles*, in addition to nineteen works of public debates, eleven commentaries on books of the Bible, twelve commentaries on works of Aristotle, four commentaries on works by other major writers, five writings on controversies of the day, six treatises on special subjects, five expert opinions, sixteen letters, and seven sermons and liturgical compositions.

■ ■ ■

What to Look For in the Selection

The selection will be analyzed in the commentary following it, but you might ask yourself the following questions as you read. Letters preceding each question correspond with the letters assigned to each of the text selections that follow.

- A. What is a human soul? Do animals and plants have souls?
- B. Must a soul be everywhere in its body? Why?
- C. What reasons do you have for thinking that the human soul is immortal?
- D, E. If the soul can exist without its body, why is its body joined to it?
- F, G. How do our senses and intellect know the physical world?
- H. How can our intellect know physical things truly if it knows them universally and yet they are singular?
- I. How did Plato solve this problem?
- J. What is a *species*? How is it involved in knowledge?
- K. Have you ever thought about how your mind knows itself? Close your eyes and think about it.
- L. If Aquinas was helped in his philosophy by his faith, how could it still be philosophy?

SELECTION FROM AQUINAS

■ ■ ■

Summa Theologiae, Part 1

A. The Nature of the Soul (Question 75, Article 1)

To seek the nature of the soul, we must premise that the soul is defined as the first principle of life in those things which live: for we call living things animate [besouled], and those things which have no life, inanimate [soulless]. Now life is shown principally by two actions, knowledge and movement. The philosophers of old, not being able to rise above their imagination, supposed that the principle of these actions was something corporeal, for they asserted that only bodies were real things, and that which is not corporeal is nothing; hence they maintained that the soul is something corporeal. This opinion can be proved to be false in many ways; but we shall make use of only one proof, based on universal and certain principles, which shows clearly that the soul is not a body.

It is manifest that not every principle of vital action is a soul, for then the eye would be a soul, as it is a principle of vision; and the same might be applied to the other instruments of the soul: but it is the *first* principle of life which we call the soul. Now, though a body may be a principle of life, as the heart is a principle of life in an animal, yet nothing corporeal can be the first principle of life. For it is clear that to be a principle of life, or to be a living thing, does not belong to a body as such, since, if that were the case, every body would be a living thing, or a principle of life. Therefore a body is a living thing, or even a principle of life, because it is a *certain kind* of body. Now, that it is actually this kind of body it owes to some principle which is called its act. Therefore the soul, which is the first principle of life, is not a body, but the act of a body; thus heat, which is the principle of warming, is not a body, but an act of a body.

B. The Soul Is Everywhere in the Body (76, 8)

If the soul were united to the body merely as its motor, we might say that it is not in each part of the body but only in one part through which it would move the others. But, since the soul is united to the body as its form, it must necessarily be in the whole body, and in each part thereof.

The soul is a substantial form; and therefore it must be the form and the act not only of the whole but also of each part. Therefore, on the withdrawal of the soul, as we do not speak of an animal or a man unless equivocally (as we speak of a painted animal or a stone animal), so is it with the hand, the eye, the flesh and bones. . . . A proof of which is that, on the withdrawal of the soul, no part of the body retains its proper action.

C. The Intellect Is Nonmaterial (75, 5)

It is clear that whatever is received into something is received according to the condition of the recipient. Now a thing is known in as far as its form is in the knower. But the intellectual soul knows a thing in its nature absolutely. For instance, it knows a stone absolutely as a stone; and therefore the form of a stone absolutely, as to its proper formal idea, is in the intellectual soul. Therefore the intellectual soul itself is an absolute form, and not something composed of matter and form. For if the intellectual soul were composed of matter and form, the forms of things would be received into it as individuals, and so it would know only the individual (just as it happens with the sensitive powers which receive forms in a corporeal organ) since matter is the principle by which forms are individualized. It follows, therefore, that the intellectual soul, and every intellectual substance which has knowledge of forms absolutely, is exempt from composition of matter and form.

D. Knowledge after Death (89, 1)

The soul united to the body can understand only by turning to phantasms [images], as experience shows. Did this not proceed from the soul's very nature, but accidentally through its being bound up with the body, as the Platonists said, the difficulty would vanish, for in that case, when the body was once removed, the soul would at once return to its own nature, and would understand intelligible things simply, without turning to the phantasms. In that case, however, the union of soul and body would not be for the soul's good (for evidently it would understand worse in the body than out of it) but for the good of the body, which would be unreasonable, since matter exists on account of the form, and not the form for the sake of matter. But, if we admit that the nature of the soul requires it to understand by turning to the phantasms, it will seem, since death does not change its nature, that it can then naturally understand nothing, as the phantasms are lacking to which it may turn.

To solve this difficulty we must consider that, as nothing acts except so far as it is actual, the mode of action in every agent follows from its mode of existence. Now, the soul has one mode of being when in the body and another when apart from it, its nature remaining always the same. But this does not mean that its union with the body is an accidental thing, for, on the contrary, such union belongs to its very nature, just as the nature of a light object is not changed when it is in its proper place (which is natural to it) and outside its proper place (which is beside its nature). The soul, therefore, when united to the body, consistently with that mode of existence, has a mode of understanding by turning to corporeal phantasms which are in corporeal organs. But, when it is separated from the body, it has a mode of understanding by turning to simply intelligible objects.

Hence it is as natural for the soul to understand by turning to the phantasms as it is for it to be joined to the body; but to be separated from the body is not in accordance with its nature, and likewise to understand without turning to the phantasms is not natural to it; and hence it is united to the body in order that it may have an existence and an operation suitable to its nature. But here again a difficulty arises. For, since a thing is always ordered to what is best, and since it is better to understand by turning to simply intelligible things than by turning to the phantasms, God should have ordered the soul's nature so that the nobler way of understanding would have been natural to it and it would not have needed the body for that purpose.

In order to resolve this difficulty we must consider that, while it is true that it is nobler in itself to understand by turning to something higher than to understand by turning to phantasms, nevertheless such a mode of understanding was not so perfect as regards what was possible to the soul. This will appear if we consider that every intellectual substance possesses intellective power by the influence of the divine light. It is one and simple in its first principle, and, the farther off intellectual creatures are from the first principle, so much the more is the light divided and diversified, as is the case with lines radiating from the centre of a circle. Hence it is that God by His one essence understands all things, while the superior intellectual substances understand by means of a number of species, which nevertheless are fewer and more universal and bestow a deeper comprehension of things, because of the efficaciouness of the intellectual power of such natures, whereas the inferior intellectual natures possess a greater number of species, which are less universal, and bestow a lower degree of comprehension, in proportion as they recede from the intellectual power of the higher natures. If, therefore, the inferior substances received species in the same degree of universality as the superior substances, since they are not so strong in understanding, the knowledge which they would derive through them would be imperfect, and of a general and confused nature.

We can see this to a certain extent in man, for those who are of weaker intellect fail to acquire perfect knowledge through the universal conceptions of those who have a better understanding, unless things are explained to them singly and in detail. Now, it is clear that in the natural order human souls hold the lowest place among intellectual substances. But the perfection of the universe required various grades of being. If, therefore, God had willed human souls to understand in the same way as separate substances, it would follow that human knowledge, so far from being perfect, would be confused and general. Therefore, to make it possible for human souls to possess perfect and proper knowledge, they were so made that their nature required them to be joined to bodies, and thus to receive the proper and adequate knowledge of sensible things from the sensible things themselves. Thus we see in the case of uneducated men that they have to be taught by sensible examples.

It is clear then that it was for the soul's good that it was united to a body, and that it understands by turning to phantasms. Nevertheless it is possible for it to exist apart from the body, and also to understand in another way.

Nor is this way of knowledge unnatural, for God is the author of the influx both of the light of grace and of the light of nature.

E. The Body Is Essential to a Human Being (75, 4)

It has been shown above that sensation is not the operation of the soul only. Since, then, sensation is an operation of man, but not proper to him, it is clear that man is not a soul only, but something composed of soul and body. Plato, through supposing that sensation was proper to the soul, could maintain man to be a soul making use of the body.

Not every particular substance is a hypostasis [or a person], but that which has the complete nature of its species. Hence a hand, or a foot, is not called a person; nor, likewise, is the soul alone so called, since it is a part of the human species.

F. The Intellect Is Passive (79, 2)

The human intellect, which is the lowest in the order of intelligence and most remote from the perfection of the divine intellect, is in potentiality with regard to things intelligible, and is at first like a clean tablet on which nothing is written, as the philosopher says. This is made clear from the fact that at first we are only in potentiality to understand, and afterwards we are made to understand actually. And so it is evident that, with us, to understand is *in a way to be passive*.

G. The Intellect Is Also Active (79, 3)

According to the opinion of Plato, there is no need for an active intellect in order to make things actually intelligible. . . . For Plato supposed that the forms of natural things subsisted apart from matter, and consequently that they are intelligible, since a thing is actually intelligible from the very fact that it is immaterial. . . . But, since Aristotle did not allow that forms of natural things exist apart from matter, and as forms existing in matter are not actually intelligible, it follows that the natures or forms of the sensible things which we understand are not actually intelligible. . . . We must therefore assign on the part of the intellect some power to make things actually intelligible, by abstraction of the species from material conditions.

H. The Object Known Has
Different Kinds of Existence (84, 1)

Now, it seems that Plato strayed from the truth because, having observed that all knowledge takes place through some kind of similitude, he thought that the form of the thing must of necessity be in the knower in the same manner as in the thing known. Then he observed that the form of the thing understood is in the intellect under conditions of universality, immateriality, and immobility, which is apparent from the very operation of the intellect, whose act of understanding has a universal extension and is subject to a certain amount of necessity. Wherefore he concluded that the things which we understand must have in themselves an existence under the same conditions of immateriality and immobility.

But there is no necessity for this. For even in sensible things it is to be observed that the form is otherwise in one sensible than in another; for instance, . . . in one we find whiteness with sweetness, in another without sweetness. In the same way the sensible form is conditioned differently in the thing which is external to the soul and in the senses which receive the forms of sensible things without receiving matter, such as the color of gold without receiving gold. So also the intellect, according to its own mode, receives, under conditions of immateriality and immobility, the species of material and mobile bodies, for the received is in the receiver according to the mode of the receiver. We must conclude, therefore, that through the intellect the soul knows bodies by a knowledge which is immaterial, universal, and necessary.

I. Objects Sensed Act on the Intellect (84, 6)

On this point the philosophers held three opinions. For Democritus held that all knowledge is caused by images issuing from the bodies we think of and entering into our souls. . . . And the reason for this opinion was that both Democritus and the other early philosophers did not distinguish between intellect and sense. . . . Consequently, since the sense is affected by the sensible, they thought that all our knowledge is affected by this mere impression brought about by sensible things. . . .

Plato, on the other hand, held that the intellect is distinct from the senses, and that it is an immaterial power not making use of a corporeal organ for its action. And, since the incorporeal cannot be affected by the corporeal, he held that intellectual knowledge is not brought about by sensible things affecting the intellect. . . . Moreover, he held that sense is a power operating of itself. Consequently neither is sense (since it is a spiritual power) affected by the sensible. But [for Plato] the sensible organs *are* affected by the sensible, the result being that the soul is in a way roused to form within itself the species of the sensible.

Aristotle chose a middle course, for with Plato he agreed that intellect and sense are different, but he held that the sense has not its proper operation without the cooperation of the body, so that to feel is not an act of the soul alone but of the composite. And he held the same in regard to all the operations of the sensitive part. Since, therefore, it is not unreasonable that the sensible objects which are outside the soul should produce some effect in the composite, Aristotle agreed with Democritus in this, that the operations of the sensitive part are caused by the impression of the sensible on the sense. But Aristotle held that the intellect has an operation which is independent of the body's cooperation. Now, nothing corporeal can make an impression on the incorporeal. And therefore, in order to cause the intellectual operation, according to Aristotle, the impression caused by the sensible does not suffice, but something more noble is required, for the agent is more noble than the patient [what it acts on]. . . . The higher and more noble agent, which he calls the active intellect, . . . causes the phantasms received from the senses to be actually intelligible, by a process of abstraction.

According to this opinion, then, on the role of the phantasms, intellectual knowledge is caused by the senses. But, since the phantasms cannot of themselves affect the receptive intellect, and require to be made actually intelligible by the active intellect, it cannot be said that sensible knowledge is the total and perfect cause of intellectual knowledge, but rather that it is in a way the material cause.

J. External Objects Are Known Directly (85, 2)

The intelligible species is to the intellect what the sensible image is to the sense. But the sensible image is not what is perceived, but rather that by which sense perceives. Therefore the intelligible species is not what is actually understood, but that by which the intellect understands.

Some have asserted that our intellectual faculties know only the impression made on them; as, for example, that sense is cognizant only of the impression made on its own organ. According to this theory, the intellect understands only its own impression, namely, the intelligible species which it has received, so that this species is what is understood.

This is, however, manifestly false for two reasons. First, because the things we understand are the objects of science; therefore, if what we understand is merely the intelligible species in the soul, it would follow that every science would not be concerned with objects outside the soul, but only with the intelligible species within the soul.

Secondly, it is untrue because it would lead to the opinion that whatever seems, is true, and that consequently contradictories are true simultaneously. For, if the faculty knows its own impression only, it can judge of that only. Now a thing seems according to the impression made on the cognitive faculty. Consequently the cognitive faculty will always judge of its own impression as such; and so every judgment will be true. . . . Thus every opinion would be equally true; in fact, every sort of apprehension.

Therefore it must be said that the intelligible species is related to the intellect as that by which it understands, which is proved thus. There is a twofold action: one which remains in the agent (for instance, to see and to understand) and another which passes into an external object (for instance, to heat and to cut). And each of these actions proceeds in virtue of some form. And, as the form from which proceeds an act tending to something external is the likeness of the object of the action, as heat in the heater is a likeness of the thing heated [that is, resembles the heat in it], so the form from which proceeds an action remaining in the agent is the likeness of the object. Hence that by which the sight sees is the likeness of the visible thing; and the likeness of the thing understood, that is, the intelligible species, is the form by which the intellect understands. But, since the intellect reflects upon itself, by such reflection it understands both its own act of intelligence and the species by which it understands. Thus the intelligible species is that which is understood secondarily. But that which is primarily understood is the object of which the species is the likeness.

K. The Intellect Also Knows Itself (87, 1)

The human intellect is only a potentiality in the genus of intelligible beings, just as primary matter is a potentiality as regards sensible beings; and hence it is called possible [potential]. Therefore in its essence the human mind is only potentially understanding. Hence it has in itself the power to understand, but not to be understood except as it is made actual. . . . As in this life our intellect has material and sensible things for its proper natural object, . . . it understands itself according as it is made actual by the species abstracted from sensible things through the light of the active intellect, which not only actuates the intelligible things themselves but also, by their instrumentality, actuates the passive intellect. Therefore the intellect knows itself not by its essence but by its act. . . .

This happens in two ways. In the first place, singularly, as when Socrates or Plato perceives that he has an intellectual soul because he perceives that he understands. In the second place, universally, as when we consider the nature of the human mind from knowledge of the intellectual act. . . .

There is, however, a difference between these two kinds of knowledge, and it consists in this: that the mere presence of the mind suffices for the first (the mind itself being the principle of action whereby it perceives itself and hence is said to know itself by its own presence) but, as regards the second kind of knowledge, the mere presence of the mind does not suffice, and there is further required a careful and subtle inquiry (hence many are ignorant of the soul's nature, and many have erred about it).

L. Philosophy Is Helped by Faith (1, 1)

It was necessary for man's salvation that there should be a knowledge revealed by God, besides philosophical science built up by human reason. First, indeed, because man is directed to God as to an end that surpasses the grasp of his reason. . . . But the end must first be known by men who are to direct their thoughts and actions to the end. Hence it was necessary for the salvation of man that certain truths which exceed human reason should be made known to him by divine revelation. Even as regards those truths about God which human reason could have discovered, it was necessary that man should be taught by a divine revelation, because the truth about God such as reason could discover would only be known by a few, and that after a long time, and with the admixture of many errors.

Extracted from *Summa Theologiae*, translated by the Fathers of the English Dominican Province, volumes 1 and 4 (Westminster, 1911 and 1913).

COMMENTARY

■ ■ ■

Analysis of the Selections

As concerns Aquinas's philosophy of the human person, he is noted for having synthesized the teachings of the greatest philosophers who came before him, such as Plato, Aristotle, and Saint Augustine. This synthesis did not consist in choosing doctrines of each of these and merely putting them side by side but in creating a new philosophy able to absorb certain teachings and reject others.

Plato had taught that the human soul is immortal (though he also taught that it transmigrates, that is, that it stays in existence but passes from a person, after that person's death, to a new body). But he had also said that the body is not really part of the human being. Aristotle had stressed the unity of the human composite but did not teach that the human soul is immortal. Saint Augustine had taught that the soul is immortal and had rejected transmigration; he had also insisted on the unity of soul and body, but had not been able to give a satisfactory explanation of why they are together. Aquinas, on the other hand, taught that the soul is immortal, that it does not transmigrate, and that it is one with its body; and was also able to give a good reason for this state of affairs.

A. For Aquinas a soul is the first principle of life in a living body. A body, as body, is not alive, just as it is not hot. To become hot it must possess the attribute of heat. Similarly, to be alive it must be informed by a life-principle, which makes it to be a certain kind of living thing. This principle is the nature of a living thing. In a human being it is a human nature.

We know that a human body has several principles of life, such as the heart and the lungs. But each of these principles is but a manifestation of one ultimate principle, a *first* principle. This principle is the soul; it is the source of all life in the body. It makes the whole body to be alive, to be human.

B. Therefore, the soul is everywhere in the body. The substantial form of any material thing, in order to make the thing be one thing, must be everywhere in the thing, so the soul, the substantial form of a living thing, is everywhere in it. Of course the soul does not exercise all its functions in each part of the living body, but rather exercises in each part the functions proper to that part. We can find experiential verification of our soul's omnipresence in our body when, for example, we experience the sense of touch in our hands and our feet at the same time. And, when we die, when the soul leaves the body, all human functions cease.

C. We will not examine Aquinas's argument for the immortality of the human soul; it is not an easy argument. But we will look at one aspect of it. The human intellect, which is one power of the human soul, has as its typical object the universal nature of a physical thing. Now, according to Aristotle's theory of the nature of physical things, each of them has a nature that is of itself universal but that is individuated by matter. Thus, in order for the intellect to be acted upon by universal natures, the universal natures must be dematerialized, released from the matter that individuates them. And, because there is always a proportion between a receiver and what it receives, the intellect itself must be immaterial. It cannot have matter in its composition. The human soul, therefore, must have a power that does not involve matter in its exercise. Thus the soul is able to function without matter. And, if it can function without matter, it must be a being that is able to exist without matter.

D. Aristotle, too, had held that the human soul is immaterial, but he did not teach that it is immortal. One important reason is that he did not see how the soul could function after death, without the body and its senses, since in this life it is so dependent on phantasms for its functioning. Phantasms are sensory representations of objects, in the senses or the sensory imagination; they cannot exist without a body.

Aquinas taught that the human intellect is indeed very dependent on sensation in this life. But he taught also that, since the soul is immaterial and capable of existing by itself, it is able to function intellectually without the body. However, he claimed that this latter functioning is less perfect than the functioning of the soul joined to the body, in so far as the natural order is concerned. In this way he was able to defend the immortality of the soul and still say that it is naturally joined to the body.

Plato, in teaching that the human soul is immortal, taught also that it is better off, in the natural order, when separated from the body. He therefore held that its being joined to the body is unnatural; he called the body a prison, a tomb. Plato believed that the higher would not be joined to the lower for the sake of the lower; thus the soul would not naturally be joined to the body for the sake of the body. But Aquinas was able to hold that the soul is joined to the body for the sake of the soul; in his philosophy the soul functions better as an intellectual substance when it is joined to the body.

For Aquinas, the human intellect is the lowest of all intellects, lower, for example, than the divine intellect or an angelic intellect. (Though philosophy cannot know of the existence of angelic intellects it can easily imagine that they might exist. Indeed it is easier to posit their existence than to think that the only created intellect is as far from the divine as ours is.) At any rate, the human intellect is indeed a lowly intellect. We are born without knowledge; our store of knowledge grows only slowly; we are not able to think of all that we know all at once; we forget things; we make mistakes; we require a large number of concepts to understand things that of themselves can be known by a single concept, and so on. And Aquinas taught that our intellect is so lowly that, in order to function as well as it can as an intellect, it needs help from the body with its senses, which would not be true of a created intellect superior to ours. Such a higher intellect could function well without a body. For Aquinas, the human intellect can function without the body, but not as well. Thus, though the human intellectual principle, the soul, is a spirit, it is of its very nature an embodied spirit.

Since the soul is a spirit, it is entitled, as it were, to knowledge by means of ideas (which Aquinas here calls *species*). But the ideas to which it is entitled simply as a spirit are not sufficient for it, as they would be sufficient for a higher type of created spirit. If we compare a learned mathematician and a seven-year-old child, we realize that the concepts mastered by the former (such as the square root of –1) would often be unsuitable for the child; the child would get nothing out of them. Similarly, the human intellect, Aquinas said, gets more out of the ideas it generates from sense knowledge than it would out of the ideas that would be given to it innately.

As to the question why God did not create only fully spiritual intellectual beings, the answer given by Aquinas is that God wanted all different kinds of beings in creation, even different kinds of intellectual beings.

One might think that the knowledge of the soul separated from its body would be a knowledge above its nature, purely supernatural, but Aquinas taught that it is not; it is natural. Some call it preternatural, to distinguish it from the supernatural and from the natural as found in this life.

E. We thus see that the nature of the human being and of the human soul is very much tied up with the nature of human knowledge. The study of human nature is therefore inextricably interwoven with the study of human knowledge. For Aquinas, as we have said, the human intellectual principle is the form of matter so that it might function properly as an intellectual principle. The human intellect needs its body, with its senses, not to exist but to function properly. So important is this doctrine for Aquinas that he said a human soul is not a human person. Only a complete human being is a person, and a complete human being is a composite of soul and matter. Just as a human hand is not a person, but only part of a person, so a human soul is not a person, but only part of a person.

F. When we are born we have no knowledge whatever. We do, however, have senses and an intellect, which are capable of acquiring knowledge. As Aristotle said, at first our mind is like a clean slate on which nothing is written. And how do things get written on this slate? Objects in the outside world act on our minds. They act on our senses, and then on our intellect. Our senses and our intellect are passive. There are ways in which both of them are active, too. But, unless they were passive, we would not need our body for intellection, or even for sensation.

G. We know that our senses are active in that they involve physiological activity. But this physiological activity is ordained to the senses receiving knowledge. Similarly, our intellect is active, and this activity is ordained to the intellect receiving knowledge. The reason this activity must precede the reception is that our intellect knows objects universally, and they exist in the outside world and in the senses only individually. These objects must be made universal before the intellect can receive them. To be universalized, their natures must be separated from the matter to which they are joined in the world and in the senses. This activity of separation is called abstraction (*abstractio* is the Latin word for separation).

H. Plato taught that there are two worlds, the physical world of individual things and the intelligible world of the universal natures of these things. He taught this because he did not see how the natures of things could be inside the things themselves. These natures are one and unchanging (that is, there is one of each kind, and it always remains the same). Things of the same kind, on the other hand, are many and changing. To safeguard the oneness and the immobility of each nature, Plato felt compelled to place it in an unchanging intelligible world.

As a result of this metaphysical principle, Plato had to say that intellectual knowledge does not come from the physical world, since intellectual knowledge is of natures and they do not exist as such in the physical world. He did not say, as his pupil Aristotle did, that we are able to know in one way what exists in the world in another way. That is, we are able to know in a universal and unchanging way the natures that exist in individuals and, indeed, in changing individuals. Plato wrongly thought that, for our intellectual knowledge to be true, we had to know things as they are. Aristotle said that we can know natures truly even if we do not know them as they exist in things. He advanced the idea that our knowledge can be true because we are aware that we know in a universal and unchanging way things that exist in reality in an individual and changing way. Therefore, we can know natures truly even though they exist as universal and immobile only in our minds.

If Plato were right, our intellectual knowledge would not come from the physical world, and we would have no need of a body in order to know intellectually. Our body would not only be unnecessary for intellectual knowledge but very likely, as Plato held, a hindrance. And we would then be forced to have a very different view of human nature.

Aquinas gave us some comparisons to show that an object can be grasped truly in knowledge without there being a grasp of all the conditions belonging to the object in reality. For example, we can truly grasp the whiteness of an object without grasping its sweetness. Our senses take in the color of gold without taking in the gold itself. Thus we can see the natures of things truly without paying attention to their individuating characteristics or their changeability.

I. We therefore see that both the unity of the human person and the immortality of the human soul are involved in a theory of human knowledge. According to Democritus, things in the world act on the human mind and produce in it likenesses of themselves, which likenesses enable the mind to know these things. These likenesses were called by Aristotle *species*. For Aristotle each thing in the world has a nature, and in order for the thing to be known, this nature must act on and specify the mind. The nature in the thing came to be called a *form*, and the nature in the mind a *species*, in order to distinguish it from the form. Democritus, however, did not distinguish sense knowledge from intellectual knowledge, which was a weakness in his theory.

Plato corrected this weakness. But, as has already been explained, he did not see how natures in the physical world could act on the intellect. He therefore disagreed with Democritus, and said that intellectual knowledge does not come from objects outside the mind acting on the mind. Aquinas also interpreted Plato as holding that, even in sensation, these objects do not act on the mind; this was certainly true for some Platonists, as, for example, Saint Augustine. Such a theory, of course, is unable to give a satisfactory account of the naturalness of the human body or even of how we know that there is a physical world or a human body.

In order to have a theory of knowledge that safeguarded the existence of the world and the human body, the naturalness of the human body, and the immaterial nature of the human mind, Aristotle had to agree with Democritus and Plato and to disagree with both of them. He agreed with Democritus that objects outside the mind act on both the senses and the intellect; and with Plato that, since the intellect is immaterial, it can be acted upon only by the immaterial. He opposed Democritus's teaching that sensation and intellection are the same, and Plato's teaching that physical things cannot act on the mind.

He achieved all this by teaching, as we have already seen, that the intellect has the power of dematerializing the natures of things in the physical world. With this teaching he was able to agree with Democritus that things in the world act on the intellect, since the intellect itself is able to give them the ability to do so. And he was able to correct Plato's teaching that material things cannot act on the immaterial intellect by showing that the intellect itself has the power to enable them to do so.

J. It is historically significant that Aquinas not only insisted that physical things can act on our senses and our intellect but also foresaw a problem in this area that would wreak devastation in the philosophy of Descartes (1596–1650) and so many philosophers following him, such as Locke, Malebranche, Berkeley, Hume, and Kant. The problem is how objects outside the mind can be known if, in order to be known, they must be inside the mind. As far as I know, Aquinas was the first person to really solve the problem explicitly. The problem is how objects outside the mind can be known if in order to be known, they must be inside the mind.

For Aquinas, as for Aristotle, knowledge takes place by the object of knowledge being present to the mind, acting on it, and specifying it. This intramental existence of the object is called a *species*. In the senses it is called a *sensory species*; in the intellect, an *intelligible species*. Aristotle and Aquinas did not see how knowledge could take place without the object known acting on and specifying the mind. But such a theory raises a question: is the object of knowledge the object outside the mind or the object inside the mind (the species)?

Aquinas's position was that the object of knowledge is the object outside the mind. Our mind is turned outward; we are, as regards our knowledge, extroverted. Otherwise we would know only what is inside our minds, we would be unable to known anything outside our minds, or even think of anything outside our minds, as Hume taught. Aquinas pointed out that we would lose our ordinary meaning of truth if such were the case. We usually take truth to be the correspondence of our mind to reality. But, if all we know is what is in our mind, and have no grasp of reality, we could not say that anything we think is false.

Aquinas taught, of course, that we can be aware of species. But our awareness of them is subsequent to our awareness of the objects they have presented to us. We are aware of them, as it were, after they have done their work. We cannot see without eyes, but we do not see our own eyes. We can know that we have them, of course, by looking in a mirror. But this is not a common occurrence with most of us. We rarely pay attention to our eyes themselves; instead, we pay attention to what they see. Similarly, we can become aware of our sensory and intelligible species, and of our act of sensing or thinking, but only after the primary object of our knowledge has been presented to us. And this reflective activity does not prevent species from doing their work, that is, presenting objects to us without themselves getting in the way. We have sensory species, intelligible species, acts of sensation, and acts of intellection, so that we can know; they are *means* whereby we know, not *obstacles* to knowledge. For Descartes, Locke, Malebranche, Berkeley, Hume, and Kant, they are obstacles to knowledge. It is as if our eyes were not a means to knowledge but an obstacle to it.

K. Aquinas had also one of the most penetrating theories of self-knowledge, that is, knowledge of our own mind. We know our sensory and intelligible species, our acts of sensing and thinking, only indirectly, without them interfering with the ordinary objects of our knowledge. We know our mind also in the same way. Though it is always possible for us to contact our mind, we usually are thinking of something else.

Aquinas saw a parallel between the way our mind knows

and the way it is known. At first our mind knows nothing; to know, it must be actualized. Similarly, the mind of itself has only potential knowledge of itself; to know itself it must be actualized; for example, by an act of knowledge or will. When we are asleep we are not aware of ourselves, unless when dreaming.

How do we know our own mind? In two ways. First, as a particular object. For this knowledge only the presence of the mind to itself is necessary, though, as we have said, it must be actualized. Second, according to its nature. This is a much fuller knowledge of our mind, and requires a great deal of study. Indeed, many disciplines study the mind: philosophy, psychology, psychiatry, and so on.

■ ■ ■

A Philosophical and Theological Reflection

L. Aquinas's theory of the human as an embodied spirit, that is, as an immortal soul intimately one with its body, incorporated the insights of Plato, Aristotle, and Saint Augustine, and yet improved on them. It will be noticed also that it is more Christian than the philosophies of these predecessors. In contrast with Plato, Aquinas made the body natural. In contrast with Aristotle, Aquinas made the soul immortal. In contrast with Saint Augustine, Aquinas gave a good reason for a spirit dwelling in matter. Now, how was Aquinas able to arrive at a more Christian understanding of the human person?

There is no doubt that in this matter, as in many others in his philosophy, Aquinas was helped by the Judeo-Christian revelation. But it is important to realize that this help was not direct. It did not substitute for philosophical reasoning. It acted merely as a spur, or as a corrective, in Aquinas's philosophy. It was a help, but an indirect, a negative, help.

At the very beginning of his *Summa Theologiae*, Aquinas asks why God has revealed truths that can be known by philosophy without revelation. He answers that there are, indeed, such truths, but that most people are not philosophers. They do not have the ability or the opportunity to become philosophers. And, even if they do have the ability and the opportunity, it would take them many, many years to become philosophers, and these truths are so important that we need them early in life. Moreover, it could well be that these philosophers would make mistakes. Indeed, Aquinas knew that all the philosophers who preceded him, who philosophized without the indirect help of revelation, had made serious philosophical mistakes about God, about the human person, and about the purpose of human life.

■ ■ ■

Religious Critique

Aquinas knew that all truth comes from God through revelation, either revelation in the natural order (in the book of nature) or revelation in the supernatural order (in the book of Scripture). He also knew that truth never contradicts itself. If something is true in the supernatural order it cannot contradict a truth of the natural order. Philosophy and science, then, can never contradict what God has revealed supernaturally. Consequently, if one comes to a conclusion in philosophy that contradicts a truth of faith, it is clear that more work has to be done in philosophy.

One must first make sure, of course, that faith has been properly understood. This requires a theological criterion, such as Scripture or the clear teaching of the Church. Then, if the faith has been properly understood, a philosophical conclusion contradicting it is necessarily false. Now, revelation does not tell the philosopher how to correct his thinking. But it offers a strong inducement to check it and to see where it can be improved. This help can be compared to that offered by answers at the back of a mathematics textbook. If one does a problem and finds that the answer is different from that given by the author of the textbook, one knows that, at least usually, one has made a mistake. And usually, too, the mistake can be detected by a careful review.

For Aquinas, then, or for anyone who knows by faith that certain things are true, it is possible to do better in philosophy for the reason stated. One has to be careful, of course, not to let faith substitute for philosophy, or to let one be fooled into thinking that poor reasoning is all right as long as it agrees with faith, but these dangers can be avoided by hard work. And Aquinas, while seeing that many of his philosophical conclusions were in line with his faith, was always careful to distinguish between faith and philosophy, and to try to ground his philosophical conclusions solely on evidence available to anyone, believer or not.

Of course, faith was only one help to Aquinas in doing philosophy, and an indirect one at that. Aquinas also made extensive use of the great philosophers who preceded him, such as Plato, Aristotle, and other pagans. They provided many philosophical truths, and even in their errors disclosed problems that had to be faced and solved.

■ ■ ■

Summary

For Aquinas the human soul is present in each part of its body, making it human and being intimately one with it. This unity is so strong that without the body there can be no person. Yet the soul has at least one power, the intellect, that transcends matter and the body in its operation, and therefore, because it is capable of functioning by itself, it is capable of existing by itself. And the reason the soul is joined to its body even though it can exist apart from it is that it functions better in its natural intellectual capacity when joined to the body than when separated from it.

Thus the nature of the human person and of the soul is connected with the nature of human knowing. The intellect needs sensation in order to develop, and sensation requires a body. Things in the physical world act on the senses and also act on the intellect. This action on the intellect requires the coaction of the intellect, however. The intellect must abstract natures from matter before they can be known, but this abstraction, though it renders knowledge incomplete, does not render it misleading. Also, although objects of knowledge must act on and specify the senses and the intellect in order to be known, the intramental presences of these objects, which are necessary conditions of knowledge, are not the primary objects of knowledge and thus are not obstacles to knowledge.

Similarly, sense knowledge and intellectual knowledge cannot take place without there being acts of sensation and intellection. These acts, however, like the sensory and intelligible species just referred to, are not the primary objects of knowledge, and thus also are not obstacles to knowledge. Like the species, they can be known in a secondary manner, by reflection on our acts of knowledge. Thus we are aware of our knowing, and of ourselves, as well as the ordinary objects of our knowledge, but one type of awareness does not prevent another.

■ ■ ■

Further Reading

E. Gilson, *The Christian Philosophy of St. Thomas Aquinas* (New York, 1956).
J. A. Weisheipl, *Friar Thomas d'Aquino* (New York, 1974).

5

RENÉ DESCARTES

. . .

THE HUMAN PERSON AS A DUALISM

Introduction and Commentary
by Desmond J. FitzGerald

INTRODUCTION

■ ■ ■

Descartes' Life and Works

René Descartes was born March 31, 1596, at La Haye, near Tours, France, into a family that, while not nobility, was part of the well-established local gentry. When he was only four Descartes' mother died, but the inheritance she left him was enough, through careful management, to make him independent for life.

When he was about ten, Descartes' father sent him to the newly founded Jesuit school at La Flèche where he remained until he was almost twenty. This school had been founded with the support of King Henry IV of France to show his gratitude to the Catholics for the support they had given him in his struggle for the throne. Descartes was later to speak of it as "one of the most celebrated schools in Europe," and here through the famous *ratio studiorum* (program of studies) he learned what would be comparable to our high school and college subjects. Unfortunately, when he graduated he was disappointed that his search for certain knowledge was left unfulfilled. "For I found myself embarrassed with so many doubts and errors

149

that it seemed to me that the effort to instruct myself had no effect other than the increasing discovery of my own ignorance." Under the influence of the writings of Montaigne (1533–92), Descartes wondered if there was to be found anywhere in the world the learning for which he had hoped.

After his graduation, it is believed that Descartes followed a family tradition and studied law for a time at Poitiers. However, not satisfied with that, he decided to be a gentleman-soldier, a soldier of fortune, and so enlisted in the army of Prince Maurice of Nassau, a principality in the Holy Roman Empire. This provided him the opportunity to travel and to use the mathematical skills he had acquired at La Flèche. While in Holland, he had serious discussions with Isaac Beeckman, a fellow mathematician, who, like Descartes, was excited at the prospect of applying mathematics to the study of the physical world. Their conversations encouraged Descartes, who later dedicated some early writings on algebra and music to his friend.

The next year found Descartes in the army's winter-quarters at the town of Ulm on the Danube. He spent the day of November 10, 1619, wondering what he should do with his life, and that night, as he slept, he had a series of dreams that decided him. He interpreted the dreams as a call from God to devote himself to the pursuit of truth; he understood that God had given him certain abilities that he had an obligation to use to reorganize science. He did not immediately change his life; he remained with the army, traveling in mid-Europe and learning from the world, and it was not until the mid-1620s that he returned to Paris to work on his project. After a few years Descartes recognized that, with his friends in Paris, he was working less efficiently than he needed to work to achieve his objective, and he was encouraged by Cardinal Berulle, who told him that he was doing the right thing in using his intellect in the service of mankind. Thus, Descartes decided to put himself into voluntary exile in 1628, by going to Holland where, among foreigners, he could work in a more concentrated fashion.

Descartes' project came into focus: he would write a treatise called *Le Monde* (The World), which integrated all the science of his day. It was a most ambitious project and began to take longer than he had anticipated. We know of his progress because he wrote regularly to his friends in France, especially to a priest friend, Marin Mersenne, with whom he shared his scientific ambitions. As the 1620s passed into the 1630s, Descartes remained confident that he was closer to finishing than was actually the case. Then, in November 1633, Descartes learned that Galileo had been condemned earlier that year in Rome for teaching the Copernican theory, and this caused a crisis; Descartes himself was using the Copernican theory in his synthesis, and Galileo's troubles concerned him greatly.

Aware now that some of what he had written in *Le Monde* would invite controversy, and controversy would obscure his achievements, Descartes must have been tempted to scrap the whole treatise, but then his life's purpose would be detoured. After some time Descartes made up his mind: he would publish some parts of *Le Monde* as an example of his work, but he would exclude the controversial parts. He selected the sections on geometry, optics, and meteors, and, to explain what he was about, he wrote an autobiographical essay, *Discourse on Method*. This introduction to his method was printed in Holland (so that he could carefully correct the proofs) and in French (so that it would reach beyond the scholarly audience). The work was published in 1637 anonymously so that Descartes could see how it was received before acknowledging that he was the author.

Descartes' book was favorably received and he was encouraged to expand on the metaphysical foundations of science by writing *Meditations on First Philosophy*. This time he worked through Mersenne in Paris in arranging publication; his friend sought the reaction of a number of contemporaries; and their comments, called *Objections*, and Descartes' *Replies*, were printed together with the work in 1641. Interestingly, the subtitle of this work was "In which the existence of God and the immortality of the soul are demonstrated."

Descartes had revealed to the world his refutation of skepticism and his metaphysical foundation for science. In his judgment he had proceeded from his universal doubt about the existence of an external world to discover his own existence, and then God's existence, and then, using God's truthfulness, had attempted to return to the world, which is where he wanted to be all along. His principal interests were mathematics and natural science; his metaphysics (the philosophy of ultimate reality) was something he invented to provide a solid foundation for science. That he was doing a service to religion as well was important to him, but he saw it more as a selling point to gain acceptance from the Sorbonne theologians than as his main concern. Nevertheless, it bothered him that his former teachers, the Jesuits, had not accepted his system to the extent that he hoped they would. He wanted them to introduce it into their schools, replacing the textbooks of late Scholasticism (late medieval philosophy) that they were using. Then it occurred to him that he needed to recast his philosophy in the form of a textbook, with numbered paragraphs and a logical development. Thus, he was led to publish his *Principles of Philosophy* in 1644. This work went beyond his metaphysics and theory or knowledge and devoted several sections to his philosophy of nature, or physics, as he analyzed natural phenomena in the physical world.

By now Descartes had international recognition. One of his correspondents was Queen Christina of Sweden. Closer at hand, in Holland, was Princess Elizabeth of Bohemia, whose late father had been a contender for the crown of Bohemia. He had lost, and so his family lived in reduced circumstances near Leiden. Descartes had met her at one of the receptions held by her mother, who styled herself Queen of Bohemia. While no longer wealthy, the mother was the daughter of James I of England and the sister of Charles I, and was well connected. Elizabeth and Descartes were able to meet occasionally because he was living nearby at Endegeest. But to preserve his privacy, they carried out their relationship by letter, and from these letters we can see that Elizabeth was one of Descartes' best students. She was also a most penetrating critic, especially of the problem of relating mind and body. She pressed Descartes for answers in areas where he had left things unclear, and generally she was an ideal student. Part of his correspondence on moral issues served as the basis for his *Passions of the Soul*, written around 1646 but not published until shortly after his death in 1650. Descartes' royal students were some compensation for his failure to win over the schools of France to his new system.

Thus in the later 1640s, when Descartes returned to Paris, he had mixed feelings about his success. Though he had made noted converts to his system, he had failed to gain the universal acceptance he judged his system merited. Nor did he receive from the French Court all the honors he had been led to expect were his for the taking. His friends Mersenne and Cardinal Richelieu were dead, and these were the connections he had counted on. So when in the summer of 1649 he received an invitation from Queen Christina to come to Sweden and personally instruct her in his philosophy and serve as her advisor with respect to a Swedish Academy of Sciences, Descartes decided to accept.

He set sail for Stockholm in the fall and arrived in November as winter had set in. He stayed with the French ambassador to Sweden whose household included a Catholic chaplain in this Lutheran country. Queen Christina was an active monarch and her busy schedule permitted philosophy lessons only at 5 A.M. Descartes had a life-long habit of staying in bed late to work at his mathematical problems and meditate. However, he rose early and met the Queen's schedule those cold winter months. Unfortunately, he became ill with, perhaps, pneumonia; his fever lasted and he drifted in and out of consciousness. In view of the seriousness of his illness, the chaplain administered the Last Sacraments, and Descartes died peacefully February 11, 1650, and was buried in Stockholm. Only much later were the French able to persuade the Swedes to return his remains to Paris, and today his remains are in the church of Saint Germain des Prés, Paris.

■ ■ ■

What to Look For in the Selection

As you read through the selection of Descartes' writings, which is organized under the six numbered headings shown here, keep the following questions in mind.

1. Methodical Doubt
Does the fact that you are thinking show conclusively that you exist?

Does it show that your mind is entirely distinct from your body?

If your mind is independent of your body, have you established your immortality?

2. Criterion of Truth

Why did Descartes choose "clearness and distinctness" as his criterion of truth? In what branch of knowledge are you most likely to know clearly and distinctly?

In establishing this criterion, is Descartes ignoring the traditional definition of truth as the conformity of knowledge to things?

3. God

Does Descartes' idea of God as a perfect being reflect your understanding of God?

Is Descartes not invoking the principle of causality? Did he intend to exclude first principles from his methodical doubt?

4. The Body

Descartes says he knows his mind better than his body. Would you agree?

Descartes here anticipates the construction of robots. What models of machinery did he have in his time?

5. Men and Brute Animals

What do you think Descartes would say to contemporary attempts to teach chimps to use sign language? What would people today say to the suggestion that humans are entirely different from brute animals?

6. The Rational Soul

Descartes believes he has been supportive of the religious teaching on immortality. What do you think? In making man's mind independent of the body, has Descartes contradicted your experience of yourself as a unity?

SELECTION FROM DESCARTES

■ ■ ■

Discourse on Method, **Parts 4 and 5**

1. Methodical Doubt

I do not know that I ought to tell you of the first meditations there made by me, for they are so metaphysical and so unusual that they may perhaps not be acceptable to everyone. And yet at the same time, in order that one may judge whether the foundations which I have laid are sufficiently secure, I find myself constrained in some measure to refer to them. For a long time I had remarked that it is sometimes requisite in the common life to follow opinions which one knows to be most uncertain, exactly as though they were indisputable, as has been said above. But because in this case I wished to give myself entirely to the search after Truth, I thought that it was necessary for me to take an apparently opposite course, and to reject as absolutely false everything as to which I could imagine the least ground of doubt, in order to see if afterwards there remained anything in my belief that was entirely certain. True, because our senses sometimes deceive us, I wished to suppose that nothing is just as they cause us to imagine it to be. And, because there are men who deceive themselves in their reasoning and fall into mistakes, even concerning the simplest matters of geometry, and judging that I was as subject to error as was any other, I rejected as false all the reasons formerly accepted by me as demonstrations. And since all the same thoughts and conceptions which we have while awake may also come to us in sleep, without any of them being at that time true, I resolved to assume that everything that ever entered into my mind was no more true than the illusions of my dreams. But immediately afterwards I noticed that, whilst I thus wished to think all things false, it was absolutely essential that the I who thought this should be something. And, remarking that this truth "I think, therefore I am" was so certain and so assured that all the most extravagant suppositions brought forward by the sceptics were incapable of shaking it, I came to the conclusion that I could receive it without scruple as the first principle of the Philosophy for which I was seeking.

And then, examining attentively that which I was, I saw that I could conceive that I had no body, and that there was no world nor place where I might be; but yet that I could not for all that conceive that *I* was not. On the contrary, I saw, from the very fact that I thought of doubting the truth of other things, it very evidently and certainly followed that I was; on the other hand, if I had only ceased from thinking, even if all the rest of what I had ever imagined had really existed, I should have no reason for thinking that I had existed. From that I knew that I was a substance the whole essence or nature of which is to think, and that for its existence there is no need of any place, nor does it depend on any material thing; so that this "me," that is to say, the soul by which I am what I am, is entirely distinct from its body, and is even more easy to know than is the latter; and even if the body were not, the soul would not cease to be what it is.

2. The Criterion of Truth

After this I considered generally what in a proposition is requisite in order for it to be true and certain; for since I had just discovered one which I knew to be such, I thought that I ought also to know in what this certainty consisted. And having remarked that there was nothing at all in the statement "I think, therefore I am" which assures me of having hereby made a true assertion, excepting that I see very clearly that, to think, it is necessary to be, I came to the conclusion that I might assume, as a general rule, that the things which we conceive very clearly and distinctly are all true—remembering, however, that there is some difficulty in ascertaining which are those that we distinctly conceive.

3. God

Following upon this, and reflecting on the fact that I doubted, and that consequently my existence was not quite perfect (for I saw clearly that it was a greater perfection to know than to doubt), I resolved to inquire whence I had learnt to think of anything more perfect than I myself was, and I recognised very clearly that this conception must proceed from some nature which was really more perfect. As to the thoughts which I had of many other things outside of me, like the heavens, the earth, light, heat, and a thousand others, I had not so much difficulty in knowing whence they came, because, remarking nothing in them which seemed to render them superior to me, I could believe that, if they were true, they were dependencies upon my nature, in so far as it possessed some perfection; and, if they were not true, that I held them from nought, that is to say, that they were in me because I had something lacking in my nature. But this could not apply to the idea of a Being more perfect than my own, for to hold it from nought would be manifestly impossible. And, because it is no less contradictory to say of the more perfect that it is what results from and depends on the less perfect, than to say that there is something which proceeds from nothing, it was equally impossible that I should hold it from myself. In this way it could but follow that it had been placed in me by a Nature which was really more perfect than mine could be, and which even had within itself all the perfections of which I could form any idea—that is to say, to put it in a word, which was God. To which I added that, since I knew some perfections which I did not possess, I was not the only being in existence (I shall here use freely, if you will allow, the terms of the School), but that there was necessary some other more perfect Being on which I depended, or from which I acquired all that I had. For if I had existed alone and independent of any other, so that I should have had from myself all that perfection of being in which I participated to however small an extent, I should have been able for the same reason to have had all the remainder which I knew that I lacked; and thus I myself should have been infinite, eternal, immutable, omniscient, all-powerful; and, finally, I should have all the perfections which I could discern in God. For, in pursuance of the reasonings which I have just carried on, in order to know the nature of God as far as my nature is capable of knowing it, I had only to consider in reference to all these things of which I found some idea in myself, whether it was a perfection to possess them or not. And I was assured that none of those which indicated some imperfection were in Him, but that all else was present; and I saw that doubt, inconstancy, sadness, and such things could not be in Him, considering that I myself should have been glad to be without them. In addition to this, I had ideas of many things which are sensible and corporeal; for, although I might suppose that I was dreaming, and that all that I saw or imagined was false, I could not at the same time deny that the ideas were really in my thoughts. But because I had already recognised very clearly in myself that the nature of the intelligence is distinct from that of the body, and observing that all composition gives evidence of dependency, and that dependency is manifestly an imperfection, I came to the conclusion that it could not be a perfection in God to be composed of these two natures, and that consequently He was not so composed. I judged, however, that if there were any bodies in the world, or even any intelligences or other natures which were not wholly perfect, their existence must depend on His power in such a way that they could not subsist without Him for a single moment.

After that I desired to seek for other truths. And, having put before myself the object of the geometricians, which I conceived to be a continuous body, or a space indefinitely extended in length, breadth, height, or depth, which was

divisible into various parts, and which might have various
shapes and sizes, and might be moved or transposed in all
sorts of ways (for all this the geometricians suppose to be in
the object of their contemplation), I went through some of
their simplest demonstrations and, having noticed that this
great certainty which everyone attributes to these demonstrations is founded solely on the fact that they are conceived of
with clearness, in accordance with the rule which I have just
laid down, I also noticed that there was nothing at all in them
to assure me of the existence of their object. For, to take an
example, I saw very well that, if we suppose a triangle to be
given, the three angles must certainly be equal to two right
angles; but, for all that, I saw no reason to be assured that
there was any such triangle in existence, while, on the contrary, on reverting to the examination of the idea which I had
of a perfect being, I found that in this case existence was
implied in it in the same manner in which the equality of its
three angles to two right angles is implied in the idea of a triangle; or, in the idea of a sphere, that all the points on its surface are equidistant from its centre; or even more evidently
still. Consequently it is at least as certain that God, who is a
Being so perfect, is, or exists, as any demonstration of geometry can possibly be.

What causes many, however, to persuade themselves that
there is difficulty in knowing this truth, and even in knowing
the nature of their soul, is the fact that they never raise their
minds above the things of sense, or that they are so accustomed to consider nothing except by imaging it, which is a
mode of thought specially adapted to material objects, that all
that is not capable of being imagined appears to them not to
be intelligible at all. This is manifest enough from the fact that
even the philosophers in the Schools hold it as a maxim that
there is nothing in the understanding which has not first of all
been in the senses, in which there is certainly no doubt that the
ideas of God and of the soul have never been. And it seems to
me that those who desire to make use of their imagination in
order to understand these ideas, act in the same way as if, to
hear sounds or smell odors, they should wish to make use of
their eyes: excepting that there is indeed this difference, that
the sense of sight does not give us less assurance of the truth

of its objects than do those of scent or of hearing, while neither our imagination nor our senses can ever assure us of anything if our understanding does not intervene.

If there are, finally, any persons who are not sufficiently persuaded of the existence of God and of their soul by the reasons which I have brought forward, I wish that they should know that all other things of which they perhaps think themselves more assured (such as possessing a body, and that there are stars and an earth and so on) are less certain. For, although we have a moral assurance of these things which is such that it seems that it would be extravagant in us to doubt them, at the same time no one, unless he is devoid of reason, can deny, when a metaphysical certainty is in question, that there is sufficient cause for our not having complete assurance, by observing the fact that when asleep we may similarly imagine that we have another body, and that we see other stars and another earth, without there being anything of the kind. For how do we know that the thoughts that come in dreams are more false than those that we have when we are awake, seeing that often enough the former are not less lively and vivid than the latter? And though the wisest minds may study the matter as much as they will, I do not believe that they will be able to give any sufficient reason for removing this doubt, unless they presuppose the existence of God. For to begin with, that which I have just taken as a rule, that is to say, that all the things that we very clearly and very distinctly conceive of are true, is certain only because God is or exists, and that He is a perfect being, and that all that is in us issues from Him. From this it follows that our ideas or notions, which to the extent of their being clear or distinct are ideas of real things issuing from God, cannot but to that extent be true. So that though we often enough have ideas which have an element of falsity, this can only be the case in regard to those which have in them something that is confused or obscure, because in so far as they have this character they participate in negation— that is, they exist in us as confused only because we are not quite perfect. And it is evident that there is no less repugnance in the idea that error or imperfection, inasmuch as it is imperfection, proceeds from God, than there is in the idea of truth or perfection proceeding from nought. But if we did not know that all that is in us of reality and truth proceeds from a perfect and infinite Being, however clear and distinct were our ideas, we should not have any reason to assure ourselves that they had the perfection of being true.

But after the knowledge of God and of the soul has thus rendered us certain of this rule, it is very easy to understand that the dreams which we imagine in our sleep should not make us in any way doubt the truth of the thoughts which we have when awake. For even if in sleep we had some very distinct idea such as a geometrician might have who discovered some new demonstration, the fact of being asleep would not militate against its truth. And as to the most ordinary error in our dreams, which consists in their representing to us various objects in the same way as do our external senses, it does not matter that this should give us occasion to suspect the truth of such ideas, because we may be likewise often enough deceived in them without our sleeping at all, just as when those who have the jaundice see everything as yellow, or when stars or other bodies which are very remote appear much smaller than they really are. For, finally, whether we are awake or asleep, we should never allow ourselves to be persuaded except by the evidence of our Reason. And it must be remarked that I speak of our Reason and not of our imagination nor of our senses; just as, though we see the sun very clearly, we should not for that reason judge that it is of the size of which it appears to be; likewise we could quite well distinctly imagine the head of a lion on the body of a goat, without necessarily concluding that a chimera exists. For Reason does not insist that whatever we see or imagine thus is a truth, but it tells us clearly that all our ideas or notions must have some foundation of truth. For otherwise it could not be possible that God, who is all perfection and truth, should have placed them within us. And because our reasonings are never so evident nor so complete during sleep as during wakefulness, although sometimes our imaginations are then just as lively and acute, or even more so, Reason tells us that, since our thoughts cannot possibly be all true, because we are not altogether perfect, that which they have of truth must infallibly be met with in our waking experience rather than in that of our dreams. . . .

4. The Body

I had explained all these matters in some detail in the Treatise which I formerly intended to publish. And afterwards I had shown there what must be the fabric of the nerves and muscles of the human body in order that the animal spirits therein contained should have the power to move the members, just as the heads of animals, a little while after decapitation, are still observed to move, and bite the earth, notwithstanding that they are no longer animate; what changes are necessary in the brain to cause wakefulness, sleep, and dreams; how light, sounds, smells, tastes, heat, and all other qualities pertaining to external objects are able to imprint on it various ideas by the intervention of the senses; how hunger, thirst, and other internal affections can also convey their impressions upon it; what should be regarded as the "common sense" by which these ideas are received, and what is meant by the memory which retains them, by the fancy which can change them in diverse ways and out of them constitute new ideas, and which, by the same means, distributing the animal spirits through the muscles, can cause the members of such a body to move in as many diverse ways, and in a manner as suitable to the objects which present themselves to its senses and to its internal passions, as can happen in our own case apart from the direction of our free will. And this will not seem strange to those who know how many different *automata* or moving machines can be made by the industry of man, without employing in so doing more than a very few parts in comparison with the great multitude of bones, muscles, nerves, arteries, veins, or other parts that are found in the body of each animal. From this aspect the body is regarded as a machine which, having been made by the hands of God, is incomparably better arranged, and possesses in itself movements which are much more admirable, than any of those which can be invented by man. Here I specially stopped to show that if there had been such machines, possessing the organs and outward form of a monkey or some other animal lacking reason, we should not have had any means of ascertaining that they were not of the same nature as those animals. On the other hand, if there were machines which bore a resemblance to our body and imitated our actions as far as it was morally possible to do so, we should always have two very certain tests by which to recognise that, for all that, they were not real men. The first is that they could never use speech or other signs as we do when placing our thoughts on record for the benefit of others. For we can easily understand a machine's being constituted so that it can utter words, and even emit some responses to action on it of a corporeal kind which brings about a change in its organs; for instance, if it is touched in a particular part it may ask what we wish to say to it; if in another part, it may exclaim that it is being hurt; and so on. But it never happens that it arranges its speech in various ways in order to reply appropriately to everything that may be said in its presence, as even the lowest type of man can do. And the second difference is that, although machines can perform certain things as well as or perhaps better than any of us can do, they infallibly fall short in others, by which means we may discover that they did not act from knowledge, but only from the disposition of their organs. For while reason is a universal instrument which can serve for all contingencies, these organs have need of some special adaptation for every particular action. From this it follows that it is morally impossible that there should be sufficient diversity in any machine to allow it to act in all the events of life in the same way as our reason causes us to act.

5. Men and Brute Animals

By these two methods we may also recognise the difference that exists between men and brutes. For it is a very remarkable fact that there are none so depraved and stupid, without even excepting idiots, that they cannot arrange different words together, forming from them a statement by which they make known their thoughts; while, on the other hand, there is no other animal, however perfect and fortunately circumstanced it may be, which can do the same. It is not the lack of organs that brings this to pass, for it is evident that magpies and parrots are able to utter words just like ourselves, and yet they cannot speak as we do, that is, so as to give evidence that they think of what they say. On the other hand, men who, being born deaf and dumb, are, in the same degree as or even more than the brutes, destitute of the organs which serve the others for talking, are in the habit of themselves inventing certain signs by which they make themselves understood by those who, being usually in their company, have leisure to learn their language. And this does not merely show that the brutes have less reason than men, but that they have none at all, since it is clear that very little is required in order to be able to talk. And when we notice the inequality that exists between animals of the same species, as well as between men, and observe that some are more capable of receiving instruction than others, it is not credible that a monkey or a parrot, selected as the most perfect of its species, should not in these matters equal the stupidest child to be found, or at least a child whose mind is clouded, unless, in the case of the brute, the soul were of an entirely different nature from ours. And we ought not to confound speech with natural movements which betray passion and may be imitated by machines as well as be manifested by animals; nor must we think, as did some of the ancients, that brutes talk although we do not understand their language. For if this were true, since they have many organs which are allied to our own, they would communicate their thoughts to us just as easily as to those of their own race. It is also a very remarkable fact that although there are many animals which exhibit more dexterity than we do in some of their actions, we at the same time observe that they do not manifest any dexterity at all in many others. Hence the fact that they do better than we do does not prove that they are endowed with mind, for in this case they would have more reason than any of us, and would surpass us in all other things. It rather shows that they have no reason at all, and that it is nature which acts in them according to the disposition of their organs, just as a clock, which is composed only of wheels and weights, is able to tell the hours and measure the time more correctly than we can do with all our wisdom.

6. The Rational Soul

I had described after this the rational soul and shown that it could not be in any way derived from the power of matter, like the other things of which I had spoken, but that it must be expressly created. I showed, too, that it is not sufficient that it should be lodged in the human body like a pilot in his ship, unless perhaps for the moving of its members, but that it is necessary that it should also be joined and united more closely to the body in order to have sensations and appetites similar to our own, and thus to form a true man. In conclusion, I have here enlarged a little on the subject of the soul, because it is one of the greatest importance. For next to the error of those who deny God, which I think I have already sufficiently refuted, there is none which is more effectual in leading feeble spirits from the straight path of virtue than to imagine that the soul of the brute is of the same nature as our own, and that, in consequence, after this life we have nothing to fear or to hope for, any more than the flies and ants. As a matter of fact, when one comes to know how greatly they differ, we understand much better the reasons which go to prove that our soul is in its nature entirely independent of its body, and in consequence that it is not liable to die with it. And then, inasmuch as we observe no other causes capable of destroying it, we are naturally inclined to judge that it is immortal.

Extracted from *Discourse on Method,* translated by E. S. Haldane and G. R. T. Ross (Cambridge, 1912).

COMMENTARY

■ ■ ■

The Background of Descartes' Philosophy

To understand Descartes' philosophy of the human person, we should know something of the time in which he lived and the background of his writing. Among the factors that influenced his thinking, three are especially important: the Copernican Revolution, the resurgence of mathematics, and the revival of skepticism.

From ancient times until well into the seventeenth century, astronomy was dominated by the theory that came to be associated with Claudius Ptolemy (c. A.D. 100–178): the planet Earth is the center of the heavens. The theory coincided with our everyday observations of the Sun rising in the east and setting in the west, and the rotation of the starry skies at night. More than that, Ptolemy's calculations in his *Almagest* served as the basis for predicting eclipses, and generally was well received by the astrologers who were part of the entourage of kings and princes. Yet there were difficulties and, to account for discrepancies between the theory and what was observed, adjustments had to be made from time to time. By the late 1400s these additions to the movement of the planets, called epicycles, made the original theory appear cumbersome to the sort of mathematical mind that prized simplicity and elegance. Thus, Nicholas Copernicus (1473–1543) was moved to wonder if there was not a better way to explain what we observe.

Copernicus posited that if the Sun were recognized as the center of the heavens, with the earth and the other planets rotating around the Sun, astronomers could eliminate many of the inaccuracies associated with Ptolemy's system. The phenomenon of the Sun's rising and setting could be better explained by proposing that our planet Earth goes through a daily rotation, while the change of seasons could be accounted for by proposing that the earth wobbles, the north pole tipping toward the sun during the northern hemisphere's summer months, and away in winter. Many objected to the Copernican theory, however, because they could not believe that we live on a moving platform and yet have no sense of movement. The man-on-the-street's reaction to Copernicus, as well as that of many learned people, was that the theory goes against common experience and so, while it may be a useful theory for astronomers, it has little to do with real life. Only in the next century, after he developed the telescope, did Galileo (1564–1642) become a convert to, and the leading proponent of, the Copernican position.

Unfortunately, Galileo's pugnacious temperament, especially when he believed he was right, led to conflicts with the university professors, who manipulated the churchmen into warning Galileo in 1616 not to teach the Copernican theory, and then condemning him in 1633 when he broke his promise by publishing his *Dialogue on the Two World Systems* (1632). However, the Copernican theory continued to gain acceptance among intellectuals like Descartes, and there were many interesting repercussions.

One such repercussion was the negative impact the Copernican theory had on Aristotle's reputation. Over time Aristotle's view of the organization of the heavens came to be aligned with the Ptolemaic theory because both centered the organization of the world on our planet Earth. To the extent that there was a growing rejection of Ptolemy, Aristotle's reputation of having all the answers suffered a setback. Descartes was motivated to replace Aristotle as the philosopher of the universities.

In the twelfth century, when the Latin West began recovering ancient Greek writings from the Moslems in Spain, one of the many treasures regained were scientific writings in astronomy and mathematics. Included was the system of arithmetical symbols we call "Arabic numerals," which came from India through the Arabs. This system, with its zero, was recognized as an improvement on Roman numerals, and the gradual adoption of these numerals, first in commerce, then in science, stimulated mathematical speculation. In the period of the Renaissance, mathematicians commonly made discoveries that they kept secret, and then challenged their contemporaries to solve the puzzles they had unravelled. Gradually, as the late Renaissance merged into the early seventeenth century, a number of achievements had become the common property of mathematicians: decimals, logarithms, and conventional signs relating to squaring or cubing numbers. To a mathematical observer like Descartes, the certitude of mathematics was impressive, and he judged that the secret to the success of mathematics was its method.

In contrast with the agreement among mathematicians with respect to the conclusions of their science, the disagreements among philosophers on almost every topic presented a scandal to someone living toward the end of the sixteenth century. Some wondered how the best minds could have debated the fundamental questions of life (the existence of God, the immortality of the soul, and freedom of choice) and failed after so many centuries to have settled these issues beyond further debate. Among those who wondered was Michel de Montaigne (1533–92). After an active period in political affairs, he retired to the estate he had inherited from his father to ponder the questions raised by his reading of the classics. After some years of study he was prompted to share his reflections in brief writings for which he coined the term *Essais* from the French verb *essayer*, to try, to test. Here his thoughts articulated a mood that characterized the intellectual atmosphere in this late Renaissance, post-Reformation period: the mood of skepticism, that scientific knowledge, with its demanding features of certainty and universality, was impossible.

These thoughts, especially in the long essay *Apology for Raimond of Sebonde,* gave voice to an attitude growing in literary and intellectual circles, and Montaigne quickly became a significant author, stimulating other writers to express similar doubts about ever knowing truth for certain. Even in church circles, this tendency to play down the power of reason, and question what it might accomplish, in order to play up the need for faith and a teaching authority, a movement called "fideism," was tried as a ploy to combat the free thinkers and reformers in post-Reformation Europe.

Descartes was one of those who came under Montaigne's influence but, unlike others who accepted the skeptical mood, he resisted it. Taking his inspiration from the success of mathematics, Descartes conceived a project that would in one blow refute the skeptics and provide the foundation for the philosophic system he sought to build. This project was to begin with methodical or universal doubt.

As Descartes begins the fourth part of his *Discourse,* he intends to give a summary of his systematic approach to philosophizing. In the selections we have a condensed version of what Descartes later presents in an expanded form in the *Six Meditations.* Already, in Part I, he has given the biographical account of his school days at La Flèche and the disappointment he felt as he concluded the course of studies. One thing pleased him, the study of mathematics: "Most of all I was delighted with mathematics, because of the certitude and evidence of its reasonings; but I did not yet notice its true usage and, thinking that it only served the mechanical arts, I was astonished that on such firm and solid foundations nothing greater had been built."

This remark is important because Descartes makes clear his intention to build a greater edifice, his system, on a foundation that is certain and evident. Like other seventeenth-century thinkers, such as his contemporary, Thomas Hobbes, Descartes has Euclid's *Geometry* in mind as a model of scientific procedure. Just as Euclid began with self-evident axioms, so Descartes is searching for some evident and unchallengeable truth on which he can build his system.

In Parts 2 and 3 of the *Discourse,* Descartes has reflected on his method of proceeding. He tells us that he was impressed with city planners who might tear down a section of a city in order to rebuild it properly according to more rational standards, and judged that something like this was possible with respect to the accumulation of opinions we acquire in the course of some years of living. But care must be taken to guide oneself with good rules for rebuilding, and so Descartes laid out certain steps for the reconstruction he was planning:

> The first of these was to accept nothing as true which I did not clearly recognize to be so: that is to say, carefully to avoid precipitation and prejudice in judgments, and to accept in them nothing more than what was presented to my mind so clearly and distinctly that I could have no occasion to doubt it. The second was to "divide up" each of the difficulties which I examined into as many parts as possible and as seemed requisite, in order that it might be resolved in the best manner possible. The third was to carry on my reflections in due order, commencing with objects that were the most simple and easy to understand, in order to rise little by little, or by degrees, to knowledge of the most complex, assuming an order, even if a fictitious one, among those which do not follow a natural sequence relatively to one another. The last was in all cases to make enumerations so complete and reviews so general that I should be certain of having omitted nothing.

Knowing that he would begin his system with a universal all-embracing doubt of what he had held up to now, Descartes took care in Part 3 to lay down some rules to guide him morally while he worked on his new philosophy. As a conservative person on social matters, he simply proposed to obey the laws and customs of his country, as well as keep his religious commitment to the Catholic faith in which he had been raised. Generally, he proposed to live moderately within his means, and certainly to avoid all extremes. In a somewhat Stoic fashion, he further proposed to conquer himself rather than fortune and, by controlling his desires, to make himself satisfied with his situation. Thus, he took care to ensure that he would live a careful moderate life while he reviewed by his doubt whatever he had accepted up to now. He was concerned to clarify his intention: he was doubting not as the skeptics doubted—to end in doubt—but rather to discover the indubitable: "Not that in this I imitated the sceptics who doubt for the sake of doubting and pretend to be always uncommitted; on the contrary my intention was only to assure myself and to cast aside the loose earth and sand in order to reach the rock or clay."

■ ■ ■

Analysis of the Selection

As Descartes begins part 4 of his *Discourse,* he is following up on his ploy to beat the skeptics at their own game. He opens up with a remark that he has some concern about sharing his approach because he recognizes that not everyone will find it suitable; however, he overcomes his hesitation on the ground that if others are to be the judges of his system, they must know how he went about building it. Noting that his objective is to devote himself to the search for truth, Descartes explains that he will first move in an opposite course by making an attempt to doubt everything. But, as he says, his intention is not to end in doubt but to discover the indubitable. And so one by one, in a methodic way, he reviews the possible sources of error in knowledge: sense experience, mistakes in reasoning, and even mixing dreams with reality. Then it dawns on him that while he is choosing to think everything false, he must at least be existing! Now he has it: if he is thinking, he must be existing! This famous *Cogito, ergo sum* (I think, therefore I am) is a landmark in the history of philosophy, and, as Descartes adds, "even the most extravagant suppositions of the skeptics are incapable of shaking it." He has found his starting point, the self-evident truth upon which to build his system.

And from this starting point, Descartes draws a critical conclusion: he is a mind, "a substance whose whole essence or nature is to think." This realization is most important, for Descartes is revealing what he judges he is as a human being: "a thing that thinks," as he will say later in his *Meditations.* But he is not finished, for he then asserts that, "even if the body were not, the soul would not cease to be." Thus Descartes, in arguing his approach to the philosophy of human nature, settles ever so simply what had been the subject of much controversy among the scholastic Aristotelians early in the sixteenth century: personal immortality.

Note that Descartes is using the word *soul* here for the sake of his readers. The Aristotelian/Thomistic theory of man as a composite of body and soul has been rejected by him, but he realizes that his audience is familiar with the word *soul*, and so in this context he uses it. Also note that, whereas Descartes uses the word *distinct* to distinguish the mind from the body, the meaning the word carries for him, as regards the mind, is more than just "distinct," that is, "different from" the body; the implication is "separate," that is, "independent of" the body. Descartes is pleased with himself for he judges that he has established personal immortality in a way supportive of his religious faith, and he believes this to be one of the key selling points of his system, and so an advantage in his effort to supplant Aristotle as the philosopher of the universities.

Having broken out of his methodical doubt with the proof of his existence, and then reflecting on himself as a mind, a mental substance, whose immateriality was viewed as a basis for incorruptibility or immortality, Descartes moves to clarify his confidence that he has achieved the truth. He asks himself what there is about the *"Je pense, donc je suis,"* as the original French version had it, that makes him certain of its truth. His answer seems too simple: the insight is clear and distinct. From these newly discovered criteria for recognizing truth, Descartes lays down a general rule: hereafter, as he proceeds to build his system, whenever any thought breaks through with clarity and distinctness comparable to that found in the *cogito,* he will hold on to it as true.

It is important to understand that Descartes defined truth according to the correspondence, or confirmation, theory, which holds that the true "corresponds" to reality. When he speaks of "clearness and distinctness," he is presenting his criteria for recognizing truth and not for defining it.

Next Descartes turns to the question of the existence of God. He proposes several different arguments to establish

God's existence, based on his understanding of God. Recognizing that he is an imperfect or limited being from the fact that he doubts, Descartes also recognizes that there is within his consciousness the idea of a perfect being. How did the idea get there? Descartes says that with respect to the ideas of many other things, the heavens, the earth, and so on, there is nothing about them that he could not have caused. (Incidentally, it can be noted in passing that, whereas Descartes claimed to have totally doubted everything that ever entered his mind, his doubt did not really extend to first principles such as the principle of contradiction.) Here he is invoking a form of the principle of causality—that the cause must be at least as great as the effect—and using it to argue to God's existence. Simply put, he infers that since he, a limited being, cannot account for the idea of a "perfect or infinite being," there must truly be a perfect or infinite being in existence to account for that effect.

Now, without even a paragraph break, Descartes elaborates on the existence of God. There is disagreement on whether what follows constitutes a new and different argument for God's existence; Etienne Gilson, a well-known Cartesian scholar, argues that Descartes judged it was but the continuation of the first argument, but a case can be made that this is a distinctly different argument because this time Descartes does not start with the idea of an infinite or perfect being but reflects on the limited nature of his own existence. Whereas the starting point of the first argument is the idea of an infinite being and what could have caused it, the starting point of this second argument is rather the question "Who caused me?"

Descartes recognizes that he is not the source of his own existence. He says that, if he were his own cause, he would have given himself all the perfections of which he had any idea, and consequently he would have made himself to be "infinite, eternal, immutable, omniscient, all-powerful." But he does not have these divine perfections. Consequently, he must infer that he is a dependent being, and from that further infer that there is a God, a necessary being upon whom he depends for his existence.

In this latter part of the argument Descartes shows that he is not entirely inattentive to the metaphysical lectures of his scholastic teachers at La Flèche, for he understands very well the profound insight that he who could cause something to be, who could cause existence, could cause anything. There would be no stopping such a being. It would have everything; it would be a necessary being, God. There are echoes of Saint Thomas Aquinas in these words of Descartes.

Descartes continues to reflect on the nature of God as creator and concludes that, in contrast to himself burdened with doubt and sometimes sadness, God would be perfect, and would be immaterial, and, if there are physical bodies in the world, would be the cause of such bodies.

There next occurs to Descartes an argument for God's existence that is only briefly treated in the *Discourse* but is more fully treated in his *Meditations*—the famous *ontological argument* (ontology is the study of being). Descartes notes that as a mathematician he often contemplates the properties of a geometrical figure; a triangle, for example. And, while he can conclude that the sum of the interior angles equals two right angles, he does not know whether there are such triangles. By contrast, when he contemplates the idea of a perfect being, he cannot escape the conclusion that such a perfect being, having all perfections including existence, must necessarily exist. In the *Discourse*, the argument is simply given, but in the *Meditations* he takes care to develop it more fully, and to raise an objection, which he then tries to answer. The objection is that, whereas a hill is inconceivable without a valley so that the ideas of hill and valley are necessarily associated, this does not mean that there is any hill or valley anywhere in existence. And consequently, although he cannot think of a perfect being without existence, perhaps there is no such being in reality.

To this Descartes replies that God is a unique case; his essence entails existence: "For I am not free to think of God without existence (that is, a supremely perfect being without a supreme perfection) as I am free to imagine a horse with or without wings."

Now that Descartes has to his satisfaction established the existence of God, his next move is to get back to the world. His way of doing so is through the truthfulness of God. In the *Discourse* this is less explicit than in the *Meditations*, but the direction is the same. Descartes was a mathematico-physical scientist who judged that before he could pursue the publication of his research on the natural world he needed to reply to the challenge of skepticism. Thus he had begun with his metaphysics and theory of knowledge to lay the groundwork for his investigation of the natural world. Having doubted the existence of the extramental world, he established his own existence, then God's existence, and now, using God's veracity, he returns to the world. As he argued in the sixth meditation: "I have ideas of corporeal objects. I wonder if there really are such things outside my mind? Of course there must be such things since God, who is all-good, has given me a very great inclination to believe these ideas are caused by such objects, and he would not deceive me on something so basic. Therefore we must conclude that corporeal objects do indeed exist."

In part 5 of the *Discourse,* after an allusion to the treatise on the world, *Le Monde,* which he decided not to publish after he learned of Galileo's condemnation, Descartes proceeded to summarize the variety of physiological questions he had investigated. In a way it is extraordinary; there in his kitchens in Holland, with the carcasses of animals he had purchased at the slaughterhouses, he had sought to learn how the brain accounts for messages in the body to control the movements of our limbs; sensations; and even the processes of falling asleep and waking up. It is an interesting list of topics, and it shows the passionate interest Descartes had in neurological problems. Note, however, the metaphor he assumes: the body is a *machine,* but a machine built by God and so incomparably more complicated than any that humans could make. He mentions in passing though that, were one to construct a mechanical monkey and then clothe it in the hide or skin of a real monkey, no one could tell that it was false. Why? Because for Descartes, reflecting the mechanism of his time, a real, natural monkey was only a machine.

In a leap of the imagination, Descartes next anticipates an innovation in technology three hundred years ahead of his time. Descartes imagined the construction of robots (to use a twentieth-century word) that could be programmed to respond to certain stimuli. He quite agrees that they could be made to say "What do you want?" but he argues forcefully that they could never carry on a conversation as even the most ordinary peasant can do. This is another landmark in the history of Western thought, for in those words Descartes threw down the gauntlet to challenge the computer technologists of our time, most especially Alan Turing whose Turing Test proposal is undoubtedly a response to Descartes. As of the present writing, Descartes is still unanswered.

Descartes further suggests that whereas machines can be made to do a special operation better than humans, such as measure the time or tell temperature, there will never be a machine that can accomplish the wide range of things humans are capable of, from carrying objects to doing calculations. We are intelligent beings and because of our minds, we have abilities that cannot be matched by machines. Here Descartes is affirming his continuity with traditional philosophy in his appreciation of man as a reasoning being able to do things other creatures cannot.

Something of this idea is presented by Descartes in his thoughts about brute animals. He notes that certain animals can imitate the sound of speech, as parrots do, but they do not understand what they say. Here one can observe that, if Descartes were alive today holding these same principles, he would be skeptical of the experimental work of a number of psychologists who claim to have taught their chimpanzees to speak American sign language. As he says, "this does not merely show that brutes have less reason than men, but that they have none at all, since it is clear that very little is required in order to be able to talk."

In his *Apology for Raymond of Sebond*, Montaigne toys with the notion that animals are as intelligent as, if not more intelligent than, we are; it is just that we do not understand each other's languages. Descartes takes pains to repudiate this view as he again affirms that we are beings of body and mind.

Having stressed the independence of our minds in relation to our bodies to protect the immortality of the soul, Descartes, in the closing paragraph of part 5 of the *Discourse,* asserts the unity of man. He is aware that a feature of scholastic Aristotelianism was that the hylomorphic theory of man as a composition of body and soul better explained our experience of ourselves as one being than did the Augustinian dualism of man as "a soul sent to rule the body." Now he wishes to assert the unity of man and distance himself from the Platonic theory that the soul is in the body as a pilot in his ship. However, an assertion is not enough. Descartes cannot offer a reason for the union of soul and body, and, affirming it as it repeatedly does, his philosophy fails to give an account of the need of their being together; there is no sufficient purpose for their union.

This failure to justify the unification of mind and body will haunt Descartes. His friend and correspondent, Princess Elizabeth, will push him on the question and Descartes will never be able to answer her satisfactorily. But history will be a harsher judge. Descartes will come to be known as the creator of the mind/body problem, and all the ingenuity of Malebranche (1638–1715) and Leibniz (1646–1715) will fail to resolve the problem. Only in the eighteenth century will Julien La Mettrie (1709–51) cut the Gordian knot and settle the problem to his satisfaction by dropping the mind from man. His *Man, a Machine* will claim to account for all mental activity by the brain with no need to appeal to an immaterial principle within man. It is this solution that will largely take over modern philosophy after the eighteenth-century so-called Enlightenment and thus pass into contemporary social sciences such as psychology. And so in the long run the support Descartes believed he gave to immortality came to nothing. Further, this exaggerated dualism of Descartes has served to undermine the position of other traditional philosophers, such as Thomas Aquinas, who maintain the immateriality of the intellect.

■ ■ ■

Philosophical and Religious Critique

In parts 4 and 5 of the *Discourse*, Descartes presented his system in brief; he later expanded it in his *Meditations*. Let us reconsider the steps of his philosophy in a summary form:

1. The Methodical Doubt
2. The *"Cogito, ergo sum"*—his first principle
3. Man—"a substance whose whole essence or nature is to think"—a mind
4. The Criterion of Truth: "clearness and distinctness"

5. The Existence of God
   (i)   What caused the idea of a perfect being?
   (ii) Who caused me?
   (iii) The idea of a perfect being involves existence
6. The existence of the extramental world

How successful has Descartes been in establishing this system? Note that Descartes intended it to proceed step by step, like the theorems in Euclid's *Geometry*. But does it?

Consider the last argument Descartes made in his attempt to get out of his mind, as it were, and back to the world of corporeal objects where he really wanted to be as a student of the natural sciences. Strictly speaking, the argument failed because it was built on a premise that involved what he wanted to believe. In the sixth meditation, Descartes speaks of "a very strong inclination" to believe that things rather than God caused his ideas. But is it prudent to make a statement about what you would like to believe when advancing a philosophical demonstration?

On a deeper level of Thomistic theory of knowledge, Etienne Gilson would argue that Descartes was doomed to failure because he was trying to answer a false question: "How do you go from thought to things?" In other words, Descartes started off wrong, for by beginning with his universal or methodical doubt, he called into question what is most evident to us as human knowers, namely, that there is something; things exist!

Thus, once Descartes had denied to himself the evidence of his senses, his human experience, he could never come up with anything more evident to serve as a premise to prove the existence of the world. It has been argued that, by beginning with his doubt, Descartes retreated, as it were, into his own mind and falsely spoke of knowing "ideas" rather than "things." Unfortunately, this was not a mistake made only by Descartes. In their different ways, other modern philosophers such as John Locke, George Berkeley, and David Hume were to follow Descartes in talking as if ideas or impressions are what we know, rather than things.

At least one further problem remains: how was it that Descartes, undoubted genius, allowed himself to be so misled as to make what some consider basic mistakes? Again Etienne

Gilson proposes an answer that makes Descartes' error understandable in human terms. Descartes was guilty of "mathematicism."

You won't find *mathematicism* in your dictionaries. Gilson coined the term in his *The Unity of Philosophic Experience* to characterize the mistake of attempting to remake philosophy according to the method of mathematics. In other words, it is the use of the mathematical method where it does not belong, that is, in philosophy.

It is perfectly proper for a mathematician to ignore the world of things and begin in his mind by analyzing the implications of mathematical entities such as numbers and geometrical figures. This is correct since mathematical entities exist only in the mind. And though mathematicians often begin with a challenge from physical problems, nevertheless numbers, circles, triangles, and so on are "beings of reason" and have only mental existence. So Descartes, outstanding mathematician that he was, was used to closing his eyes and withdrawing to the world of mathematical beings and proceeding logically step by step to infer the implications of his mathematical definitions and axioms. When he arrived at a conclusion, that was it; he did not have to go back to the world of things.

The mathematicism of Descartes is, perhaps, best illustrated in the fallacy of his argument for the existence of God, based on the accepted definition of God as an all-perfect being. In considering the implications of that definition, Descartes argued that it implied the perfection of existence, and so God, an all-perfect being, must exist, by definition as it were. That way of reasoning is suitable for the properties of triangles but, as the classic criticism of the ontological argument goes, you cannot make "the illicit transition from the mental order to the extramental order" since you cannot have something in your conclusion that was not in some way in your premises. Thus the simple concept of "existence" cannot yield extramental existence in the world of things.

Descartes stands as a giant at the beginning of modern philosophy. He is linked by his education to the late medieval scholastic philosophy of his teachers, and his intention is to preserve what he had learned to value in his Jesuit education:

the importance of establishing the existence of God, the immortality of the soul, and freedom of choice. Yet in his very effort to create a philosophy that would serve the Church, the mistakes he made had an effect opposite to what he intended. He not only created a mind/body problem that led in the long run to the denial of anything immaterial in man; his ontological argument for God came to be viewed by thinkers like Immanuel Kant as typical of all metaphysical arguments for God's existence.

Even worse though, many would contend that Descartes started the fashion of making our ideas the object of knowledge rather than the means of knowing things. This in turn led in time to the skepticism of David Hume (1711–76). And it was as a response to Hume that Immanuel Kant (1724–1804) and the nineteenth-century German philosophers invented philosophies severed from the physical world.

■ ■ ■

Further Reading

J. Cottingham, *Descartes* (Oxford, 1986).

J. Cottingham, ed., *The Cambridge Companion to Descartes* (Cambridge, 1992).

E. Gilson, *The Unity of Philosophical Experience* (London, 1938), chapters 5–8.

M. Grene, *Descartes* (Minneapolis, 1985).

J. Maritain, *The Dream of Descartes* (New York, 1940).

J. Maritain, *Three Reformers* (New York, 1929), part 2.

6

DAVID HUME

...

THE HUMAN PERSON
AS A CONSTRUCT

Introduction and Commentary by Hunter Brown

INTRODUCTION

■ ■ ■

Hume's Life and Works

David Hume was born in 1711 in Edinburgh, Scotland. As a young man he rejected his parents' wishes that he pursue a career in law, devoting himself instead to philosophical and literary endeavors. His commitment to these endeavors was manifested in his willingness to live under austere conditions in France from 1734 to 1737 while working on *A Treatise of Human Nature*. Undaunted by the failure of that work to attract public attention, he went on to publish *Essays Moral and Political* in 1741–42, a work that did become successful. A revision of the earlier *Treatise* under the new title *An Enquiry Concerning Human Understanding* followed this success, as did works on the history of England and three further philosophical books, including *Dialogues on Natural Religion* published after his death. In 1763 he became secretary to the British ambassador in France and was undersecretary of state from 1767 to 1769. In subsequent years he developed friendships with a wide variety of people whose intellectual diversity attests to Hume's breadth of interests. He died in 1776.

■ ■ ■

Hume's Philosophical Importance

Hume's philosophical importance rests in great part upon his participation in traditions of thought that preceded him and that have been very significant since his time. On a fairly large historical scale, Hume worked during a period that continued a movement away from a God-centered understanding of the world, which had been greatly advanced by the thirteenth-century Christian thinker Thomas Aquinas. Such a theological frame of reference was continuing to give way during Hume's time in favor of one centering upon the human being.

It should be added in this connection, however, that while the prominent philosophers during Hume's general period contributed in their own fashion to this shift away from the predominance of theological influence upon philosophical thought, one cannot conclude from this fact that such philosophers were necessarily irreligious or antireligious. On the contrary, George Berkeley (1685–1753) was a bishop, and René Descartes (1596–1650), John Locke (1632–1704), and Immanuel Kant (1724–1804) were all very much affected, both personally and philosophically, by theological considerations. Hume, for his part, notwithstanding his harsh criticisms of the conventional natural theology of his time in *Dialogues on Natural Religion,* was not indiscriminately anti-theistic. His criticisms can be understood as having been directed toward certain specific forms of religious argumentation rather than toward theism as such.

In addition to locating Hume in terms of the general historical decline of a theological center of gravity for philosophy, it is important to discuss Hume's more immediate relation to philosophers of his own period. Hume stands in a succession of thinkers who contributed in crucial ways to the philosophical development of their time. Every member of this succession, from Descartes to Kant, was deeply indebted to the insights of his forerunners, insights that allowed each to move forward philosophically. In order to understand properly Hume's view of personal identity, it is necessary to consider some features of this movement. In particular, we will focus on the issue of philosophical *method* because Hume's conclusions on the nature of selfhood are in great part a function of his methodological commitments.

One of the many important questions asked by Plato early in the history of Western philosophy was How, if a person is not presently in possession of the truth, would he or she be able to recognize the truth when it is encountered? This question brings to prominence the dependence of the truth-seeking process upon certain decisions about the signs that will be taken as indicating the presence of truth. For example, do we know that a conviction is true because of the force with which it strikes us? Is truth a function of certain properties of ideas?

It is initially appealing to hold that truth is a function of the way in which certain ideas strike us. This notion, however, must withstand the challenge of other experiences that potentially undermine it. For example, when a person discovers the falsity of an idea he once held as true, that person must question the very properties of the idea that he had originally used as indicators of truth.

If the presence of certain properties of ideas is not necessarily a sure indication of truth, what other criteria might be available? Perhaps recourse to concrete experience holds some promise. Empiricist method, of which Hume is widely considered to be a preeminent representative, looks in this direction. In Hume's system, ideas are copies of the impressions found in concrete experience. The term *impressions* here refers to sensory experiences of realities in the world. Consequently, according to Hume the truth of our conceptions about such ideas as selfhood would be something that can be determined only by searching for the ideas' originating impressions. Within Hume's rigorous pursuit of such originating impressions lies the compelling challenge of his philosophy as well as its distinguishability from the philosophies of his immediate empiricist predecessors.

Increasing rigor in the application of empiricist method had been developing for some time in the work of Hume's predecessors, namely, Locke and Berkeley. Berkeley had criticized the lack of such rigor in Locke's work as Hume would go on to criticize such lack in the philosophy of Berkeley. In reflection upon the experience of physical realities, for example, John Locke had observed the phenomena of color, sound, taste, and odor. He claimed that such qualities must inhere *in* something, in some more basic reality, in a *substance*. Coffee, for example, would seem to be more than just dark, brown, and granular. Is there not some*thing* "standing under" such qualities—*sub* (under) *stance* (standing)—something that supports such perceptible qualities? Locke thought so. There must be more to the identity of an object than just its sensible qualities. What that more might be, however, he could not say. Thus, he concluded the underlying substance is an "I know not what." In the same spirit, but for other reasons, Locke affirmed that some*thing* must also stand beneath mental phenomena—a mental substance; a self.

Locke's contention that something must lie beneath and support sensory and mental phenomena has a good deal of intuitive appeal, as Hume would later readily concede. Notwithstanding such appeal, however, it is difficult to justify such a contention according to the canons of empiricism. Locke had not identified an impression that corresponded with his idea of substance. Nor had he identified one that corresponded with his idea of self. Locke's decision to posit such entities nevertheless would be, for Hume, a deficiency in the application of empiricist method.

Locke's successor, Bishop Berkeley, was convinced of Locke's failure in this regard. Sense experience does indeed disclose color, sound, taste, and odor, agreed Berkeley. What is more, he also agreed, there is a powerful intuitive tendency to ascribe such qualities to a substance to which they could be said to belong. Is there, however, any *empirical* justification for subscribing to such a position? Berkeley concluded that there was not, and so he favored an abandonment of Locke's notion of physical substance. As to mental substance, however, Berkeley reached different conclusions. He retained the conviction that the self is a real entity that underlies the different kinds of mental events that are experienced day to day.

The empiricist attempt to screen out convictions for which there is no originating impression was taken up with particular diligence by Hume. As Berkeley had found insufficient rigor in Locke's analyses, so Hume found insufficient rigor in the analyses of Berkeley. At Hume's hands, a substantive notion of selfhood would fail. However intuitively attractive,

Hume insisted, the impulse to posit such a self can claim no exemption from the empiricist demand for originating impressions. Hume's rigorous application of this empiricist requirement to conventional beliefs about God, the world, and causality, as well as about selfhood—an application that has been characterized as a "wrecking ball"—had a devastating effect upon long-standing, widespread convictions about such subjects. The concepts of God, world, cause, and self were all put to the Humean test with an empiricist commitment surpassing that of Berkeley and Locke.

In what impression, Hume would ask relentlessly, could one find the origin of the supposed ideas of cause or of self, of God, or of the world? If one could not identify such impressions, then upon what grounds could one claim to have an idea of such things? To what impression, for example, does the notion of *cause* correspond? Certainly there are impressions that give rise to common convictions about causality, Hume realized. But are those impressions actually impressions of a specific reality to which one refers by means of the term *cause?* No, said Hume. The impressions that support such convictions about causality are impressions of contiguity, temporal priority, and constant conjunction. *These* impressions give rise to conventional convictions about causality. As to an impression of a specific phenomenon to which the term could be said to refer, however, none is to be found, concluded Hume. What, then, about selfhood?

■ ■ ■

What to Look For in the Selection

With this background in mind, read the selection from Hume's *A Treatise of Human Nature.* Ask yourself particularly about one aspect of his efforts by asking the following questions. Is Hume making his inquiry into selfhood *with* anyone else? Does this matter? To what extent do we come into contact with selfhood simply by looking inward by ourselves, and to what extent by means of contact with other persons? Ask yourself whether the self that Hume eventually comes up with is a moral agent who can be held responsible, in the long run, for his or her actions? By Hume's account, are you exactly the same person when you are middle-aged as you were when you were a teenager? If you are not, what implications does this difference have for moral accountability?

SELECTION FROM HUME

■ ■ ■

A Treatise of Human Nature, **Book 1, Part 4, Section 6: Personal Identity**

There are some philosophers who imagine we are every moment intimately conscious of what we call our *self*; that we feel its existence and its continuance in existence; and are certain, beyond the evidence of a demonstration, of both its perfect identity and simplicity. The strongest sensation, the most violent passion, they say, instead of distracting us from this view, only fix it the more intensely, and make us consider their influence on *self* either by their pain or pleasure. To attempt a further proof of this is to weaken its evidence since no proof can be derived from any fact of which we are so intimately conscious; nor is there anything of which we can be certain, if we doubt of this.

Unluckily all these positive assertions are contrary to that very experience which is pleaded for them, nor have we any idea of *self* after the manner here explained. For from what impression could this idea be derived? This question is impossible to answer without a manifest contradiction and absurdity; and yet it's a question which must necessarily be answered if we would have the idea of self pass for clear and intelligible. It must be some one impression that gives rise to every real idea. But self or person is not any one impression, but that to which our several impressions and ideas are supposed to have a reference. If any impression gives rise to the idea of self, that impression must continue invariably the same, through the whole course of our lives, since self is supposed to exist after that manner. But there is no impression constant and invariable. Pain and pleasure, grief and joy, passions and sensations, succeed each other, and never all exist at the same time. It cannot, therefore, be from any of these impressions, or from any other, that the idea of self is derived; and consequently there is no such idea.

But further, what must become of all our particular perceptions upon this hypothesis? All these are different, and distinguishable, and separable from each other, and may be separately considered, and may exist separately, and have no need of any thing to support their existence. After what manner, therefore, do they belong to self; and how are they connected with it? For my part, when I enter most intimately into what I call *myself*, I always stumble on some particular perception or other, of heat or cold, light or shade, love or hatred, pain or pleasure. I never can catch *myself* at any time without a perception, and never can observe anything but the perception. When my perceptions are removed for any time, as by sound sleep, so long am I insensible of *myself*, and may truly be said not to exist. And were all my perceptions removed by death, and could I neither think, nor feel, nor see, nor love, nor hate after the dissolution of my body, I should be entirely annihilated, nor do I conceive what is further requisite to make me a perfect non-entity. If anyone, upon serious and unprejudiced reflexion, thinks he has a different notion of *himself*, I must confess I can no longer reason with him. All I can allow him is that he may be in the right as well as I, and that we are essentially different in this particular. He may, perhaps, perceive something simple and continued, which he calls *himself*, though I am certain there is no such principle in me.

But, setting aside some metaphysicians of this kind, I may venture to affirm of the rest of mankind that they are nothing but a bundle or collection of different perceptions, which succeed each other with an inconceivable rapidity, and are in a perpetual flux and movement. Our eyes cannot turn in their sockets without varying our perceptions. Our thought is still more variable than our sight; and all our other senses and faculties contribute to this change; nor is there any single power of the soul which remains unalterably the same, perhaps for one moment. The mind is a kind of theatre where several perceptions successively make their appearance, pass, re-pass, glide away, and mingle in an infinite variety of postures and situations. There is properly no *simplicity* in it at one time, nor *identity* at different times, whatever natural propensity we may have to imagine that simplicity and identity. The comparison with the theatre must not mislead us. They are the successive perceptions only that constitute the mind; nor have we the most distant notion of the place where these scenes are represented, or of the materials of which it is composed.

What then gives us so great a propensity to ascribe an identity to these successive perceptions, and to suppose ourselves possessed of an invariable and uninterrupted existence through the whole course of our lives? In order to answer this question, we must distinguish between personal identity as it regards our thought or imagination, and as it regards our passions or the concern we take in ourselves. The first is our present subject; and to explain it perfectly we must take the matter pretty deep, and account for that identity which we attribute to plants and animals, there being a great analogy between it and the identity of a self or person.

We have a distinct idea of an object that remains invariable and uninterrupted through a supposed variation of time; and this idea we call that of *identity* or *sameness*. We have also a distinct idea of several different objects existing in succession, and connected together by a close relation; and this to an accurate view affords as perfect a notion of *diversity* as if there were no manner of relation among the objects. But though these two ideas, of identity and a succession of related objects, be in themselves perfectly distinct, and even contrary, yet it is certain that in our common way of thinking they are generally confounded with each other. That action of the imagination by which we consider the uninterrupted and invariable object, and that by which we reflect on the succession of related objects, are almost the same to the feeling, nor is there much more effort of thought required in the latter case than in the former. The relation facilitates the transition of the mind from one object to another, and renders its passage as smooth as if it contemplated one continued object. This resemblance is the cause of the confusion and mistake, and makes us substitute the notion of identity instead of that of related objects. However at one instant we may consider the related succession as variable or interrupted, we are sure the next to ascribe to it a perfect identity, and regard it as invariable and uninterrupted. Our propensity to this mistake is so great from the resemblance above-mentioned that we fall into it before we are aware; and though we incessantly correct ourselves by reflexion, and return to a more accurate method of thinking, yet we cannot long sustain our philosophy, or take off this bias from the imagination. Our last resource is to yield to it, and boldly assert that these different related objects are in effect the same, however interrupted and variable. In order to justify to ourselves this absurdity, we often feign some new and unintelligible principle that connects the objects together, and prevents their interruption or variation. Thus we feign the continued existence of the perceptions of our senses to remove the interruption; and run into the notion of a *soul*, and *self*, and *substance*, to disguise the variation. But we may farther observe that, where we do not give rise to such a fiction, our propensity to confound identity with relation is so great that we are apt to imagine something unknown and mysterious, connecting the parts, besides their relation; and this I take to be the case with regard to the identity we ascribe to plants and vegetables. And, even when this does not take place, we still feel a propensity to confound these ideas, though we are not able fully to satisfy ourselves in that particular, nor find anything invariable and uninterrupted to justify our notion of identity.

Thus the controversy concerning identity is not merely a dispute of words. For, when we attribute identity, in an improper sense, to variable or interrupted objects, our mistake is not confined to the expression, but is commonly attended with a fiction, either of something invariable and uninterrupted, or of something mysterious and inexplicable, or at least with a propensity to such fictions. What will suffice to prove this hypothesis to the satisfaction of every fair enquirer is to show, from daily experience and observation, that the objects which are variable or interrupted, and yet are supposed to continue the same, are such only as consist of a succession of parts, connected together by resemblance, contiguity, or causation. For, as such a succession answers evidently to our notion of diversity, it can only be by mistake that we ascribe to it an identity; and, as the relation of parts, which leads us into this mistake, is really nothing but a quality which produces an association of ideas, and an easy transition of the imagination from one to another, it can only be from the resemblance which this act of the mind bears to that by which we contemplate one continued object that the error arises. Our chief business, then, must be to prove that all objects to which we ascribe identity, without observing their invariableness and uninterruptedness, are such as consist of a succession of related objects.

In order to do this, suppose any mass of matter, of which the parts are contiguous and connected, to be placed before us; it's plain we must attribute a perfect identity to this mass, provided all the parts continue uninterruptedly and invariably the same, whatever motion or change of place we may observe either in the whole or in any of the parts. But, supposing some very *small* or *inconsiderable* part to be added to the mass or subtracted from it; though this absolutely destroys the identity of the whole, strictly speaking, yet, as we seldom think so accurately, we scruple not to pronounce a mass of matter the same where we find so trivial an alteration. The passage of the thought from the object before the change to the object after it is so smooth and easy that we scarce perceive the transition, and are apt to imagine that it's nothing but a continued survey of the same object.

There is a very remarkable circumstance that attends this experiment, which is that, though the change of any considerable part in a mass of matter destroys the identity of the whole, yet we must measure the greatness of the part, not absolutely, but by its *proportion* to the whole. The addition or diminution of a mountain would not be sufficient to produce a diversity in a planet, though the change of a very few inches would be able to destroy the identity of some bodies. It will be impossible to account for this but by reflecting that objects operate upon the mind, and break or interrupt the continuity of its actions, not according to their real greatness, but according to their proportion to each other. And therefore, since this interruption makes an object cease to appear the same, it must be the uninterrupted progress of the thought which constitutes the identity.

This may be confirmed by another phenomenon. A change in any considerable part of a body destroys its identity; but it is remarkable that, where the change is produced *gradually* and *insensibly,* we are less apt to ascribe to it the same effect. The reason can plainly be no other than that the mind, in following the successive changes of the body, feels an easy passage from surveying its condition in one moment to viewing it in another, and at no particular time perceives any interruption in its actions, from which continued perception it ascribes a continued existence and identity to the object.

But whatever precaution we may use in introducing the changes gradually, and making them proportionable to the whole, it is certain that, where the changes are at last observed to become considerable, we make a scruple of ascribing identity to such different objects. There is, however, another artifice by which we may induce the imagination to advance a step farther; and that is by producing a reference of the parts to each other, and a combination to some *common end* or purpose. A ship, of which a considerable part has been changed by frequent repairs, is still considered the same; nor does the difference of the materials hinder us from ascribing an identity to it. The common end to which the parts conspire is the same under all their variations, and affords an easy transition of the imagination from one situation of the body to another.

But this is still more remarkable when we add a *sympathy* of parts to their *common end,* and suppose that they bear to each other the reciprocal relation of cause and effect in all their actions and operations. This is the case with all animals and vegetables, where not only the several parts have a reference to some general purpose, but also a mutual dependence on, and connexion with, each other. The effect of so strong a relation is that, though everyone must allow that in a very few years both vegetables and animals endure a *total* change, yet we still attribute identity to them, while their form, size, and substance are entirely altered. An oak that grows from a small plant to a large tree is still the same oak, though there be not one particle of matter, or shape of its parts, the same. An infant becomes a man, and is sometimes fat, sometimes lean, without any change in his identity.

We may also consider the two following phenomena, which are remarkable in their kind. The first is that, though we commonly are able to distinguish pretty exactly between numerical and specific identity, yet it sometimes happens that we confound them, and in our thinking and reasoning employ the one for the other. Thus a man who hears a noise that is frequently interrupted and renewed says it is still the same noise, though it is evident the sounds have only a specific identity or resemblance, and there is nothing numerically the same but the cause which produced them. In like manner it may be said without breach of the propriety of language that a church which was formerly of brick fell to ruin, and that the parish rebuilt the same church of free-stone, and according to modern architecture. Here neither the form nor materials are the same, nor is there anything common to the two objects except their relation to the inhabitants of the parish; and yet this alone is sufficient to make us denominate them the same. But we must observe that in these cases the first object is in a manner annihilated before the second comes into existence, by which means we are never presented in any one point of time with the idea of difference and multiplicity, and for that reason are less scrupulous in calling them the same.

Secondly, we may remark that, though in a succession of related objects it is, in a manner, requisite that the change of parts be not sudden nor entire in order to preserve the identity, yet, where the objects are in their nature changeable and inconstant, we admit of a more sudden transition than would otherwise be consistent with that relation. Thus as the nature of a river consists in the motion and change of parts, though in less than twenty-four hours these be totally altered, this does not hinder the river from continuing the same during several ages. What is natural and essential to anything is, in a manner, expected; and what is expected makes less impression, and appears of less moment, than what is unusual and extraordinary. A considerable change of the former kind seems really less to the imagination than the most trivial alteration of the latter and, by breaking less the continuity of the thought, has less influence in destroying the identity.

We now proceed to explain the nature of *personal identity*, which has become so great a question in philosophy, especially of late years in England, where all the more abstruse sciences are studied with a peculiar ardour and application. And here, it is evident, the same method of reasoning must be continued which has so successfully explained the identity of plants, and animals, and ships, and houses, and of all the compounded and changeable productions either of art or of nature. The identity which we ascribe to the mind of man is only a fictitious one, and of a like kind with that which we ascribe to vegetables and animal bodies. It cannot, therefore, have a different origin, but must proceed from a like operation of the imagination upon like objects.

But lest this argument should not convince the reader, though in my opinion perfectly decisive, let him weigh the following reasoning, which is still closer and more immediate. It is evident that the identity which we attribute to the human mind, however perfect we may imagine it to be, is not able to run the several different perceptions into one, and make them lose their characters of distinction and difference, which are essential to them. It is still true that every distinct perception which enters into the composition of the mind is a distinct existence, and is different, and distinguishable, and separable from every other perception, either contemporary or successive. But, as, notwithstanding this distinction and separability, we suppose the whole train of perceptions to be united by identity, a question naturally arises concerning this relation of identity: whether it be something that really binds our several perceptions together, or only associates their ideas in the imagination. That is, in other words, whether, in pronouncing concerning the identity of a person, we observe some real bond among his perceptions, or only feel one among the ideas we form of them. This question we might easily decide if we would recollect what has been already proved at large, that the understanding never observes any real connexion among objects, and that even the union of cause and effect, when strictly examined, resolves itself into a customary association of ideas. For from thence it evidently follows that identity is nothing really belonging to these different perceptions and uniting them together, but is merely a quality which we attribute to them because of the union of their ideas in the imagination, when we reflect upon them. Now the only qualities which can give ideas a union in the imagination are these three relations above-mentioned. These are the uniting principles in the world of ideas, and without them every distinct object is separable by the mind, and may be separately considered, and appears not to have any more connexion with any other object than if disjoined by the greatest difference and remoteness. It is, therefore, on some of these three relations of resemblance, contiguity, and causation, that identity depends, and, as the very essence of these relations consists in their producing an easy transition of ideas, it follows that our notions of personal identity proceed entirely from the smooth and uninterrupted progress of the thought along a train of connected ideas, according to the principles above-explained.

The only question, therefore, which remains is by what relations this uninterrupted progress of our thought is produced when we consider the successive existence of a mind or thinking person. And here it is evident that we must confine ourselves to resemblance and causation, and must drop contiguity, which has little or no influence in the present case.

To begin with *resemblance:* suppose we could see clearly into the breast of another, and observe that succession of perceptions which constitutes his mind or thinking principle, and suppose that he always preserves the memory of a considerable part of past perceptions; it is evident that nothing could contribute more to bestow a relation on this succession amidst all its variations. For what is the memory but a faculty by which we raise up the images of past perceptions? And, as an image necessarily resembles its object, must not the frequent placing of these resembling perceptions in the chain of thought convey the imagination more easily from one link to another, and make the whole seem like the continuance of one object? In this particular, then, the memory not only discovers the identity but also contributes to its production, by producing the relation of resemblance among the perceptions. The case is the same whether we consider ourselves or others.

As to *causation:* we may observe that the true idea of the human mind is to consider it as a system of different perceptions or different existences, which are linked together by the relation of cause and effect, and mutually produce, destroy, influence, and modify each other. Our impressions give rise to their corresponding ideas; and these ideas in their turn produce other impressions. One thought chases another, and draws after it a third, by which it is expelled in its turn. In this respect, I cannot compare the soul more properly to any thing than to a republic or commonwealth, in which the several members are united by the reciprocal ties of government and subordination, and give rise to other persons, who propagate the same republic in the incessant changes of its parts. And, as the same individual republic may not only change its members, but also its laws and constitutions, in like manner the same person may vary his character and disposition, as well as his impressions and ideas, without losing his identity. Whatever changes he endures, his several parts are still connected by the relation of causation. And in this view our identity with regard to the passions serves to corroborate that with regard to the imagination, by making our distant perceptions influence each other, and by giving us a present concern for our past or future pains or pleasures.

As memory alone acquaints us with the continuance and extent of this succession of perceptions, it is to be considered, upon that account chiefly, as the source of personal identity. Had we no memory, we never should have any notion of causation, nor consequently of that chain of causes and effects which constitute our self or person. But, having once acquired this notion of causation from the memory, we can extend the same chain of causes, and consequently the identity of our persons, beyond our memory, and can comprehend times, and circumstances, and actions, which we have entirely forgot, but suppose in general to have existed. For how few of our past actions are there of which we have any memory? Who can tell me, for instance, what were his thoughts and actions on the first of January 1715, the 11th of March 1719, and the 3rd of August 1733? Or will he affirm, because he has entirely forgot the incidents of these days, that the present self is not the same person with the self of that time, and by that means overturn all the most established notions of personal identity? In this view, therefore, memory does not so much *produce* as *discover* personal identity, by showing us the relation of cause and effect among our different perceptions. It will be incumbent on those who affirm that memory produces entirely our personal identity, to give a reason why we can thus extend our identity beyond our memory.

The whole of this doctrine leads us to a conclusion, which is of great importance in the present affair, that is, that all the nice and subtle questions concerning personal identity can never possibly be decided, and are to be regarded rather as grammatical than as philosophical difficulties. Identity depends on the relations of ideas; and these relations produce identity by means of that easy transition they occasion. But as the relations, and the easiness of the transition, may diminish by insensible degrees, we have no just standard by which we can decide any dispute concerning the time when they acquire or lose a title to the name of identity. All the disputes concerning the identity of connected objects are merely verbal, except so far as the relation of parts gives rise to some fiction or imaginary principle of union, as we have already observed.

Extracted from the original edition of *A Treatise of Human Nature*, edited by L. A. Selby-Bigge, book 1, part 4, section 6 (London, 1888, 1896), with a modernization of spelling, punctuation, and usage by L. A. Kennedy.

COMMENTARY

■ ■ ■

Analysis of the Selection

Hume begins book 1, part 4, section 6 of *A Treatise of Human Nature* by identifying his position on the question of selfhood. Some philosophers, he tells us, claim that selfhood is something that can be an object of introspective reflection. Hume, therefore, undertakes such reflection. He does so in the spirit of his methodological commitment to empiricism, faithfully attempting not to read into his introspection what he might conventionally expect would be found there. His search is geared exclusively toward what is disclosed by experience. If personal identity is a constant feature of an individual's life, he reasons, then an impression of self could be expected not only to exist but to be an enduring presence throughout life. With his philosophical attention resolutely turned away from speculation and toward the deliverances of actual experience, then—to the results of "serious and unprejudiced reflexion"— Hume undertakes the search for such a self.

What Hume finds in the end is that introspection does not yield an impression of a self. Rather, it yields a *number* of impressions, impressions of pains, pleasures, and sensations, for example. Do these phenomena *belong* to an underlying self? The result of Hume's efforts to find one, he reports, has been negative. "I never can catch *myself* at any time without a perception, and never can observe any thing but the perception." What basis is there in experience, then, he asks, for arguing that something lies *beneath* sensations, thoughts, and emotions, beneath the "bundle or collection of different perceptions, which succeed each other . . . in a perpetual flux and movement?" Hume is aware of the counterintuitive force of the suggestion that no such self exists. He acknowledges a powerful "propension" to posit a self as the enduring seat of the experiences that he has found. He remains loyal, however, to his methodological antipathy toward any conclusions that are not empirically defensible, and he resists the intuitive attractiveness of positing such a self.

Hume is well aware that, as in the case of causality, so too in the present case there must be elements of experience that give rise to the propensity to postulate a self. There must be impressions of *some* kind that underwrite such a desire. The issue, for Hume, is not so much whether there are such deliverances of experience that give rise to this propensity, but rather what deliverances these actually are, and what exactly one is warranted in believing on the basis of them. Hume's inquiry into this matter leads to an understanding of personal identity framed in terms of his theory of identity in general.

Philosophical reflection, says Hume, allows one to appreciate the difference between *identity*—"a distinct idea of an object that remains invariable and uninterrupted through a supposed variation of time"—and *diversity*—"a distinct idea of several different objects existing in succession, and connected together by a close relation." Unfortunately, most of life is lived superficially, not philosophically, as a result of which the lines between identity and diversity become blurred. Such superficiality obscures the imagination's capacity to unite diverse entities, allowing thereby for the development of the sense that such entities share a common identity. Human thought's preoccupation with unity, in other words, breeds a habitual indifference to diversity and change. For example, diversity is usually overlooked when it is proportionately minor or when a rate of change involved is small or when a diversity of entities function in relation to a single purpose. The parts of a boat, for instance, dedicated as they are to a common end, are thought of as "belonging" to some common substrate. In some cases, even very great diversity is overlooked. In incidents of the complete transformation of some forms of animal or vegetable life, as in the case of the sapling turning into a tree, a single entity is commonly assumed. In an even more striking way, sometimes entities that are totally distinct both physically and historically (such as a church built to replace an earlier one ruined by fire) are identified. Such identity might be expressed in a statement to the effect, for example, that the parishioners have rebuilt *the* church. Even greater diversity than this is overlooked when it is expected as a matter of course, as is the rise and fall of the water level in *a* river. In short, argues Hume, human beings habitually overlook a vast range of diversity that argues against the conviction that there exists some deeper identity beneath such phenomena. Human beings, in other words, continually misinterpret relation as identity.

In Hume's thought, the succession of psychological phenomena is as susceptible to being misinterpreted (in this way) as belonging to a deeper "self," as are qualities susceptible of being misinterpreted as inhering in an underlying physical substance. The erroneous tendency to posit a self can be counteracted only by means of diligent allegiance to the empiricist analysis of experience. What such analysis discloses is not a deep underlying entity but relations that pertain among the elements synthesized by imagination. Such analysis discloses that "our notions of personal identity proceed entirely from the smooth and uninterrupted progress of the thought along a train of connected ideas, according to the principles above explained."

In the final passages of the accompanying section of the *Treatise,* Hume rounds out the foregoing picture. At the root of the sense of personal identity, he says, is memory, for memory allows the sense of relation among so many diverse elements of experience to "seem like the continuance of one object," and it "acquaints us with the continuance and extent of this succession of perceptions." Memory is, therefore, "to be considered, upon that account chiefly, as the source of personal identity."

Such a view of selfhood, for Hume, is able to take account of the many variations of identity that can be found among actual personalities. As the relations among impressions and ideas change and are held in different forms by memory, so "the same person may vary his character and disposition, as well as his impressions and ideas, without losing his identity." What, then, about the fallibility and inconsistency of memory? If personal identity is tied so closely to memory and if memory cannot recall this or that past event, must one then conclude that "the present self is not the same person with the self of that time?" Memory, replies Hume, is capable of moving beyond specific remembrances and extending itself in the abstract to past events now forgotten. Moreover, memory does not have an unlimited role in the constitution of identity. One also "discovers" relations among perceptions that also contribute to the sense of identity.

In the end, concludes Hume, identity has to do with relation and not with deeper foundations. What is more, when philosophical reflection scrutinizes experience closely enough to recognize this fact, it becomes apparent that in the case of selfhood, as in cases of nonpsychological identity claims, the relations of ideas upon which such claims are made are so elusive that "all the disputes concerning the identity of connected objects are merely verbal, except so far as the relation of parts gives rise to some fiction or imaginary principle of union, as we have already observed."

■ ■ ■

Philosophical Critique

There is a great deal of religious significance in Hume's understanding of self, not the least of which is related to the general philosophical tenor of the modern period that is reflected in his work. Much philosophy after the seventeenth century, including Hume's, has possessed characteristics of thought that are typical in a number of respects of the philosophical mentality of Descartes, the reputed father of modern philosophy. What is particularly significant about the thought of Descartes in this regard is his attempt to undertake philosophical reflection *independently* of tradition, including cultural and philosophical as well as religious tradition. Descartes' famous *Discourse on Method* represents a radical and important turning point in the history of philosophy in this regard. It begins with an explicit methodological attempt to reflect apart from the influence of such traditions. Convinced that received convictions were at least in part the Trojan horse of error, Descartes was determined to develop a philosophical method that would be capable of circumventing misleading influences. Since we are unable to identify readily which traditions and assumptions are vehicles of error, he thought, philosophical reflection ought initially to set aside all such traditions and assumptions, accepting only what can be seen *introspectively* and *by the individual* to be indubitably true. In his determination to set aside everything that could be imagined as a potential vehicle of error, Descartes endeavoured to wipe his intellectual slate clean, as it were, so as to begin afresh the search for truth, free from all potentially distorting influences.

What Descartes sought—and this continues to have a profound effect upon philosophy to this day—were *foundations*. Deeply impressed with human beings' susceptibility to philosophical error, and equally influenced by philosophy's lack of progress as a discipline by comparison with the scientific disciplines, Descartes sought a secular, methodological foundation upon which he could build an edifice of reliable philosophical truth. Since tradition could not serve such a foundational role, he had to look elsewhere. Where he looked was within.

While in a very different tradition, Hume's empiricist inquiry into selfhood shares the same kind of introspective tendency that we find in Descartes. Hume's search for self is individualistic, private, and introspective. Moreover, in its mentalistic focus it lacks essential links with corporeality or mortality. In addition, Hume's efforts presuppose that the fullness of experience can be adequately captured by the form of introspective analysis to which he is methodologically committed. Hume assumes that if a self exists it would be available *to itself* upon introspection as an *object* of its own knowledge. All of these characteristics of Hume's philosophical reflections have an immediate relevance to the religious significance of his work on selfhood.

More specifically, to begin with the last observation concerning Hume's confidence in his method, there is no doubt that one of the compelling aspects of Hume's philosophy is its methodological discipline, a discipline that results in a particular astuteness in his reflections upon experience. Hume often exhibits an uncanny capacity for raising difficult questions about the experiential foundations of many conventional beliefs. In the case at hand, the apparent absence of an objectifiable self lends great initial strength to Hume's case.

Such strength must be viewed in a larger context, however. As noted above, the Humean individualistic pursuit of self presupposes the possibility that such a self, if it did exist, would be able to constitute itself as an object for itself. As Hume points out, this does not happen. The failure of self to materialize upon introspective reflection forces Hume's philosophical hand. Having admitted that there is a powerful intuitive impulse to posit such a self, but having been unable to find that self, Hume is forced to account in some other way for such an impulse. He accounts for it by applying to the subject of selfhood his general theory of identity. That is, he concludes that the positing of such a self is the result of a mistaken understanding of certain relations within experience. It is important to be clear about this. At bottom, it is Hume's inability to find an objectifiable self that is the principal influence behind his recourse to a theory of relations and memory.

The assumption that a self would be accessible to itself as an object of knowledge in the first place, however, is highly problematic, not only philosophically but religiously as well. Philosophically, there are some who would challenge the adequacy of Hume's entire approach to the analysis of experience, an approach that appears to underwrite Hume's expectation that a self could have an impression of itself. William James (1841–1910), for example, has argued that Hume overlooked a major feature of reflection and thereby inadvertently scuttled his own empiricist project. What Hume failed to recognize, argued James, were the limits of atomistic abstract reflection's capacity to capture the true dynamic nature of what is actually transpiring in experience. A Humean analysis, James contended, must artificially carve up *lived* life in order to grasp it. One might envision James's point by analogy with the way in which movie film records a scene by reducing it to a series of static frames. For James, Hume had failed to recognize that his reflections had missed what is most important in experience—its dynamism. It is worthwhile inquiring into the potential philosophical significance of James's criticism of Hume in connection with the topic at hand. How philosophically feasible is it to expect that Humean atomistic introspection would be able to lay hold fully and objectively of a dynamic self beyond the unity of experience afforded by memory, should such a self exist?

■ ■ ■

Religious Critique

Theologically, Hume's presumption of the availability of self as an object of individual, private introspection is very much out of line with significant patterns of both Jewish and Christian thought. These traditions place a great deal of weight not upon the self's objective accessibility to itself but upon its indebtedness, both in existing and knowing itself, to other selves, both human and divine. That is to say, these traditions are profoundly communitarian, not individualistic, in their treatment of this subject; the self is constituted and known principally *in relation* to other persons and to God. Implicit in centuries of theological thought has been an approach to selfhood that insists upon understanding it in such relational terms. Saint Augustine, for example, says that his heart is restless because outside of a proper relation to God it falls short of what it could be and desires to be. In this, Augustine has ample scriptural precedent. The deeply communitarian Jewish Scriptures place at the center of the early chapters of the Genesis narrative a powerful condemnation of pursuit of self apart from proper relation with God and with one's fellow creatures. Christian Scriptures likewise propose that one is truly known only by God who is the source of identity (*Rev.* 2:17). Twentieth-century reflections by the Jewish philosopher Martin Buber, the Christian monk Thomas Merton, and the Russian Orthodox bishop Anthony Bloom, among many others, carry on the tradition of making the centerpiece of their work the contention that personal identity is not something that is constituted or known apart from relation with the world and with God. From both philosophical and theological points of view, then, one must question the introspective individualism of Hume's pursuit of self and its presumption that self would necessarily be objectively accessible to itself.

In addition to being highly individualistic, Hume's pursuit of self also lacks serious consideration of human corporeality. This omission has great religious as well as philosophical significance in relation to the question of an afterlife and also in relation to the question of the role of corporeality in the constitution of human selfhood.

In addition to its individualism and its lack of attention to corporeality, Hume's account of self is affected, from a religious point of view, by some of its moral dimensions. From its inception, the Christian community has made salvation the centerpiece of its theological reflection. The centrality of salvation raises issues of moral rectitude, accountability, and judgment, which in turn directly implicate the subject of selfhood. For example, in order to be held accountable for one's deeds, the human agent must be the *same person* over the period of his or her existence. John Locke acknowledged this issue more fully in his analysis of selfhood than did Hume. Whether Hume's account of selfhood is capable of supporting major religious beliefs concerning accountability and divine judgment is an important subject of further inquiry.

In the end, the individualistic, introspective, and private character of Hume's approach to selfhood is deeply at odds with the communitarian and self-transcending pursuit of selfhood in the Christian tradition. His approach is also heavily indebted to methodological principles that ought to be seriously questioned in the light of the work of such philosophers as William James and Henri Bergson (1859–1941).

■ ■ ■

Further Reading

A study of Hume's thought that takes account of his views concerning religion can be found in A. Flew, *Hume's Philosophy of Belief* (London, 1961). On the issues of identity, morality, resurrection, and corporeality, the following books are useful:

P. Geach, *God and the Soul* (New York, 1969), chapter 2.

J. Hick, *Philosophy of Religion*, 3rd ed. (New Jersey, 1983), 122–27.

W. Kasper, *Jesus the Christ* (New York, 1976), 124–60.

J. Locke, *An Essay Concerning Human Understanding* (1690), 2.27.

B. Russell, *Why I Am Not a Christian* (London, 1957), 88–93.

7

SØREN KIERKEGAARD

. . .

THE HUMAN PERSON AS A
COLLISION OF OPPOSITES
Introduction and Commentary by Dennis L. Hudecki

INTRODUCTION

■ ■ ■

Kierkegaard's Early Life

Kierkegaard (1813–55) was born in Copenhagen, Denmark, into an unusually difficult set of circumstances. His upbringing was shaped by the fact that his mother and five of his siblings died before he reached the age of twenty-two. Furthermore, his interpretation of these deaths, and of everything else in his early life, was colored by the morbid and overly severe version of Christianity that his guilt-ridden father had passed on to him. Kierkegaard wrote in his journals that he "never felt the joy of childhood" and that his childhood had never for a day been completely free of suffering and melancholy. His entire life was marked by what today we would informally call "depression." He vowed early on not to become enslaved by it but rather to press it into a higher service by thinking about its religious and philosophical implications.

When Kierkegaard was twenty-seven, he became engaged to Regina Olsen, who was just seventeen at the time. Immediately afterward, however, he experienced misgivings and, after a year, decided to break off the engagement. Even though Kierkegaard discussed the engagement at length in his journals, it is still not clear to scholars why the relationship did not last. Was it that Regina was too young and unreflective, as Kierkegaard on occasion seemed to suggest? Or was it that Kierkegaard was too full of morbidity and anxiety to be married? Years later, Kierkegaard raised the possibility that it was his lack of faith that prevented him from going forward. In particular, he believed that his marriage would not be in keeping with his divine calling, which he took to be his writing. (In fact, after his engagement broke down, he went on to write over thirty works in the next eleven years.)

Let us take a closer look at Kierkegaard's spiritual development. As a young man, due to his father's warped religiosity, Kierkegaard experienced religion as a crushing, terrible burden. To the young Kierkegaard, God was cruel and punishing. Perhaps to escape from the burden, Kierkegaard spent his university days developing a distant and critical view of Christianity. During this time he lived in the fast lane, and his life veered back and forth from high excitement to suicidal despair. At the age of twenty-five, however, his spiritual crisis came to an end. He came to a better understanding of his father's weaknesses, and was no longer so victimized by them. His faith in Christianity returned, but now it was more mature and intelligent.

■ ■ ■

Kierkegaard's Goal as a Writer

Kierkegaard claimed that his goal as a writer remained consistent throughout his life: to bring Christianity forward into the intellectually sophisticated modern world in which he lived. Kierkegaard addresses himself to the scientists, theologians, philosophers, and other intellectuals of his age, and to the special set of confusions that he felt stood between them and a proper understanding of Christianity. In Kierkegaard's time, science was advancing at a breathtaking pace—its credibility was at an all-time high. Generally, in the intellectual world, it was taken for granted that reason could be trusted, reality was intelligible, and an absolute understanding of the whole of reality was in theory attainable. This attitude is at the heart of the philosophy of Georg Hegel (1770–1831), for example, who was the most influential philosopher of the time and Kierkegaard's main antagonist. Hegel, along with many other intellectuals of the time, saw Christianity, and other historical religions, as being full of falsehoods and superstitions not only at their margins but in some of their core beliefs. These intellectuals were of the view that faith was a throwback to early, more primitive times. Reason, they believed, had superseded faith. In fact, for Hegel, faith was a symptom of intellectual alienation. It was into this world, then, that Kierkegaard wanted to reintroduce religion, in general, and Christianity in particular.

■ ■ ■

Introductory Comments on Kierkegaard's Style

Kierkegaard was well aware of the highly rationalistic and antifaith climate of his time, and he shaped his writings so as to engage the age in which he lived. In so doing, Kierkegaard was simultaneously mounting an even deeper protest against the impersonal, rationalistic tendencies he found in Western philosophy that held up abstract, distant truth as the one and only goal of philosophical inquiry.

Kierkegaard claims that certain "essential" questions (e.g., ethical and religious questions) require a different approach than, say, mathematical questions or those of the natural sciences. Inquiries into essential questions must be carried out in such a way as to *engage* the individual and provoke self-reflection. One of the main techniques Kierkegaard uses to bring about this kind of engagement is to present the reader with various points of view, using fictional or false names. In so doing, Kierkegaard hopes to lure readers into the process of thinking for themselves, rather than providing them with ready-made intellectual positions.

An even more fundamental aspect of Kierkegaard's style of thinking is that his work adopts more of a literary model than of either a scientific or a mathematical one. Indeed, professional philosophers sometimes are inclined to say of Kierkegaard's work: "That's not philosophy, it's poetry." Kierkegaard is drawn to the literary model by his desire to do justice to the full complexities and subtleties of human reality, and to present them back to the reader in the form of a challenge to live better. As we shall see below, Kierkegaard's way of characterizing the "self"—as a series of inner collisions— exemplifies his poetic, challenging, and nonscientific way of philosophizing.

■ ■ ■

What to Look For in the Selections

The selections we have chosen from Kierkegaard's writings illustrate his concept of the self. We have organized these selections into nine categories, each with a different heading. The following list of numbered paragraphs corresponds with the text selections and provides a short introduction to each selection.

1. The Young Kierkegaard Speaks

Throughout the whole of his adult life, Kierkegaard kept an intellectual journal, and this is one of his earliest entries. It contains some of Kierkegaard's deepest hopes as a thinker and provides for us a context in which to understand his philosophy as a whole.

2. What Is Existence?

This is Kierkegaard's abstract definition of the self. The self consists of a series of opposites.

3. Thinking Must Reflect the Structure of Existence

All of the remaining selections, beginning with this one, examine the personal and intellectual implications of this abstract definition of the self. In this selection, Kierkegaard is suggesting that our main task must be to reflect in our thinking and the way we live the structure of our existence. Thus, if our existence consists of opposite and colliding tendencies, as he suggests it does, then these opposites must be reflected by us and not ignored or forgotten.

4. Despair

In this selection, Kierkegaard claims that the penalty for not addressing all parts of the self is despair. Furthermore, despair is such that one can be in a state of deep despair and not even realize it.

5. An Aesthete Speaks

This selection is from the writing of a fictional character in Kierkegaard's *Either/Or*. The character's name in the book is unknown; he is simply referred to as "A." This person, whom Kierkegaard calls an "aesthete," lives according to the maxim: "Seek the interesting and avoid the boring. Pleasure is the main goal. Being a morally good person is not a priority." As long as A can find something new and interesting, he can avoid facing many aspects of himself, and his inner despair. This lifestyle, Kierkegaard suggests, is characterized on one level by exciting, casual, relationships. However, deep and lasting friendships and love-relationships must be avoided, since they tend to force a person to inwardly face himself or herself.

6. An Ethicist Responds to the Aesthete

This is a piece of writing from another fictional character in *Either/Or*. This character is referred to as "B." B, who deeply believes in the importance of being ethical, comes across the writings of A and decides to respond to them in the form of a letter. According to B, an aesthete like A pays a stiff price to maintain a self-escaping lifestyle. Without realizing it, B argues, A is severely limiting his freedom.

7. On the Difference between Ethics and Religion

Kierkegaard does not believe that ethics is the highest way of life, even though it seems more appropriate for a human being than does the aesthetic way of life. The ethical way of life is characterized by Kierkegaard in this selection as a life lived in accordance with universal moral values and maxims. The patriarch Abraham's life, however, transcends the ethical. Kierkegaard calls Abraham a "knight of faith" and suggests that our human self is constituted in such a way that all of us need religious faith (along with morality) to fully deal with our inner contradictions. Otherwise, our lives will hopelessly and tragically remain dissatisfied. Kierkegaard characterizes the ethical way of life, without faith, as "tragic heroism." He suggests, however, that in the religious way of life one can overcome this inner sense of tragedy.

8. Paradoxical Religiousness

What if our existence is so hardened against truth that the ordinary, everyday virtues of faith and hope are useless to us? What if we have lost touch with ourselves to such an extent that we are in no position to know what to hope for or to have faith in? What if our lives are in need of a higher-than-human *Saviour?* Given what Kierkegaard thinks the self is, these possibilities are all real. In this selection, Kierkegaard explores some of their implications.

9. How Christianity Comes to the Conflicted Self

This short selection sums up how Kierkegaard thinks the self stands before God.

SELECTIONS FROM KIERKEGAARD

■ ■ ■

1. The Young Kierkegaard Speaks

What I really lack is to be clear in my mind *what I am to do*, not what I am to know, except in so far as a certain understanding must precede every action. The thing is to understand myself, to see what God really wishes *me* to do; the thing is to find a truth which is true *for me*, to find *the idea for which I can live and die*. What would be the use of discovering so-called objective truth, of working through all the systems of philosophy and of being able, if required, to review them all and show up the inconsistencies within each system—what good would it do me to be able to develop a theory of the state and combine all the details into a single whole, and so construct a world in which I did not live, but only held up to the view of others— what good would it do me to be able to explain the meaning of Christianity if it had no deeper significance *for me and for my life*—what good would it do me if truth stood before me, cold and naked, not caring whether I recognised her or not, and producing in me a shudder of fear rather than a trusting devotion? I certainly do not deny that I still recognise an *imperative of understanding* and that through it one can work upon men,

221

but it must be taken up into my life, and *that* is what I now recognise as the most important thing. That is what my soul longs after, as the African desert thirsts for water. . . . One must know oneself before knowing anything else. . . . It is only after a man has thus understood himself inwardly, and has thus seen his way, that life acquires peace and significance; only then is he rid of that tiresome, ill-omened fellow-traveller, the irony of life, which shows itself in the sphere of understanding, bidding true understanding begin with ignorance (as Socrates said) like God creating the world out of nothing.[1]

■ ■ ■

2. What is Existence?

But what is existence? Existence is the child that is born of the infinite and the finite, the eternal and the temporal, and is therefore a constant striving. . . .[2]

■ ■ ■

3. Thinking Must Reflect the Structure of Existence

The subjective existing thinker is as bi-frontal as existence itself. . . .

The thinker who can forget, in all his thinking, also to think that he is an existing individual, will never explain life. He merely makes an attempt to cease to be a human being, in order to become a book or an objective something. . . . It is not denied that objective thought has validity; but in connection with all thinking where subjectivity must be accentuated, it is a misunderstanding. . . .

The task . . . is to transform . . . [oneself] into an instrument that clearly and definitely expresses in existence whatever is essentially human.[3]

■ ■ ■

4. Despair

Socrates proved the immortality of the soul from the fact that the sickness of the soul (sin) does not consume it as sickness of the body consumes the body. So also we can demonstrate the eternal in man from the fact that despair cannot consume his self, that this precisely is the torment of contradiction in despair. If there were nothing eternal in a man, he could not despair; but if despair could consume his self, there would still be no despair.

Thus it is that despair, this sickness in the self, is the sickness unto death. The despairing man is mortally ill. In an entirely different sense than can appropriately be said of any disease, we may say that the sickness has attacked the noblest part; and yet the man cannot die. Death is not the last phase of the sickness, but death is continually the last. To be delivered from this sickness by death is an impossibility, for the sickness and its torment . . . and death consist in not being able to die.

This is the situation in despair. And however thoroughly it eludes the attention of the despairer, and however thoroughly the despairer may succeed (as in the case of that kind of despair which is characterized by unawareness of being in despair) in losing himself entirely, and losing himself in such a way that it is not noticed in the least—eternity nevertheless will make it manifest that his situation was despair, and it will so nail him to himself that the torment nevertheless remains that he cannot get rid of himself, and it becomes manifest that he was deluded in thinking that he succeeded. And thus it is eternity must act, because to have a self, to be a self, is the greatest concession made to man, but at the same time it is eternity's demand upon him. . . .

Therefore it is as far as possible from being true that the vulgar view is right in assuming that despair is a rarity; on the contrary, it is quite universal. It is as far as possible from being true that the vulgar view is right in assuming that everyone who does not think or feel that he is in despair is not so at all, and that only he is in despair who says that he is. On the contrary, one who without affectation says that he is in despair is after all a little bit nearer, a dialectical step nearer, to being cured than all those who are not regarded, and do not regard themselves, as being in despair. But precisely this is the common situation (as the physician of souls will doubtless concede), that the majority of men live without being thoroughly conscious that they are spiritual beings—and to this is referable all the security, contentment with life, etc., etc., which precisely is despair. Those, on the other hand, who say that they are in despair are generally such as have a nature so much more profound that they must become conscious of themselves as spirit, or such as by the hard vicissitudes of life and its dreadful decisions have been helped to become conscious of themselves as spirit—either one or the other, for rare is the man who truly is free from despair.[4]

■ ■ ■

5. An Aesthete Speaks

Starting from a principle is affirmed by people of experience to be a very reasonable procedure; I am willing to humor them, and so begin with the principle that all men are bores. . . . [I]f my principle is true, one need only consider how ruinous boredom is for humanity. . . .

In the case of children, the ruinous character of boredom is universally acknowledged. Children are always well-behaved as long as they are enjoying themselves. . . .

The history of this can be traced from the very beginning of the world. The gods were bored, and so they created man. Adam was bored because he was alone, and so Eve was created. Thus boredom entered the world, and increased in proportion to the increase of population. Adam was bored alone; then Adam and Eve were bored together; then Adam and Eve and Cain and Abel were bored *en famille* [as a family]; then the population of the world increased, and the peoples were bored *en masse* [as a group]. To divert themselves they conceived the idea of constructing a tower high enough to reach the heavens. This idea is itself as boring as the tower was high, and constitutes a terrible proof of how boredom gained the upper hand. The nations were scattered over the earth, just as people now travel abroad, but they continued to be bored.

Consider the consequences of this boredom. Humanity fell from its lofty height, first because of Eve, and then from the Tower of Babel. What was it, on the other hand, that delayed the fall of Rome; was it not *panis et circenses* [bread and circuses]? And is anything being done now? Is anyone concerned about planning some means of diversion? Quite the contrary, the impending ruin is being accelerated. It is proposed to call a constitutional assembly. Can anything more tiresome be imagined, both for the participants themselves, and for those who have to hear and read about it? It is proposed to improve the financial condition of the state by practising economy. What could be more tiresome? Instead of increasing the national debt, it is proposed to pay it off. As I understand the political situation, it would be an easy matter for Denmark to negotiate a loan of fifteen million dollars. Why not consider this plan? Every once in a while we hear of a man who is a genius, and therefore neglects to pay his debts—why should not a nation do the same, if we were all agreed? Let us then borrow fifteen million, and let us use the proceeds, not to pay our debts, but for public entertainment. Let us celebrate the millennium in a riot of merriment. Let us place boxes everywhere, not, as at present, for the deposit of money, but for the free distribution of money. Everything would become gratis: theatres gratis, women of easy virtue gratis, one would drive to the park gratis, be buried gratis, one's eulogy would be gratis; I say gratis, for when one always has money at hand, everything is in a certain sense free. No one should be permitted to own any property. Only in my own case would there be an exception. I reserve to myself securities in the Bank of London to the value of one hundred dollars a day, partly because I cannot do with less, partly because the idea is mine, and finally because I may not be able to hit upon a new idea when the fifteen million are gone . . . .

Now since boredom as shown above is the root of all evil, what can be more natural than the effort to overcome it? . . .

My own dissent from the ordinary view is sufficiently expressed in the use I make of the word "rotation." This word might seem to conceal an ambiguity, and if I wished to use it so as to find room in it for the ordinary method, I should have to define it as a change of field. But the farmer does not use the word in this sense. I shall, however, adopt this meaning for a moment, in order to speak of the rotation which depends on change in its boundless infinity, its extensive dimension, so to speak.

This is the vulgar and inartistic method, and needs to be supported by illusion. One tires of living in the country, and moves to the city; one tires of one's native land, and travels abroad; one is *europamüde* [tired of Europe], and goes to America, and so on; finally one indulges in a sentimental hope of endless journeyings from star to star. Or the movement is different but still extensive. One tires of porcelain dishes and eats on silver; one tires of silver and turns to gold; one burns half of Rome to get an idea of the burning of Troy. This method defeats itself; it is plain endlessness. And what did Nero gain by it? Antonine was wiser; he says: "It is in your power to review your life, to look at things you saw before from another point of view." My method does not consist in change of field, but resembles the true rotation method in changing the crop and the mode of cultivation. . . .

The more resourceful in changing the mode of cultivation one can be, the better; but every particular change will always come under the general categories of *remembering and forgetting.* . . .

To forget—all men wish to forget, and when something unpleasant happens, they always say: Oh, that one might forget! But forgetting is an art that must be practised beforehand. . . . No moment must be permitted so great a significance that it cannot be forgotten when convenient; each moment ought, however, to have so much significance that it can be recollected at will. . . .

The art of remembering and forgetting will also insure against sticking fast in some relationship of life, and make possible the realization of a complete freedom.

One must guard against *friendship.* . . .

But because you abstain from friendship it does not follow that you abstain from social contacts. On the contrary, these social relationships may at times be permitted to take on a deeper character, provided you always have so much more momentum in yourself that you can sheer off at will, in spite of sharing for a time in the momentum of the common movement. . . . The essential thing is never to stick fast, and for this it is necessary to have oblivion back of one. The experienced farmer lets his land lie fallow now and then, and the theory of social prudence recommends the same. . . .

One must never enter into the relation of *marriage*. Husband and wife promise to love one another for eternity. . . . And how does a marriage usually work out? In a little while one party begins to perceive that there is something wrong, then the other party complains, and cries to heaven: faithless! faithless! A little later the second party reaches the same standpoint, and a neutrality is established in which the mutual faithlessness is mutually cancelled, to the satisfaction and contentment of both parties. But it is now too late, for there are great difficulties connected with divorce. . . .

Friendship is dangerous, marriage still more so; for woman is and ever will be the ruin of a man, as soon as he contracts a permanent relation with her. . . . But because a man does not marry, it does not follow that his life need be wholly deprived of the erotic element. And the erotic ought also to have infinitude; but poetic infinitude, which can just as well be limited to an hour as to a month. When two beings fall in love with one another and begin to suspect that they were made for each other, it is time to have the courage to break it off; for by going on they have everything to lose and nothing to gain. This seems a paradox, and it is so for the feeling, but not for the understanding. In this sphere it is particularly necessary that one should make use of one's moods; through them one may realize an inexhaustible variety of combinations.[5]

■ ■ ■

6. An Ethicist Responds to the Aesthete

But in reality you have not chosen at all, or it is in an improper sense of the word you have chosen. Your choice is an aesthetic choice, but an aesthetic choice is no choice. The act of choosing is essentially a proper and stringent expression of the ethical. Whenever in a stricter sense there is question of an either/or, one can always be sure that the ethical is involved. The only absolute either/or is the choice between good and evil, but that is also absolutely ethical. The aesthetic choice is either entirely immediate and to that extent no choice, or it loses itself in the multifarious. Thus, when a young girl follows the choice of her heart, this choice, however beautiful it may be, is in the strictest sense no choice, since it is entirely immediate. When a man deliberates aesthetically upon a multitude of life's problems . . . he does not easily get one either/or, but a whole multiplicity, because the self-determining factor in the choice is not ethically accentuated, and because when one does not choose absolutely one chooses only for the moment, and therefore can choose something different the next moment. The ethical choice is therefore in a certain sense much easier, much simpler, but in another sense it is infinitely harder. He who would define his life task ethically has ordinarily not so considerable a selection to choose from; on the other hand, the act of choice has far more importance for him. If you will understand me aright, I should like to say that in making a choice it is not so much a question of choosing the right as of the energy, the earnestness, the pathos with which one chooses. Thereby the personality announces its inner infinity, and thereby, in turn, the personality is consolidated. Therefore, even if a man were to choose the wrong, he will nevertheless discover, precisely by reason of the energy with which he chose, that he had chosen the wrong. For, the choice being made with the whole inwardness of his personality, his nature is purified and he himself brought into immediate relation to the eternal Power whose omnipresence interpenetrates the whole of existence. This transfiguration, this higher consecration, is never attained by that man who chooses merely aesthetically. . . .

What is it, then, that I distinguish in my either/or? Is it good and evil? No, I would only bring you up to the point where the choice between the evil and the good acquires significance for you. Everything hinges upon this. As soon as one can get a man to stand at the crossways in such a position that there is no recourse but to choose, he will choose the right. Hence, if it should chance that, while you are in the course of reading this somewhat lengthy dissertation, which again I send you in the form of a letter, you were to feel that the instant for choice had come, then throw the rest of this away, never concern yourself about it, you have lost nothing—but choose, and you shall see what validity there is in this act; yea, no young girl can be so happy with the choice of her heart as is a man who knows how to choose. So then, one either has to live aesthetically or one has to live ethically. In this alternative, as I have said, there is not yet in the strictest sense any question of a choice; for he who lives aesthetically does not choose, and he who after the ethical has manifested itself to him chooses the aesthetical is not living aesthetically, for he is sinning and is subject to ethical determinants even though his life may be described as unethical.[6]

■ ■ ■

7. On the Difference between Ethics and Religion

In Luke 14:26, as everybody knows, there is a striking doctrine taught about the absolute duty toward God: "If any man cometh unto me and hateth not his own father and mother and wife and children and brethren and sisters, yea, and his own life also, he cannot be my disciple." This is a hard saying; who can bear to hear it? . . .

But how hate them? I will not recall here the human distinction between loving and hating—not because I have much to object to in it (for after all it is passionate), but because it is egoistic and is not in place here. However, if I regard the problem as a paradox, then I understand it, that is, I understand it in such a way as one can understand a paradox. The absolute duty may cause one to do what ethics would forbid, but by no means can it cause the knight of faith to cease to love. This is shown by Abraham. The instant he is ready to sacrifice Isaac the ethical expression for what he does is this: he hates Isaac. But if he really hates Isaac, he can be sure that God does not require this, for Cain and Abraham are not identical. Isaac he must love with his whole soul; when God requires Isaac he must love him if possible even more dearly, and only on this condition can he sacrifice him; for in fact it is this love for Isaac which, by its paradoxical opposition to his love for God, makes his act a sacrifice. But the distress and dread in this paradox is that, humanly speaking, he is entirely unable to make himself intelligible. Only at the moment when his act is in absolute contradiction to his feeling is his act a sacrifice, but the reality of his act is the factor by which he belongs to the universal, and in that aspect he is and remains a murderer. Moreover, the passage in Luke must be understood in such a way as to make it clearly evident that the knight of faith has no higher expression of the universal (i.e. the ethical) by which he can save himself. . . .

People commonly refrain from quoting such a text as this in Luke. They are afraid of giving men a free rein, are afraid that the worst will happen as soon as the individual takes it into his head to comport himself as the individual. Moreover, they think that to exist as the individual is the easiest thing of all, and that therefore people have to be compelled to become the universal. . . .

Let us consider a little more closely the distress and dread in the paradox of faith. The tragic hero renounces himself in order to express the universal, the knight of faith renounces the universal in order to become the individual. As has been said, everything depends upon how one is placed. He who believes that it is easy enough to be the individual can always be sure that he is not a knight of faith, for vagabonds and roving geniuses are not men of faith. The knight of faith knows, on the other hand, that it is glorious to belong to the universal. He knows that it is beautiful and salutary to be the individual who translates himself into the universal, who edits as it were a pure and elegant edition of himself, as free from errors as possible and which everyone can read. He knows that it is refreshing to become intelligible to oneself in the universal so that he understands it and so that every individual who understands him understands through him in turn the universal, and both rejoice in the security of the universal. He knows that it is beautiful to be born as the individual who has the universal as his home, his friendly abiding place, which at once welcomes him with open arms when he would tarry in it. But he knows also that higher than this there winds a solitary path, narrow and steep; he knows that it is terrible to be born outside the universal, to walk without meeting a single traveller. He knows very well where he is and how he is related to men. Humanly speaking, he is crazy and cannot make himself intelligible to anyone. And yet it is the mildest expression, to say that he is crazy. If he is not supposed to be that, then he is a hypocrite, and the higher he climbs on this path, the more dreadful a hypocrite he is.

The knight of faith knows that to give up oneself for the universal inspires enthusiasm, and that it requires courage, but he also knows that security is to be found in this, precisely because it is for the universal.[7]

■ ■ ■

8. Paradoxical Religiousness

Now, if things are to be otherwise, the Moment in time must have a decisive significance, so that I will never be able to forget it either in time or eternity; because the Eternal, which hitherto did not exist, came into existence in this moment. Under this presupposition let us now proceed to consider the consequences for the problem of how far it is possible to acquire a knowledge of the Truth.

The Antecedent State

We begin with the Socratic difficulty about seeking the Truth, which seems equally impossible whether we have it or do not have it. The Socratic thought really abolishes this disjunction, since it appears that at bottom every human being is in possession of the Truth. This was Socrates' explanation; we have seen what follows from it with respect to the moment. Now if the latter is to have decisive significance, the seeker must be destitute of the Truth up to the very moment of his learning it; he cannot even have possessed it in the form of ignorance, for in that case the moment becomes merely occasional. What is more, he cannot even be described as seeker; for such is the expression we must give to the difficulty if we do not wish to explain it Socratically. He must therefore be characterized as beyond the pale of the Truth, not approaching it like a proselyte, but departing from it; or as being in error. He is then in a state of Error. But how is he now to be reminded, or what will it profit him to be reminded of what he has not known, and consequently cannot recall?

The Teacher

Now if the learner is to acquire the Truth, the Teacher must bring it to him; and not only so, but he must also give him the condition necessary for understanding it. For if the learner were in his own person the condition for understanding the Truth, he need only recall it. The condition for understanding the Truth is like the capacity to inquire for it: the condition contains the conditioned, and the question implies the answer. (Unless this is so, the moment must be understood in the Socratic sense.)

But one who gives the learner not only the Truth, but also the condition for understanding it, is more than teacher. . . .

The Teacher is then the God himself, who in acting as an occasion prompts the learner to recall that he is in Error, and that by reason of his own guilt. But this state, the being in Error by reason of one's own guilt, what shall we call it? Let us call it *Sin*.

The Teacher, then, is the God, and he gives the learner the requisite condition and the Truth. What shall we call such a Teacher?—for we are surely agreed that we have already far transcended the ordinary functions of a teacher. In so far as the learner is in Error, but in consequence of his own act (and in no other way can he possibly be in this state, as we have shown above), he might seem to be free; for to be what one is by one's own act is freedom. And yet he is in reality unfree and bound and exiled; for to be free from the Truth is to be exiled from the Truth, and to be exiled by one's own self is to be bound. But since he is bound by himself, may he not loose his bonds and set himself free? For, whatever binds me, the same should be able to set me free when it wills; and since this power is here his own self, he should be able to liberate himself. But first at any rate he must will it. Suppose him now to be so profoundly impressed by what the Teacher gave him occasion to remember (and this must not be omitted from the reckoning); suppose that he wills his freedom. In that case, i.e., if by willing to be free he could by himself become free, the fact that he had been bound would become a state of the past, tracelessly vanishing in the moment of liberation; the moment would not be charged with decisive significance. He was not aware that he had bound himself, and now he has freed himself. Thus interpreted the moment receives no decisive significance, and yet this was the hypothesis we proposed to ourselves in the beginning. By the terms of our hypothesis, therefore, he will not be able to set himself free.—And so it is in very truth; for he forges the chains of his bondage with the strength of his freedom, since he exists in it without compulsion; and thus his bonds grow strong, and his powers unite to make him the slave of sin.—What now shall we call such a Teacher, one who restores the lost condition and gives the learner the Truth? Let us call him *Saviour*, for he saves the learner from his bondage and from himself; let us call him *Redeemer*, for he redeems the learner from the captivity into which he had plunged himself, and no captivity is so terrible and so impossible to break, as that in which the individual keeps himself. And still we have not said all that is necessary; for by his self-imposed bondage the learner has brought upon himself a burden of guilt, and, when the Teacher gives him the condition and the Truth, he constitutes himself an *Atonement*, taking away the wrath impending upon that of which the learner has made himself guilty.

Such a Teacher the learner will never be able to forget. . . .

The Socratic principle is that the learner, being himself the Truth and in possession of the condition, can thrust the teacher aside; the Socratic art and the Socratic heroism consisted precisely in helping men to do this. But Faith must steadily hold fast to the Teacher. In order that he may have the power to give the condition, the Teacher must be the God; in order that he may be able to put the learner in possession of it he must be Man. This contradiction is again the object of Faith, and is the Paradox, the Moment. That the God has once for all given man the requisite condition is the eternal Socratic presupposition, which comes into no hostile collision with time, but is incommensurable with the temporal and its determinations. The contradiction of our hypothesis is that man receives the condition in the Moment, the same condition which, since it is requisite for the understanding of the eternal Truth, is *eo ipso* [by that very fact] an eternal condition. If the case is otherwise we stand at the Socratic principle of Recollection.[8]

■ ■ ■

9. How Christianity Comes to the Conflicted Self

If Christ is to come and take up his abode in me, it must happen according to the title of to-day's Gospel in the *Almanac:* Christ came in through locked doors.[9]

Extracted from the titles listed in the following notes.

1. S. Kierkegaard, *The Journals of Kierkegaard* (New York, 1959), 44, 46.
2. S. Kierkegaard, *Concluding Unscientific Postscript to the Philosophical Fragments* (Princeton, 1941), 85.
3. Ibid., 83, 85–86, 318.
4. S. Kierkegaard, [*Fear and Trembling* and] *The Sickness unto Death* (New York, 1954), 153–54, 159.
5. S. Kierkegaard, *Either/Or* (New York, 1959), 1.281–83, 287–94.
6. Ibid., 2.170–72.
7. S. Kierkegaard, *The Sickness unto Death,* 82, 84–86.
8. S. Kierkegaard, *Philosophical Fragments, or a Fragment of Philosophy* (Princeton, 1962), 16–21, 77.
9. *Journals,* 58.

COMMENTARY

■ ■ ■

The Concept of the Self:
A Synthesis (or Collision) of Opposites

If one combs Kierkegaard's writings (whether under his own name or under his pen name) one will be struck by the consistency in the way Kierkegaard conceptualizes the self. Most often, he defines the self as a synthesis of two ill-fitting or colliding parts. For example, he often defines the self as a synthesis of the temporal and eternal. How much these colliding parts can form a synthesis is his central question. The answer, to the end, is left open.

Kierkegaard uses various formulae throughout his authorship to capture the duality that he thinks constitutes the self. The following list provides the most frequently mentioned combination of elements Kierkegaard uses to discuss the self:

1. The temporal and the eternal
2. The finite and the infinite
3. Necessity and freedom
4. The particular and the universal
5. Beast and angel
6. Body and soul

One should not be put off by each of these pairs of words. One of the things that Kierkegaard is saying with the use of these formulae is that there is a limit to which the self can be conceptualized. The more "spiritual" terms on the right-hand side of the list defy precise definition: they are meant to be suggestive and evocative. They negate to some extent the more "worldly" terms on the left-hand side. Furthermore, the words on the right operate in Kierkegaard's philosophy as ways to mark off areas that Kierkegaard believes to be essentially beyond our understanding, but that nevertheless lie at the core of human existence. In other words, Kierkegaard's definition of the self is partly an antidefinition. Part of its function is to ward off other Western philosophical concepts of the self (e.g., the mechanistic or materialist views of the self) that, in Kierkegaard's mind, pretend to know too much about the self.

Kierkegaard's intellectual hero is the early Socrates, as found in Plato's *Apology* or *Euthyphro*. Kierkegaard interprets Socrates as claiming that we *do not* know the answers to such questions about ourselves as (1) Where did I come from? (2) How important is it that I am here? and (3) How exactly is human existence constituted? Yet, these are the *most important* questions about our existence. Thus Kierkegaard's definition of the self contains within itself room for these Socratic unknowings.

Having said all of this, however, the question still remains: what are we to make of such concepts as the *eternal* or the *infinite*? Very briefly, let us work our way down the right-hand side of the previous list. In Kierkegaard's writings, the *eternal* not only stands for unchanging truths and principles of goodness, but also for that aspect of our existence that is most served by such truths and principles and that might have a more-than-temporal destiny. The *infinite* refers to the structural limits on our capacity for knowledge about essential aspects of our existence. About the *infinite* we have no knowledge, just imagined possibilities. *Freedom* refers to that part of our existence wherein the capacity for choice resides. It is the morally responsible part of ourselves and the part of ourselves that cannot be explained in terms of the laws of natural science. The *universal* in us refers to that part of our self—the essentially human part—that is shared by all other human beings and that, among other things, is subject to the same ethical imperatives as is the case with everyone else. The terms *angel* and *soul* are catch-all concepts that gather up the different aspects of the duality to which the more specific terms point.

By using these formulae, Kierkegaard is attempting to capture a fundamental duality or conflict in the self. One typical occasion wherein this duality reveals itself is in a crisis of conscience. Suppose, for example, that I am faced with an opportunity to quickly become very rich. All I have to do is perjure myself in court and participate in a few illegal maneuvers. Here my worldly concerns stand to gain, but at the cost of having to shirk one or more of the unchanging, universal ethical obligations to which I may be subject. So, if I steal and lie in order to get rich, there may be a trade-off between two sides of my self: my *worldly* part seems to gain, while my *eternal* part loses. I may be maiming myself spiritually while helping myself temporally. Such choices reveal the duality to which Kierkegaard is referring.

The task of the individual is to properly deal with both sides of himself or herself, the temporal and the eternal. As Kierkegaard says, existence is "bifrontal." The task is to establish a workable synthesis inwardly or existentially—not just intellectually—and to do so in terms of the unique details of each of our lives. This synthesis must become integrated into our actual way of being, so that it is reflected at all times in what we do and what we think. Because the self is ultimately "spirit," and not just a bundle of instincts, the synthesis will not just automatically come about. Instead, each individual has the fundamental responsibility of shaping his or her existence so that it properly reflects the essential structure of this existence. Each individual has the choice to face up to this responsibility or to evade it.

Up to this point, Kierkegaard has not said anything that has not already been said in ancient Greece. Plato, for example, characterized the self as a body/soul duality, as being spiritual, and as facing fundamental choices. Where Kierkegaard parts ways with views such as those found in Plato, for example, is right here: Kierkegaard sees the conflicts in the self as deeper, more complex, and more anxiety-provoking than does

Plato, and sees more and deeper possible ways of going wrong in the attempt to reconcile these conflicts. Let us look at why Kierkegaard thinks this is so.

The major problem we face, according to Kierkegaard, is the pain or anxiety of living with parts of ourselves that strongly resist working together. To properly care for both the temporal and the eternal in us requires an almost *divine* devotion. Most find it too difficult. The difficulty, and the strong possibility of failure, in turn give rise to a painful anxiety. Kierkegaard is one of the first thinkers in Western philosophy to argue that anxiety is a *universal human phenomenon* and that it resides at the *core* of our existence. This anxiety is *structural*—it is different from neurotic anxiety that is often caused by major hurts in our life and which is potentially removable by psychotherapy. Ultimately, the reason why we tend to go wrong in coming to grips with our true structure, then, is our desire to escape the challenge, and the anxiety with which it presents us.

It should also be noted that the human psyche is such that escape routes are possible. Here Kierkegaard fully anticipates Freud. Humans can and do deceive themselves. Humans can and do shunt off into what today, after Freud, can be called their unconscious, truths they find too painful to face. Humans can and do conveniently *forget* about certain essential aspects of their existence. Indeed when Kierkegaard, with his most philosophical pseudonym, Johannes Climacus, attempts to explain the spiritual *malaise* of his time, his ultimate explanation is that, in his day, the individual has "forgotten what it means to exist as a human being."

What is behind this self-deception or forgetting? For Kierkegaard, the answer can be expressed in one word: despair. Buried deeply in the dark recesses of the individual is an unspoken thought that goes something like this:

> I cannot simultaneously hold together in myself *both* the temporal and eternal. I am therefore going to convince myself that one of them is not there or is not important. Maybe if I pretend convincingly enough, the whole problem will disappear.

Despair, however, is not inevitable. The anxiety caused by the collision of opposites in us can be *educative*. In fact, for Kierkegaard, understanding anxiety in the right light is the *ultimate* education for a human being. For Kierkegaard, the "right light" will turn out to be a kind of religious faith. With the proper kind of religious faith, one can be saved from the formerly destructive collision of opposites. A deeper grasp of Kierkegaard's concept of religiousness, however, requires an understanding of his famous theory of the "stages" or "spheres" of existence, and it is to this theory we now turn.

■ ■ ■

The Stages of Existence

According to Kierkegaard, all humans exist in one of three mutually exclusive stages of existence, namely the aesthetic, the ethical, or the religious. Very simply, an individual in the aesthetic stage gives priority to the temporal side of existence relative to the eternal, while an individual in the ethical stage privileges the eternal side, at the cost of the temporal. In the religious stage, the individual "impossibly" holds together the seemingly irreconcilable opposites.

Before moving on, a word of warning about the theory of stages is in order. Kierkegaard takes great liberties in expanding or contrasting the number of stages in his theory by sometimes collapsing two together (e.g., the ethical and religious stages into the "ethico-religious" stage), subdividing one or more (e.g., the religious stage into "religiousness A" or "religiousness B"), or introducing names for the boundaries between stages (e.g., "irony" and "humor"). For Kierkegaard, then, how the stages are ordered and their actual make-up depend upon the particular context. For the purpose of discussing Kierkegaard's concept of the self, the three-stage schema, with one subdivision, seems best. The stages we will discuss, then, are the aesthetic, the ethical, religiousness A, and religiousness B.

■ ■ ■

The Aesthetic Stage

The "aesthetic" stage, as Kierkegaard calls it, consists of a number of similar styles, attitudes, and approaches toward life. Generally, someone who lives in this stage takes one or more of the following as the highest good: physical pleasure, intellectual pleasure, excitement, beauty, power, or some other natural, immediate good. Furthermore, certain (Socratic) kinds of self-knowledge and self-reflection are foreign to the aesthete's sensibility. Truth, for the aesthete, exists somewhere "out there" (i.e., in the objective world) and self-knowledge has no important role to play in the attainment of it.

The name "aesthetic" is appropriate for a number of reasons, but to understand why this is so we need to examine some of the factors that give rise to this life-view in the first place. The aesthetic stage represents an attempt to escape the anxiety caused by the clash of opposites embedded in the core structure of the self. The fundamental reality behind the aesthete's life is despair—the despair of ever successfully meeting the demand of all sides of the self. In his or her despair, then, the aesthete looks for ways to neutralize the deep pain within, believing that there is no happy solution to the inner collision of opposites.

Kierkegaard includes, under the concept of "aesthetic" phenomena, pleasure, beauty, drama, excitement, and transcendence. The aesthetic "escape-route" makes use of the fact that humans have access to countless of these aesthetic things— things that can, at least for the moment, make one's life bearable, or even sweet, and can safely insulate a person from the pain and anxiety of being alive. Such things are so powerful and all-encompassing that they can provide their own meaning and direction to existence, even if it is usually only for short periods of time; such things can do away altogether with the need for the individual to deal with personal questions of meaning, so long as the individual is under their spell.

Sex, for example, is an almost inexhaustible source of ecstasy that nature itself provides. When one partakes of it, one is momentarily transported out of the ordinary realities of life. Art, too, transports us from the everyday. When we enjoy a piece of music or a movie, say, it is almost as if our lives are one with the music or movie. All of these things function in a similar way. All have within them an almost guaranteed capacity for high pleasure. When we experience them, life seems to need no other justification. Life in such moments is so overwhelmingly rewarding that questions about our nature and purpose can be ignored, along with the anxiety that such questions provoke.

So far, we have seen that art and other things like art have a capacity for intensely positive, exciting experiences. They give us "highs," so to speak. Another aspect of aesthetic reality that Kierkegaard draws upon is concern with the *outer* appearance of things. For example, an aesthetic person, in this sense, might center his or her life on physical health and beauty. Another might seek happiness by possessing only the outer trappings of such things as religion or goodness—things that by their very nature require an inward commitment. Still another might equate "success" with money, regardless of how the money is made. The aesthete who is intellectually inclined is someone who is dazzled by knowledge—scientific or otherwise—but who uses this knowledge as a substitute for, or a distraction from, the difficult task of seeking a solution to his or her inner despair. Such knowledge, then, pertains only to outer reality, not inner.

On the surface, the aesthetic individual's life follows two simple rules: (1) Avoid "the boring" and (2) Seek "the interesting." The aesthetically successful person will not let "the boring" take over "the interesting." One of the techniques the aesthetic individual uses to avoid such a takeover is the use of "the rotation method." Just as a farmer rotates fields to keep them fertile, the aesthetic individual plans a systematic rotation of pleasures so that fresh, new ones will constantly keep blossoming. "I may be enjoying the company of this lover now," says the aesthete, "but I had better make sure that I do not stop planting the seeds for future affairs."

A second technique is to choose "highs" that are more enduring than the ones provided by the sexual act, for example, or by a work of art. The aesthete notices not only that "first love" especially, and "romantic love" generally, provide intense and all-consuming experiences, but also that they can last months or perhaps years. But the aesthete also sadly recognizes that romantic love of this sort cannot be artificially manufactured by the mere willing of it. Instead, turning to "Don Juanism," the aesthete sees in the art of seduction a somewhat long-lasting and controllable way to escape boredom.

Can the aesthetic way of life work? For Kierkegaard, the answer is yes and no. Some people are completely successful in escaping the essential issues of life, and they do so by making use of nature's aesthetic gifts. The aesthete runs risks, however. First, in trying to plan a life around immediate, natural goods, the aesthete may become jaded, perverse, or addicted. If so, life may become painful, in spite of his or her best efforts. Second, by letting such immediate goods as beauty, excitement, and pleasure govern life, a person is likely to forfeit many other types of possible choices. How could someone who lives for immediate pleasure spend several years writing a novel, getting a Ph.D., or, as we shall see in a moment, participate in the difficult task of making a marriage (or other relationships) work? Nevertheless, Kierkegaard seems convinced that such problems are not fatal to the aesthetic life. There's enough of "the interesting" to last a lifetime. From Kierkegaard's point of view, however, people who choose this kind of life remain victims of despair.

■ ■ ■

The Ethical Stage

Like the aesthetic stage, the ethical stage in Kierkegaard's writings has a number of different but similar approaches. Using one of his fictitious names, Judge William, Kierkegaard sees the ethical as being perfectly symbolized in the good husband (or wife) and the good citizen. Such a person is steady, sober, responsible, and civic-minded. Under another fictitious name, Kierkegaard, in *Fear and Trembling,* characterizes the ethical in a Kantian manner, emphasizing universal moral imperatives. Under his own name, in *Purity of Heart* and *Works of Love,* he portrays the ethical person as one whose way of being is characterized by a steady, inwardly based love. Finally, there is the existentialist Kierkegaard who, under his pen name Johannes Climacus, sees the highest ethical task as that of becoming a genuine human being. To become this, according to Climacus, one is required to appropriate into one's way of being all that is essentially human. (Climacus thinks that the early Socrates is, in this sense, an ethical hero.)

What these approaches have in common is that the ethical person gives the eternal priority over the temporal. This is not to suggest that he or she thinks that there is anything wrong with aesthetic, temporal, goods. In fact, the ethical person sees aesthetic pleasures as good in exactly the same way as the aesthete sees them—but only so long as they do not interfere with the ethical. What is true, however, is that the ethical person must renounce the aesthetic, in the sense that he or she must be prepared to give it up, at once, if it clashes with the ethical. The idea in Kierkegaard's philosophy that life has "suffering" structured into its very essence, and that the higher one's consciousness the more one is aware of this, begins with his claim that the ethical stage requires a "renunciation" of the temporal.

Is the ethical viewpoint adequate? Plato, Aristotle, Kant, and Mill (1806–73), as spokespersons for the ethical, would all say yes. The existential, Christian, Freudian-like Kierkegaard, however, is less optimistic. For him, there is still more to the "self" than what ethical categories can account for. Ethical categories can neither (1) explain the high failure rate that humans have at being ethical, even among those who explicitly strive toward ethical goodness, nor (2) provide individuals with a satisfying way of dealing with their ethical failures. Let us speak about each of these inadequacies in turn.

How is it that we so often fail at the ethical? Kierkegaard, once again anticipating Freud's discovery of the unconscious, suggests that buried deep inside the individual is a negative or ambivalent attitude toward the ethical, in spite of surface intentions and ideas. We are so often passively ignorant about the ethical, or actively hostile toward it, that Kierkegaard strongly suspects there is a conflict deep within us that tends to subvert our ethical aims.

The problem—once again—is that the ethical cannot meet the demands of the whole self. This time it is the temporal or worldly part of us that feels cheated. The individual becomes *resigned* to not getting a greater share of the temporal. The ethical individual is a "knight of resignation" or a "tragic hero." He or she is a good person, but somewhat depressed as a result. Because of this, resignation may even turn into full-blown resentment against "life's unfair demands." It is as if the individual says to himself or herself:

> I am obligated to be good, but I really want much more than what the so-called Good Life has to offer. I don't like being split in half between what I really desire, on the one hand, and what is ethically good, on the other. My real thoughts and desires do not and never will conform to "the good."

Plato, Aristotle, Kant, and Mill would try to persuade this individual that, with practice and discipline, one's desires *can* be made to conform to the good. Human nature, they would say, has this potential. Kierkegaard disagrees. The ethical life, he argues, will lead to frustration, guilt, and conscious or unconscious resignation or resentment. The challenges are too numerous and too great. A God-relationship is what is needed. We then must move on to the next stage.

■ ■ ■

Religiousness A

Religiousness A is an intensified version of the ethical. Instead of making "the ethical good" one's highest priority, the religious person makes the quality of his or her God-relationship the highest priority. In this stage, the individual confesses to God his or her ethical failures, and ambivalence or hostility toward the ethical good, admits to being nothing before God, recognizes his or her complete dependence on God, and does all of this in the expectation of an eternal happiness. Kierkegaard, under his pen name Climacus, captures all of this when he says: "The totality of guilt-consciousness in the particular individual before God in relation to an eternal happiness is religiousness."

Given Kierkegaard's theory of the self as a synthesis of the temporal and the eternal, the religiousness A stage seems now to have finally exhausted the logical possibilities. It is the only stage at which seemingly no part of the self needs to be repressed. The temporal is acknowledged as being in collision with the eternal, and the resulting ethical failure is not hidden, but *confessed* before God. In the place of self-deception, religiousness A features self-disclosure. Instead of despair, the religious person hopes for eternal happiness. Is this not an articulate account of what religion-in-general, at its best, is all about? What more is there to say?

Yet, Kierkegaard is not finished. What if, regarding the individual's relationship to God and truth, "things are to be otherwise?" Climacus asks in the *Philosophical Fragments*. How could things be otherwise? As we turn to the final stage in Kierkegaard's theory, religiousness B, we must notice how he will generate his account by raising questions about a key, but hitherto unquestioned, assumption in religiousness A.

■ ■ ■

Religiousness B

Kierkegaard questions the assumption in religiousness A that within the individual there is a healthy capacity for the attainment of truth. For example, in religiousness A it was assumed that when the individual "confesses" before God, the resulting confession is a genuine self-disclosure. Is it not possible, however, Kierkegaard asks, that such confessions are phoney or idealized? Is it not possible that the hatred of the eternal or ambivalence toward it, which we noticed to be operative in the ethical stage, and which was confessed in the religiousness A stage, extends even farther, so that there is in each of us a hatred of, or ambivalence towards, *truth* itself? Kierkegaard, under his pen name in the *Philosophical Fragments*, forms these speculations into an hypothesis. What are the logical and existential implications for the individual, he asks, if individuals in the religiousness A stage (who, for Kierkegaard, include even Socrates) are too optimistic about their capacity to make a *truthful* assessment of their self before God? Some of the main implications, for Kierkegaard, are as follows:

1. The individual's guilt consciousness would no longer be taken as the "truth" about what he or she really feels or thinks about the good, the eternal, or God, but would now come under suspicion. The individual would be in a state of "Error" or "Sin," invisibly out of touch with himself or herself, and all efforts to be "sincere" or "truthful" would only compound the Error.

2. Any movement toward the deepest truths (i.e., truths about one's relationship to the eternal) will require that the learner first be *made over* or *reconstructed* in order to be given the requisite condition for attaining the truth. Until this happens, no method of inquiry known to humans will bring them closer to truth, but instead will leave them on a path that more and more entrenches them in Error.

3. Since no human can re-create another, this hypothesis requires the existence of a God. As Kierkegaard puts it, using a pen name, "The Teacher then, is the God, and this God gives the learner the requisite Condition and the Truth."

4. Error or Sin must have been caused by the individual and not by the God who is, by hypothesis, a Teacher of Truth. No one forced the individual to despair over the truth and to go to war against it.

5. Such a Teacher would be a "saviour" and a "redeemer."

6. This hypothesis is, paradoxically, unthinkable, unless there *really has been* such a Teacher-God since, by the hypothesis, all humans are in Error or Sin and therefore incapable of even *imagining* the truth about themselves.

Regarding this last implication, Kierkegaard is in the strongest possible terms denying that he has anything whatever to do with the genesis of the hypothesis. Instead, he attributes this hypothesis to Christianity since it is the only historical religion that perfectly fits the logic of his hypothesis. Furthermore, Kierkegaard is claiming that there is a self-authenticating dimension to this hypothesis. Since it would be nonsensical for a human, or a group of humans, to claim that humans are in Sin, when Sin is by definition invisible to humans, it seems as though the very existence of the Sin/Teacher hypothesis is, in and of itself, evidence for its having a higher-than-human origin.

■ ■ ■

Conclusion

We have now seen where Kierkegaard's concept of the self as a collision between the temporal and the eternal leads. The collision may be so direct, and the despair and subsequent self-deception so great, that a divine Teacher, who is both a saviour and a redeemer, may be the only possible antidote to despair. Whether such a Teacher exists, whether Christ was such a teacher, or indeed even whether God exists, however, are not questions to which Kierkegaard believes we can know the answer, in the sense of "know" employed by the universal court of human reason. The Teacher-God-Saviour idea is just a *possibility:* a possible item for faith, but not an item of knowledge. Kierkegaard, like the Socrates of Plato's *Apology*, believes that reason, on its own, is not capable of answering life's most important questions. What Kierkegaard leaves us with, then, are unanswered questions about the self and a marking out of the role that certain kinds of religious faith could play in dealing with these questions.

■ ■ ■

Philosophical Critique

Kierkegaard's thought advances philosophical thinking about the self in two ways. First, Kierkegaard, seeing himself in the footsteps of Socrates, challenges traditional philosophy by calling attention not to what is already known about the self, but rather to *all that is not known*. In particular, Kierkegaard puts forward the genuine possibility, which he attributes to Christianity, that there is in each of us a *fundamental disharmony* that is greater than what anyone has hitherto imagined—or, perhaps, could imagine, using rational capacities alone. Second, Kierkegaard develops a concept of the self, as a collision of ethically significant opposites, that has several strengths:

1. It allows for exploration of the new possibilities and questions about the self that he raises, or which he thinks Christianity raises.
2. It has deep historical roots, and yet anticipates, and is compatible with, twentieth-century discoveries about the self. For example: (a) it builds on, and does not contradict, the ancient Greek views of the self (especially those of Socrates and Plato); (b) it is compatible with the possibilities about the self raised by Christianity; (c) it anticipates and is compatible with Freud's concept of the unconscious. Kierkegaard's thought, then, connects the early Socrates, Plato, Christ, and Freud, and, in so doing, throws more light on what each says about the self.
3. It seems to prompt in the reader, as Kierkegaard had hoped, newer and deeper levels of self-reflection.

■ ■ ■

Religious Critique

It can perhaps be argued that Kierkegaard's thought is significant for religious faith in the following four ways:

1. It makes a strong and updated case for the view that there are *limits* to what philosophy can discover about the self and that ultimate beliefs about the self are matters for faith or revelation.
2. It successfully restores Christianity's stature in the intellectual world by showing how it puts forth a unique and now indispensable theory of how the self is related to truth.
3. It effectively fights against the scientific and materialistic attacks on the self as a spiritual entity.
4. It effectively reminds us that the basis of religious belief is not knowledge, but (a) a Socratic awareness of all that we do not know about our existence, and (b) faith.

■ ■ ■

Further Reading

J. Collins, *The Mind of Kierkegaard* (Chicago, 1953).
H. A. Nielsen, *Where the Passion Is* (Florida, 1983).

8

KARL MARX

■ ■ ■

THE HUMAN PERSON AS WORKER
Introduction and Commentary by Michael T. Ryan

INTRODUCTION

The Industrial Revolution took place in England during the years 1760 to 1830, and somewhat later in other European countries. It brought dramatic change to traditional ways of life, a breakdown of social bonds, and great suffering to those who became the working class in the new industrial enterprises. The reigning capitalist philosophy of *laissez faire* (hands off) ensured a workplace relatively free from such government restrictions as minimum wage laws, or the regulation of either hours or conditions of work. The widespread condition of human suffering that resulted among workers and their families came to be referred to as "the social problem." One of the major responses to this social problem was the "scientific socialism" of Karl Marx and Frederick Engels.

■ ■ ■

Marx's Life and Works

Karl Marx was born in 1818 in Trier, in the Rhineland, where his father, a Jewish lawyer, had "converted," along with his family, to Lutheranism, when Karl was six years old. The "conversion" was really a move to help the elder Marx carry on his profession in a society whose laws discriminated against Jews.

The young Karl studied law, history, and philosophy, first in Bonn, and then in Berlin, where he received his doctorate in 1841. Philosophy is the first important element in Marx's thought. His training was primarily in the philosophy of Hegel. Marx simultaneously revolted against Hegel's views and borrowed heavily from them. From Hegel, for example, he derived his messianic view that after a period of strife, and a great final upheaval, there would come a new age of peace and fulfillment.

After graduation, Marx became editor of a left-wing newspaper in Cologne. Eventually the paper was suppressed in 1843, and Marx went to Paris. Here he became immersed in a movement that contributed the second important element to his thought: socialism. The socialists deepened his conviction that there must be concerted action to change the very structure of society.

Expelled from Paris in 1845, Marx went to Brussels, but was expelled from there in 1848. He returned to Paris, then left for Cologne, and eventually came back to Paris. Expelled again, he went to England in 1849, where he lived for the rest of his life. There he was able to pursue what had become the third great formative influence in his thought: economics. His reading of the classical economists convinced him that the ultimate breakdown of capitalism was inevitable.

In Paris, Marx had met Frederick Engels (1820–95), a German industrialist who also had holdings in England, and the two became lifelong friends and collaborators.

Marx had married Jenny von Westphalen in 1843, and she bore him several children, only three of whom lived to adulthood. Their life together, which was at first quite poor, became reasonably comfortable by the 1850s when, in addition to financial help from Engels and others, Marx secured regular employment as a journalist, and Jenny received money by inheritance. Marx's daughter paints a picture of a happy home life, and portrays Marx as a warm and caring father. He died in 1883.

From 1843 onward, Marx had considerable contact with workers' groups, and he carried on a devastating critique of capitalism. In a sense, he was a prophet crying out in the midst of human misery. His voice was not, however, one of compassion, since he had no use for such "virtues." Instead he was convinced that objective natural laws governed society's evolution, and, according to those laws, capitalism was doomed. It would be followed by a society in which people would be able to experience their true humanity.

Among his principal writings are the following:

The Economic and Philosophical Manuscripts (1844)
The German Ideology (1844–45) (in collaboration with Engels)
The Poverty of Philosophy (1846)
The Communist Manifesto (1848) (together with Engels)
The Eighteenth Brumaire of Louis Bonaparte (1852)
Grundrisse (1857–58)
Capital (1865–66)

■ ■ ■

What to Look For in the Selections

The selections chosen from Marx's writings have been organized under the following four headings to highlight four prominent elements in Marx's image of the human person. As you read through the selections, keep the following questions in mind.

1. The Human Person Is Naturally Social

Humans are not individuals who simply agree to form societies, but are beings who can develop as humans only within societies. In the first selection, *On the Jewish Question*, ask yourself why Marx criticizes the French Revolution's concept of the rights of man. In the selection from *Grundrisse*, why is Marx so opposed to the claims that individuals are prior to society in time, and superior to it in dignity? How does Marx explain a character like Robinson Crusoe?

2. The Human Person Is Essentially a Worker

Humans are sometimes described as rational animals, political animals, or animals that can make free choices. For Marx, the feature that distinguishes humans from other animals is the ability to work. From this he argues that the manner of life dictated by our work largely determines the kind of persons we will be. In the selection from *The German Ideology,* ask yourself how many of the differences between people and structures in a rural community and those in an industrial center are traceable to the principal form of work in that community. In the selection from *Capital,* why does Marx say that the activity of spiders or bees is not work? Can you see why Marx regards work as the means toward human liberation?

3. The Human Person and Religion

Is the human person naturally religious or is religion an outdated, even harmful, way of viewing reality? For Marx, the latter was the case. As you read the passage from *Toward a Critique of Hegel's Philosophy of Right,* ask what Marx means by religion's "inverted attitude toward the world," and why he refers to religion as "the opium of the people."

4. The Materialist Conception of Human History

We ask questions about the kind of beings humans are so that we can draw conclusions about how human beings should act, and what their goals, both personal and social, should be. As you read through these selections from *The Communist Manifesto,* see how all that Marx says about the goal of history is rooted in his understanding of the human person as worker, as social being, and as someone who needs to be freed from religion. Keep the following questions in mind. Is the goal of history, as described by Marx, something dependent on our free choices, or will it come about inevitably? Does Marx supply any details of what society will be like when that goal is reached?

SELECTIONS FROM MARX

■ ■ ■

1. The Human Person Is Naturally Social

On the Jewish Question

Thus none of the so-called rights of man goes beyond egoistic man, man as he is in civil society, namely an individual withdrawn behind his private interests and whims and separated from the community. Far from the rights of man conceiving of man as a species-being, species-life itself, society appears as a framework exterior to individuals, a limitation of their original self-sufficiency. The only bond that holds them together is natural necessity, need, and private interest, the conservation of their property and egoistic person.

It is already paradoxical that a people that is just beginning to free itself, to tear down all barriers between different sections of the people and form a political community, should solemnly proclaim (in the French *Declaration* of 1791) the justification of egoistic man separated from his fellow men and the community. Indeed, this proclamation is repeated at a moment when only the most heroic devotion can save the nation, and is therefore peremptorily demanded; at a moment when the sacrifice of all the interests of civil society is raised to the order of the day and egoism must be punished as a crime (*Declaration of the Rights of Man,* 1793). This fact appears to be even more paradoxical when we see that citizenship, the political community, is degraded by the political emancipators to a mere means for the preservation of these so-called rights of man; that the citizen is declared to be the servant of egoistic man; that the sphere in which man behaves as a communal being is degraded below the sphere in which man behaves as a partial being; finally, that it is not man as a citizen but man as a bourgeois who is called the real and true man.

Grundrisse

The subject of our discussion is first of all *material* production. Individuals producing in society, thus the socially determined production of individuals, naturally constitutes the starting-point. The individual and isolated hunter or fisher who forms the starting-point with Smith [1723–90] and Ricardo [1772–1823] belongs to the insipid illusions of the eighteenth century. They are Robinson Crusoe stories which do not by any means represent, as students of the history of civilization imagine, a reaction against over-refinement and a return to a misunderstood natural life. They are no more based on such a naturalism than is Rousseau's *contrat social* which makes naturally independent individuals come in contact and have mutual intercourse by contract. They are the fiction, and only the aesthetic fiction, of the small and great adventure stories. They are, rather, the anticipation of "civil society," which had been in the course of development since the sixteenth century and made gigantic strides towards maturity in the eighteenth. In this society of free competition the individual appears free from the bonds of nature, etc., which in former epochs of history made him part of a definite, limited human conglomeration. To the prophets of the eighteenth century, on whose shoulders Smith and Ricardo are still standing, this eighteenth-century individual, constituting the joint product of the dissolution of the feudal form of society and of the new forces of production which had developed since the sixteenth century, appears as an ideal whose existence belongs to the past; not as a result of history, but as its starting-point. Since that individual appeared to be in conformity with nature and corresponded to their conception of human nature, he was regarded not as developing historically but as posited by nature. This illusion has been characteristic of every new epoch in the past. Steuart [1712–81], who, as an aristocrat, stood more firmly on historical ground and was in many respects opposed to the spirit of the eighteenth century, escaped this simplicity of view.

The farther back we go into history, the more the individual and, therefore, the producing individual seems to depend on and belong to a large whole: at first it is, quite naturally, the family and the clan, which is but an enlarged family; later on, it is the community growing up in its different forms out of the clash and the amalgamation of clans. It is only in the eighteenth century, in "civil society," that the different forms of social union confront the individual as a mere means to his private ends, as an external necessity. But the period in which this standpoint—that of the isolated individual—became prevalent is the very one in which the social relations of society (universal relations according to that standpoint) have reached the highest state of development. Man is in the most literal sense of the word a political animal, not only a social animal but an animal which can develop into an individual only in society. Production by isolated individuals outside society—something which might happen as an exception to a civilized man who by accident got into the wilderness and already potentially possessed within himself the forces of society—is as great an absurdity as the idea of the development of language without individuals living together and talking to one another. We need not dwell on this any longer.

■ ■ ■

2. The Human Person Is Essentially a Worker

The German Ideology

The way in which men produce their means of subsistence depends first of all on the nature of the actual means of subsistence they find in existence and have to reproduce. This mode of production must not be considered simply as being the production of the physical existence of the individuals. Rather it is a definite form of activity of these individuals, a definite form of expressing their life, a definite mode of life on their part. As individuals express their life, so they are. What they are, therefore, coincides with their production, both with what they produce and with *how* they produce. The nature of individuals thus depends on the material conditions determining their production.

Capital, volume 1

Labour is, in the first place, a process in which both man and Nature participate, and in which man of his own accord starts, regulates, and controls the material reactions between himself and Nature. He opposes himself to Nature as one of her own forces, setting in motion arms and legs, head and hands, the natural forces of his body, in order to appropriate Nature's productions in a form adapted to his own wants. By thus acting on the external world and changing it, he at the same time changes his own nature. He develops his slumbering powers and compels them to act in obedience to his sway. We are not now dealing with those primitive instinctive forms of labour that remind us of the mere animal. An immeasurable interval of time separates the state of things in which a man brings his labour power to market for sale as a commodity, from that state in which human labour was still in its first instinctive stage. We presuppose labour in a form that stamps it as exclusively human. A spider conducts operations that resemble those of a weaver, and a bee puts to shame many an architect in the construction of her cells. But what distinguishes the worst architect from the best of bees is this, that the architect raises his structure in imagination before he erects it in reality. At the end of every labour process, we get a result that already existed in the imagination of the labourer at its commencement. He not only effects a change of form in the material on which he works, but he also realizes a purpose of his own that gives the law to his *modus operandi* [way of working], and to which he must subordinate his will. And this subordination is no mere momentary act. Besides the exertion of the bodily organs, the process demands that, during the whole operation, the workman's will be steadily in consonance with his purpose. This means close attention. The less he is attracted by the nature of the work, and the mode in which it is carried on, and the less, therefore, he enjoys it as something which gives play to his bodily and mental powers, the more close his attention is forced to be.

■ ■ ■

3. The Human Person and Religion

Toward a Critique of Hegel's Philosophy of Right: Introduction

The foundation of irreligious criticism is this: man makes religion, religion does not make man. Religion is indeed the self-consciousness and self-awareness of man who either has not yet attained to himself or has already lost himself again. But man is no abstract being squatting outside the world. Man is the world of man, the state, society. This state, this society, produces religion's inverted attitude to the world, because they are an inverted world themselves. Religion is the general theory of this world, its encyclopaedic compendium, its logic in popular form, its spiritual *point d'honneur*, its enthusiasm, its moral sanction, its solemn complement, its universal basis for consolation and justification. It is the imaginary realization of the human essence, because the human essence possesses no true reality. Thus, the struggle against religion is indirectly the struggle against the world whose spiritual aroma is religion.

Religious suffering is at the same time an expression of real suffering and a protest against real suffering. Religion is the sigh of the oppressed creature, the feeling of a heartless world, and the soul of soulless circumstances. It is the opium of the people.

The abolition of religion as the illusory happiness of the people is the demand for their real happiness. The demand to give up the illusions about their condition is a demand to give up a condition that requires illusion. The criticism of religion is therefore the germ of the criticism of the valley of tears whose halo is religion.

Criticism has plucked the imaginary flowers from the chains not so that man may bear chains without any imagination or comfort, but so that he may throw away the chains and pluck living flowers. The criticism of religion disillusions man so that he may think, act, and fashion his own reality as a disillusioned man come to his senses; so that he may revolve around himself as his real sun. Religion is only the illusory sun which revolves around man as long as he does not revolve around himself.

■ ■ ■

4. The Materialist Conception of Human History

The Communist Manifesto, **part 1**

1. The history of all hitherto existing society is the history of class struggles.
2. Freeman and slave, patrician and plebeian, lord and serf, guild-masters and journeyman, in a word, oppressor and oppressed, stood in constant opposition to one another, carried on an uninterrupted, now hidden, now open fight, a fight that each time ended either in a revolutionary re-constitution of society at large or in the common ruin of the contending classes.

3. In the earlier epochs of history, we find almost everywhere a complicated arrangement of society into various orders, a manifold gradation of social rank. In ancient Rome we have patricians, knights, plebeians, slaves; in the Middle Ages, feudal lords, vassals, guild-masters, journeymen, apprentices, serfs; in almost all of these classes, again, subordinate gradations.

4. The modern bourgeois society that has sprouted from the ruins of feudal society has not done away with class antagonisms. It has but established new classes, new conditions of oppression, new forms of struggle, in place of the old ones.

5. Our epoch, the epoch of the bourgeoisie, possesses, however, this distinctive feature: it has simplified the class antagonisms. Society as a whole is more and more splitting up into two great hostile camps, into two great classes directly facing each other: bourgeoisie and proletariat.

6. From the serfs of the Middle Ages sprang the chartered burghers of the earliest towns. From these burgesses the first elements of the bourgeoisie were developed.

7. The discovery of America, the rounding of the Cape, opened up fresh ground for the rising bourgeoisie. The East-Indian and Chinese markets, the colonisation of America, trade with the colonies, the increase in the means of exchange and in commodities generally, gave to commerce, to navigation, to industry, an impulse never before known, and thereby, to the revolutionary element in the tottering feudal society, a rapid development.

8. The feudal system of industry, under which industrial production was monopolised by closed guilds, now no longer sufficed for the growing wants of the new markets. The manufacturing system took its place. The guild-masters were pushed on one side by the manufacturing middle class; division of labour between the different corporate guilds vanished in the face of division of labor in each single workshop.

9. Meantime the markets kept ever growing, the demand ever rising. Even manufacture no longer sufficed. Thereupon, steam and machinery revolutionized industrial

production. The place of manufacture was taken by the giant, Modern Industry; the place of the industrial middle class, by industrial millionaires, the leaders of whole industrial armies, the modern bourgeois.

10. Modern industry has established the world market, for which the discovery of America paved the way. This market has given an immense development to commerce, to navigation, to communication by land. This development has, in its turn, reacted on the extension of industry; and in proportion as industry, commerce, navigation, and railways extended, in the same proportion the bourgeoisie developed, increased its capital, and pushed into the background every class handed down from the Middle Ages.

11. We see, therefore, how the modern bourgeoisie is itself the product of a long course of development, of a series of revolutions in the modes of production and of exchange.

12. Each step in the development of the bourgeoisie was accompanied by a corresponding political advance of that class. An oppressed class under the sway of the feudal nobility; an armed and self-governing association in the medieval commune; in one place an independent urban republic (as in Italy and Germany); in another place a taxable "third estate" of the monarchy (as in France); afterwards, in the period of manufacture proper, serving either the semi-feudal or the absolute monarchy as a counterpoise against the nobility; and, in fact, corner stone of the great monarchies in general, the bourgeoisie has at last, since the establishment of Modern Industry and of the world market, conquered for itself, in the modern representative State, exclusive political sway. The executive of the modern State is but a committee for managing the common affairs of the whole bourgeoisie.

13. The bourgeoisie, historically, has played a most revolutionary part.

14. The bourgeoisie, wherever it has got the upper hand, has put an end to all feudal, patriarchal, idyllic relations. It has pitilessly torn asunder the motley feudal

ties that bound man to his "natural superiors," and has left remaining no other nexus between man and man than naked self-interest, than callous "cash payment." It has drowned the most heavenly ecstasies of religious fervor, of chivalrous enthusiasm, of philistine sentimentalism, in the icy water of egotistical calculation. It has resolved personal worth into exchange value, and, in place of the numberless indefeasible chartered freedoms, has set up that single, unconscionable freedom—Free Trade. In one word, for exploitation, veiled by religious and political illusions, it has substituted naked, shameless, direct, brutal exploitation.

15. The bourgeoisie has stripped of its halo every occupation hitherto honored and looked up to with reverent awe. It has converted the physician, the lawyer, the priest, the poet, the man of science, into its paid wage-earners.

16. The bourgeoisie has torn away from the family its sentimental veil, and has reduced the family relation to a mere money relation.

17. The bourgeoisie has disclosed how it came to pass that the brutal display of vigor in the Middle Ages, which Reactionists so much admire, found its fitting complement in the most slothful indolence. It has been the first to show what man's activity can bring about. It has accomplished wonders far surpassing Egyptian pyramids, Roman aqueducts, and Gothic cathedrals; it has conducted expeditions that put in the shade all former Exoduses of nations and crusades.

18. The bourgeoisie cannot exist without constantly revolutionising the instruments of production, and thereby the relations of production, and with them the whole relations of society. Conservation of the old modes of production in unaltered form, was, on the contrary, the first condition of existence for all earlier industrial classes. Constant revolutionising of production, uninterrupted disturbance of all social conditions, everlasting uncertainty and agitation distinguish the bourgeois epoch from all earlier ones. All fixed, fast-frozen relations, with their train of ancient and venerable prejudices and

opinions, are swept away, all new-formed ones become antiquated before they can ossify. All that is solid melts into air, all that is holy is profaned, and man is at last compelled to face with sober senses his real conditions of life, and his relations with his kind.

19. The need of a constantly expanding market for its products chases the bourgeoisie over the whole surface of the globe. It must nestle everywhere, settle everywhere, establish connexions everywhere.

20. The bourgeoisie has through its exploitation of the world market given a cosmopolitan character to production and consumption in every country. To the great chagrin of Reactionists, it has drawn from under the feet of industry the national ground on which it stood. All old-established national industries have been destroyed or are daily being destroyed. They are dislodged by new industries, whose introduction becomes a life-and-death question for all civilised nations, by industries that no longer work up indigenous raw material, but raw material drawn from the remotest zones; industries whose products are consumed, not only at home, but in every quarter of the globe. In place of the old wants, satisfied by the productions of the country, we find new wants, requiring for their satisfaction the products of distant lands and climes. In place of the old local and national seclusion and self-sufficiency, we have intercourse in every direction, universal interdependence of nations. And as in material, so also in intellectual production. The intellectual creations of individual nations become common property. National one-sidedness and narrow-mindedness become more and more impossible, and from the numerous national and local literatures there arises a world-literature.

21. The bourgeoisie, by the rapid improvement of all instruments of production, by the immensely facilitated means of communication, draws all, even the most barbarian, nations into civilisation. The cheap prices of its commodites are the heavy artillery with which it batters down all Chinese walls, with which it forces the barbarians' intensely obstinate hatred of foreigners to

capitulate. It compels all nations, on pain of extinction, to adopt the bourgeois mode of production; it compels them to introduce what it calls civilisation into their midst, that is, to become bourgeois themselves. In one word, it creates a world after its own image.

22. The bourgeoisie has subjected the country to the rule of the towns. It has created enormous cities, has greatly increased the urban population as compared with the rural, and has thus rescued a considerable part of the population from the idiocy of rural life. Just as it has made the country dependent on the towns, so it has made barbarian and semi-barbarian countries dependent on the civilised ones, nations of peasants on nations of bourgeois, the East on the West.

23. The bourgeoisie keeps more and more doing away with the scattered state of the population, of the means of production, and of property. It has agglomerated population, centralised means of production, and concentrated property in a few hands. The necessary consequence of this was political centralisation. Independent or but loosely connected provinces, with separate interests, laws, governments, and systems of taxation, became lumped together into one nation, with one government, one code of laws, one national class-interest, one frontier, and one customs-tariff.

24. The bourgeoisie, during its rule of scarce one hundred years, has created more massive and more colossal productive forces than have all preceding generations together. Subjection of Nature's forces to man, machinery, application of chemistry to industry and agriculture, steam-navigation, railways, electric telegraphs, clearing of whole continents for cultivation, canalisation of rivers, whole populations conjured out of the ground—what earlier century had even a presentiment that such productive forces slumbered in the lap of social labor?

25. We see then that the means of production and of exchange, on whose foundation the bourgeoisie built itself up, were generated in feudal society. At a certain stage in the development of these means of production

and of exchange, the conditions under which feudal society produced and exchanged, the feudal organisation of agriculture and manufacturing, industry, in one word, the feudal relations of property, become no longer compatible with the already developed productive forces; they became so many fetters. They had to be burst asunder; they were burst asunder.

26. Into their place stepped free competition, accompanied by a social and political constitution adapted to it, and by the economic and political sway of the bourgeois class.

27. A similar movement is going on before our own eyes. Modern bourgeois society with its relations of production, of exchange, and of property, a society that has conjured up such gigantic means of production and of exchange, is like the sorcerer, who is no longer able to control the powers of the nether world which he has called up by his spells. For many a decade past, the history of industry and commerce is but the history of the revolt of modern productive forces against modern conditions of production, against the property relations that are the conditions for the existence of the bourgeoisie and of its rule. It is enough to mention the commercial crises that by their periodical return put on its trial, each time more threateningly, the existence of the entire bourgeois society. In these crises a great part not only of the existing products, but also of the previously created productive forces, are periodically destroyed. In these crises there breaks out an epidemic that, in all earlier epochs, would have seemed an absurdity—the epidemic of over-production. Society suddenly finds itself put back into a state of momentary barbarism; it appears as if a famine, a universal war of devastation, had cut off the supply of every means of subsistence; industry and commerce seem to be destroyed; and why? Because there is too much civilisation, too much of the means of subsistence, too much industry, too much commerce. The productive forces at the disposal of society no longer tend to further the development of the conditions of bourgeois property; on the contrary, they have become too powerful for these conditions, by

which they are fettered, and, so soon as they overcome these fetters, they bring disorder into the whole of bourgeois society, and endanger the existence of bourgeois property. The conditions of bourgeois society are too narrow to comprise the wealth created by them. And how does the bourgeoisie get over these crises? On the one hand by enforced destruction of a mass of productive forces; on the other, by the conquest of new markets, and by the more thorough exploitation of the old ones. That is to say, by paving the way for more extensive and more destructive crises, and by diminishing the means whereby crises are prevented.

28. The weapons with which the bourgeoisie felled feudalism to the ground are now turned against the bourgeoisie itself.

29. But not only has the bourgeoisie forged the weapons that bring death to itself; it has also called into existence the men who are to wield those weapons—the modern working class, the proletarians.

30. In proportion as the bourgeoisie, that is, capital, is developed, in the same proportion is the proletariat, the modern working class, developed—a class of laborers, who live only so long as they find work, and who find work only so long as their labor increases capital. These laborers, who must sell themselves piecemeal, are a commmodity, like every other article of commerce, and are consequently exposed to all the vicissitudes of competition, to all the fluctuations of the market.

31. Owing to the extensive use of machinery and to division of labor, the work of the proletarians has lost all individual character, and, consequently, all charm for the workman. He becomes an appendage of the machine, and it is only the most simple, most monotonous, and most easily acquired knack that is required of him. Hence the cost of production of a workman is restricted, almost entirely, to the means of subsistence that he requires for his maintenance and for the propagation of his race. But the price of a commodity, and therefore also of labor, is equal to its cost of production. In proportion, therefore, as the repulsiveness

of the work increases, the wage decreases. Nay more, in proportion as the use of machinery and division of labor increases, in the same proportion the burden of toil also increases, whether by prolongation of the working hours, by increase of the work exacted in a given time, by increased speed of the machinery, etc.

32. Modern industry has converted the little workshop of the patriarchal master into the great factory of the industrial capitalist. Masses of laborers, crowded into the factory, are organised like soldiers. As privates of the industrial army they are placed under the command of a perfect hierarchy of officers and sergeants. Not only are they slaves of the bourgeois class and of the bourgeois State; they are daily and hourly enslaved by the machine, by the overlooker, and, above all, by the individual bourgeois manufacturer himself. The more openly this despotism proclaims gain to be its end and aim, the more petty, the more hateful, and the more embittering it is.

33. The less the skill and exertion of strength implied in manual labor, in other words, as modern industry becomes more developed, the more is the labour of men superseded by that of women. Differences of age and sex have no longer any distinctive social validity for the working class. All are instruments of labor, more or less expensive to use, according to their age and sex.

34. No sooner is the exploitation of the laborer by the manufacturer so far at an end that he receives his wages in cash, than he is set upon by the other portions of the bourgeoisie: the landlord, the shopkeeper, the pawnbroker, etc.

35. The lower strata of the middle class—the small tradespeople, shopkeepers, and retired tradesmen generally, the handicraftsmen and peasants—all these sink gradually into the proletariat, partly because their diminutive capital does not suffice for the scale on which Modern Industry is carried on, and is swamped in the competition with the large capitalists, partly because their specialised skill is rendered worthless by new methods of

production. Thus the proletariat is recruited from all classes of the population.

36. The proletariat goes through various stages of development. With its birth begins its struggle with the bourgeoisie. At first the contest is carried on by individual laborers, then by the workpeople of a factory, then by the operatives of one trade, in one locality, against the individual bourgeois who directly exploits them. They direct their attacks not against the bourgeois conditions of production but against the instruments of production themselves; they destroy imported wares that compete with their labor; they smash machinery to pieces, they set factories ablaze, they seek to restore by force the vanished status of the workman of the Middle Ages.

37. At this stage the laborers still form an incoherent mass scattered over the whole country, and broken up by their mutual competition. If anywhere they unite to form more compact bodies, this is not yet the consequence of their own active union but of the union of the bourgeoisie, which class, in order to attain its own political ends, is compelled to set the whole proletariat in motion, and is moreover yet, for a time, able to do so. At this stage, therefore, the proletarians do not fight their enemies, but the enemies of their enemies: the remnants of absolute monarchy, the landowners, the non-industrial bourgeois, the petty bourgeoisie. Thus the whole historical movement is concentrated in the hands of the bourgeoisie; every victory so obtained is a victory for the bourgeoisie.

38. But with the development of industry the proletariat not only increases in number; it becomes concentrated in greater masses, its strength grows, and it feels that strength more. The various interests and conditions of life within the ranks of the proletariat are more and more equalised in proportion as machinery obliterates all distinctions of labor, and nearly everywhere reduces wages to the same low level. The growing competition among the bourgeois, and the resulting commercial crises, make the wages of the workers ever more fluctuating. The

unceasing improvement of machinery, ever more rapidly developing, makes their livelihood more and more precarious; the collisions between individual workmen and individual bourgeois take on more and more the character of collisions between two classes. Thereupon the workers begin to form combinations (Trades' Unions) against the bourgeois; they club together in order to keep up the rate of wages; they found permanent associations in order to make provision beforehand for these occasional revolts. Here and there the contest breaks out into riots.

39. Now and then the workers are victorious, but only for a time. The real fruit of their battles lies not in the immediate result but in the ever-expanding union of the workers. This union is helped on by the improved means of communication that are created by modern industry and that place the workers of different localities in contact with one another. It was just this contact that was needed to centralise the numerous local struggles, all of the same character, into one national struggle between classes. But every class struggle is a political struggle. And that union, to attain which the burghers of the Middle Ages, with their miserable highways, required centuries, the modern proletarians, thanks to railways, achieve in a few years.

40. This organisation of the proletarians into a class, and consequently into a political party, is continually being upset again by the competition between the workers themselves. But it ever rises up again, stronger, firmer, mightier. It compels legislative recognition of particular interests of the workers, by taking advantage of the divisions among the bourgeoisie itself. Thus the ten-hours' bill in England was carried.

41. Altogether, collisions between the classes of the old society further, in many ways, the course of development of the proletariat. The bourgeoisie finds itself in a constant battle: at first with the aristocracy; later on, with those portions of the bourgeoisie itself whose interests have become antagonistic to the progress of industry; at all times, with the bourgeoisie of foreign

countries. In all these battles it sees itself compelled to appeal to the proletariat, to ask for its help, and thus to drag it into the political arena. The bourgeoisie itself, therefore, supplies the proletariat with its own elements of political and general education; in other words, it furnishes the proletariat with weapons for fighting the bourgeoisie.

42. Further, as we have already seen, entire sections of the ruling classes are, by the advance of industry, precipitated into the proletariat, or are at least threatened in their conditions of existence. These also supply the proletariat with fresh elements of enlightenment and progress.

43. Finally, in times when the class struggle nears the decisive hour, the process of dissolution going on within the ruling class, in fact within the whole range of old society, assumes such a violent, glaring character that a small section of the ruling class cuts itself adrift and joins the revolutionary class, the class that holds the future in its hands. Just as, therefore, at an earlier period, a section of the nobility went over to the bourgeoisie, so now a portion of the bourgeoisie goes over to the proletariat, and, in particular, a portion of the bourgeois ideologists, who have raised themselves to the level of comprehending theoretically the historical movement as a whole.

44. Of all the classes that stand face to face with the bourgeoisie today, the proletariat alone is a really revolutionary class. The other classes decay and finally disappear in the face of modern industry; the proletariat is its special and essential product.

45. The lower middle class, the small manufacturer, the shopkeeper, the artisan, the peasant, all these fight against the bourgeoisie to save themselves from being eliminated as parts of the middle class. They are therefore not revolutionary but conservative. Nay more, they are reactionary, for they try to roll back the wheel of history. If by chance they are revolutionary they are so only in view of their impending transfer into the proletariat. They thus defend not their present but their future

interests; they desert their own standpoint to place themselves at that of the proletariat.

46. The "dangerous class," the social scum, that passively rotting mass thrown off by the lowest layers of old society, may, here and there, be swept into the movement by a proletarian revolution; its conditions of life, however, prepare it far more for the part of a bribed tool of reactionary intrigue.

47. For the proletariat the former conditions of society in general have virtually disappeared. The proletarian is without property; his relation to his wife and children has no longer anything in common with the bourgeois family-relations; modern industrial labor, modern subjection to capital, the same in England as in France, in America as in Germany, has stripped him of every trace of national character. Law, morality, religion, are to him so many bourgeois prejudices, behind which lurk in ambush just as many bourgeois interests.

48. All preceding classes that got the upper hand sought to fortify their already acquired status by subjecting society at large to their conditions of ownership. The proletarians cannot become masters of the productive forces of society except by abolishing their own previous mode of ownership and thereby also every other previous mode of ownership. They have nothing of their own to secure and to fortify; their mission is to destroy all previous securities for, and insurances of, individual property.

49. All previous historical movements were movements of minorities, or in the interest of minorities. The proletarian movement is the self-conscious, independent movement of the immense majority, in the interest of the immense majority. The proletariat, the lowest stratum of our present society, cannot stir, cannot raise itself up, without the whole superincumbent strata of official society being sprung into the air.

50. Though not in substance, yet in form, the struggle of the proletariat with the bourgeoisie is at first a national struggle. The proletariat of each country must, of

course, first of all settle matters with its own bourgeoisie.

51. In depicting the most general phases of the development of the proletariat, we traced the more or less veiled civil war, raging within existing society, up to the point where that war breaks out into open revolution, and where the violent overthrow of the bourgeoisie lays the foundation for the sway of the proletariat.

52. Hitherto, every form of society has been based, as we have already seen, on the antagonism of oppressing and oppressed classes. But in order to oppress a class, certain conditions must be assured to it under which it can, at least, continue its slavish existence. The serf, in the period of serfdom, raised himself to membership in the commune, just as the petty bourgeois, under the yoke of feudal absolutism, managed to develop into a bourgeois. The modern laborer, on the contrary, instead of rising with the progress of industry, sinks deeper and deeper below the conditions of existence of his own class. He becomes a pauper, and pauperism develops more rapidly than population and wealth. And here it becomes evident that the bourgeoisie is unfit any longer to be the ruling class in society and to impose its conditions of existence upon society as an over-riding law. It is unfit to rule because it is incompetent to assure an existence to its slave within his slavery, because it cannot help letting him sink into such a state that it has to feed him, instead of being fed by him. Society can no longer live under this bourgeoisie; in other words, its existence is no longer compatible with society.

53. The essential condition for the existence, and for the sway, of the bourgeois class is the formation and augmentation of capital; the condition for capital is wage-labor. Wage-labor rests exclusively on competition between the laborers. The advance of industry, whose involuntary promoter is the bourgeoisie, replaces the isolation of the laborers, due to competition, by their revolutionary combination, due to association. The development of Modern Industry, therefore, cuts from

under its feet the very foundation on which the bourgeoisie produces and appropriates products. What the bourgeoisie, therefore, produces, above all, is its own grave-diggers. Its fall and the victory of the proletariat are equally inevitable.

The Communist Manifesto, **part 2 (selection)**

We have seen above that the first step in the revolution by the working class is to raise the proletariat to the position of ruling class, to win the battle of democracy.

The proletariat will use its political supremacy to wrest, by degrees, all capital from the bourgeoisie; to centralise all instruments of production in the hands of the State, that is, of the proletariat organised as the ruling class; and to increase the total of productive forces as rapidly as possible.

When, in the course of development, class distinctions have disappeared, and all production has been concentrated in the hands of a vast association of the whole nation, the public power will lose its political character. Political power, properly so called, is merely the organised power of one class for oppressing another. If the proletariat during its contest with the bourgeoisie is compelled, by the force of circumstances, to organise itself as a class, if, by means of a revolution, it makes itself the ruling class, and, as such, sweeps away by force the old conditions of production, then it will, along with these conditions, have swept away the conditions for the existence of class antagonisms and of classes generally, and will thereby have abolished its own supremacy as a class.

In place of the old bourgeois society, with its classes and class antagonisms, we shall have an association in which the free development of each is the condition for the free development of all.

Extracted from *The Communist Manifesto,* translated by S. Moore (London, 1888) and *Karl Marx: Selected Writings,* translated and edited by D. McLellen (Oxford, 1977), 54, 63–64, 160–61, 345–46, and 455–56.

COMMENTARY

■ ■ ■

1. The Human Person Is Naturally Social

On the Jewish Question

This selection is from an article that Marx wrote for a German philosophical journal in 1843, and was intended as a review of two articles that had been written by the philosopher, Bruno Bauer.

Marx attacks the modern state. The picture of the human person that pervades classical economics, and the liberal state with which it is associated, is that of an atomic being, utterly individual and fundamentally selfish. This individual is regarded as finding fulfillment in the acquisition of property. Since the resources that individuals seek to acquire are relatively scarce and limited, it is therefore concluded that the basic relationship among humans is one of competition.

Since this competition cannot take place without some basic rules that make it possible, the state, in the form of government and laws, becomes a necessity. Such was the view put forward by some political philosophers of the seventeenth and eighteenth centuries. Here the political entity is a mere means to the survival of "civil society," that is, the pursuit of personal and economic goals by individuals. In this sense, the modern state is said to guarantee our "rights."

Hegel had offered a much more exalted view of the state. For him, there is an immanent Reason that expresses itself and unfolds itself in human history. (Hegel capitalizes terms like *reason, state,* and *whole* because for him they represent a reality that is, in some sense, divine.) If this Reason is sometimes visible in great individuals, it can be especially manifest in the State, in which Reason can appear in universal form. Modern democracies, in which people elect their own representatives, and, through them, make their own laws, would appear to bring about a rule of Reason, and so a type of State that offers human fulfillment. Here was a different, and, in Hegel's view, more noble view of human rights as guaranteed by the state. Individuals find their fulfillment in the Whole, because the Whole most fully expresses what they seek as individuals.

Marx opposes both of these pictures of the state. In his view, both of them involve a wrong image of the human person. Humans are not, says Marx, primarily individuals, but rather "species-beings." What he means is that humans find their fulfillment, not in the pursuit of their private interests, but in thinking and acting as part of society, as members of the universal community. If this is so, then human emancipation is not something that requires the creation of the state, but is something that can come about only by abolishing the state entirely. It is when all the artificial barriers are removed, and institutions that drive people to selfishness are gone, that people will discover their true humanity in living and acting as part of the human community.

Grundrisse

This selection is from a work that Marx wrote in 1857–58 but never published himself. Though it stands in need of severe editing and revision, it does show us how some of Marx's most basic ideas from his earlier years had become deepened and enlarged through his reflection and reading.

The selection from *On the Jewish Question* had criticized both the liberal and Hegelian views of the state on the grounds that both of them erred in thinking of the individual, rather than of the "species-being," that is, human community itself, as the basic given. The present selection clarifies why, in Marx's mind, human community is a more fundamental notion than that of the "individual." It is because humans, like the social insects, produce what they need socially. Our basically social character is intimately connected with the way in which we carry out human work.

The "individual," as Marx points out, is really a modern creation, which, once created, also tended to be romanticized. Humans, moderns claim, started out as individuals. It is society and social institutions that have corrupted them. Hence the road to human fulfillment is the development of a society and an economy in which free initiative and free enterprise can proceed unimpeded.

To this picture, Marx opposes two arguments. First, a historical one. The closer we study the earliest periods of human history (and the nineteenth century had great interest in such prehistory), the more we will find that human community was the norm, because human production of the necessities of life demanded it. Social production, says Marx, is as primitive and universal a fact of human existence as is human language.

Second, Marx points to an obvious fact of his own day. Human development and social progress have been intimately tied to the growth in social forms of production. If there was one feature of the Industrial Revolution that was evident to even the most casual observer, it was that modern production is supremely a social process. If today people have gained some freedom from the necessity imposed by nature, and have been able to accomplish marvels in production and trade, it is because they have found production techniques that are more fully social than anything the world has ever seen before. It was the Industrial Revolution itself that bore witness to our social nature.

■ ■ ■

2. The Human Person Is Essentially a Worker

The German Ideology

This particular book represents a turning-point in Marx's writing. He feels that he has left "philosophy" behind, and is now engaged in a "value-free science." As an empirical scientist, Marx says, he is investigating the plain facts of history as they bear on human society.

The most basic "fact" that Marx claims to have discovered is that "man produces himself through his labour."

Humans, says Marx, are animals that work. This is their distinguishing characteristic. Whereas other animals simply consume nature as it is (and are consumed by it in turn), humans actually *produce* from nature what they need. "Production" implies altering nature, adapting it to human needs. Moreover such alteration is always associated with some particular mode of cooperation, some particular type of social relationship. It is in this way that the human mode of work determines the particular mode of human society.

To explain this further: one can distinguish between fixed drives in humans (for example, hunger and sex) and relative drives. The latter derive from the way our society is organized, the kinds of social structures and institutions that we have. The way we come to see the world, the sorts of things we value, the way we see ourselves, will thus, in final analysis, be a reflection of the way we produce to meet our human needs. One can see what Marx had in mind if one thinks of a people like the Vikings, whose social structure, religion, and literature so clearly reflect their mode of "production": long-range piracy over the seas.

Capital, volume 1

In this oft-quoted passage, Marx is more explicit still in showing why he considers humans to be "animals that work," thus making work our most distinguishing characteristic.

What makes us capable of genuine work, in contrast with the social insects, for example, is that we form a plan in our mind before we do the work. As Charles Taylor has pointed out, this emphasis on the ability to plan (and so improve) our activity is the ultimate reason Marx's philosophy is so often looked upon as a philosophy of liberation.

Human work involves having a plan in our mind ahead of time, and this means that we can change that plan and so change the way we do our work. The ability to change—in contrast with the bees and spiders—means that we can find better ways of doing our work. In short, we are capable of progress. That progress shows up in two ways. First, as our ways of working improve we gradually get an edge over nature, and so secure greater freedom for ourselves. Second, as we find better ways of working, we discover how to make our work itself, and the ways in which we relate to one another in it, a more satisfying and humanly fulfilling activity. So work should be, for humans, the road to freedom and to fulfillment.[1] Of course, it is precisely as a social process that work accomplishes these two goals.

■ ■ ■

3. The Human Person and Religion

Toward a Critique of Hegel's
Philosophy of Right: Introduction

This selection is from an article that Marx wrote for a journal in 1844, and it brings out clearly one of the major reasons why Marx rejected religion: he saw it as a form of alienation.

In general, for Marx, alienation is the situation of a subject who has been compelled to live in a subjective world, a false world, because that subject is cut off from the real world. As the *Communist Manifesto* will state, Marx is convinced that the most fundamental realm of human life, that of work, is one of alienation for most people. This is the case because most people have no control over their work. Hence they have no control over the kind of society that is being created by work, and so no control over the forces that are making them into a particular kind of person. This basic, economic alienation supplies the foundation for other forms of alienation: social, political, cultural, religious.

Marx makes it clear then that religious alienation is not, in his view, the fundamental one. It is rather an "opium," that is, a self-administered alienation that people invent in order to ease the pain of living with the more basic alienations in their lives. It is an illusion, but one that can be finally destroyed only by attacking the most basic of all alienations, that in the world of work, where most working people are simply "hired hands."

There is another reason too why Marx was disposed to regard the world of religion as a world of illusion: because of his reaction against Hegel (1770–1831). For Hegel, the material world is really just a reflection of Spirit. Marx sees only one possible alternative to such a position, and insists that the realm of Spirit is only a reflection of the material world.

A further motive at work in Marx's opposition to religion was his determination to be "scientific." Once he had made up his mind that he was not doing philosophy but was engaged in social science, Marx began rejecting everything that smacked of the "old-fashioned" way of viewing reality, all that was magical or superstitious. For him, religion fell into that category; it was a prescientific way of viewing the world.

The overcoming of all alienations would mean that humanity, in control of the work process, would also be in control of those social forces that mold people and make them the kind of people they are. In that situation, people would no longer dream of some heavenly world that awaits them, but would create a truly human world for themselves now. They would not look for a divine savior, but would save themselves. They would view themselves, not some higher reality, as the source of their humanity.

■ ■ ■

4. The Materialist Conception of Human History

The Communist Manifesto, **parts 1 and 2**

At the first International Communist Congress in London in June 1847, the delegates expressed the need for some sort of communist "creed." Frederick Engels made a beginning on this, and his ideas were presented to the second Communist Congress, also in London, in December 1847. The Congress asked Marx to carry the work further. Making some use of Engels's material, but relying principally on his own writing, Marx produced the *Communist Manifesto* in February 1848. It is divided into four parts, of which the first part is by far the most important, and provides us with an overall picture of Marx's "scientific socialism."

The document opens with a statement of its basic thesis, one that appears several times in the *Manifesto:* history is the story of class struggle; it is, in fact, class struggle that makes history take place.

According to Marx and Engels, the original society was classless. However, the effort to make progress in productive capability brought about a division of society into classes. Whatever other differences there might be, the basic difference between classes is ultimately an economic one, and turns on who owns the means of production. Society has seen a development from one type of class division to another: from a primitive communal (classless) society to a slave society in the ancient world, to a feudal society in the Middle Ages, and to a capitalist society in modern times. The next and final step, it is claimed, will be to a developed communal (classless) society.

What Marx, in his early work, calls "alienation" is the condition of those who do not own the means of production, and so have no control over their work or its products, and hence no control over the kind of society that makes them the kind of people they are. Marx later comes to call this alienation "division of labour," and he means by this a "natural" division of labour that is imposed on certain people, rather than a voluntary one. Associated with the "natural" division of labor is the private ownership of productive property, which gives control of the work process, and all that it involves, to certain select classes instead of to society as a whole.

The transition from one type of society to another, for example from feudal society to capitalist, and now from capitalist to developed communist, is a *dialectical* one, that is, one in which the new arises from the heart of the old, and by contradicting the old. In this first part of the *Manifesto*, Marx illustrates this process by showing that the very success of feudal society, for example, is what gave rise to the forces that would overcome it. So too, he argues, it is the very success of capitalism that is giving rise to the forces that will overthrow it.

The great advantage that capitalist society has over previous historical societies, according to Marx, is that the division between classes is becoming much sharper. More and more, the various class divisions are giving way to just one division, that between the bourgeoisie and the proletariat, that is, between the owners of the means of production and the workers. As Marx names and describes these two classes, he means the contrast to be one between oppressors and oppressed, between evil and good. *Bourgeoisie*, from *burg*, meaning "a walled town," summons up the picture of wealth protecting itself. *Proletariat*, from the Latin *proles*, meaning "offspring," recalls the class in Roman society that was so poor the only thing it had to give to the Empire was its children. In this context, Marx refers to those people who are so poor that the only thing they have to give is their work.

It is important also to see that *bourgeoisie* and *proletariat* are meant to picture the two sides of the same coin. Implicit in the *Manifesto* (but to be developed later in *Capital*) is the notion of *surplus value*. The bourgeoisie takes over the product of the proletariat's work, and sells it for more than the cost of materials and wages. This creates a "surplus value" that the bourgeoisie uses to purchase bigger and better instruments of production, which therefore represent "stored labour" or "dead labour." These lead to the employment of more members of the proletariat. Living labor therefore constantly serves dead labor.

Marx does not object to using some savings from the work process in order to purchase or produce better means of production (capital). What he objects to is that this capital is owned by one class of people rather than by society as a whole. *Capital* is therefore not just an economic notion for Marx, but also a social one.

As Marx describes the dialectical transition from feudalism to capitalism, and now (he believes) from capitalism to developed communism, he speaks of productive forces developing until they outstrip the relations of production. This is an important notion, and needs to be looked at carefully.

Everything other than the economic in life—which social classes are dominant, what form political life takes, what style of music or literature predominates—will be a reflection of the economic. Since humans are "animals that work," their mode of production or work will be the most important fact about them, and so the way their work is organized will be reflected in every other feature of life. To use terms that will appear in a later Marxist writing, the economic *substructure* of society will be mirrored in the *superstructure* of society, that is, in social patterns, political arrangements, cultural life, literature, religion, and so on. Thus, in a capitalist society, where the bourgeoisie or capitalists own the means of production, the capitalist "stamp" will be on every other feature of social life.

At present, says Marx, the productive forces (the machines and instruments of work, the people, and the skills) are beginning to outstrip the relations of production (that is, the form of ownership of the means of production). Whereas the ownership of the means of production is still in private hands, those very means have become so huge, so organized, so utterly social in their nature, that they literally cry out for social ownership. Capitalism has created a giant so big that it can no longer be controlled by private hands. Under communism this great social instrument will be socially owned and controlled. The work process will once again be in the hands of the whole of society, and people will be in charge of those forces that shape them. Alienations will come to an end. Conflict will disappear. The need for religion will cease. Human fulfillment will become a reality.

The *Manifesto* pictures capitalism's success as leading to its downfall in two ways. First, its very size will make of it a monster that no private owners can control; second, it will tend to create, through the modern processes of large-scale production, that huge disciplined army of workers that will rise up as a revolutionary force to overthrow it.

The balance of Part 1 of the *Manifesto* traces Marx's interpretation of the development of the proletariat, and prophesies an outcome of this development.

The condition of the proletariat is shown as one that worsens with the development of capitalist production, because workers come to be treated more and more as mere appendages of machines, as commodities. Capitalist growth also leads to the disappearance of other classes, such as that of small shopowners or tradespersons, and their absorption into a growing proletariat. Meanwhile, the discipline of factory life serves the purpose of organizing workers into an "army." The 1811 Luddite revolt of British workers (who destroyed textile machinery in the belief that it would diminish unemployment) is pictured as an early expression of worker discontent. The most important fact, however, is a steady growth in worker consciousness. This growth is symbolized by the development of trade unions, and the acquisition of sufficient strength to force some legislative changes. Even some of the educated bourgeoisie begin to take the side of the proletariat (Marx and Engels have themselves in mind, for example). Slowly, the proletariat develops a different lifestyle from that of its capitalist masters. With its growing impoverishment it begins national struggles against the bourgeoisie. Eventually this leads to the revolutionary replacement of capitalism by communism, an event that in time will assume worldwide proportions.

Part 2 of the *Manifesto*, which deals with the relationship of the Communist Party to the growth of worker consciousness and the coming revolution, closes with a description of what is to come. After the revolution, the proletariat will assume power. For a time, it will have to function as a government, until various political, economic, and social changes have been carried out. Eventually, however, as these changes take place and the ownership of the means of production becomes vested in the people as a whole, all the reasons for class division will cease. With the disappearance of classes, there will also be a disappearance of conflict (because all conflict has been class-based). A new type of human being will emerge, in a classless, and therefore conflictless, society. The state itself will cease to exist in any modern form. Human fulfillment in the social process of work will become a reality.

Finally, one needs to keep in mind that Marx puts all this forward, not as a theory, but as his reading of the facts. He describes his position as "scientific socialism." He believes that he has uncovered the "laws of history," and that those laws are as predictable in their results as is the law of gravity formulated by Isaac Newton. As he got older, Marx tended to stress even more this note of "inevitability" of a future class-less society that would most surely come about, whether people acknowledged that fact now or not.

■ ■ ■

Assessment of the Marxist Position: Strengths

The Social Nature of the Person

Marx's writings serve as an important reminder that human beings are thoroughly social beings. We become what we are only in human society. We reflect the society of which we are a part. We are as much social types as we are individual persons. It is true that Marx went too far. He spoke at times of human beings as having their meaning and identity only as part of the whole, and so downplayed in some respects the inviolable dignity of every human person as an individual.

Yet Marx was correct in pointing the finger at that modern creation of "the individual." As persons who live in a society that is generally characterized as very individualistic, we need the kind of reminders that Marx supplies. We are as fundamentally social as we are individual. We are not autonomous beings who can divorce ourselves from either history or social life. We see reality in ways that are thoroughly conditioned by the society of which we are a part. This brings out the fact that personal conversion is never enough all by itself. In final analysis, one must also change many of the social structures, customs, and laws, that help to make human beings in a given society the kind of persons they are. It also shows how much we must be conscious of the fact that to be human is to be part of a social family, with which we must be in solidarity.

The Philosophy of Work

Marx's writing on the centrality of work in human life, and the role of human social production in giving a shape to other elements of human existence, is a great contribution to human self-understanding. There is no philosophy of work today that does not owe some debt to the insights of Karl Marx.

That human work so clearly distinguishes us from the rest of the animal kingdom, and that it represents a distinctive relationship to nature for us, is a very important truth. That the forms of human work throughout the ages have been crucial to growth in freedom and in levels of human awareness seems beyond question. That humans rightly look for some form of fulfillment in work seems confirmed again and again. People want to work, and they find that good work makes them more complete.

Since work is so central to human life, it is not surprising that the modes of work in a given society do in fact color other aspects of social life. This truth also, overstated as it was by Marx, is still a most important insight.

It is interesting to see how thoroughly Pope John Paul II agrees with many aspects of Marx's thought on this subject, in the Pope's 1981 encyclical letter *Laborem Exercens* (On Human Work). He too insists that "only human beings work." He too points out that work is, as a general rule, fundamental to our human condition; we need to work, and we find a certain fulfillment and perfection in our work. Again, he also severely criticizes those aspects of the workplace that prevent work from being what it ought to be for everyone. Work, he says, is for the sake of persons, not persons for the sake of work.

At the same time, it is revealing to see the ways in which the Pope goes beyond Marx on this topic. He states that the reason why we are, in a sense, "animals that work," and find a certain fulfillment in work, is because we are the "images of God." It is because we have been made, like God, beings who are able to take command of their own lives, and who, through the exercise of intelligence and freedom, can assume genuine responsibility for other persons and things, that we can be entrusted by God with the care of this world. God made us something like God, so that God could entrust to us a task somewhat like God's own: the care and development of this world. We carry out this role especially through our work. Human work is, at its best, a participation in God's providential care of all persons and things.

The Critique of Capitalism

Not all of Marx's criticisms of capitalism turned out to be accurate. In fact many of his prophecies were proved false. For one thing, he had not foreseen the growth of a large middle class in many capitalist countries. For another, he misjudged the direction that would be taken by most labor unions.

It must not be forgotten, however, that Marx spoke out against the terrible abuses of early capitalism at a time when far too many others were largely silent. He was aware of the conditions that workers and their families faced, and his voice, whatever its weaknesses, was a loud and clear one on behalf of the working class.

There is also a fundamental criticism of capitalism that Marx put forth and that has been echoed by Pope John Paul II to which we need to pay close attention. Without subscribing to Marx's theory of "surplus value," one can at least see the truth in his claim that there is something inherently wrong in a system that puts living labor at the service of dead labor (capital). This is very close to what the pope means when he speaks of the priority of labor, in his *Laborem Exercens*. As he points out, it is labor that should hire capital, not capital that should hire labor. Involved here is a call for the radical overhaul of the workplace. Structures that give working people a genuine share in the management, ownership, and profits of the business enterprises of which they are part, will have workers actually "working for themselves."

■ ■ ■

Assessment of the Marxist Position: Weaknesses

The Basic Thesis

As Louis Dupré points out,[2] the basic thesis stated in the opening lines of the *Communist Manifesto* simply cannot be supported by an appeal to the facts. That thesis, once again, is: "The history of all hitherto existing society is the history of class struggles."

This thesis contends (1) that all history is reducible to social conflicts; (2) that all social conflicts are really forms of class struggle; and (3) that class is defined solely by a group's place in the process of production. None of these propositions can be sustained.

Clearly history is not reducible to social conflict. Some of the most important factors affecting human history result, not from conflict, but from the creative spirit of human beings. How much the course of human events has been influenced by great works of art, masterpieces of literature, beautiful creations in music! How many discoveries, including scientific discoveries, had nothing whatsoever to do with conflict! In fact it is interesting to see how many of them resulted from theological interest.

Even if history could be reduced to a series of social conflicts, it is clear that social conflicts cannot themselves be reduced to class conflicts. The realities of international politics make this very clear, as do such facts as racial conflict. It is also interesting to see that successful movements for social change have not been ones that neglected other ties among people in favor of their "proletariat" tie, but have been ones that paid a great deal of attention to the cultural, religious, and ethnic symbols in people's lives.[3]

Finally, it is widely acknowledged today that class cannot be defined in economic terms alone. The fundamental reason is that human labor is never simply an economic activity. Human occasions of eating and drinking are regularly associated with other meanings besides the mere satisfaction of bodily need. Human habitation is nearly always more than bare shelter, and has important aesthetic and cultural aspects as well. Human dress, even the most basic, almost always has elements that serve as symbols of social status and sex, for example. Humans are animals that work, but they are not *simply* animals that work.

The Understanding of Alienation

Marx's notion of alienation is extreme. While it is true that people do suffer from various forms of alienation, and that the Industrial Revolution introduced terrible alienation into the lives of working people, Marx tended to regard humans as alienated if they were subject to anything. "The criticism of religion," Marx said, "ends with the doctrine that man is for himself the highest being." Marx's theory of alienation was, therefore, necessarily atheistic.

In fact, Marx represents the culmination of a process of reversal that began in Hegel. In the ancient world, "alienation" could have a positive meaning, since it was believed that humans found their fulfillment *beyond* themselves. The Latin *alienation* had a kinship with the Greek *ecstasy*. To overcome preoccupation with self in order to enter into union with God was a perfecting of the human. For Hegel, the Divine was immanent in the world, and was to be found within humanity itself. It was but a step to Marx's view that humanity was to find its fulfillment only in itself.[4]

The Place of Human Freedom

As a philosophy of human liberation, Marxism is very attractive. It looks forward to a society in which the conditions for human work will be such that persons can find the freedom and fulfillment that work ideally could promote. Yet, as a "scientific" theory that insists on the inevitability of history's processes, Marxism clearly seems to downplay the role of human freedom. If the future is to be a realm of great human freedom, how is this consistent with the view that the processes bringing it about are natural forces that overrule human freedom?[5]

Related to this observation is the fact that Marx's picture of the human person is unreal. On the one hand, it expects too little of the human person, picturing humans as largely determined by the society of which they are a part. This is scarcely a noble view of the person. On the other, it expects far too much of the person, when it pictures the future society as one in which, with the disappearance of classes, there will also come the disappearance of conflict. Such a view totally neglects the reality of human sinfulness.

The Bourgeoisie and the Proletariat

In one sense, there seems to be a lot of evidence to support Marx's view that the bourgeoisie and the proletariat are two sides of the same coin. We see many situations in which it appears that the riches of the rich depend upon the poverty of the poor. There has long been evidence that the lifestyle of the northern hemisphere in our world could not exist without the poverty of those in the southern hemisphere. Again, within industrialized societies, the distribution of income and wealth remains remarkably unequal, in about the same proportions year after year, in spite of social programs and so-called tax reforms. A society like that of South Africa looks like the kind of society that Marx had in mind, for it does appear that the rich white population in that country maintains its comfortable situation by a systematic denial of equal benefits to the black majority.

Yet, in spite of the empirical evidence, there is a feature of Marx's analysis that seems to have the character simply of a dogma. One suspects that this may be due to his Hegelian background. Hegel is filled with the notion that one concept generates its opposite. We cannot, for example, think of blindness without simultaneously thinking of sight. So too, we cannot think of poverty without thinking of riches. For Hegel, this interrelatedness manifested itself also in the real world. Is Marx influenced by Hegel when he insists that riches necessarily generate poverty in actuality?

■ ■ ■

Conclusion

Both the strengths and the weaknesses of Marxism raise the following particularly important consideration for the Christian: Marxism has filled a gap where Christian social teaching was neglected. During the past 150 years, the major Christian denominations have developed important bodies of social teaching that address the main issues that concerned Marx. His philosophy should be seen as a call to Christians to look more deeply into their own treasures of social teaching.

■ ■ ■

Notes

1. C. Taylor, "Marxist Philosophy," in B. Magee, ed., *Men of Ideas* (New York, 1979), 45–50.
2. L. Dupré, *The Philosophical Foundation of Marxism* (New York, 1966).
3. H. Boyte, *The Background Revolution* (Philadelphia, 1980).
4. N. Rotenstreich, *Basic Problems of Marx's Philosophy* (Indianapolis, 1965).
5. Taylor, p. 49.

■ ■ ■

Further Reading

A. McGovern, *Marxism, An American Christian Perspective* (Maryknoll, N.Y., 1980).
D. McLellan, *Karl Marx, His Life and Thought* (London, 1973).
R. Tucker, *Philosophy and Myth in Karl Marx* (Cambridge, 1961).

9

WILLIAM JAMES

...

THE HUMAN PERSON AS ELUSIVE

Introduction and Commentary by Hunter Brown

INTRODUCTION

■ ■ ■

James's Life and Works

William James was born in New York City in 1842. He was the grandson of William James of Bailieborough, Ireland, who had emigrated to the United States and settled in Albany, New York. William of Albany's extraordinary success in business and civic life—typified by investments as shrewd as his purchase of the entire village of Syracuse, New York, while still in its nascency—would provide a level of wealth and social standing extending forward to and beyond the time of William and his famous brother, novelist Henry James. William's father, Henry—one of William of Albany's thirteen offspring—received an inheritance that made possible a very diversified and cosmopolitan education for his son William who, from early adolescent years, traveled and studied throughout Europe, forming himself intellectually in an international setting.

William inherited more than money from his family. His father was by temperament an inquisitive person who created in his household a spirit of debate and inquiry. Never far from the surface of such inquiry was a deep theological vein, mined during Henry's youthful studies at Princeton Theological Seminary and further developed throughout his life. William would have occasion to reflect upon and rekindle his father's theological influence upon him when later in life after his father's death he collected his writings and published them in 1884 as *The Literary Remains of the Late Henry James.*

William's talents were as varied and diverse as his education had been. When an adolescent, he showed great promise as an artist and studied art in Paris under Léon Coigniet, and later in New York under William Hunt. He also studied science at the Collège Imperial in Boulogne-sur-mer, and chemistry and comparative anatomy at the Lawrence Scientific School at Harvard. In 1864 he entered Harvard Medical School where he would study on and off during subsequent years, eventually becoming a qualified physician. In 1872 he was appointed instructor of physiology at Harvard where for some years he taught both physiology and psychology, establishing in 1875 the first psychology laboratory in the United States. He married in 1879 during which year his first son, Henry, was born and during which he produced some of the initial sections of his famous later work, *Principles of Psychology.* In 1880 he was appointed assistant professor of philosophy at Harvard. Five years later he founded an American branch of the Society for Psychical Research and two years after that began teaching philosophy of religion. In 1890, at the age of 48, William published his famous *Principles of Psychology* and firmly established his fame.

The publication of *Principles* marked the beginning of an impressive scholarly output during William's remaining twenty years. In 1897 he published *The Will to Believe and Other Essays in Popular Philosophy,* and four years later the *Varieties of Religious Experience,* originally prepared for the 1901 Gifford Lectures in Edinborough. In 1906 he resigned after thirty-five years of teaching, but he certainly did not flag in his productivity. In that same year he presented at Columbia University the substance of his famous work, *Pragmatism.* Three years later he gave the Hibbert Lectures at Oxford, which were subsequently published as *A Pluralistic Universe.* Early in the year of his death, 1910, he published yet eighteen more essays under the title *The Meaning of Truth*.

William's capacity to function as physician, artist, philosopher, psychologist, scientist, and so on made possible an extraordinary breadth in his thought. Some philosophers have found such breadth unsettling, interpreting it as a lack of focus. Others have lauded it as enabling James to produce what was recently described as a historically important "radical reconstruction of philosophy" that may yet turn out to have even greater significance in the twentieth century than has heretofore been accorded it.[1]

■ ■ ■

What to Look For in the Selections

There are some basic features of James's thought to keep in mind as you read the selections from James's *Principles of Psychology* and *Psychology: Briefer Course*. The human person, in James's philosophy, is an integral part of an evolving world, and human intelligence is the instrument by means of which a person adapts to that world. Rational activity, then, is inherently *practical*, oriented toward the well-being and survival of the person. It should be immediately underscored in this connection, however, that such well-being applies to human welfare at *all* levels, spiritual and intellectual, for example, as well as physical and economic. Saying, then, that reason is inherently "practical" is not intended to reduce its activity to the pursuit of crassly egotistical and materialistic ends.

It is out of such an understanding of the human being that James designated his philosophy as *pragmatic*, a term that looks to its Greek origins in the notion of *pragma*, "action." By means of this designation he wished to emphasize that intellectual insight is *always situated* within a deep and indissoluble union between the life of thought and the life of the whole person actively immersed in a concrete world at a particular time and in a particular place. The term *pragmatism*, then, was intended to enshrine James's central conviction that human rationality and the concrete processes of actually living in the world are inseparable; understanding is not an immutable, timeless mirror of an unchanging reality but is a fluid, intellectual relation with the world arising out of purposeful living.

James realized full well that such an emphasis on utility cuts against the grain of the usual vocabulary about truth, which depicts truth as having to do not with "working" but with accurately "picturing" or mirroring the world outside the mind.[2] He often accepted such picturing language but pressed his readers to inquire into its experiential origins. Such language obviously cannot come from an intellectual comparison of what is believed about the world with the world outside the believer, for no one can get outside the mental world in order to make such a comparison. Confidence that knowledge in some manner objectively represents the extramental world, James concluded, is closely associated with the life of *action* that spontaneously generates a felt union of agent and world. It is the failure of certain conceptions in the midst of such activity to bring about anticipated results, James thought, that raises doubts about the representational accuracy of those conceptions, while it is the success of other conceptions in bringing about their anticipated results that inculcates confidence in them.

Truth, then, is what *works,* to use James's famous phrase. For example, the claim that the rocket theory produced by General Dynamics is true (or that Thomas Merton's spirituality truthfully depicts the inner life) is essentially rooted in anticipating or discovering through actual experience that they do or do not facilitate an efficacious form of living under the specific circumstances in which they are applicable, whether these circumstances have to do with orbiting the earth or with seeking God. Because of this link between reason and human aspirations, moreover, it is not ultimately possible, in James's view, to separate knowing from valuing. Knowledge involves the recognition of what is valuable for the person, what is *good* for the person under specific circumstances.

It is important to emphasize the communitarian nature of James's thought. James describes truth as "funded," drawing thereby upon an analogy between the truths held by a community and the community's monetary currency, both of which rely on collective confidence. Truth, like an economic system, has a deeply social character; it is not up to, or even within the capacity of, the individual to reinvent it or to tailor it exclusively to his or her individual self-interests. Rather, the lessons of concrete experience over many generations enter into the cultural ethos of a community and are passed on through the community's language, traditions, practices, and mores. Most of what the members of any culture believe to be true is a function of such enculturation, a function of believing the instruction of trusted persons. But such trusted persons' convictions are in turn related to other persons' convictions, including the convictions of generations now long passed. Truth "builds up" in a community, says James, like the rings of a tree. Because of this long and tested historical and cultural experience that lies behind conventionally accepted truths, it is appropriate, says James, that such truths be accorded respect and the benefit of the doubt. On the other hand, however, realizing that many widely accepted truths in the past have turned out to be erroneous, the possibility of inadequacy on the part of any particular present truth must be left open. James is a fallibilist; that is, he thinks error is possible.

Notwithstanding such fallibilism, it would be seriously inaccurate to construe James's insistence upon a close link between truth and utility as entailing subjectivistically that it is up to the individual to make the world anything he or she pleases. There is a distinctive objectivist core in James's philosophy. Time and again he depicts the world as *resisting* the wishes, aspirations, and beliefs of individuals and even of the community. What the world is, independently of what one may want or selfishly desire, will make itself known, insists James, often contrary to the individual's desires and intentions. "Woe to him," James warns ominously, who makes of the world anything he pleases. While the subjectivity of personal involvement in the world is always the *medium* through which the world is known, it is nevertheless the world which is known through, albeit within the limitations of, that medium.

This objectivist thread in James's philosophy also emerges in his account of *a priori* knowledge, that is, knowledge we have independently of experience. It is true that, for James, conceptual systems of mathematics, logic, ethics, religion, and so on have deeply subjective origins, arising out of the highly inventive mental capacities of the human being that are exercised in the context of purposeful living. In James's account of the attempted application of these systems to the world, however, a distinctive objectivist side of his account appears. Having invented such systems, human beings thereupon see if they will "fit" the world. The world, says James, "resists" certain of these applications and "accepts" others. A straight line, for example, "allows itself" to be described as running from east to west as well as from west to east. Unlike the tree or the earthworm, however, it does not admit of an organic description that the biologist might apply to living beings. To say that the application of a certain concept to the line *works* is to say that that particular feature of the world admits of being meaningfully described in such terms. Overall, then, what is preeminently characteristic of James's description of the human person as a knower is a distinctive integration of subjectivity and objectivity.

James's foregoing convictions regarding human beings' capacity to know underwrite one of the most distinctive features of his philosophy, a feature that greatly affects his approach to the human person. James's philosophy insists that experience in *all* the rich, bewildering complexity to which the blending of subjectivity and objectivity gives rise, be the touchstone of philosophy; that a consultation of *no less than* that full range of complexity is imperative in the development of philosophy. For James, this means refusing to think only in terms of abstractions at the price of ignoring the teeming diversity of actual, concrete reality. It means no less, however, refusing to think only in terms of such concrete diversity when that diversity points beyond itself to philosophical truths. Thus, one finds in James's writing from his early days the presence of scientific criticisms of philosophers for their neglect of empirical attention to the concrete world, and also philosophical criticisms of empirical scientists for their neglect of more abstract truths.

James fought tenaciously against the confinement of truth to either science or philosophy, insisting that the mysterious human capacity to know the world simultaneously as "one-and-many" required allegiance to both the abstract theoretical unity available to human beings through their capacity to form universal concepts, and also allegiance to the concrete "manyness" of experience available through their immersion in a world of particulars, a manyness from which so often emerge exceptions to human generalizations. If this imperative of attending scrupulously to both particularity and universality entails that any present grasp of truth is inherently tentative and fallible, James would say, then such consequences have to be accepted. If it means that comprehensiveness of understanding has to be postponed to the indefinite future or even to be surrendered completely, that too has to be accepted. In either case, such tentativeness would be demanded by the careful observer's recognition of a surpassing richness in reality that at least temporarily if not permanently eludes full intelligibility. When reading James's account of selfhood, ask yourself whether his position reflects this open-endedness. Ask yourself, as well, whether such open-endedness would necessarily be a deficiency in a philosophical quest of this kind.

■ ■ ■

Notes

1. C. H. Seigfried, *William James's Radical Reconstruction of Philosophy* (Albany, N.Y., 1990).
2. The student may wish to check Richard Rorty's brief comments about the "spectator theory of knowledge" in J. P. Murphy, *Pragmatism: From Peirce to Davidson* (Boulder, Colo., and Oxford, 1990), 1–5, or his more extended work in *Philosophy and the Mirror of Nature* (Princeton, 1979). See also C. G. Prado, *The Limits of Pragmatism* (Atlantic Highlands, N.J., 1987), 1–21.

SELECTIONS FROM JAMES

■ ■ ■

The Consciousness of Self

Let us begin with the Self in its widest acceptation, and follow it up to its most delicate and subtle form, advancing from the study of the empirical Ego, as the Germans call it, to that of the pure Ego.

The Empirical Self or Me

The Empirical Self of each of us is all that he is tempted to call by the name of *me*. But it is clear that between what a man calls *me* and what he simply calls *mine* the line is difficult to draw. We feel and act about certain things that are ours very much as we feel and act about ourselves. Our fame, our children, the work of our hands, may be as dear to us as our bodies are, and arouse the same feelings and the same acts of reprisal if attacked. And our bodies themselves, are they simply ours, or are they *us*? Certainly men have been ready to disown their very bodies and to regard them as mere vestures, or even as prisons of clay from which they should some day be glad to escape.

We see then that we are dealing with a fluctuating material. The same object being sometimes treated as a part of me, at other times as simply mine, and then again as if I had nothing to do with it at all. *In its widest possible sense, however, a man's self is the sum total of all that he CAN call his,* not only his body and his psychic powers, but his clothes and his house, his wife and children, his ancestors and friends, his reputation and works, his lands and horses, and yacht and bank-account. All these things give him the same emotions. If they wax and prosper, he feels triumphant; if they dwindle and die away, he feels cast down—not necessarily in the same degree for each thing, but in much the same way for all. . . .

1. *The constituents of the Self* may be divided into four classes, those which make up respectively—
   (a) The Material Self;
   (b) The Social Self;
   (c) The Spiritual Self; and
   (d) The Pure Ego.

(a) The body is the innermost part of the Material Self in each of us; and certain parts of the body seem more intimately ours than the rest. The clothes come next. The old saying that the human person is composed of three parts—soul, body, and clothes—is more than a joke. . . . Next, our immediate family is a part of ourselves. Our father and mother, our wife and babes, are bone of our bone and flesh of our flesh. When they die, a part of our very selves is gone. If they do anything wrong, it is our shame. If they are insulted, our anger flashes forth as readily as if we stood in their place. Our home comes next. Its scenes are part of our life; its aspects awaken the tenderest feelings of affection; and we do not easily forgive the stranger who, in visiting it, finds fault with its arrangements or treats it with contempt. All these different things are the objects of instinctive preferences coupled with the most important practical interests of life. We all have a blind impulse to watch over our body, to deck it with clothing of an ornamental sort, to cherish parents, wife, and babes, and to find for ourselves a home of our own which we may live in and "improve."

An equally instinctive impulse drives us to collect property; and the collections thus made become, with different degrees of intimacy, parts of our empirical selves. The parts of our wealth most intimately ours are those which are saturated with our labor. There are few men who would not feel personally annihilated if a life-long construction of their hands or brains—say an entomological collection or an extensive work in manuscript—were suddenly swept away. The miser feels similarly towards his gold, and although it is true that a part of our depression at the loss of possessions is due to our feeling that we must now go without certain goods that we expected the possessions to bring in their train, yet in every case there remains, over and above this, a sense of the shrinkage of our personality, a partial conversion of ourselves to nothingness, which is a psychological phenomenon by itself. . . .

(b) A man's Social Self is the recognition which he gets from his mates. We are not only gregarious animals, liking to be in sight of our fellows, but we have an innate propensity to get ourselves noticed, and noticed favorably, by our kind. No more fiendish punishment could be devised, were such a thing physically possible, than that one should be turned loose in society and remain absolutely unnoticed by all the members thereof. If no one turned round when we entered, answered when we spoke, or minded what we did, but if every person we met "cut us dead," and acted as if we were non-existing things, a kind of rage and impotent despair would ere long well up in us, from which the cruellest bodily tortures would be a relief; for these would make us feel that, however bad might be our plight, we had not sunk to such a depth as to be unworthy of attention at all.

Properly speaking, a man has as many social selves as there are individuals who recognize him and carry an image of him in their mind. To wound any one of these his images is to wound him. But as the individuals who carry the images fall naturally into classes, we may practically say that he has as many different social selves as there are distinct groups of persons about whose opinion he cares. He generally shows a different side of himself to each of these different groups. Many a youth who is demure enough before his parents and teachers, swears and swaggers like a pirate among his "tough" young friends. We do not show ourselves to our children as to our club-companions, to our customers as to the laborers we employ, to our own masters and employers as to our intimate friends. From this there results what practically is a division of the man into several selves; and this may be a discordant split-ting, as where one is afraid to let one set of his acquaintances know him as he is elsewhere; or it may be a perfectly harmo-nious division of labor, as where one tender to his children is stern to the soldiers or prisoners under his command.

The most peculiar social self which one is apt to have is in the mind of the person one is in love with. The good or bad fortunes of this self cause the most intense elation and dejec-tion—unreasonable enough as measured by every other stan-dard than that of the organic feeling of the individual. To his own consciousness he is not, so long as this particular social self fails to get recognition, and when it is recognized his con-tentment passes all bounds.

A man's *fame*, good or bad, and his *honor* or dishonor, are names for one of his social selves. The particular social self of a man called his honor is usually the result of one of those splittings of which we have spoken. It is his image in the eyes of his own "set," which exalts or condemns him as he con-forms or not to certain requirements that may not be made of one in another walk of life. Thus a layman may abandon a city infected with cholera; but a priest or a doctor would think such an act incompatible with his honor. A soldier's honor requires him to fight or to die under circumstances where another man can apologize or run away with no stain upon his social self. A judge, a statesman, are in like manner debarred by the honor of their cloth from entering into pecu-niary relations perfectly honorable to persons in private life. Nothing is commoner than to hear people discriminate between their different selves of this sort: "As a man I pity you, but as an official I must show you no mercy; as a politi-cian I regard him as an ally, but as a moralist I loathe him"; etc., etc. What may be called "club-opinion" is one of the very strongest forces in life. The thief must not steal from other thieves; the gambler must pay his gambling-debts, though he pay no other debts in the world.

(c) By the Spiritual Self, so far as it belongs to the Empirical Me, I mean a man's inner or subjective being, his psychic faculties or dispositions, taken concretely; not the bare principle of personal Unity, or "pure" Ego, which remains still to be discussed. These psychic dispositions are the most enduring and intimate part of the self, that which we most verily seem to be. We take a purer self-satisfaction when we think of our ability to argue and discriminate, of our moral sensibility and conscience, of our indomitable will, than when we survey any of our other possessions.

Now this subjective life of ours, distinguished as such so clearly from the objects known by its means, may, as aforesaid, be taken by us in a concrete or in an abstract way. Of the concrete way I will say nothing just now, except that the actual "section" of the stream will ere long, in our discussion of the nature of the principle of unity in consciousness, play a very important part. The abstract way claims our attention first. If the stream as a whole is identified with the Self far more than any outward thing, a certain portion of the stream abstracted from the rest is so identified in an altogether peculiar degree, and is felt by all men as a sort of innermost centre within the circle, of sanctuary within the citadel, constituted by the subjective life as a whole. Compared with this element of the stream, the other parts, even of the subjective life, seem transient external possessions, of which each in turn can be disowned, whilst that which disowns them remains. Now, what is this self of all the other selves?

Probably all men would describe it in much the same way up to a certain point. They would call it the active element in all consciousness, saying that whatever qualities a man's feelings may possess, or whatever content his thought may include, there is a spiritual something in him which seems to go out to meet these qualities and contents, whilst they seem to come in to be received by it. It is what welcomes or rejects. It presides over the perception of sensations, and by giving or withholding its assent it influences the movements they tend to arouse. It is the home of interest—not the pleasant or the painful, not even pleasure or pain, as such, but that within us to which pleasure and pain, the pleasant and the painful, speak. It is the source of effort and attention, and the place from which appear to emanate the fiats of the will. . . .

One may, I think, . . . believe that all men must single out, from the rest of what they call themselves, some central principle of which each would recognize the foregoing to be a fair general description—accurate enough, at any rate, to denote what is meant—and keep it unconfused with other things. The moment, however, they came to closer quarters with it, trying to define more accurately its precise nature, we should find opinions beginning to diverge. Some would say that it is a simple active substance, the soul, of which they are thus conscious; others, that it is nothing but a fiction, the imaginary being denoted by the pronoun I; and between these extremes of opinion all sorts of intermediaries would be found. . . .

It may be all that Transcendentalists say it is, and all that Empiricists say it is into the bargain, but it is at any rate no mere *"ens rationis,"* cognized only in an intellectual way, and no mere summation of memories or mere sound of a word in our ears. It is something with which we also have direct sensible acquaintance, and which is as fully present at any moment of consciousness in which it is present as in a whole lifetime of such moments. When, just now, it was called an abstraction, that did not mean that, like some general notion, it could not be presented in a particular experience. It only meant that in the stream of consciousness it never was found all alone. But when it is found, it is felt, just as the body is felt, the feeling of which is also an abstraction, because never is the body felt all alone, but always together with other things. . . .

But when I forsake such general descriptions and grapple with particulars, coming to the closest possible quarters with the facts, it is difficult for me to detect in the activity any purely spiritual element at all. Whenever my introspective glance succeeds in turning round quickly enough to catch one of these manifestations of spontaneity in the act, all it can ever feel distinctly is some bodily process, for the most part taking place within the head. . . .

In a sense, then, it may be truly said that, in one person at least, the "Self of selves," when carefully examined, is found to consist mainly of the collection of these peculiar motions in the head or between the head and throat. I do not for a moment say that this is all it consists of, for I fully realize how desperately hard is introspection in this field. But I feel quite sure that these cephalic motions are the portions of my innermost activity of which I am most distinctly aware. If the dim portions which I cannot yet define should prove to be like unto these distinct portions in me, and I like other men, it would follow that our entire feeling of spiritual activity, or what commonly passes by that name, is really a feeling of bodily activities whose exact nature is by most men overlooked. . . .

(d) The Pure Ego. Our decks are consequently cleared for the struggle with that pure principle of personal identity which has met us all along our preliminary exposition, but which we have always shied from and treated as a difficulty to be postponed. Ever since Hume's time, it has been justly regarded as the most puzzling puzzle with which psychology has to deal; and whatever view one may espouse, one has to hold his position against heavy odds.

The Sense of Personal Identity

Each of us when he awakens says "Here's the same old self again," just as he says "Here's the same old bed, the same old room, the same old world."

The sense of our own personal identity . . . is exactly like any one of our other perceptions of sameness among phenomena. It is a conclusion grounded either on the resemblance in a fundamental respect, or on the continuity before the mind, of the phenomena compared.

And it must not be taken to mean more than these grounds warrant, or treated as a sort of metaphysical or absolute Unity in which all differences are overwhelmed. The past and present selves compared are the same just so far as they *are* the same, and not farther. A uniform feeling of "warmth," of bodily existence (or an equally uniform feeling of pure psychic energy?), pervades them all; and this is what gives them a *generic* unity, and makes them the same in *kind*. But this generic unity coexists with generic differences just as real as the unity. And if from the one point of view they are one self, from others they are as truly not one but many selves. And similarly of the attribute of continuity: it gives its own kind of unity to the self—that of mere connectedness, or unbrokenness, a perfectly definite phenomenal thing—but it gives not a jot or tittle more. And this unbrokenness in the stream of selves, like the unbrokenness in an exhibition of "dissolving views," in no wise implies any farther unity or contradicts any amount of plurality in other respects.

And accordingly we find that, where the resemblance and the continuity are no longer felt, the sense of personal identity goes too. We hear from our parents various anecdotes about our infant years, but we do not appropriate them as we do our own memories. Those breaches of decorum awaken no blush, those bright sayings no self-complacency. That child is a foreign creature with which our present self is no more identified in feeling than it is with some stranger's living child to-day. Why? Partly because great time-gaps break up all these early years—we cannot ascend to them by continuous memories—and partly because no representation of how the child *felt* comes up with the stories. We know what he said and did; but no sentiment of his little body, of his emotions, of his psychic strivings as they felt to him, comes up to contribute an element of warmth and intimacy to the narrative we hear, and the main bond of union with our present self thus disappears. It is the same with certain of our dimly recollected experiences. We hardly know whether to appropriate them or to disown them as fancies, or things read or heard and not lived through. Their animal heat has evaporated; the feelings that accompanied them are so lacking in the recall, or so different from those we now enjoy, that no judgment of identity can be decisively cast.

Resemblance among the parts of a continuum of feelings (especially bodily feelings), experienced along with things widely different in all other regards, *thus constitutes the real and verifiable "personal identity" which we feel.* There is no other identity than this in the "stream" of subjective consciousness which we described in the last chapter. Its parts differ, but under all their differences they are knit in these two ways; and if either way of knitting disappears, the sense of unity departs. If a man wakes up some fine day unable to recall any of his past experiences, so that he has to learn his biography afresh, or if he only recalls the facts of it in a cold abstract way as things that he is sure once happened; or if, without this loss of memory, his bodily and spiritual habits all change during the night, each organ giving a different tone, and the act of thought becoming aware of itself in a different way; he *feels*, and he *says*, that he is a changed person. He disowns his former me, gives himself a new name, identifies his present life with nothing from out of the older time. Such cases are not rare in mental pathology. . . .

[Nevertheless] common-sense insists that the unity of all the selves is not a mere appearance of similarity or continuity, ascertained after the fact. She is sure that it involves a real belonging to a real Owner, to a pure spiritual entity of some kind. Relation to this entity is what makes the self's constituents stick together as they do for thought.

The "Soul" of Metaphysics and the "Transcendental Ego" of the Kantian Philosophy are, as we shall soon see, but attempts to satisfy this urgent demand of common-sense. But, for a time at least, we can still express without any such hypotheses that appearance of never-lapsing ownership for which common-sense contends. . . .

Each pulse of cognitive consciousness, each Thought, dies away and is replaced by another. The other, among the things it knows, knows its own predecessor, and finding it "warm," in the way we have described, greets it, saying "Thou art *mine*, and part of the same self with me." Each later Thought, knowing and including thus the Thoughts which went before, is the final receptacle—and appropriating them is the final owner—of all that they contain and own. Each Thought is thus born an owner, and dies owned, transmitting whatever it realized as its Self to its own later proprietor. As Kant says, it is as if elastic balls were to have not only motion but knowledge of it, and a first ball were to transmit both its motion and its consciousness to a second, which took both up into *its* consciousness and passed them to a third, until the last ball held all that the other balls had held, and realized it as its own. It is this trick which the nascent thought has of immediately taking up the expiring thought and "adopting" it, which is the foundation of the appropriation of most of the remoter constituents of the self. Who owns the last self owns the self before the last, for what possesses the possessor possesses the possessed.

But the Thought never is an object in its own hands, it never appropriates or disowns itself. It appropriates *to* itself, it is the actual focus of accretion, the hook from which the chain of past selves dangles, planted firmly in the Present, which alone passes for real, and thus keeping the chain from being a purely ideal thing. Anon the hook itself will drop into the past with all it carries, and then be treated as an object and appropriated by a new Thought in the new present which will serve as living hook in turn. The present moment of consciousness is thus . . . the darkest in the whole series. It may feel its own immediate existence—we have all along admitted the possibility of this, hard as it is by direct introspection to ascertain the fact—but nothing can be known *about* it till it be dead and gone. Its appropriations are therefore less to *itself* than to the most intimately felt *part of its present Object, the body, and the central adjustments,* which accompany the act of thinking, in the head. *These are the real nucleus of our personal identity,* and it is their actual existence, realized as a solid present fact, which makes us say "As sure *as I exist,* those past facts were part of myself." They are the kernel to which the *represented* parts of the Self are assimilated, accreted, and knit on; and even were Thought entirely unconscious of itself in the act of thinking, these "warm" parts of its present object would be a firm basis on which the consciousness of personal identity would rest. Such consciousness, then, as a psychologic fact, can be fully described without supposing any other agent than a succession of perishing thoughts, endowed with the functions of appropriation and rejection, and of which some can know and appropriate or reject objects already known, appropriated, or rejected by the rest. . . .

The passing Thought then seems to be the Thinker; and though there *may* be another non-phenomenal Thinker behind that, so far we do not seem to need him to express the facts. But we cannot definitively make up our mind about him until we have heard the reasons that have historically been used to prove his reality.

■ ■ ■

The Question of "Free Will"

The fact is that the question of free-will is insoluble on strictly psychologic grounds. After a certain amount of effort of attention has been given to an idea, it is manifestly impossible to tell whether either more or less of it *might* have been given or not. To tell that, we should have to ascend to the antecedents of the effort, and, defining them with mathematical exactitude, prove, by laws of which we have not at present even an inkling, that the only amount of sequent effort which could *possibly* comport with them was the precise amount that actually came. Such measurements, whether of psychic or of neural quantities, and such deductive reasonings as this method of proof implies, will surely be forever beyond human reach. No serious psychologist or physiologist will venture even to suggest a notion of how they might be practically made. Had one no motives drawn from elsewhere to make one partial to either solution, one might easily leave the matter undecided. But a psychologist cannot be expected to be thus impartial, having a great motive in favor of determinism. He wants to build a *Science;* and a Science is a system of fixed relations. Wherever there are independent variables, there Science stops. So far, then, as our volitions may be independent variables, a scientific psychology must ignore that fact, and treat of them only so far as they are fixed functions. In other words, she must deal with the *general laws* of volition exclusively; with the impulsive and inhibitory character of ideas; with the nature of their appeals to the attention; with the conditions under which effort may arise, etc.; but not with the precise amounts of effort, for these, if our wills be free, are impossible to compute. She thus abstracts from free-will, without necessarily denying its existence. Practically, however, such abstraction is not distinguished from rejection; and most actual psychologists have no hesitation in denying that free-will exists.

For ourselves, we can hand the free-will controversy over to metaphysics. Psychology will surely never grow refined enough to discover, in the case of any individual's decision, a discrepancy between her scientific calculations and the fact. Her prevision will never foretell whether the effort be completely predestinate or not, the way in which each individual emergency is resolved. Psychology will be psychology, and Science science, as much as ever (as much and no more) in this world, whether free-will be true in it or not.

■ ■ ■

The Ethical Importance
of the Phenomenon of Effort

But whilst eliminating the question about the amount of our effort as one which psychology will never have a practical call to decide, I must say one word about the extraordinarily intimate and important character which the phenomenon of effort assumes in our own eyes as individual men. Of course we measure ourselves by many standards. Our strength and our intelligence, our wealth and even our good luck, are things which warm our heart and make us feel ourselves a match for life. But deeper than all such things, and able to suffice unto itself without them, is the sense of the amount of effort which we can put forth. Those are, after all, but effects, products, and reflections of the outer world within. But the effort seems to belong to an altogether different realm, as if it were the substantive thing which we *are*, and those were but externals which we *carry*. If the "searching of our heart and reins" be the purpose of this human drama, then what is sought seems to be what effort we can make. He who can make none is but a shadow; he who can make much is a hero. The huge world that girdles us about puts all sorts of questions to us, and tests us in all sorts of ways. Some of the tests we meet by actions that are easy, and some of the questions we answer in articulately formulated words. But the deepest question that is ever asked admits of no reply but the dumb turning of the will and tightening of our heart-strings as we say, *"Yes, I will even have it so!"* When a dreadful object is presented, or when life as a whole turns up its dark abysses to our view, then the worthless ones among us lose their hold on the situation altogether, and either escape from its difficulties by averting their attention or, if they cannot do that, collapse into yielding masses of plaintiveness and fear. The effort required for facing and consenting to such objects is beyond their power to make. But the heroic mind does differently. To it, too, the objects are sinister and dreadful, unwelcome, incompatible with wished-for things. But it can face them if necessary, without for that losing its hold upon the rest of life. The world thus finds in the heroic man its worthy match and

316

mate; and the effort which he is able to put forth to hold himself erect and keep his heart unshaken is the direct measure of his worth and function in the game of human life. He can *stand* this Universe. He can meet it and keep up his faith in it in presence of those same features which lay his weaker brethren low. He can still find a zest in it, not by "ostrich-like forgetfulness," but by pure inward willingness to face it with these deterrent objects there. And hereby he makes himself one of the masters and the lords of life. He must be counted with henceforth; he forms a part of human destiny. Neither in the theoretic nor in the practical sphere do we care for, or go for help to, those who have no head for risks, or sense for living on the perilous edge. Our religious life lies more than it used to, our practical life lies less, on the perilous edge. But just as our courage is so often a reflex of another's courage, so our faith is apt to be a faith in some one else's faith. We draw new life from the heroic example. The prophet has drunk more deeply than anyone of the cup of bitterness, but his countenance is so unshaken and he speaks such mighty words of cheer that his will becomes our will, and our life is kindled at his own.

Thus not only our morality but our religion, so far as the latter is deliberate, depend on the effort which we can make. *"Will you or won't you have it so?"* is the most probing question we are ever asked; we are asked it every hour of the day, and about the largest as well as the smallest, the most theoretical as well as the most practical, things. We answer by *consents or non-consents* and not by words. What wonder that these dumb responses should seem our deepest organs of communication with the nature of things! What wonder if the effort demanded by them be the measure of our worth as men! What wonder if the amount [of effort we put forth] were the one strictly underived and original contribution which we make to the world!

Extracted from W. James, *Principles of Psychology* (1890), vol. 1, chap. 10, and *Psychology: Briefer Course* (1892).

COMMENTARY

■ ■ ■

Analysis of the Selections

In these readings from James, one can see the presence of his philosophical priorities, as described earlier in the introduction to his work. In his pursuit of self, James vigilantly focuses from the outset not upon philosophical disputes but upon what experience of self concretely yields, upon "just how this central nucleus of the Self may *feel*"; upon the "palpitating" awareness of things, the dynamic process of "welcoming or opposing, appropriating or disowning, striving with or against, saying yes or no"; upon the "*whole* fact" of inner life, to use one of his favored expressions. He searches carefully, in laying the groundwork of philosophical speculation, for the presence of conventionally neglected elements of the experience of selfhood, and also for the presence of elements erroneously imputed to experience on ideological grounds.

Such a concrete point of departure causes him to reject an approach that begins with an abstract notion of the individual, substantial self standing apart from the real world, and so to reject as well the commonplace division of the human person into *who* he or she is and what *belongs* to him or her (e.g., he *is* generous; she *has* two arms). Appealing, rather, to the reader's concrete experience of links between the sense of selfhood and the condition of one's body, family, or even possessions, as well as of psychological states, James depicts selfhood in terms of the wide range of relations between a human being and the universe of persons and objects with which he or she is in constant contact: the body, the artifacts that one has made, possessions, children, reputation, and more. Taking all these into account he offers an initial, broad definition of the person as "the sum total of all that he *can* call his." Only thereafter does he narrow his focus by considering the self in its material, social, and spiritual dimensions and then, finally, as Pure Ego.

As *material*, the self exists not only in and through the body but through extensions of bodiliness such as the garments with which one presents oneself to the world, through artifacts and possessions that, being "saturated with our labour," are material manifestations of the self, and through the family with which one shares a common physical heritage, a present standing in the human community, and an identity-shaping future involvement.

As *social*, personhood involves multiple self-images and a wide repertoire of distinctive behaviors geared toward the constituencies with which one has ongoing contact: parents, children, spouses, peers, employers, and so on. Of necessity, not all such selves can coexist harmoniously and so some must be sacrificed to others—the capitalist to the saint, for instance, or the athlete to the party-goer. The decisions involved in this process cause some such selves to fade into insignificance while others acquire increasing prominence. The distinctive priorities of the dominant self-images shape, in turn, one's relation to the world. The committed athlete, for example, may eye with keen interest or jealousy the physique of his or her colleague of superior strength while remaining completely oblivious to another companion's superior intellect. As with bodiliness, however, so here, reputation is not experienced as something wholly *external* to an impervious inner core of identity, but as inseparable from it. Identity can be built up or badly shaken by physiological, psychological, and social events, as one discovers through the jarring experiences of serious illness, severe family turmoil, or public assaults upon one's reputation.

By the *spiritual* self James means primarily "psychic dispositions," intellectual, moral, and volitional. Inquiry into this dimension of self moves toward the "innermost centre within the circle . . . constituted by the subjective life as a whole," raising the question: "What is this self of all the other selves?" Such a self, many would say, is a "spiritual something" that presides over the wider range of psychological activities; it is the "home of interest," the home of attention.

James's commitment to a close consultation of the full range of experience in the foregoing domains creates an initial, superficial resemblance between his position and that of Hume. With Hume, James finds no isolatable self objectively available to introspection. James soon goes his own way, however, charging Hume with having read experience incorrectly. The key problem with Hume's analysis, thinks James, is Hume's having failed to recognize how experience is transformed by being reflected upon. In its most basic form, "pure experience," for James, is undifferentiated and immediate, lacking a sense of division between self and world or between self and itself. In order to live, however, such immediate experience must be structured, and it is the purpose of the activity of conceptualization and reflection to introduce structure and compartmentalization into the superabundant and seamless character of pure experience. This structuring of experience involves a radical alteration of the basic experience itself, however. Innumerable sensory impressions, phenomena, and relations that are not immediately relevant to one's present state and purposes are screened out. As I resolutely head for my car in the parking lot, for instance, I may not even hear the airplane overhead or notice the students lounging on the nearby hillside.

What is particularly significant vis-à-vis the pursuit of selfhood, for James, is that in this process of conceptually structuring pure experience, the dynamism of such experience is lost, for an attempt to objectify such dynamism through introspective analysis is "like seizing a spinning top to catch its motion, or trying to turn up the gas quickly enough to see how the darkness looks."[1] The loss of such dynamism involves the loss of the felt unity of self and world in pure experience as well as the loss of an immediate nonconceptual awareness of self of a form that James calls direct "knowledge-by-acquaintance."

Finding no such living relations in experience as reflected upon, Hume threw the baby of selfhood out with the substantialist bath water, laments James. As advocates of a theory of soul "say the self is nothing but Unity, . . . Hume says it is nothing but Diversity." Hume's philosophical preoccupation with analytically seeking some kind of necessary connection among the parts of the stream of consciousness, James thinks, compromised his powers of philosophical reflection, blinding him to the striking relations that do suffuse the diverse parts of pure experience, and particularly to the "core of sameness, running through the ingredients of the Self." Having reflectively chopped up the stream of consciousness, removing from it thereby its living unity and continuity, Hume had had to resort to "recurrences" and "resemblances," and to acts of intellectual synthesis in the vain attempt to knit back together what he had conceptually unravelled into an assortment of discreet, atomistically separate strands.

The deep sense of selfhood that is typical of most people's experience, however, says James—the sense of "I" and "mine"—cannot be represented by such a Humean "assembly" of discreet parts of the psychic life. There is in addition to, and suffusing, the Humean assembly of psychological elements, says James, a *feeling* of continuity that constitutes the sense of self. While common sense awareness of such feeling has underwritten many a theory of soul, transcendental ego, and the like, says James, he resists speculation about such views in deference to continued close analysis of the phenomena that give rise to those theories.

The feeling at the core of selfhood is deeply indebted, James thinks, to certain physiological experiences that most philosophers who lack his medical training had neglected. It is also indebted to a particular characteristic of consciousness. If one directs reflection not toward a hoped-for objectifiable self but toward immediate experience, one finds a special relation between the *present* moment of conscious life—to which James commonly refers as "Thought"—and the moments of conscious life that have passed by and are now gone. The present living moment of Thought is not just another occurrence in an atomistic succession of discreet psychological events. If scrutinized closely, James suggests, rather, the present moment of Thought discloses itself as capable of *taking up* the past stream of conscious life into itself; of "adopting" preceding but now-expired states; of making what was contained in those previous states its own; of inheriting their mantle and carrying forward the personal character that conscious life had acquired cumulatively through the complex process of living. The present moment of living Thought is capable of creating not just an intellectual synthesis (as Kant [1728–1804] said) but a subjective feeling of being the *same* person. What Hume had missed in experience, James contends, then, and what James says is available to the reader's attentive reflection, is this unique dynamic capacity of present Thought to *take up* consciousness's past into itself, its capacity to be *"cognizant* and *appropriative* of the old."

Clinical information to which James the psychologist was privy encouraged him to hold onto such a view. Certain medical conditions erode the capacity of consciousness to sustain this adoptive activity, impairing the integrative process and occasioning thereby the collapse of a sense of personal identity. Much less dramatically, even the normal developmental processes in human beings create long-term discontinuity of identity. At a certain mature age, for example, it becomes difficult to identify with some experiences that one may have had many years prior. Anecdotal reports about one's childhood behavior sometimes have a peculiarly distant feel, as though they are about another person. One can intellectually accept them as part of one's history, but if this is done without the *feeling* of their being one's own, James points out, they do not enter into the sense of selfhood. Thus, he argues, such feeling, and not just intellectual integration, lies at the core of the experience of self.

Whether in the foregoing dramatic or in normal cases, there is a demonstrable precariousness in human identity, James points out, which, he thinks, must figure prominently in any viable philosophy of the person. The frailty and fluidity of selfhood did not seem to him to be well represented by the relative invulnerability of self suggested by transcendental theories of selfhood involving a simple unchangeable soul or a remote Transcendental Ego. Such theories, James argued, were not adequate in this regard. Neither were they necessary to account for the sense of mysteriousness of self. Self is experienced as mysterious, he says, because present Thought eludes being grasped as an *object*. "Nothing can be known *about* [present Thought that embodies the sense of self] . . . until it be dead and gone." But *of* the elusive activity of such Thought there can be a genuine, intuitive awareness rooted in the immediate sense of physiological and of psychological events, a true "knowledge-by-acquaintance" that relieves the philosopher of the necessity of positing another philosophical entity behind this self to know it.

Whether the foregoing account of the person does justice to the experience of self is up to the student to assess. It has been subject to thoughtful analysis, especially regarding the "adoptive" capacity of present thought, the prominence of the role of "feeling," and other issues.[2] In pursuing the question of its adequacy, however, Jamesian philosophy would press two points above all others: Are there aspects of the *actual* experience of selfhood that would demand adding to this theory of thought a soul or ego? And, if there are, *exactly* what explanatory role do such entities have in relation to these additional phenomena? In the remainder of chapter 10 of the *Principles*, James himself puts these questions to prominent philosophical theories that have proposed such positions.

The foregoing reflections by James are only part of a larger, incomplete picture, for his analysis of Thought ultimately lacks philosophical resolution. As he confronts the mysterious phenomenon of "cognizing," which he has described in terms of Thought, James rejects *both* standard monistic and dualistic theories (that is, that the self is composed of *one* element or of *two* elements, respectively). As to materialistic monism, he says: "The 'Thought' which we have relied upon in our account *is* not the brain, closely as it seems connected with it." As John Wild has pointed out, James "clearly rejects the charge of materialism that has often been raised against his own position."[3] On the other hand, however, James finds a dualistic appeal to an immaterial soul transcending the body to be unhelpful, for such appeal, in his view, only introduces an entity that is too mysterious to explain anything but which imposes the weighty demand of producing explanations of it. In the end, for James, whether one appeals monistically to brain, or dualistically to soul in addition to body, "the great difficulty is in seeing how a thing can cognize *anything*."

The volitional capacities of the human person as well—the freedom of which James defended vigorously all his life—are every bit as perplexing to him as is the activity of cognizing. As the final brief excerpt from his writings brings out, freedom, while related to outside stimulation, motives, and character is, in the end, "independent" of these and, as such, stands outside the purview of any monistically materialistic analysis. Volitional effort is experienced as belonging to "an altogether different realm," he says; it is the seat of perhaps the only "strictly *underived*" contribution that the human being can make to the world in the form of moral effort. While James is unwilling to account for such activity dualistically with a theory of soul, neither is he altogether at ease with the monistic alternatives. In the end, his account remains open.

■ ■ ■

Philosophical and Religious Critique

James's overall account of self is incomplete. One would not be without justification in criticizing such incompleteness. Groping vainly for some kind of unconventional mixture of prevailing theories, his view could be written off as a failed exercise, however insightful may be some of the individual observations made along the way. Before minimizing the significance of his work for this reason, however, it is noteworthy that such theoretical incompleteness, in theorizing about selfhood, has distinctive echoes in the contemporary debate about the human person among Christian philosophers. In the interests of bringing out the religious significance of James's thought by aligning him with such discussions, I will pass over the more obvious religious elements of his philosophy with which his work on the person might otherwise be linked—his moral repugnance toward God's providence being used as a basis for taking a "moral holiday" from the pursuit of social justice; his installation of human "character" and its ennoblement at the heart of philosophy; his consistent defense of belief in an afterlife, and of the importance of religious experience, and so on.

One of the major challenges before Christian philosophers today is the need to formulate a response to the widespread rejection, in this century, of a recurrent dualism in Christian thought about the human person. This rejection of dualism has built upon the increasing scholarly recognition of the differences between the original Semitic cultural setting of Christianity and its subsequent adopted non-Jewish setting. Such recognition, in turn, has given rise to the recovery of a current in Jewish thought about the human person that emphasizes the person's *oneness*. The human person is one entity (monistic) and not a composite of two separate entities, soul and body (dualistic). Not only many biblical scholars of virtually all mainline denominations but also a number of contemporary Christian philosophers have sought to recover this monistic current in recent times.[4]

While rescuing distinctive monistic elements of ancient thought about the person, the recent abandonment of dualism has been achieved at a price, however. Neurophysiological categories, for example, do not lend themselves automatically to Christian beliefs regarding an interim period between death and final judgement, or identity after death, or biblical depictions of demon possession or of free will. Extensive academic discussion of John Hick's work has brought out many difficulties involved in a theory that postulates the recreation of a soulless individual after death.[5] In short, monistic theories of the person do not seem to provide all the answers.

Christian philosophers are faced with the job of trying to maintain continuity between the thought of present-day philosophy and that of Christian antiquity. That is, which contemporary philosophical view best embodies canonical Christian thought about the human person? It is important to recognize that being *continuous* with Scripture does not necessarily require that subsequent thought be *conceptually identical* with Scripture, as much modern work on the development of dogma has made very clear. Even if it were true, then, that

Scripture entirely lacked any dualism in its view of the person—a view that will be questioned below—this would not by itself preclude the possibility that some later form of philosophical dualism might be satisfactorily continuous with the early Christian tradition. The fact that the Christian dualisms developed over the centuries were not Jewish in character and are absent from Scripture, then, is not in and of itself a bad thing. There is a challenge to Christian philosophers, then, to identify what is really central in the way that the early church understood the human person, and to find a way to express this understanding clearly in contemporary terms. On the one hand, antiquity seems sometimes dualistic in its portrayal of the afterlife, for example. On the other hand, there are some features of the tradition that are strikingly monistic in character. How can contemporary philosophers do justice to both trends; how can a material body and an immaterial soul, for example, truly be united and genuinely (not just superficially) interdependent?

Thomas Aquinas stands out historically as a philosopher who was particularly aware of the need to control his use of the Greek philosophical tradition within the bounds dictated by the demands of early Christian thought. While subscribing to the existence of a soul whose nature entailed the possibility of its living in a disembodied form, he was very much aware of the Christian tradition's strong emphasis upon the centrality of bodiliness in human existence. His position attempts to graft the latter onto the former, holding that while disembodied existence is possible for the human being, it is inferior to the embodied state originally intended by God. Whether or not the Thomistic position deals adequately with corporeality is a topic of debate that surpasses the focus of this essay.[6] There is no doubt, at least, that Aquinas's doctrine of the inseparability of matter and form greatly strengthens the monistic character of Aquinas's position.

Whatever the success of Aquinas's efforts, it is crucial to recognize one particular feature of the religious tradition with which the philosophy of Aquinas and contemporary philosophy are both attempting to grapple. When all is said and done, the ancient tradition is *ambiguous,* being neither straightforwardly monistic nor straightforwardly dualistic.

The scriptural portrayal of the human person is characterized most fundamentally, rather, by a *tension* between monistic and dualistic elements that together create the ancient tradition's distinctive but ambiguous anthropology.

From the monistic side, ancient Judaism uses the Hebrew vocabulary that portrays the human as a single being in the act of running, thinking, feeling, praying, and so on. From the dualistic side, however, notwithstanding such unity, the human form of creation is singled out in *Genesis* and elsewhere as in some way more than simply body. It is uniquely the result of special divine deliberation and creative activity, and as such is capable, in the image and likeness of God, of a form of "god-like" intellectual and volitional conduct that equips it to be deputed to custodial responsibility for the earth. These capacities underwrite Paul's imputation to the human being of potential to become more than just a physical existent.

Become, however, is a key word here. For Paul, what distinguishes life "in the Spirit" from life "in the flesh" is the exercise of the unique human capacity to choose God rather than one's self as the guiding force of life. One could argue that it has been part of the function of the concept of soul in Christian history to act as a sort of "place-holder" for this unique feature of human life that, according to Scripture, somehow sets human life apart from the rest of the material order from which it is portrayed as otherwise inseparable.

Whether a philosophical entity such as soul need be posited by the Christian in order to secure this belief remains a matter of significant variation among Christian thinkers such as, for example, the aforementioned Thomists and perspectivalists. While less concerned with Christian orthodoxy than either of these groups, William James's unconventional shyness toward both monism and dualism anticipates in some ways the discussions among contemporary Christian philosophers.[7] In his own distinctive way, James tries to mine the insights of both monism and dualism. While rejecting a conventional dualism, he doubts the ability of available monisms to account for the puzzling and philosophically challenging character of cognizing, of freedom of the will, of moral intuition, and of the heroic dignity of the person that the exercise of such intuition makes possible, and of afterlife and so on.

It is up to the student to decide the degree to which James's account may contribute in whole or in part to the contemporary effort to seek continuity between ancient and contemporary thought about the person by looking beyond conventional monisms and dualisms. Perhaps his work points toward the need for further exploration of an appropriate form of what is sometimes called "double aspect" theory. In any event, one thing is clear: The effort to create a philosophical anthropology that can claim genuine continuity with the ambiguity of canonical antiquity, while at the same time answering credibly to the penetrating questions that have been put to both monism and dualism by modern philosophy, is no small task. James's characteristic strong tendency to resist conventional philosophical polarizations such as those between empiricism and rationalism, or monism and dualism, may well have a particular relevance to today's discussions of the human person among Christian philosophers faced with such a challenge.

■ ■ ■

Notes

1. J. J. McDermott, *The Writings of William James: A Comprehensive Edition* (Chicago, 1977), 37.
2. J. Wild, *The Radical Empiricism of William James* (Garden City, N.Y., 1969), 100, 113–14.
3. Ibid., 107.
4. This strand of thought can be found among "perspectivalist" authors.
5. For the location of Hick's work and his replies to critics on this subject, see S. Voss, "Understanding Eternal Life," *Faith and Philosophy* 9 (January 1992), note 18. See also J. C. Yates, "Survival as Replication," *Sophia* 27, pp. 2–9.
6. See F. C. Copleston, *Aquinas* (Penguin Books, 1961), 151–73.
7. See, for example, the criticisms of both monistic and dualistic theories in S. Voss's aforementioned article.

■ ■ ■

Further Reading

R. B. B. Lewis, *The Jameses: A Family Narrative* (New York, 1991).

J. J. McDermott, *The Writings of William James: A Comprehensive Edition* (Chicago, 1977).

C. H. Seigfried, *William James's Radical Reconstruction of Philosophy* (Albany, N.Y., 1990).

J. Wild, *The Radical Empiricism of William James* (Garden City, N.Y., 1969), chapter 4.

10

FRIEDRICH NIETZSCHE

■ ■ ■

THE HUMAN PERSON
AS WILL TO POWER

Introduction and Commentary by John J. Snyder

INTRODUCTION

Friedrich Nietzsche was a nineteenth-century thinker whose ideas have strongly influenced many contemporary philosophers and writers. A version of his philosophy, falsified by his sister for her own political gain, was used by the German Nazis to justify many of their philosophical positions. Existentialists and modern literary critics have found in his writings the basis for many of their own ideas. Even religious thinkers, familiar with his critique of Christianity, have modified their approaches to religion to meet Nietzsche's valid criticisms.

■ ■ ■

Nietzsche's Life and Works

Nietzsche was born in Röcken, a small Prussian village, in 1844. His father, a Lutheran minister, died when he was five. The young Nietzsche originally intended to follow in his father's footsteps, but during his university years he abandoned his religious faith. Instead, he became a student of philology, the study of word origins and development.

Eventually he took a position teaching classical philology at the Swiss University of Basel.

Despite his philological training, from his earliest years Nietzsche was interested in philosophy. In conjunction with his classical studies, he read the ancient Greek philosophers and felt that the pre-Socratic thinkers were more in touch with our passionate nature than Plato or Aristotle. By chance, while browsing in a bookstore in 1865, he picked up *The World as Will and Representation* of Arthur Schopenhauer (1788–1860). The work convinced Nietzsche that irrational passions and volitions are at the heart of human existence, and that human reason, lacking any real insight into why we act the way we do, simply tries to rationalize these actions after the fact. Although Nietzsche would later repudiate many of Schopenhauer's ideas, he retained Schopenhauer's basic voluntarist vision throughout his writings.

Another strong influence on Nietzsche was the famous composer, Richard Wagner (1813–83). As a student, Nietzsche met Wagner. Nietzsche deeply admired the man, his music, and his thought. He saw him as the ideal of what a human person could become, a superior individual who could shape an era. However, by 1876 Nietzsche became disillusioned with Wagner, thinking that his work was catering to the masses and becoming overly Christianized. The friendship ended but Nietzsche never ceased to admire the ideal that Wagner represented.

Due to bad health, Nietzsche was forced to resign his teaching position in 1879. For the next ten years he wandered from health spa to health spa searching for medical relief. Despite constant headaches and nausea, he continued writing. His most famous work, *Thus Spake Zarathustra,* and several others were published during this period. In 1889 Nietzsche broke down, mentally insane, never to recover. He died August 25, 1900. After he died, his sister published a set of his notes, known as *The Will to Power.*

■ ■ ■

What to Look For in the Selection

The Will to Power, from which the following selections are taken, consists of a set of notes written by Nietzsche between 1883 and 1888. After his death, these notes were collected, organized, and published by his sister. Although they do not always represent Nietzsche's final word on a topic, they do provide a good insight into his later thought on many significant issues.

The following selection of Nietzsche's notes, from *The Will to Power,* will provide the reader with some of Nietzsche's basic thoughts regarding the human person. In reading these notes, it will help to focus on several key questions.

1. Why does Nietzsche attack the Christian understanding of human nature? (See notes 159, 160, 168, 169, 176, 221, 222, and 246.)
2. What does Nietzsche mean by *perspectivism?* (See notes 481 and 616.)
3. How does Nietzsche understand the self and consciousness? (See notes 480, 492, 517, 524, and 611.)
4. What does Nietzsche mean by the will to power and why is it so important? (See notes 619, 641, 658, 668, 671, and 704.)
5. For Nietzsche, who is the "higher type" of human being? (See notes 684, 987, 997, 998, and 1001.)

SELECTION FROM NIETZSCHE

■ ■ ■

The Will to Power

No. 480 (March–June 1888). There exists neither "spirit," nor reason, nor thinking, nor consciousness, nor soul; nor will; nor truth: all are fictions that are of no use. There is no question of "subject and object," but of a particular species of animal that can prosper only through a certain relative rightness; above all, regularity of its perceptions (so that it can accumulate experience).

Knowledge works as a tool of power. Hence it is plain that it increases with every increase of power.

The meaning of "knowledge": here, as in the case of "good" or "beautiful," the concept is to be regarded in a strict and narrow anthropocentric and biological sense. In order for a particular species to maintain itself and increase its power, its conception of reality must comprehend enough of the calculable and constant for it to base a scheme of behavior on it. The utility of preservation—not some abstract-theoretical need not to be deceived—stands as the motive behind the development of the organs of knowledge—they develop in such a way that their observations suffice for our preservation. In other words:

the measure of the desire for knowledge depends upon the measure to which the will to power grows in a species: a species grasps a certain amount of reality in order to become master of it, in order to press it into service.

481 (1883–1888). Against positivism, which halts at phenomena—"There are only *facts*")—I would say: No, facts is precisely what there is not, only interpretations. We cannot establish any fact "in itself"; perhaps it is folly to want to do such a thing.

"Everything is subjective," you say; but even this is interpretation. The "subject" is not something given; it is something added and invented and projected behind what there is.—Finally, is it necessary to posit an interpreter behind the interpretation? Even this is invention, hypothesis.

In so far as the word "knowledge" has any meaning, the world is knowable; but it is *interpretable* otherwise, it has no meaning behind it, but countless meanings.—"Perspectivism."

It is our needs that interpret the world; our drives, and their For and Against. Every drive is a kind of lust to rule; each one has its perspective that it would like to compel all the other drives to accept as a norm.

492 (1885). The body and physiology the starting point: why?—We gain the correct idea of the nature of our subject-unity, namely as regents at the head of a communality (not as "souls" or "life forces"), also of the dependence of these regents upon the ruled and of an order of rank and division of labor as the conditions that make possible the whole and its parts. In the same way, how living unities continually arise and die and how the "subject" is not eternal. In the same way, that the struggle expresses itself in obeying and commanding, and that a fluctuating assessment of the limits of power is part of life. The relative ignorance in which the regent is kept concerning individual activities and even disturbances within the communality is among the conditions under which rule can be exercised. In short, we also gain a valuation of *not-knowing*, of seeing things on a broad scale, of simplification and falsification, of perspectivity. The most important thing, however, is: that we understand that the ruler and his subjects are of the same kind, all feeling, willing, thinking—and that, wherever we see or divine movement in a body, we learn to conclude that there is a subjective, invisible life appertaining to it.

Movement is symbolism for the eye; it indicates that something has been felt, willed, thought.

The danger of the direct questioning of the subject *about* the subject, and of all self-reflection of the spirit, lies in this, that it could be useful and important for one's activity to interpret oneself *falsely*. That is why we question the body and reject the evidence of the sharpened senses: we try, if you like, to see whether the inferior parts themselves cannot enter into communication with us.

517 (Spring–Fall, 1887). In order to think and infer it is necessary to assume beings: logic handles only formulas for what remains the same. That is why this assumption would not be proof of reality: "beings" are part of our perspective. The "ego" of a being (—not affected by becoming and development).

The fictitious world of subject, substance, "reason," etc., is needed; there is in us a power to order, simplify, falsify, artificially distinguish. "Truth" is the will to be master over the multiplicity of sensations: to classify phenomena into definite categories. In this we start from a belief in the "in-itself" of things (we take phenomena as *real*).

The character of the world in a state of becoming as incapable of formulation, as "false," as "self-contradictory." Knowledge and becoming exclude one another. Consequently, "knowledge" must be something else; there must first of all be a will to make knowable, a kind of becoming must itself create the deception of beings.

524 (Nov. 1887–March 1888). *The role of "consciousness."* It is essential that one should not make a mistake over the role of "consciousness": it is our relation with the "outer world" that evolved it. On the other hand, the direction or protection and care in respect of the coordination of the bodily functions does *not* enter our consciousness, any more than spiritual accumulation: that a higher court rules over these things cannot be doubted—a kind of directing committee on which the various chief desires make their votes and power felt. "Pleasure," "displeasure," are hints from this sphere; also the act of will; also ideas.

In summa: That which becomes conscious is involved in causal relations which are entirely withheld from us—the sequence of thoughts, feelings, and ideas in consciousness does not signify that this sequence is a causal sequence; but apparently it is so, to the highest degree. Upon this *appearance* we have founded our whole idea of spirit, reason, logic, etc. (—none of these exist: they are fictitious syntheses and unities), and projected these *into* things and *behind* things.

Usually one takes consciousness itself as the general sensorium and supreme court; nonetheless, it is only a means of communication; it is evolved through social intercourse and with a view to the interests of social intercourse—"Intercourse" here understood to include the influences of the outer world and the reactions they compel on our side; also our effect upon the outer world. It is not the directing agent but an organ of the directing agent.

556 (1885–86). A "thing-in-itself" just as perverse as a "sense-in-itself," a "meaning-in-itself." There are no "facts-in-themselves," for a sense must always be projected into them before there can be "facts."

The question "what is that?" is an imposition of meaning from some other viewpoint. "Essence," the "essential nature," is something perspective and already presupposes a multiplicity. At the bottom of it there always lies "What is that for *me* (for us, for all that lives, etc.)?"

A thing would be defined once all creatures had asked "what is that?" and had answered their question. Supposing one single creature, with its own relationships and perspectives for all things, were missing, then the thing would not yet be "defined."

In short: the essence of a thing is only an *opinion* about the "thing." Or rather: "it is considered" is the real "it is," the sole "this is."

One may not ask: "who then interprets?" for the interpretation itself is a form of the will to power, exists (but not as a "being" but as a process, a becoming) as an affect.

The origin of "things" is wholly the work of that which imagines, thinks, wills, feels. The concept "thing" itself just as much as all its qualities.—Even "the subject" is such a created entity, a "thing" like all others: a simplification with the object of defining the force which posits, invents, thinks, as distinct from all individual positing, inventing, thinking, as such. Thus a capacity as distinct from all that is individual—fundamentally, action collectively considered with respect to all anticipated actions (action and the probability of similar actions).

569 (Spring–Fall, 1887). Our psychological perspective is determined by the following:

(1) that communication is necessary, and that for there to be communication something has to be firm, simplified, capable of precision (above all in the [so-called] *identical* case). For it to be communicable, however, it must be experienced as adapted, as "recognizable." The material of the senses adapted by the understanding, reduced to rough outlines, made similar, subsumed under related matters. Thus the fuzziness and chaos of sense impressions are, as it were, logicized;

(2) the world of "phenomena" is the adapted world which we feel to be real. The "reality" lies in the continual recurrence of identical, familiar, related things in their logicized character, in the belief that here we are able to reckon and calculate;

(3) the antithesis of this phenomenal world is not "the true world," but the formless unformulable world of the chaos of sensations—*another kind* of phenomenal world, a kind "unknowable" for us;

(4) questions, what things "in themselves" may be like, apart from our sense receptivity and the activity of our understanding, must be rebutted with the question: how could we know that things exist? "Thingness" was first created by us. The question is whether there could not be many other ways of creating such an apparent world, and whether this creating, logicizing, adapting, falsifying, is not itself the best-guaranteed reality; in short, whether that which "posits things" is not the sole reality; and whether the "effect of the external world upon us" is not also only the result of such active subjects.—The other "entities" act upon us; our adapted apparent world is an adaptation and overpowering of their actions; a kind of defensive measure. The subject alone is demonstrable; hypothesis that only subjects exist—that "object" is only a kind of effect produced by a subject upon a subject—a *modus of the subject*.

611 (1883–88). We find that the strongest and most constantly employed faculty at all stages of life is thought—even in every act of perceiving and apparent passivity! Evidently, it thus becomes most powerful and demanding, and in the long run it tyrannizes over all other forces. Finally it becomes "passion-in-itself."

616 (1885–86). That the value of the world lies in our interpretation (—that other interpretations than merely human ones are perhaps somewhere possible—); that previous interpretations have been perspective valuations by virtue of which we can survive in life, i.e., in the will to power, for the growth of power; that every elevation of man brings with it the overcoming of narrower interpretations; that every strengthening and increase of power opens up new perspectives and means believing in new horizons—this idea permeates my writings. The world with which we are concerned is false, i.e., is not a fact but a fable and approximation on the basis of a meager sum of observations; it is "in flux," as something in a state of becoming, as a falsehood always changing but never getting near the truth: for there is no "truth."

619 (1885). The victorious concept "force," by means of which our physicists have created God and the world, still needs to be completed; an inner will must be ascribed to it, which I designate as "will to power," i.e., as an insatiable desire to manifest power; or as the employment and exercise of power, as a creative drive, etc. Physicists cannot eradicate "action at a distance" from their principles; nor can they eradicate a repellent force (or an attracting one). There is nothing for it: one is obliged to understand all motion, all "appearances," all "laws," only as symptoms of an inner event and to employ man as an analogy to this end. In the case of an animal, it is possible to trace all its drives to the will to power; likewise all the functions of organic life to this one source.

641 (1883–88). A multiplicity of forces, connected by a common mode of nutrition, we call "life." To this mode of nutrition, as a means of making it possible, belong all so-called feelings, ideas, thoughts; that is, (1) a resistance to all other forces; (2) an adjustment of the same according to form and rhythm; (3) an estimate in regard to assimilation or excretion.

657 (1886–87). What is "passive"?—To be hindered from moving forward: thus an act of resistance and reaction.

What is "active"?—Reaching out for power.

"Nourishment"—is only derivative; the original phenomenon is: to desire to incorporate everything.

"Procreation"—only derivative; originally: where one will was not enough to organize the entire appropriated material, there came into force an opposing will which took in hand the separation; a new center of organization, after a struggle with the original will.

"Pleasure"—as a feeling of power (presupposing displeasure).

658 (1885). 1. The organic functions translated back to the basic will, the will to power—and understood as offshoots.

2. The will to power specializes as will to nourishment, to property, to tools, to servants (those who obey) and masters: the body as an example.—The stronger will directs the weaker. There is absolutely no other kind of causality than that of will upon will. Not explained mechanistically.

3. Thinking, feeling, willing, in all living beings. What is a pleasure but: an excitation of the feeling of power by an obstacle (even more strongly by rhythmic obstacles and resistances)—so it swells up. Thus all pleasure includes pain.—If the pleasure is to be very great, the pains must be very protracted and the tension of the bow tremendous.

4. The spiritual functions. Will to shape, to assimilate, etc.

668 (Nov. 1887–March 1888). "Willing" is not "desiring," striving, demanding: it is distinguished from these by the affect of commanding.

There is no such thing as "willing," but only a willing *something*: one must not remove the aim from the total condition—as epistemologists do. "Willing" as they understand it is as little a reality as "thinking": it is pure fiction.

It is part of willing that something is commanded (—which naturally does not mean that the will is "effected").

That state of tension by virtue of which a force seeks to discharge itself—is not an example of "willing."

671 (1883–88). Freedom of will or no freedom of will?—There is no such thing as "will"; it is only a simplifying conception of understanding, as is "matter."

684. *My general view.*

First proposition: man as a species is not progressing. Higher types are indeed attained, but they do not last. The level of the species is not raised.

Second proposition: man as a species does not represent any progress compared with any other animal. The whole animal and vegetable kingdom does not evolve from the lower to the higher—but all at the same time, in utter disorder, over and against each other. The richer and more complex forms—for the expression "higher type" means no more than this—perish more easily: only the lowest preserve an apparent indestructibility. The former are achieved only rarely and maintain their superiority with difficulty; the latter are favored by a compromising fruitfulness.

Among men, too, the higher types, the lucky strokes of evolution, perish most easily as fortunes change. They are exposed to every kind of decadence: they are extreme, and that almost means decadents.

The brief spell of beauty, of genius, of Caesar, is *sui generis:* such things are not inherited. The *type* is hereditary; a type is nothing extreme, no "lucky stroke"—

This is not due to any special fatality or malevolence of nature, but simply to the concept "higher type": the higher type represents an incomparably greater complexity—a greater sum of coordinated elements; so its disintegration is also incomparably more likely. The "genius" is the sublimest machine there is—consequently the most fragile.

Third proposition: the domestication (the "culture") of man does not go deep.—Where it does go deep it at once becomes degeneration (type: the Christian). The "savage" (or, in moral terms, the evil man) is a return to nature—and in a certain sense his recovery, his *cure* from "culture"—

704 (Nov. 1887–March 1888). How does it happen that the basic articles of faith in psychology are one and all the most arrant misrepresentations and counterfeits? "Man strives after happiness," e.g.—how much of that is true? In order to understand what "life" is, what kind of striving and tension life is, the formula must apply as well to trees and plants as to animals. "What does a plant strive after?"—but here we have already invented a false unity which does not exist: the fact of

a millionfold growth with individual and semi-individual initiatives is concealed and denied if we begin by positing a crude unity, "plant." That the very smallest "individuals" cannot be understood in the sense of a "metaphysical individuality" and atom, that their sphere of power is continually changing—that is the first thing that becomes obvious; but does each of them strive after happiness when it changes in this way?—

But all expansion, incorporation, growth, means striving against something that resists; motion is essentially tied up with states of displeasure; that which is here the driving force must in any event desire something else if it desires displeasure in this way and continually looks for it. For what do the trees in a jungle fight each other? For "happiness"?—*For power!*—

Man, become master over the forces of nature, master over his own savagery and licentiousness (the desires have learned to obey and be useful)—man, in comparison with a preman—represents a tremendous quantum of *power—not* an increase in "happiness"! How can one claim that he has *striven* for happiness?—

987 (1884). The most difficult and highest form of man will succeed most rarely: thus the history of philosophy reveals a superabundance of failures, of accidents, and an extremely slow advance; whole millennia intervene and overwhelm what has been achieved; the continuity is broken again and again. It is an appalling history—the history of the highest man, the *sage.*—

What is most harmed is precisely the memory of the great, for the semi-failures and the failures misunderstand them and vanquish them by means of "successes." Every time "an influence" shows itself, a mob crowds upon the scene; the chatter of the petty and the poor in spirit is a terrible torment for the ears of those who remember with a shudder *that the destiny of humanity depends upon the attainment of its highest type.*

From my childhood I have pondered the conditions for the existence of the sage, and I will not conceal my joyous conviction that he is again becoming *possible* in Europe—perhaps only for a short time.

997 (1884). I teach: that there are higher and lower men, and that a single individual can under certain circumstances

justify the existence of whole millennia—that is, a full, rich, great, whole human being in relation to countless incomplete fragmentary men.

998 (1884). The highest men live beyond the rulers, freed from all bonds; and in the rulers they have their instruments.

1001 (1884). Not "mankind" but *overman* is the goal!

159 (Nov. 1887–March 1888). The entire Christian teaching as to what shall be believed, the entire Christian "truth," is idle falsehood and deception: and precisely the opposite of what inspired the Christian movement in the beginning. Precisely that which is Christian in the ecclesiastical sense is anti-Christian in essence: things and people instead of symbols; history instead of eternal facts; forms, rites, dogmas, instead of a way of life. Utter indifference to dogmas, cults, priests, church, theology, is Christian.

The Christian way of life is no more a fantasy than the Buddhist way of life: it is a means to being happy.

160 (Nov. 1887–March 1888). Jesus starts directly with the condition the "Kingdom of Heaven" in the heart, and he does not find the means to it in the observances of the Jewish church; the reality of Judaism itself (its need to preserve itself) he regards as nothing; he is purely inward.—

He likewise ignores the entire system of crude formalities governing intercourse with God; he opposes the whole teaching of repentance and atonement; he demonstrates how one must live in order to feel "deified"—and how one will not achieve it through repentance and contrition for one's sins: "Sin is of no account" is his central judgment.

Sin, repentance, forgiveness—none of this belongs here—it is acquired from Judaism, or it is pagan.

168 (Nov. 188–March 1888). —The church is precisely that against which Jesus preached—and against which he taught his disciples to fight.—

169 (Nov. 1887–March 1888). A god who died for our sins: redemption through faith, resurrection after death—all these are counterfeits of true Christianity for which that disastrous wrong-headed fellow [St. Paul] must be held responsible.

The exemplary life consists of love and humility, in a fullness of heart that does not exclude even the lowliest; in a formal repudiation of maintaining one's rights, of self-defense, of victory in the sense of personal triumph; in faith in blessedness here on earth, in spite of distress, opposition, and death; in reconciliation; in the absence of anger; not wanting to be rewarded; not being obliged to anyone; the completest spiritual-intellectual independence; a very proud life beneath the will to a life of poverty and service.

After the church had let itself be deprived of the entire Christian way of life and had quite specifically sanctioned life under the state, that form of life that Jesus had combatted and condemned, it had to find the meaning of Christianity in something else: in faith in unbelievable things, in the ceremonial of prayers, worship, feasts, etc. The concept "sin," "forgiveness," "reward"—all quite unimportant and virtually excluded from primitive Christianity—now comes into the foreground.

An appalling mishmash of Greek philosophy and Judaism; asceticism; continual judging and condemning; order of rank; etc.

176 (March–June 1888). *Reaction of the little people.*

Love gives the greatest feeling of power. To grasp to what extent not man in general but a certain species of man speaks here. This is to be exhumed more precisely.

"We are divine through love, we become 'children of God'; God loves us and wants nothing whatever from us save love"; this means: no morality, obedience, or activity produces that feeling of power that love produces; one does nothing bad from love, one does much more than one would do from obedience and virtue.Here is the happiness of the herd, the feeling of community in great and small things, the living feeling of unity experienced as the sum of the feeling of life. Being helpful and useful and caring for others continually arouses the feeling of power; visible success, the expression of pleasure, underlines the feeling of power; pride is not lacking, in the form of community, the abode of God, the "chosen."

What has in fact happened is that man has again experienced an *alteration* of personality: this time he calls his feeling of love God. One must picture to oneself what the awakening of such a feeling is like: a kind of ecstasy, a strange language, a "gospel"—it was this novelty that forbade him to ascribe love to himself—: he thought God was walking before him and coming alive within him.—"God descends to man," one's "neighbor" is transfigured into a god (in so far as he arouses the feeling of love). Jesus is one's neighbor as soon as he is conceived as godhead, as a cause of the feeling of power.

221 (Nov. 1887–March 1888). We have recovered the Christian ideal; it remains to determine its value.

1. What values are *negated* by it? What does its *counter-ideal* comprise?— Pride, pathos of distance, great responsibility, exuberance, splendid animality, the instincts that delight in war and conquest, the deification of passion, of revenge, of cunning, of anger, of voluptuousness, of adventure, of knowledge—; the noble ideal is negated: the beauty, wisdom, power, splendor, and dangerousness of the type "man": the man who fixes goals, the "man of the future" (—here Christianity appears as a logical consequence of Judaism—).

2. Can it be *realized?* Yes, under the right climatic conditions, as the Indian ideal was. Work is missing in both.— It detaches the individual from people, state, cultural community, jurisdiction; it rejects education, knowledge, cultivation of good manners, gain, commerce—it lets everything go that comprises the usefulness and value of man—it shuts him off by means of an idiosyncracy of feeling. Unpolitical, anti-national, neither aggressive nor defensive—possible only within the most firmly ordered political and social life, which allows these holy parasites to proliferate at public expense—

3. It is a consequence of the will to *pleasure* and of nothing else! "Blessedness" counts as something self-evident, which no longer requires any justification—everything else (how to live and let live) is only a means to an end—

But this way of thinking is base: fear of pain, of defilement, of corruption, as a sufficient motive for letting everything go—This is a *wretched* way of thinking—Sign of an *exhausted race*—One should not let oneself be deceived. ("Become as little children"—. Of related nature: Francis of Assisi, neurotic, epileptic, a visionary, like Jesus.)

222 (Nov. 1887–March 1888). The higher man is distinguished from the lower by his fearlessness and his readiness to challenge misfortune: it is a sign of degeneration when eudaemonistic valuations begin to prevail (—physiological fatigue, feebleness of will—). Christianity, with its perspective of "blessedness," is a mode of thought typical of a suffering and feeble species of man. Abundant strength wants to create, suffer, go under: the Christian salvation-for-bigots is bad music to it, and its hieratic posture an annoyance.

246 (Jan.–Fall 1888). In moving the doctrine of selflessness and love into the foreground, Christianity was in no way establishing the interests of the species as of higher value than the interests of the individual. Its real *historical* effect, the fateful element in its effect, remains, on the contrary, in precisely the enhancement of egoism, of the egoism of the individual, to an extreme (—to the extreme of individual immortality). Through Christianity, the individual was made so important, so absolute, that he could no longer be sacrificed: but the species endures only through human sacrifice—All "souls" became equal before God, but this is precisely the most dangerous of all possible evaluations! If one regards individuals as equal, one calls the species into question, one encourages a way of life that leads to the ruin of the species: Christianity is the counter-principle to the principle of *selection*. If the degenerate and sick ("the Christian") is to be accorded the same value as the healthy ("the pagan"), or even more value, as in Pascal's judgment concerning sickness and health, then unnaturalness becomes law—

This universal love of men is in practice the *preference* for the suffering, underprivileged, degenerate: it has in fact lowered and weakened the strength, the responsibility, the lofty duty, to sacrifice men. All that remains, according to the Christian scheme of values, is to sacrifice oneself: but this residue of human sacrifice that Christianity concedes and even advises has, from the standpoint of general breeding, no meaning at all. The prosperity of the species is unaffected by the self-sacrifice of this or that individual (—whether it be in the monkish and ascetic manner or, with the aid of crosses, pyres, and scaffolds, as "martyrs" of error). The species requires that the ill-constituted, weak, degenerate, perish: but it was precisely to them that Christianity turned as a conserving force; it further enhanced that instinct in the weak, already so powerful, to take care of and preserve themselves and to sustain one another. What is "virtue" and "charity" in Christianity if not just this mutual preservation, this solidarity of the weak, this hampering of selection? What is Christian altruism if not the mass-egotism of the weak, which divines that if all care for one another each individual will be preserved as long as possible?—

If one does not feel such a disposition as an extreme immorality, as a crime against life, one belongs with the company of the sick and possesses its instincts oneself—

Genuine charity demands sacrifice for the good of the species—it is hard, it is full of self-overcoming, because it needs human sacrifice. And this pseudo-humaneness called Christianity wants it established that no one should be sacrificed—

Extracted from *The Will to Power*, translated by W. Kaufmann and R. J. Hollingdale (New York, 1967), 98, 101–2, 107–8, 129–30, 141–42, 266–67, 271–72, 280, 284, 301–2, 306–7, 329–30, 332–33, 341–42, 346–47, 353–54, 363–64, 374–75, 515–16, 518–19.

COMMENTARY

■ ■ ■

Perspectivism

Nietzsche described his philosophical point of view as "perspectivism." He held that there is no such thing as preexisting data capable of being confronted and known by consciousness. There is no extramental world of facts and substances waiting to be understood by the intellect. Rather, the "given" is a formless chaos of "impressions" that receives an intelligible perspective through the organizing activity of consciousness.

Nietzsche viewed consciousness as the source of whatever permanence, order, and unity exist within the world. According to him, the process of arbitrarily selecting roughly similar traits from the sensory multiplicity and unifying them under one concept allows consciousness to create permanent unchanging structures. These essences or things-in-themselves, created to give some stability and unity to the everchanging multiplicity, do not really exist. They are simply intellectual fabrications invented to help human beings relate better in the world. Therefore, Nietzsche believed that all so-called intellectual, moral, and scientific truths are merely human interpretations of the sensory flux.

■ ■ ■

Physical Reality

By Nietzsche's theory, then, the physical world cannot accurately be described as a set of things or substances. No things or substances exist. Physical reality is composed of dynamic clusters of forces in a relation of tension to all other forces. An individual body, as arbitrarily singled out by consciousness, is a multiple phenomenon, a plurality of irreducible forces that vie with each other and outside forces for growth and development. A rock, for example, is a complex set of energized physical and chemical forces contending with each other for inner supremacy and acting together against surrounding elements and bodies. The rock gives the impression of being a unity but is really a mutiplicity of forces.

Within every force, an inner will exists, which Nietzsche calls the "will to power." The will to power is the active "striving" within a force to control and subdue other forces. It is the commanding element within a force, and accounts for its strength and quality. Nietzsche goes so far as to say that the will to power is "the innermost essence of being." All that is, is, at bottom, will to power.

Nietzsche saw evidence for the will to power everywhere. Physical forces such as fire and acids consume everything in their paths. Living things compete for the sun's rays, water, and the minerals in the soil. Animals fight for food and territory. Humans continuously battle each other for wealth, fame, and domination. Will to power is central to existence.

The material world has no cause of its existence. It has always existed and always will. No God is needed to explain it. Historically, gods were created by human beings to give meaning, permanence, and stability to the flux. Like essences and substances, the gods are just one more attempt to help explain an inherently unexplainable flux.

■ ■ ■

The Human Body

Although Nietzsche understood human beings to be the most developed organic beings, all organisms, humans included, are simply physical bodies. In saying that a human being is just a physical body, it must be understood that the term *body* does not signify some permanent physical "thing." Instead, it stands for a complex community of interrelated forces. A human being, like any other being, is a multiplicity of ever-changing forces struggling with each other for supremacy. No spiritual soul animates the body. *Soul* is just a word signifying specific conscious forces in the body.

These multiple forces are called "living" insofar as they work together to nourish themselves. Nutrition is nothing other than the joint but unequal effort of bodily forces to appropriate and assimilate other materials to increase their mutual strength.

■ ■ ■

Consciousness

Consciousness originally evolved as an instrument of the body's need to nourish itself. By having sensations, images, thoughts, feelings, and the corresponding organs that produce them, an organism is better able to appropriate and incorporate outside materials. Being aware of objects at a distance and their potential benefits or threats is a distinct evolutionary advantage.

Consciousness does not belong to a "knowing subject" or a "thinking thing." Rather, what is called "consciousness" is in reality nothing more than a set of feelings, sensations, images, and thoughts. Philosophers such as Plato and Descartes mistakenly assumed that these conscious acts were unified by a knowing subject that initiates them. Nietzsche, however, held that there is no conscious subject acting as their source. All that exists is a stream of conscious acts. We have no experience of any "subject" doing the thinking.

Why, then, do these thoughts and feelings occur in a definite sequence? Nietzsche held that the existence and arrangement of mental phenomena are the result of numerous unconscious bodily forces. We are often unaware of what forces actually cause our thoughts and feelings. For example, when we feel hunger pangs, it is not "consciousness" that causes them but some unknown bodily force. The awareness of hunger is just that: an awareness of hunger. "Consciousness" does not cause the hunger. It is not the directing agent, but only the organ of unconscious directing forces. These unconscious commanding forces are like regents at the head of a communality. They vie with each other and the forces they command for control of the person.

Among conscious activities is the unifying of similar sensations or images. "Consciousness" unifies a multiplicity of impressions by picking out what is common to them and overlooking what is not. For example, by arbitrarily selecting roughly similar aspects and omitting differentiating characteristics among "leafy" images, the concept "leaf" is formed. No essence or substance "leaf" actually exists. The concept "leaf" is simply an arbitrary mental construct that unifies a set of similar impressions under a unifying perspective.

This unifying activity of consciousness operates even at the level of sensation. Two impressions that are close neighbors are sensed as being the same. The judgment "the grass is green" presumes that the different green colors in a million blades of grass are already experienced as being the same green.

The known world, then, as conceptualized through conscious activity, is ultimately a construct. The permanence and stability created by consciousness does not really exist. Consciousness, in effect, creates falsehoods; it creates entities that do not really exist.

Once created, these new conceptual perspectives are retained in memory and used to categorize future perceptions. New impressions and images are received and classified under these ideas. In this way, stability and unity are given to the realm of sensory chaos.

Why does consciousness engage in this activity, effectively creating falsehoods? The simple answer is biological need. Over time, human beings evolved the capacity for abstractive thought as a practical way of maintaining themselves and increasing their power. This power was developed, not for the sake of acquiring truth for truth's sake, but for the practical purpose of surviving in the best way. Only when images and impressions are categorized do they become usable. A world constructed of regularities and constancies, though it be false, provides a better basis for behavior than a world of chaotic change. Human knowledge is valuable only to the extent that it enables human beings to control their environment.

Knowledge, then, is an instrument of power that gives humans an evolutionary advantage. Every generalization is a means of power for the self because it involves a personal interpretation of the flux. To impose one's own truths and meanings on reality is in effect to gain control over others. For example, interpreting "human being" to include whites but not blacks, teenagers but not fetuses, Aryans but not Jews, has been a source of power for many individuals in this century.

■ ■ ■

Self-Consciousness

For Nietzsche, humans, unlike other conscious beings, are able to reflect on their thoughts and feelings. But, as he points out, reflective thought constitutes only a small proportion of our thinking and is always done by using words. Therefore, most of our sensing, feeling, imagining, and thinking takes place without reflection.

Nietzsche conjectured that the evolution of self-consciousness is tied to the necessity of communication. Because human beings needed to communicate to survive, it became necessary for them to develop the ability to know themselves reflectively. They had to know what they lacked, how they felt, and what they thought, before they could convey any of this information. Since their thinking was geared toward communicating with others, it was done in the symbols of communication: words. Self-reflection, then, is not an inborn power but is a tool developed for survival. It gave humans an evolutionary advantage.

■ ■ ■

The Human Will

For Nietzsche, "will," too, is not a power of the soul. What we call "will" is really an admixture of thought, feeling, and willing. There is no unified will that is the cause of human actions. The feeling of willing is experienced but no definitive connection can be made between the feeling of willing and what is willed. The cause of any action is rooted in physical forces that are ultimately unable to be known.

Since "will" is simply a mental construct that has no real existence, all discussions of a "free" or an "unfree" will have no basis. Historically, notions like "free will" or "unfree will" have been used by persons in power to gain control over other persons. Whether the underlying physical forces that ultimately control an individual are free simply cannot be known.

■ ■ ■

Human Growth: Become What You Are

Every human being, then, is composed of a unique set of forces that manifest themselves through feelings, urges, desires, imaginings, thoughts, volitions, and actions. These forces continually vie with each other for internal supremacy. There is no separate "self" or "I" that unifies them. The self is a multiplicity of forces, not a single entity.

Personal growth occurs when the will to power of the strongest forces within a person triumphs, when weakness is overcome.[1] Only when a person is able to overcome fears and inner weaknesses, allowing inner strengths to prevail, can the person truly become what he or she is. For example, if a young man has strong musical abilities and desires, he will attain self-realization if, and only if, these talents dominate his life. If he allows his fear of failure or his lethargic practice habits to prevail over his inner talents, his life will be diminished.

■ ■ ■

Degrees of Power

The extent of the power present in a being is measured by the *extent* of what is commanded, by the *way* in which it is commanded, and by the *strength of the opposition*. The power of a general, for example, is determined by the number of troops under his command, by their discipline and their ability to fight as a unit, and by the strength of the armies they have battled. In a human being, power is measured by the number of strong forces that exist. These drives must be harnessed so that the strongest rule, and the weakest are subordinate.[2] The weaker forces must not be suppressed or eliminated but must be allowed their fullest strength commensurate with the rule of the stronger forces. The strength and harmonizing of these forces are enhanced by the surmounting of great obstacles. As in a tennis match, the better the opponent, the more one's abilities will be tested and sharpened.

■ ■ ■

The Overman

Composed of forces of differing strengths, human beings are not equal in talent or ability. Some are more gifted physically, intellectually, and emotionally than others. There is an order of rank among humans that is ultimately determined by the power they have. The strong will inevitably command the weak.

The highest type of person is what Nietzsche called the "overman" (*übermensch*).[3] He is that unique gifted specimen who represents the uppermost limit of human perfection. He is blessed with great intelligence and strong passions. These gifts he has channeled into one harmonious whole without destroying the force of any one of them. The overman is not just physically strong nor does he have his power simply by virtue of wealth or position. He is intellectually gifted but is not merely an "intellectual." He may be a social or political leader, but not necessarily. The overman is a creative genius whose will to power stamps an age with new insights and directions. Individuals like Caesar, Leonardo da Vinci,

Napoleon, Bismarck, and Goethe all approached the ideal of the overman. These people were geniuses who gave new meaning to their eras. They established the frameworks within which many lesser persons have toiled for generations. Yet even these great men did not fully realize Nietzsche's ideal of the overman. All had their deficiencies. In *Thus Spake Zarathustra*, Nietzsche tells us that "never yet has there been an overman."[4]

The ideal of the overman is difficult and can be reached only by a few select individuals. Most human beings do not have the talents or the appropriate accident of birth (being in the right place at the right time) to become an overman. Even among those who have the talents and opportunity, most cannot face up to the sufferings and dangers involved. The process of becoming a person who can harness passions and channel intellectual and social energies into creative work takes time, patience, and great discipline. The creation of new ideas and values does not come easy, nor are they always well accepted. It takes great courage and strength of character for a person to stand by his or her ideas. Great innovators like Galileo, Wagner, and Darwin were not well received and suffered much because of their new ideas and values. They had to fight hard against the intellectual or the religious establishment for their ideals to prevail. Most persons, even superior individuals, do not have the talent or strength of character to create new ideas and values, and to stand by them. They fall prey to social pressures and personal weaknesses, and are unable to realize their full potential. They would rather follow than lead.

In Nietzsche's philosophical system, in which there are no God or absolute truths or values, and in which traditional religion is steadily losing support, the overman is humankind's greatest hope for providing the meaning needed to keep us from despair and nihilism. The superman alone has the gifts and the daring to think new thoughts and to conceive new values. His spirit is not constrained by the powers of the status quo. Just as Richard Wagner gave a new meaning to the art and life of his day, so too, in a similar way, does the overman in his era.

■ ■ ■

Christianity and the Person

Nietzsche saw the Christian religion as the major obstacle to the realization of the ideal of the overman. He saw Christianity as an antilife force that opposed the will to power and taught an unrealistic doctrine of the equality of human beings. The Christian Church, for him, was the most active force in preventing the strong from assuming their natural leadership over the mediocre and the weak.

Surprisingly, Nietzsche was not overly critical of Jesus, whom he interpreted as a "flower child" rebelling against the rigid legalism of the Jewish religious hierarchy, and eventually being put to death for his rebellion. According to Nietzsche, Jesus was not God; he was a simple peace-loving carpenter who believed he could solve all the world's problems through love. His disciples, especially Paul, motivated by revenge against the Jewish priests for crucifying Jesus, made Him into the Son of God. The disciples interpreted his death as a sacrifice for the forgiveness of sins, and created the myth of the Resurrection. The risen Christ would be the new judge of right and wrong. As the new priestly class, these vengeance-filled Christians now had the power of God's judgment on their side. Their message of love, and hatred of the powerful, appealed to the poor and the slaves within the Roman empire, and Christianity quickly spread among them.

Since they were inherently weak and vengeful individuals, Nietzsche did not believe that the early Christians had the strength of character to create an original value-system. They could only react against the values of the ruling classes. What the Jewish priests and governing Romans wanted, they devalued. Pride, ambition, and power were seen as vices. Opposing traits, like humility, meekness, gentleness, equality, and love, were applauded. The weak and downtrodden were exalted at the expense of the strong and powerful.

Nietzsche saw this aversion to power and elitism as a sorry state of affairs. The Christian values of selfless love and human equality prevented the strong overman types from ascending to their natural positions of command. Proud and powerful individuals were viewed as sinners and were actively oppressed by the Christian community. The view that all humans are equal also kept the Christians from accepting any notion of the natural superiority of some persons over others. The weak, the sickly, and the naturally deficient were valued just the same as the naturally gifted. There was little room within the Christian community for a unique, powerful individual to rise above the masses. In the name of humility and equality, all such attempts were put down. Christianity became the breeding-ground of mediocrity and conformity. The gospel of love is diametrically opposed to Nietzsche's philosophy of power and the overman. Only when Christianity is repudiated can the aristocratic cream rise to the top and provide the life-affirming values needed to give the masses meaning in life.

Nietzsche not only criticized Christianity's suppression of the overman type; he also saw the basic Christian understanding of the person to be false. As we have seen earlier, he denied the existence of a spiritual soul and free will, calling them imaginary constructs having no basis in reality. He also repudiated, as religious fabrications, the so-called debilitating effects of original sin on the soul and the hidden motivating power of divine grace. The Christian belief in an afterlife was similarly rejected. To deny this world in favor of the next makes no sense since this is the only life we have to live.

Christianity's vilification of basic human instincts and drives also troubled Nietzsche. He strongly criticized Christian writers and saints who considered feelings like pride, ambition, and sensuality to be evil temptations. Although following these passions to excess can be a danger, said Nietzsche, the solution is not to exterminate them, as is recommended by Christian writers, but to control and sublimate them. In that way, the strength of these drives can be maintained or redirected in enriching ways.

Finally, Nietzsche was also highly critical of the Christian practice of love of neighbor. Although the Christian ideal is to love one's neighbor selflessly, Nietzsche thought that most Christians are incomplete persons who are actually seeking self-affirmation from others. What passes as love is really an attempt to use others to make up for personal inadequacies. As deficient persons, Christians are so wrapped up in their own needs that they cannot truly give themselves to others. In opposition to love of neighbor, Nietzsche teaches the doctrine of the friend. Friendship is a love that flows from a strong self-love. When persons see themselves as valuable and are content with their inner selves, they are willing to give of themselves to others. They love not because they need to be loved but because they want to love. Their love flows from a satisfied ego, not from a weak ego that seeks satisfaction from others.

■ ■ ■

Philosophical and Religious Critique

Although Friedrich Nietzsche has provided several important insights into the nature of the human person, there are some difficulties in his thought that warrant mention. To begin with, Nietzsche's perspectivist viewpoint is not without serious philosophical difficulties. The crux of his position is that reality, at bottom, is an "unformulable" chaos of impressions, having no permanence or unity; in itself, it is neither definable nor knowable. According to Nietzsche, then, consciousness, in an effort to gain some control over this unintelligible sea of becoming, creates general concepts to give some unity and permanence to the flux. Consequently, reality as we know it is simply an artificial creation of our minds.

Although this position seems initially tenable, there is a fundamental difficulty with it. We must ask, are the basic presuppositions that form the core of Nietzsche's perspectivist point of view statements about what reality really is or are they themselves simply perspectives he has created? If these are true statements about what is real, then there is a contradiction: contrary to Nietzsche's own teaching, reality at base is knowable and able to be described in intelligible terms. And if they are simply hypotheses, another conundrum arises. When statements like "there exists an 'unformulable' sea of becoming" or "consciousness is able to give unity and permanence to the flux" are regarded simply as hypotheses, there is no reason to believe them any more than any other hypothesis. To say that these interpretations are "truer" than any other perspectives ignores the fact that there is no absolute standard for truth in Nietzsche's philosophy. Thus Nietzsche's basic philosophical assumptions have no more reason to be believed than any other assumptions.

In fact, Nietzsche "presupposes and even insists upon the truth of his own claims."[5] There are many places in his works where he unquestionably acted upon the presumption that his basic premises are true, without seeming to realize the inherent contradiction in his position.[6] Clearly, his assumptions have no factual support.

Nietzsche's view that the will to power is the ultimate motivating force in all human beings also has a ring of truth to it. There is no question that concerns over power continually arise in human relationships. Nations, governments, and big corporations are consistently involved in conflicts over power. Even familial and interpersonal relationships often involve issues of control. But the question remains whether *all* human relationships are power relationships. Is the will to command the underlying desire in all human relationships?

While acknowledging that many human relationships, rightly or wrongly, are power relationships, it is also the case that many of our relationships are rooted in a caring love. Although marital partners and personal friends often try to control each other, openly or subtly, there are many times when they act out of a genuine care for each other, seeking the other's well-being without any desire for personal gain. Nietzsche's doctrine of the friend seems to point to this kind of caring relationship, but he does not develop its implications sufficiently. Granted, some persons, Christians included, *use* one another in their relationships, but this is not always the case. Even at the larger levels of government and business, where power and profit are often the primary motives, altruistic motives are sometimes present. Altruism exists, not as often as we would like, but it does exist. The will to power, then, is not the universal basis for all human actions.

Although Nietzsche argued that Christian altruism is rooted in personal weakness—Christians choose to love because they are too weak to control the powerful—many contemporary psychologists of love[7] contend that a caring love flows not from personal weakness but from personal strength. Only after persons have developed to the point where they feel secure and confident in themselves are they willing to involve themselves lovingly in the life of others. When persons are unloved and feel personally deficient, then they are more concerned with filling personal needs than with loving others. Their relationships are viewed more in functional terms than in loving terms. Love flows from strength of character, not weakness.

Finally, Nietzsche's position that the human self is not a unified single substance raises serious difficulties. His point is well made that many processes and feelings take place within ourselves that show little or no conscious connection with some directing self. Digestion, blood circulation, and growth patterns are clear examples. Unexpected hunger pangs, sexual desires, and ideas that just pop into our heads, are others. However, to conceive of the self as simply a multiplicity of independent forces loses sight of the fact that humans often do act purposefully, under a central direction. My conscious life is not just a random set of thoughts, feelings, volitions, and imaginings, happening in a haphazard fashion. There is often a clear direction to my conscious thought and, by implication, a director of it. A conscious identical self is needed to account for my deliberate reflections and actions. This conscious self unifies and directs my thoughts and actions throughout the course of my life.

■ ■ ■

Summary

Nietzsche saw the physical world as composed of clusters of dynamic forces in constant tension with each other. There are no things or substances, only collections of forces. Within each force there exists a will to power, an active striving to rule and command. The human person is just a more highly evolved cluster of ever-changing forces capable of living activities. Human consciousness is simply one force among many vying for power and control. Having conscious activity gives humans an evolutionary advantage because it enables them to create concepts that unify their experience, thereby giving them greater control over their surroundings. Consciousness does not discover truth but creates conceptual frameworks that best enable it to have power over its surroundings.

Human beings are not equal in power. Some are more gifted intellectually and physically than others. The strong will inevitably command the weak. The highest type of person is what Nietzsche calls the "overman," that rare and gifted individual having great intelligence, passion, and will to power. In an era when "God is dead" and traditional ideals and values no longer hold sway, these "overmen" will create new visions and give human beings new meanings in a despairing age. Only these "overmen" can provide hope for the future of humankind.

For Nietzsche, the greatest obstacle preventing the strong from assuming their rightful leadership over the weak is the Christian religion. The Christian gospel of love, humility, and peace stands in strong opposition to his ideals of power, strength, and ambition. Therefore, throughout his life, he vehemently attacked Christianity as presenting an antilife vision of humankind.

Nietzsche has many important insights into the being of the human person. However, several objections may be raised about his position. There is a clear inconsistency between his position that there are no absolute truths and the truth claims that he makes for his own basic philosophical presuppositions. Also, objections may be raised against his claims that the will to power is the ultimate motivating force in human beings and that Christian altruism is rooted in personal weakness.

■ ■ ■

Notes

1. "What is good? Everything that heightens the feeling of power in man, the will to power, power itself. What is bad? Everything that is born of weakness. What is happiness? The feeling that power is growing, that resistance is overcome." F. Nietzsche, *The Antichrist*, 1.2 in *The Portable Nietzsche* (New York, 1964), 570.

2. "The highest man would have the greatest multiplicity of urges, in the relatively greatest strength that can be endured." F. Nietzsche, *The Will to Power* (New York, 1968), 507.

3. "The word 'overman' is the designation of a type of supreme achievement, as opposed to 'modern' men, to 'good' men, to Christians and other nihilists—a word that in the mouth of Zarathustra, the annihilator of morality, becomes a very utmost innocence in the sense of those very values whose opposite Zarathustra was meant to represent—that is, an 'idealistic' type of a higher kind of man, half 'saint,' half 'genius'." F. Nietzsche, *Ecce Homo*, in *On the Genealogy of Morals* and *Ecce Homo* (New York, 1967), 261.
4. F. Nietzsche, *Thus Spake Zarathustra*, part 2, in *The Portable Nietzsche*, 202–5.
5. J. T. Wilcox, *Truth and Value in Nietzsche: A Study of His Metaethics and Epistemology* (Ann Arbor, 1974), 45.
6. F. Nietzsche, *Ecce Homo*, in *On the Geneaology of Morals* and *Ecce Homo* (New York, 1967), 327–28, 330–31; *Beyond Good and Evil* (Chicago, 1955), 44–46.
7. For example, see Erich Fromm, *The Art of Loving* (New York, 1956).

■ ■ ■

Further Reading

G. Deleuze, *Nietzsche and Philosophy*, translated by H. Tomlinson (New York, 1983).

W. Kaufmann, *Nietzsche: Philosopher, Psychologist, Antichrist*, 4th ed. (Princeton, 1974).

G. A. Morgan, Jr., *What Nietzsche Means* (Cambridge, Mass., 1941).

11

SIGMUND FREUD

...

THE HUMAN PERSON AS SEXUAL

Introduction and Commentary by Deal W. Hudson

INTRODUCTION

■ ■ ■

Freud's Life and Works

Sigmund Freud was born in 1856 in Czechoslovakia, but spent most of his life in Vienna, Austria. Though not technically a philosopher, he influenced the philosophy of the human person to a great extent. Freud was a psychiatrist, the founder of the school of psychiatry that became known as Psychoanalysis. He left Austria because of the Nazi occupation just before the Second World War and went to England, where he died in 1939. He is known especially for his emphasis on, indeed his obsession with, the sexual aspect of the human person.

Freud wrote prolifically throughout his career, publishing numerous essays, articles, and books. Among his most important works are the following: *The Interpretation of Dreams* (1900), *Introductory Lectures on Psycho-Analysis* (1916–17), *Beyond the Pleasure Principle* (1920), *The Ego and the Id* (1923), *The Future of an Illusion* (1927), and *Civilization and Its Discontents* (1930).

Freud's method of treating mental and emotional disorders stresses the role of both unconscious mental states and instinctual desire in understanding human behavior. Freud began to devise his revolutionary theory of human nature in the 1890s while attempting to treat patients by means of hypnosis. He soon found that his patients did not require hypnosis to reveal the sources of their anxieties. Through a process of free association of dreams and possible meanings, patients, with the help of the therapist, were able to recall and to reconstruct the painful experiences at the root of their symptoms.

Freud was particularly interested in those memories that patients repressed and experienced difficulty in summoning back into conscious awareness. Behind this repression, for Freud, lay the powerful drive of the *libido,* or each individual's instinctual urge toward sexual gratification. His tripartite theory of personality—*id, ego, superego*—was devised against this backdrop. The id represents the unconscious, its drives and impulses; the ego represents conscious and preconscious functions, such as simple perception and ordinary cognition; while the superego contains the normative content of human personality, the values and directives that govern conscious thought and action. Freud's story of *Civilization and Its Discontents* is his personality theory in relation to society as a whole: the libido demands what a civilized society, made up of persons guided by a strong superego, simply cannot allow.

Although Freud was one of the truly original thinkers of the twentieth century, it would be a mistake to consider his views of human nature and happiness without a brief reminder of their historical context. Freud considered himself a scientist but did not seek to cut himself off from the inherited wisdom of the past, although he dramatically reinterpreted it. Freud was deeply conversant with the traditions of his European culture, its philosophy, literature, and mythology, becoming an expert in the visual arts, especially Italian Renaissance painting. That he allowed all of these influences to find their way into his theories surprises contemporary readers who expect scientists of a more purely experimental type.

Thus, in spite of his originality, Freud belongs to the culture of late nineteenth-century Europe. His theories reflect the empiricism of the eighteenth-century Enlightenment, the resigned pessimism of Arthur Schopenhauer (1788–1860), the evolutionary theory of Darwin (1809–82), and the discovery of the will-to-power by Nietzsche (1844–1900). For example, Freud accepts without question the hedonistic assumption of John Locke that the universal human desire for happiness is a desire for maximum pleasure and minimal pain. Locke and most of his contemporaries, however, still regarded the pleasure of eternal life as the final object of the drive to happiness. Later eighteenth-century philosophers employed this hedonism to devise a "science of happiness" by measuring amounts of pain and pleasure. And as historical existence came increasingly to be viewed as final, the attempt to quantify happiness would lead to utopianism (a zealous but impractical reformation of society) and utilitarianism. The utilitarians Jeremy Bentham (1748–1832) and John Stuart Mill (1806–73), for example, would seek to reform society through applying the "principle of utility" that purported to measure the pleasure or happiness of individuals and societies.

Bentham and Mill were the last philosophers to treat happiness with the same urgent optimism found in antiquity: the desire for happiness they still regarded as a sign of the human difference, an expression of that aspect of human life that distinguished it from the life of other animals. Freud accepted the identification of happiness with pleasure but rejected any necessary connection of the drive toward happiness with the needs of the human intellect. On the contrary, he viewed human happiness (the German word is *Glück*) solely as the satisfaction of instinctual drives.[1] This is eighteenth-century hedonism given a Darwinian twist: the drive for happiness belongs to the animal side of human nature and arises from the dynamism of the human nervous system toward gratification, especially sexual gratification. For Freud, it becomes the job of human rationality to limit and to sublimate this happiness impulse in ways that keep it from being destructive to self and society.

Thus, it is not surprising that *Civilization and Its Discontents*, published in 1930, was originally entitled "Unhappiness in Culture." Freud had recognized a "Catch-22" in the universal human desire for a happiness such as he had defined it. The universal human drive for instinctual gratification is destined to frustration; the external world will not conform to our desires for an uninterrupted immediacy of pleasure. The requirements of civilization explicitly prohibit the acts of incest, polygamy, and murder, which would make it possible to enjoy the constant gratification, or *happiness*, of the libidinal urge. It is a mistake to consider Freud as offering a radical or libertine solution to the problem of happiness, as some of his followers did. Freud remained throughout his life a cultural conservative and a moralist, in contrast with the fact that psychoanalysis, at least in the popular mind, became the justification for overthrowing the old "repressive" sexual mores. For example, Herbert Marcuse, who was one of the most influential philosophers of the 1960s, argued in his *Eros and Civilization* (1955) for the liberation of the pleasure principle and for complete license regarding instinctual development. Social repression, for Marcuse, was simply another method of domination by the purveyors of capitalism who require a class of industrious workers committed to an ethics of work and to sharing an abhorrence of socially subversive pleasure.[2]

However, the conservative realism of Freud's original position is clearly seen in his comments here: "There is no possibility at all of its being carried through. . . . One feels inclined to say that the intention that man should be 'happy' is not included in the plan of 'creation'." Civilization demands the restriction of genital gratification for the sake of a cohesive social existence. Complete sexual freedom would, for example, destroy the family and the fabric of friendship: it would begin with sexual conquest and end with murder. Thus, it is no surprise that the very nature of happiness for Freud remains epitomized by the experience of the adult in sexual orgasm and of the child within its mother's womb.

The sheer intensity of gratification required by such exemplary experiences, of course, stands in sharp contrast with ordinary life. In spite of the fact that the dynamic of the "pleasure principle" limits happiness to momentary experience, Freud holds fast to his biological, instinctual understanding of human nature, insisting that the ideal of human happiness should be derived from it.

■ ■ ■

What to Look For in the Selection

As you read the following selection from Freud's *Civilization and Its Discontents*, ask yourself the following questions:

1. For Freud, what is the purpose of life?
2. Is this purpose obtainable?
3. What "palliative measures" do people substitute for it?
4. Is religion a palliative measure? How?
5. How does the human purpose of life differ from that of animals?
6. What serious problems arise from Freud's teaching in this matter?

■ ■ ■

Notes

1. S. Freud, *Civilization and Its Discontents* (New York, 1989), 25. One of the best treatments of Freud's views on happiness is G. Kalin, *The Utopian Flight from Unhappiness: Freud Against Marx on Social Problems* (Chicago, 1974).
2. H. Marcuse, *Eros and Civilization* (New York, 1962). See also the treatment of Marcuse by A. MacIntyre, *Herbert Marcuse* (New York, 1970).

SELECTION FROM FREUD

■ ■ ■

Civilization and Its Discontents, Chapter 2

The question of the purpose of human life has been raised countless times; it has never yet received a satisfactory answer and perhaps does not admit of one. Some of those who have asked it have added that if it should turn out that life has *no* purpose, it would lose all value for them. But this threat alters nothing. It looks, on the contrary, as though one had a right to dismiss the question, for it seems to derive from human presumptuousness, many other manifestations of which are already familiar to us. Nobody talks about the purpose of the life of animals, unless, perhaps, it may be supposed to lie in being of service to man. But this view is not tenable either, for there are many animals of which man can make nothing, except to describe, classify, and study them; and innumerable species of animals have escaped even this use, since they existed and became extinct before man set eyes on them. Once again, only religion can answer the question of the purpose of life. One can hardly be wrong in concluding that the idea of life having a purpose stands and falls with the religious system.

We will therefore turn to the less ambitious question of what men themselves show by their behavior to be the purpose and intention of their lives. What do they demand of life and wish to achieve in it? The answer to this can hardly be in doubt. They strive after happiness; they want to become happy and to remain so. This endeavor has two sides, a positive and a negative aim. It aims, on the one hand, at an absence of pain and "unpleasure," and, on the other, at the experiencing of strong feelings of pleasure. In its narrower sense the word "happiness" only relates to the latter. In conformity with this dichotomy in his aims, man's activity develops in two directions, according as it seeks to realize—in the main, or even exclusively—the one or the other of these aims.

As we see, what decides the purpose of life is simply the program of the pleasure principle. This principle dominates the operation of the mental apparatus from the start. There can be no doubt about its efficacy, and yet its program is at loggerheads with the whole world, with the macrocosm as much as with the microcosm. There is no possibility at all of its being carried through; all the regulations of the universe run counter to it. One feels inclined to say that the intention that man should be "happy" is not included in the plan of "creation." What we call happiness in the strictest sense comes from the (preferably sudden) satisfaction of needs which have been dammed up to a high degree, and it is from its nature only possible as an episodic phenomenon. When any situation that is desired by the pleasure principle is prolonged, it only produces a feeling of mild contentment. We are so made that we can derive intense enjoyment only from a contrast, and very little from a state of things. Thus our possibilities of happiness are already restricted by our constitution. Unhappiness is much less difficult to experience. We are threatened with suffering from three directions: from our own body, which is doomed to decay and dissolution and which cannot even do without pain and anxiety as warning signals; from the external world, which may rage against us with overwhelming and merciless forces of destruction; and, finally, from our relations to other men. The suffering which comes from this last source is perhaps more painful to us than any other. We tend to regard it as a kind of gratuitous addition, although it cannot be any less fatefully inevitable than the suffering which comes from elsewhere.

It is no wonder if, under the pressure of these possibilities of suffering, men are accustomed to moderate their claims to happiness—just as the pleasure principle itself, indeed, under the influence of the external world, changed into the more modest reality principle—if a man thinks himself happy merely to have escaped unhappiness or to have survived his suffering, and if in general the task of avoiding suffering pushes that of obtaining pleasure into the background. Reflection shows that the accomplishment of this task can be attempted along very different paths; and all these paths have been recommended by the various schools of worldly wisdom and put into practice by men. An unrestricted satisfaction of every need presents itself as the most enticing method of conducting one's life, but it means putting enjoyment before caution, and soon brings its own punishment. The other methods, in which avoidance of "unpleasure" is the main purpose, are differentiated according to the source of "unpleasure" to which their attention is chiefly turned. Some of these methods are extreme and some moderate; some are one-sided and some attack the problem simultaneously at several points. Against the suffering which may come upon one from human relationships the readiest safeguard is voluntary isolation, keeping oneself aloof from other people. The happiness which can be achieved along this path is, as we see, the happiness of quietness. Against the dreaded external world one can only defend oneself by some kind of turning away from it, if one intends to accomplish the task by oneself. There is, indeed, another and better path: that of becoming a member of the human community, and, with the help of a technique guided by science, going over to the attack against nature and subjecting her to the human will. Then one is working with all for the good of all. But the most interesting methods of averting suffering are those which seek to influence our own organism. In the last analysis, all suffering is nothing else than sensation; it only exists in so far as we feel it, and we only feel it in consequence of certain ways in which our organism is regulated.

The crudest, but also the most effective among these methods of influence is the chemical one—intoxication. I do not think that anyone completely understands its mechanism, but it is a fact that there are foreign substances which, when present in the blood or tissues, directly cause us pleasurable sensations; and they also so alter the conditions governing our sensibility that we become incapable of receiving unpleasurable impulses. The two effects not only occur simultaneously but seem to be intimately bound up with each other. But there must be substances in the chemistry of our own bodies which have similar effects, for we know at least one pathological state, mania, in which a condition similar to intoxication arises without the administration of any intoxicating drug. Besides this, our normal mental life exhibits oscillations between a comparatively easy liberation of pleasure and a comparatively difficult one, parallel with which there goes a diminished or an increased receptivity to "unpleasure." It is greatly to be regretted that this toxic side of mental processes has so far escaped scientific examination. The service rendered by intoxicating media in the struggle for happiness and in keeping misery at a distance is so highly prized as a benefit that individuals and peoples alike have given them an established place in the economics of their libido. We owe to such media not merely the immediate yield of pleasure but also a greatly desired degree of independence from the external world. For one knows that, with the help of this "drowner of cares," one can at any time withdraw from the pressure of reality and find refuge in a world of one's own, with better conditions of sensibility. As is well known, it is precisely this property of intoxicants which also determines their danger and their injuriousness. They are responsible, in certain circumstances, for the useless waste of a large quota of energy which might have been employed for the improvement of the human lot.

The complicated structure of our mental apparatus admits, however, of a whole number of other influences. Just as a satisfaction of instinct spells happiness for us, so severe suffering is caused us if the external world lets us starve, if it refuses to sate our needs. One may therefore hope to be freed from a part of one's sufferings by influencing the instinctual impulses. This type of defense against suffering is no longer brought to bear on the sensory apparatus; it seeks to master the internal sources of our needs. The extreme form of this is brought about by killing off the instincts, as is prescribed by the worldly wisdom of the East and practised by Yoga. If it succeeds, then the subject has, it is true, given up all other activities as well—he has sacrificed his life; and, by another path, he has once more only achieved the happiness of quietness. We follow the same path when our aims are less extreme and we merely attempt to control our instinctual life. In that case, the controlling elements are the higher psychical agencies, which have subjected themselves to the reality principle. Here the aim of satisfaction is not by any means relinquished; but a certain amount of protection against suffering is secured, in that non-satisfaction is not so painfully felt in the case of instincts kept in dependence as in the case of uninhibited ones. As against this, there is an undeniable diminution in the potentialities of enjoyment. The feeling of happiness derived from the satisfaction of a wild instinctual impulse untamed by the ego is incomparably more intense than that derived from sating an instinct that has been tamed. The irresistibility of perverse instincts, and perhaps the attraction in general of forbidden things, finds an economic explanation here.

Another technique for fending off suffering is the employment of the displacements of libido which our mental apparatus permits of, and through which its function gains so much in flexibility. The task here is that of shifting the instinctual aims in such a way that they cannot come up against frustration from the external world. In this, sublimation of the instincts lends its assistance. One gains the most if one can sufficiently heighten the yield of pleasure from the sources of psychical and intellectual work. When that is so, fate can do little against one. A satisfaction of this kind, such as an artist's joy in creating, in giving his phantasies body, or a scientist's in solving problems or discovering truths, has a special quality which we shall certainly one day be able to characterize in metapsychological terms. At present we can only say figuratively that such satisfactions seem "finer and higher." But their intensity is mild as compared with that derived from the sating of crude and primary instinctual impulses; it does not convulse our physical being. And the weak point of this method is that it is not applicable generally; it is accessible to only a few people. It presupposes the possession of special dispositions and gifts which are far from being common to any practical degree. And even to the few who do possess them, this method cannot give complete protection from suffering. It creates no impenetrable armour against the arrows of fortune, and it habitually fails when the source of suffering is a person's own body.

While this procedure already clearly shows an intention of making oneself independent of the external world by seeking satisfaction in internal, psychical processes, the next procedure brings out those features yet more strongly. In it, the connection with reality is still further loosened; satisfaction is obtained from illusions, which are recognized as such without the discrepancy between them and reality being allowed to interfere with enjoyment. The region from which these illusions arise is the life of the imagination; at the time when the development of the sense of reality took place, this region was expressly exempted from the demands of reality-testing and was set apart for the purpose of fulfilling wishes which were difficult to carry out. At the head of these satisfactions through phantasy stands the enjoyment of works of art—an enjoyment which, by the agency of the artist, is made accessible even to those who are not themselves creative. People who are receptive to the influence of art cannot set too high a value on it as a source of pleasure and consolation in life. Nevertheless the mild narcosis induced in us by art can do no more than bring about a transient withdrawal from the pressure of vital needs, and it is not strong enough to make us forget real misery.

Another procedure operates more energetically and more thoroughly. It regards reality as the sole enemy and as the source of all suffering, with which it is impossible to live, so that one must break off all relations with it if one is to be in any way happy. The hermit turns his back on the world and will have no truck with it. But one can do more than that; one can try to re-create the world, to build up in its stead another world in which its most unbearable features are eliminated, and replaced by others that are in conformity with one's own wishes. But whoever, in desperate defiance, sets out upon this path to happiness will as a rule attain nothing. Reality is too strong for him. He becomes a madman, who for the most part finds no one to help in carrying through his delusion. It is asserted, however, that each one of us behaves in some one respect like a paranoiac, corrects some aspect of the world which is unbearable to him by the construction of a wish, and introduces this delusion into reality. A special importance attaches to the case in which this attempt to procure a certainty of happiness and a protection against suffering through a delusional remolding of reality is made by a considerable number of people in common. The religions of mankind must be classed among the mass-delusions of this kind. No one, needless to say, who shares a delusion ever recognizes it as such.

I do not think that I have made a complete enumeration of the methods by which men strive to gain happiness and keep suffering away, and I know too that the material might have been differently arranged. One procedure I have not yet mentioned—not because I have forgotten it but because it will concern us later in another connection. And how could one possibly forget, of all others, this technique in the art of living? It is conspicuous for a most remarkable combination of characteristic features. It, too, aims of course at making the subject independent of Fate (as it is best to call it), and to that end it locates satisfaction in internal mental processes, making use, in so doing, of the displaceability of the libido of which we have already spoken. But it does not turn away from the external world; on the contrary, it clings to the objects belonging to that world and obtains happiness from an emotional relationship to them. Nor is it content to aim at an avoidance of "unpleasure"—a goal, as we might call it, of weary resignation; it passes this by without heed and holds fast to the original, passionate striving for a positive fulfillment of happiness. And perhaps it does in fact come nearer to this goal than any other method. I am, of course, speaking of the way of life which makes love the centre of everything, which looks for all satisfaction in loving and being loved. A psychical attitude of this sort comes naturally enough to all of us; one of the forms in which love manifests itself—sexual love—has given us our most intense experience of an overwhelming sensation of pleasure and has thus furnished us with a pattern for our search for happiness. What is more natural then that we should persist in looking for happiness along the path on which we first encountered it? The weak side of this technique of living is easy to see; otherwise no human being would have thought of abandoning this path to happiness for any other. It is that we are never so defenseless against suffering as when we love, never so helplessly unhappy as when we have lost our loved object or its love. But this does not dispose of the technique of living based on the value of love as a means to happiness. There is much more to be said about it.

We may go on from here to consider the interesting case in which happiness in life is predominantly sought in the enjoyment of beauty, wherever beauty presents itself to our senses and our judgment—the beauty of human forms and gestures, of natural objects and landscapes, and of artistic and even scientific creations. This aesthetic attitude to the goal of life offers little protection against the threat of suffering, but it can compensate for a great deal. The enjoyment of beauty has a peculiar, mildly intoxicating quality of feeling. Beauty has no obvious use; nor is there any clear cultural necessity for it. Yet civilisation could not do without it. The science of aesthetics investigates the conditions under which things are felt as beautiful, but it has been unable to give any explanation of the nature and origin of beauty, and, as usually happens, lack of success is concealed beneath a flood of resounding and empty words. Psychoanalysis, unfortunately, has scarcely anything to say about beauty either. All that seems certain is its derivation from the field of sexual feeling. The love of beauty seems a perfect example of an impulse inhibited in its aim. "Beauty" and "attraction" are originally attributes of the sexual object. It is worth remarking that the genitals themselves, the sight of which is always exciting, are nevertheless hardly ever judged to be beautiful; the quality of beauty seems, instead, to attach to certain secondary sexual characteristics.

In spite of the incompleteness of my enumeration, I will venture on a few remarks as a conclusion to our enquiry. The program of becoming happy, which the pleasure principle imposes on us, cannot be fulfilled; yet we must not—indeed, we cannot—give up our efforts to bring it nearer to fulfillment by some means or other. Very different paths may be taken in that direction, and we may give priority either to the positive aspect of the aim, that of gaining pleasure, or to its negative one, that of avoiding "unpleasure." By none of these paths can we attain all that we desire. Happiness, in the reduced sense in which we recognize it as possible, is a problem of the economics of the individual's libido.

Extracted from *Civilization and Its Discontents* (New York, 1989), 24–34.

COMMENTARY

■ ■ ■

Analysis of the Selection

Sigmund Freud's analysis of human striving in the second chapter of *Civilization and Its Discontents* starts from the assumption that, given the "economics of the individual's libido, . . . every man must find out for himself in what particular fashion he can be saved. . . . It is a question of how much real satisfaction he can expect to get from the external world, how far he is led to make himself independent of it, and, finally, how much strength he feels he has for altering the world to suit his wishes." The problem, as Freud points out, is that the world cannot be altered without serious consequences, both for society and for the renegade individual. What could be called a tragic vision in Freud's view of happiness was strongly foreshadowed in the *Candide* of Voltaire (1694–1778), the *Rasselas* of Samuel Johnson (1709–84), and the *Foundations of the Metaphysics of Morals* of Immanuel Kant (1724–1804).

Like Kant, who argues that morality cannot be based on the desire for happiness, Freud disassociates the object of psychoanalytic therapy from the happiness of the patient. Patients may in fact seek psychoanalytic help as a result of their suffering, but they should not be led to expect an existence free from all pain or frustration. This distinction, implying that those seeking the care of a therapist should give up on achieving happiness, also contradicts the popularly held view of Freudian therapy.

Freud, as is well known, also based his critique of religion on the same premise—that a God was being delusionally projected into the universe in order to assuage human suffering. Social existence requires the repression resulting from the regulation of the libido: "Civilization is built upon a renunciation of instinct." Therefore, Freud concludes that the object of therapy is not happiness at all but the "common unhappiness."[1] The therapist can help patients accept inhibited aims and redirect their instincts into other activities, such as aesthetic enjoyment, creativity, or simple work. This recommendation of resignation is a key to Freud's brand of realism.

Looking at Freud's assumptions about happiness itself against the larger historical background of the concept, one cannot help but notice the diminished value of happiness in human life. The pursuit of happiness has become a problem that the analyst has to solve through more realistic and socially beneficial expectations. In Freud's mind, the desire for happiness has become the cause of mental and emotional pathology in some, and constant frustration in all. As a product of our instinctual drive for gratification, happiness does not belong to intellectual or psychical capacities; rather, these powers must mediate the inherent dispute between the pleasure principle and the reality principle in favor of renunciation, which is often the cause of common unhappiness. The so-called reality principle enables a person to delay the gratification of impulses for the higher purpose of serving familial and social ends. Yet the central point to be made is about the pursuit of happiness itself: it no longer arises from the rational difference specifying human nature as different from other animal natures. "Happiness" as sexual gratification simply names the experience of libidinal satisfaction available to other animals as well, the only difference being that human beings can reflect upon their acts.

One of the strengths in Freud's theory of happiness is its critique of blatant hedonism. This critique stands in marked contrast to the uses of happiness in empirically based psychologies and sociology. Recent psychological researchers tend to accept any and all reports of pleasure and satisfaction as symptomatic of a "happy" state. In contrast, a recent psychoanalytic theorist takes Freud's notion of the pleasure principle, and the compulsion to repeat, as a basis to caution those who "would like to live in a state of unlimited narcissistic indulgence, to drift in a vast orgiastic ocean, disregarding reality and decrying its limitations." The caution is: "Can we call the resulting feeling happiness?"[2] Unlike classical philosophers such as Plato, Aristotle, and Epicurus, who based their critique of false pleasure on a theory of virtue and moral action, psychoanalysis limits itself to a language of psychic "health" and social "adjustment."

Again, the reason for this approach is Freud's view of sexual gratification as the model of human happiness. "Genital love" exemplifies those greatest experiences of happiness that come as unexpected satisfactions of sudden untamed instinctual impulses. Although Freud clearly points out the futility of pursuing happiness in a compulsive or violent manner, his emphasis on the biological aspects of human nature make it impossible for him to view happiness as the product of an immaterial act such as contemplation. For Freud, as was also the case for Immanuel Kant, the biological desire to obtain happiness dominates human beings "from below": arising from the sexual impulses of the body, the need for gratification often "dominates the mental apparatus."

Contrary to the tradition of the classical understanding of happiness, the desire for happiness in Freud's analysis does not arise, as has been said, from the distinguishing characteristic of the species—human rationality and its appetite for knowledge; it arises instead from certain drives that humans have in common with other species of animals. Reason enters in not to regulate the pursuit of happiness but to oppose it. Our "higher" mental activities allow a redirection of these instinctual energies so that we may collectively profit from the benefits of an orderly society.

Because the very thing that human beings most deeply desire cannot be possessed, Freud recommends the path of "sublimation," release of these instinctual energies into "higher" activities such as art and work. It is this same desire to escape the suffering that results from the restrictions on the libido that leads to the strategies of obtaining happiness, which are exhibited by the Stoic, the Yoga devotee, the hermit, the drunk, the aesthete. Indeed, the perennial struggle of mankind is between the individual's instinctual need for gratification and the needs of the group.

Freud, to a great extent, accomplished a reversal of the classical tradition: the idea of happiness now becomes fundamentally at odds with what is most praiseworthy in human life. A philosopher of Greece, Rome, medieval Paris, Renaissance Florence, or eighteenth-century Glasgow would have taught that the pursuit of happiness leads toward the perfecting of both the individual and society. But for Freud the unrestrained pursuit of happiness leads to violence. As he ironically comments elsewhere, the happy victor who succeeds in constantly gratifying his libidinal desires can only hope to convince society of at least one "thou shalt not," namely, thou shalt not murder, so that he can avoid being killed.[3] In other words, if a person is aggressive enough to seek his gratifying happiness whenever and wherever he desires it, he had better hope that those people who are hurt and offended by his willful breaking of moral rules are themselves unwilling to commit murder. The sexual profligate may indeed find that society will protect itself against those who threaten to destroy its most basic elements—its families. Such a person, far from being deemed heroic, is looked upon by Freud as weak, one who has been unable to bring the power of distinguishing between better and worse social outcomes to bear upon his own character and behavior.

Freud's seeming preoccupation with sexual desire can be misleading; he was far from being the intended harbinger of the loose sexual mores of the late twentieth century. Freud, as has been said, was a moralist. Although he recognized that human beings are driven by instinctual needs, he did not share the utilitarian confidence in measuring the goodness of morality and politics by the aggregates of pleasure they succeeded in producing. The pleasure principle on its own leads to a destructive compulsion to repeat, and ultimately comes to represent a death principle. Thus, we observe the dilemma of a typical hedonist caught in the web of his addictions, unable to rise above the self-destructive repetitions of behavior he may know to be harmful.

The way out of this compulsive behavior is marked by Freud's reality principle, which restricts the enjoyment of pleasure to what can be socially beneficial. This principle is supplied by human reason in an effort to bring freedom and order to the exercise of the instincts.[4] The reality principle stands for the learned ability of people to defer gratification according to the demands of their social conditions. Indeed, it is Freud's conviction that reason can guide human life away from destructive violence that keeps him linked to models of Greek and Roman rationality, particularly that underlying the cultivation of Stoic detachment.

However, with Freud, what was once identified as the greatest good of human life has become the motive for aggression, war, and annihilation. His analysis of culture contains a "portrayal of the tensions which civilized manners impose on central, unfulfilled human instincts, . . . as do hints . . . that there is in human interrelations an inescapable drive towards war, towards a supreme assertion of identity at the cost of mutual destruction."[5] In Freud's hands, the ideal of happiness has changed from an ideal of personal and political human perfection to the primary motive and explanation of human destruction. The same satisfaction that as late as Immanuel Kant was still thought to belong to a *summum bonum* [a highest good], the merited enjoyment of God in eternity, Freud specified as an inexorable human motive toward socially destructive ends. With Freud's theory of human nature and civilization, the ancient dualism of body and soul has reemerged, pitting the animal within us against the angel under the guise of sexual instinct, and sublimating reason.

Freud's attitude toward religion can be seen in the first chapter of *Civilization and Its Discontents*. Freud introduces his discussion by alluding to a letter he had received from Romain Rolland, a famous French novelist of the time, objecting to Freud's treatment of religion in *The Future of an Illusion*

(1927). In his letter Rolland had explained to Freud that the source of religious feelings was not based in existential insecurity but rather in what Freud calls "a sensation of 'eternity', a feeling of something limitless, unbounded—as it were, 'oceanic'." Rolland had carefully qualified his remarks as being applicable only to religious sentiments in general, not to his Catholic faith, which of course had more specific, revealed foundations.

Freud answers Rolland with scientific detachment: this is a feeling, he says, that he does not share; he cannot find it in himself. He is not denying that Rolland possesses a primal sense of being "at one" with the universe, but Freud does question whether he is properly interpreting the source of that feeling.

Freud then proceeds to analyze religious feelings in terms of his theory of the ego and the id. Under normal conditions, he explains, the individual ego does not reveal itself to consciousness as something unified with anything other than itself—the ego is "autonomous and unitary, marked off distinctly from everything else." One exception is the experience of love in which we feel our egos dissolve into union of subject and object: the lover and the beloved believe themselves to be "one." While such misconstruals of the ego's actual situation in the world are acceptable in the case of love, they are similar to pathological cases in which persons are unable to distinguish between what perceptions originate in the self and what actually arise from the not-self or world.

The ability to make these distinctions between the ego and the external world is for Freud precisely what the child must learn to acquire in becoming an adult. The opposition to the pleasure principle given by the pain of frustration accomplishes this division, except in those who seek "to throw it outside and to create a pure pleasure-ego." Experience will inevitably wear down the walls of the pleasure-ego, forcing it both to give up its delusional claim to immediacy and to accept the suffering integral to becoming a self. In such a manner, the reality principle becomes decisive in the development of the healthy, mature adult.

Freud concludes that the genesis of Rolland's "oceanic" feelings is in the vestiges of the affinity that the child's ego once felt with the external world. Those feelings that Rolland considered as religious in origin, Freud describes as infantile. This remark is not intended to sound either critical or condescending. It is both natural and common for the residue of primitive experiences to be retained not only in the development of a single individual but also in the evolution of the species itself.

It is typical of Freud's mind that he would choose to illustrate his point by beginning with an example not from biology but from the architecture of Rome. A visitor to the "Eternal City," he explains, is able to distinguish the various stages in its development, from early settlements along the river to the center of a federation and a republic and an empire. He asks his reader "by flight of imagination" to suppose that Rome is not a city but a "psychical entity with a similarly long and copious past." In this way, we can gaze upon the Coliseum while simultaneously picturing the Golden House of Nero, which no longer stands. In Rome, all that was past is preserved in the present; the same is true of the human mind if it has not been physically damaged.

Turning to the example of the human body, Freud points out that the earliest stages of physical development have been completely replaced by the adult's body. Consequently, it is the mind itself that makes possible the preservation of the child in the adult and that becomes the source of the early "ego-feelings" identified by Rolland as religious. It is not surprising then, argues Freud, that the preservation of these earliest of feelings would provide the source of religious *needs*:

> The derivation of religious needs from the infant's helplessness and the longing for the father aroused by it seems to me incontrovertible, especially since the feeling is not simply prolonged from childhood days, but is permanently sustained by fear of the superior power of Fate. I cannot think of any need in childhood as strong as the need for a father's protection. . . . The origin of the religious attitude can be traced back in clear outlines as far as the feeling of infantile helplessness.

Freud's critique of religion begins with the assumption that the ego, once it distinguishes itself from the external world, wishes to return to its state of immediate "oneness with the universe." Religious beliefs and practices become for adults a consoling but false substitute for the loss of their childhood security. Adult faith re-creates the security fostered by parental love; this time, however, the parent is God the Father. In this way, Freud gave a kind of scientific corroboration to the projectionist critique of religion that starts in Ludwig Feuerbach (1804–72), proceeds through Karl Marx (1818–83), and flowers in Friedrich Nietzsche.

Yet, unlike many of the disciples of these earlier figures, Freud wanted nothing to do with the founding of new ersatz religions to replace the old ones.[6] Many such ventures were already going strong in the period between the two world wars, and Freud considered them also to be guilty of escaping from the consequences of adult development. If anything, Freud's remarks at the beginning of our selection suggest that he took an even dimmer view of attempts to transpose traditional religious beliefs into more acceptable, humanistic, categories. Freud as a scientist did not want his critique of religion used to subvert institutional faiths so that more respectable, philosophical ones could be put in their place. Again, we meet another aspect of Freud's conservatism, his respect for his inherited culture, and perhaps even his Hebrew roots.

Although he may have been a cultural conservative, he was also, like Nietzsche, the opponent of any and all "afterworlds." As we see in the reading, Freud was intensely aware of the unavoidable suffering that drives human beings to console themselves with beliefs in redemption, eternity, and an afterlife. As a realist Freud knew that some type of relief from suffering must be allowed: humanity cannot be expected to stand totally naked before the fact of human meaninglessness.

■ ■ ■

Summary

For Freud, human beings strive primarily for bodily pleasure, but society is not possible if this striving goes unchecked.

People therefore resort to substitute pleasures, such as can be found in work or knowledge or art, or they flee from reality by using intoxicating substances. For Freud there is no *given* purpose to human life. Religion, he knows, offers an explanation of this purpose, but is mistaken. Religion, for him, is merely a childish wish in an adult, a wish for the protective father of childhood. It is really a neurotic symptom, different from an individual neurosis only in that many people share it.

For Freud the purpose of human life is not the fulfillment of our intellectual nature but of our animal nature; the role of the intellect is to restrain our animal nature in its search for pleasure and find substitutes for this pleasure. The intellect is really thus opposed to the purpose of our life. We seek happiness but life cannot provide it.

■ ■ ■

Philosophical and Religious Critique

The question becomes What type of mechanisms for finding comfort are going to be encouraged? Obviously the comforts of religion are going to be rejected since they deter human maturation, but certain forms of "sublimation," especially those involving intellectual or artistic projects, are found to be beneficial. The parallel between Freud and John Stuart Mill at this point is instructive. As has been said, Freud accepts the hedonist assumptions about the nature of happiness held a century earlier by the utilitarians. Mill himself, however, could not retain his allegiance to a purely quantitative account of hedonic happiness. His distinction between "higher and lower" pleasures was an attempt to move toward a qualitative theory of happiness while retaining its scientific basis in hedonism.[7] Freud makes the same type of connection of "higher" pleasures with those activities that traditionally have been accorded high honors in Western culture—artistic appreciation and creativity, and the intellectual exercises of reading, writing, and thinking.

The reader should bear in mind that Mill was writing in London during the first half of the nineteenth century and Freud in a Vienna not yet decimated by the Second World

War. Both figures had the advantage of appealing to models of civility and taste that have long since been destroyed by the ascendency of popular culture and its undercurrents of hatred toward high culture. Earlier readers of both Mill and Freud may in fact have been persuaded by their distinctions between higher and lower based upon a shared sense of what was of lasting importance in Western civilization. Appeals to the philosophical or artistic exertions of a Socrates or a Michelangelo may indeed have persuaded their readers of the distinction, in spite of the fact that in both cases it did not fit well into their overall perspective on happiness.

The contemporary reader is likely to share little of Freud's enthusiasm for Europe's high culture, while at the same time feel relatively familiar with his psychoanalytic critique of religion. This places the reader is an awkward situation: he or she may, on the one hand, accept the truth of the critique, especially since it comes with the *imprimatur* [permission] of science, but, on the other hand, be unsure about the sublimations that Freud seems to recommend. Does one have to become a "highbrow" in order to be psychoanalytically correct? No, it would be a misreading of Freud to make his theory strictly dependent upon the level of culture he could count on meeting in his Viennese patients. Here one must distinguish between the kind of education and articulateness that provides for the best therapeutic experience and Freud's theory of culture itself. It could be argued that his therapeutic method of free association requires a rather unusual level of verbal and imaginative dexterity. However, Freud's recommendation of work and artistic pleasure can be applied to all levels of cultural sophistication and expertise. His concern is not with the quality of the work or the artistic merit of the art objects but with the opportunity to redirect and to express our instinctual energies. Ironically, Freud, a true connoisseur of European culture, may have been in an ideal position to understand the explosion of interest in pop culture, its soap operas, its videos and MTV, and its cult of short-lived celebrityhood. Although he probably would have disdained them, Freud would have understood the powerful need for the consolation being expressed through their popularity. After all, if "God is dead" and if religion is "infantile," then we have to find some "adult" forms of comfort. Popular culture, Freud might say, has undoubtedly resulted as an antidote to the loss of confidence in religious traditions.

■ ■ ■

Notes

1. S. Freud, *Studies in Hysteria*, 2.305, quoted in P. Rieff, *Freud: The Mind of the Moralist* (New York, 1961), 358.
2. I. Silbermann, "On Happiness," *The Psychoanalytic Study of the Child* 40 (1985): 461.
3. S. Freud, *The Future of an Illusion* (New York, 1964), 19–20.
4. P. Rieff, *The Mind of the Moralist*, 355–57.
5. G. Steiner, *In Bluebeard's Castle* (New Haven, 1971), 24.
6. For further background see E. Vogelin, "Ersatz Religion," *Science, Politics, and Gnosticism* (Chicago, 1968), 83–114.
7. J. S. Mill, *Utilitarianism* (Indianapolis, 1957), 12.

■ ■ ■

Further Reading

E. Fromm, *Sigmund Freud's Mission* (New York, 1959).
P. Rieff, *Freud: The Mind of the Moralist* (London, 1960).

12

EDITH STEIN

...

THE HUMAN PERSON
AS MALE AND FEMALE

Introduction and Commentary by Prudence Allen

INTRODUCTION

. . .

Stein's Life and Works

Born in Breslau, Germany, in 1891, the seventh and youngest child in a Jewish family, Edith Stein is significant for three innovations in the history of philosophy: the reconciliation of Thomism with phenomenology, the integration of psychology and philosophy in the particular study of empathy, and the consideration of "woman" as a fundamental category for philosophical research. She also stands out in the history of the West through the profound witness of her personal life, which included conversion to Roman Catholicism in 1922, entry into the Carmelite order in Cologne in 1934, and arrest by the Gestapo and execution in the gas chambers of Auschwitz in 1942.

The intellectual life was always attractive to Stein, and she excelled in it from her early childhood. Studying Germanic literature, history, and philosophy at the University of Breslau from 1911, she discovered the thought of Edmund Husserl. His philosophical method (called *phenomenological*) drew the young student irresistibly, and in 1913 she left Breslau to transfer to the University of Göttingen to work directly with her mentor. She also began to study with Max Scheler, whose recent conversion from Judaism to Catholicism made an impression on her sensitive mind.

Stein graduated with a Ph.D. *summa cum laude* in 1916; her dissertation was entitled "On the Problem of Empathy." She worked briefly as a Red Cross nurse during World War I. A year later, when Husserl was appointed to a new position at the University of Freiburg, she moved there to work as his assistant and to edit his manuscripts. During the years in Göttingen, she had become very trusted by Husserl, and he would refer to her as the one who best understood his thought.

During this time of working with Husserl, Stein converted to Catholicism. While many factors paved the way, the moment of illumination occurred in 1921 as she read Saint Teresa of Avila's *Life,* and concluded that it was the truth. Edith Stein's love of the truth was, she claimed, her guide and constant prayer. After a period of instruction, she entered the Church on New Year's Day, 1922. Shortly afterward, the new Catholic began teaching German literature and philosophy at a Dominican Girls' College in Speyer, a job she held for eight years.

Two very important intellectual directions unfolded for her during this next period of her life: the discovery of Saint Thomas Aquinas, and a dedication to a philosophical reflection on woman. From 1925 to 1931 she entered into a close professional relationship with Erich Przywara, S.J., who led her to translate Cardinal Newman's *Letters and Journals* and *The Idea of a University* as well as Saint Thomas's *Disputed Questions on Truth.* Throughout her life she sought to integrate the original thought of Saint Thomas and Husserl, or scholasticism and phenomenology, and for this reason she is credited with being a main force in developing a German neo-Scholasticism.

In 1928 Stein began her public addresses on women, first to the Catholic women teachers of Bavaria on "The Function of Woman in National Life." Then as a result of her growing popularity she gave an address to the Congress of the German Association of Catholic Graduates, in Salzburg in 1930, on "The Ethos of Women's Vocations." In 1932 Dr. Stein accepted a position as lecturer at the Educational Institute at Münster to develop a Catholic science of the education of women. Soon after, she further developed her thinking in "Problems of

Women's Education," the text that is excerpted in this chapter. In these works Stein's knowledge of phenomenology and Thomism are brought to bear on the question of the differences and similarities of man and woman.

As Hitler rose to power, the opportunities for Jewish citizens to work in Germany became more limited. Even though Edith Stein was a convert to Catholicism, her teaching appointment was not renewed. Interpreting this as a sign from God that she would now be free to follow her prompting towards a religious vocation, on October 14, 1933, the philosopher became a postulant in the Carmelite Priory in Cologne. One year later she was received into the novitiate in the presence of many university professors, and given the name Sister Teresa Benedicta of the Cross. Shortly afterward her Provincial Superior requested that Sister Benedicta finish her treatise on potency and act. It was completed as *Finite and Eternal Being* in 1936.

Sister Benedicta spent her remaining years in the convent working on a book, *The Science of the Cross*, which was an analysis of the thought of Saint John of the Cross. In the preface to this work she noted that "only modern philosophy has set itself the task of working out a philosophy of the person," and that she was going to interpret Saint John as beginning to develop a theology of the person.[1] Most commentators claim that this work in fact was not really theological, but rather an interpretation of her own contemplative experience. It was interrupted by her need to leave Cologne suddenly when the synagogue was burned and Jewish residents were persecuted.

Sister Benedicta had previously felt the sting of anti-Semitism while she was living in Carmel: in 1935 some reviews she had written on Catholic women's education had already been accepted for publication, but then were returned unpublished because of her Jewish heritage. She, and her sister Rosa who had also entered Carmel, were sent to another monastery in Echt, Holland, only to be arrested there in a German retaliation against the Dutch Catholic Church for refusing to give over Jewish children who had converted to Catholicism.

Sister Benedicta had decided as early as 1933 (the year Hitler came to power) to offer her life to God in deep union with her people, and as a sacrifice for peace. She also wrote a letter during that same year to Pope Pius XI to ask him to write an encyclical against the persecution of the Jews. Then in a letter written to her Prioress after her arrest on August 2, 1942, she reaffirmed this call: "One can gain a *scientia Crucis [a knowledge of the Cross]* only if one is made to feel the Cross oneself to the depth of one's being. Of this I have been convinced from the first moment and have said it with all my heart. *Ave Crux, spes unica [Hail, Cross, the only hope]!*"[2]

Sister Benedicta of the Cross was immediately deported to Auschwitz, Poland, where she met her death in the gas chambers on August 9. Declared "Blessed" by Pope John Paul II in 1987, Edith Stein (Sister Teresa Benedicta of the Cross) is now recognized as a model for men and women seeking to live a holy Catholic life.

■ ■ ■

What to Look For in the Selection

The following questions are suggested as a way of looking for key ideas in the selection from Edith Stein's "Problems of Women's Education." The questions are grouped under the headings found in the selection itself.

Its Significance in the Process of Formation and Education

1. What does Stein mean by *species?* How does she think that woman and man can be considered as species? How does *species* differ from *type?* How is species related to form?
2. What, according to Stein, is the difference between ontology and philosophical anthropology? What are their proper areas of study?

Methods of Analysis

3. How would you describe the philosophical method articulated in this essay? What premises does Edith Stein start with and what steps does she take in studying her topic, "woman"?

4. How does the philosophical method, as Stein articulates it, differ from methods in the natural sciences or liberal arts?
5. What does Stein mean by *cognition?* How does it compare with abstraction, with feeling, with intuition?

Potential of the Individual Methods for an Understanding of the Content of Women's Education

6. How do philosophy and theology approach sex and gender identity in different but complementary ways?
7. What does Stein think is the goal of education? What implications for education follow from gender and sex differentiation?

A Sketch of the Subjects to Be Educated

8. What is the difference between the human species, the species woman or man, and an individual woman or man?
9. How does Stein describe the relation of body and soul as different or the same in women and men?

General Questions

10. What are the different structures present in the human being, and how are they related to gender and sex differentiation?
11. How do women and men relate to masculine and feminine types of characteristics?

■ ■ ■

Notes

1. H. Graef, *The Scholar and the Cross: The Life and Work of Edith Stein* (Westminster, Md., 1955), 207. See Edith Stein (Teresa Benedicta of the Cross, OCD), *The Science of the Cross (A Study of St. John of the Cross)* (Chicago, 1960).

2. Graef, *The Scholar and the Cross*, 223. See also J. M. Oesterreicher, "Edith Stein: Witness of Love," in *Walls are Crumbling* (New York, 1952), 288–329.

SELECTION FROM STEIN

■ ■ ■

The Nature of Woman:
Its Relation to the Content of Education

Its Significance in the Process of Formation and Education

By the term *education* we mean that formation experienced by a person designated for development. Such formation is either an inner instinctive process or a planned program carried out either independently or directed by others. It is thus evident that it is basic to understand the *object* which is being formed. If we limit *education* here to a planned program, there is a fundamental practical requirement to understand the nature of the person for whom this work is designed.

When we stand in front of the class, we see at first glance that no child is exactly like another. And not only do we notice external differences, but we perceive together *with* them inner ones as well. (We cannot explore here what these inner differences signify nor *which* external differences are particularly important in discerning them.) We see they are so many different human beings, so many unique *individuals*. After having known them awhile, we shall perceive that they also constitute groups, groups united by common characteristics and separated from each other by typically different characteristics. Now it appears that each individual also represents a *type,* and, in addition to the types represented within one age group, a comparison of students from different classes reveals types characteristic of their age groups. (In addition, we have the *class type* which is to be differentiated completely from the age group.)

For the time being, we must defer the question of what causes these types, several of which can coexist in one individual. Should we compare a class of girls to a class of boys, we would again find typical differences. And, in addition, the question is whether we are dealing with types in the same sense as those *within* the girls' or boys' class respectively or whether we have discovered a universal type common to both.

I have spoken before of the species "woman." By *species* we understand a permanent category which does not change. Thomistic philosophy designates it by the term *form,* meaning an *inner* form which determines structure. The type is not unchanging in the same sense as the species. An individual can develop from one type to another. For instance, this happens in the process when the individual advances from childhood to adolescence and then to adulthood. Hence, this progress is prescribed within the individual by an inner form. Also, a child can change type if transferred from one class into another (i.e., among other children) or displaced from one family into another. Such changes are attributed to the influence of environment. But such influences are limited by inner form. And types can vary within the limits of inner form or species.

It is quite clear that species is the core of all questions concerning *woman.* If such a "species" exists, then it cannot be modified by environmental, economic, cultural, or professional factors. If we question the concept of species, if *man* and *woman* are to be considered as types as we have defined them, then the transformation of one type to another is possible under certain conditions. This is not as absurd as it may appear at first glance. At one time this view was considered valid on the basis that although physical differences were unchanging, the psychological differences were capable of infinite variation. But certain facts, such as the existence of hybrid and transitory forms, can be quoted to dispute the immutability of physical differences.

However, this question of species as a principle affecting women's problems is related to philosophical principles. In order to answer the question properly, we must understand the relationship between gender, species, type, and individual, i.e., we must be clear about the basic problems of formal ontology; in this I perceive what Aristotle means by his concept of *First Philosophy*. The material disciplines involving their specific subjects must needs investigate what is clarified in formal universality by this fundamental philosophy. The inquiry into the essence of woman has its logical place in a *philosophical anthropology*. Anthropology clarifies the meaning of sexual differences and proves the substance of the species; moreover, it is proper to this work to prove the place of the species in the structure of the individual human being, the relationship of the types to the species and to the individual, and the relationship of types to conditions in which they develop. . . .

■ ■ ■

Methods of Analysis

How, then, should we begin to lay the theoretical foundation of girls' education? From the abundant literature on women's problems, where can we get a standard for selecting the components for such a solid foundation? We must ask ourselves what methods there are at our disposal to attain this knowledge; and if we should try to evaluate an existing inquiry, we must then ascertain what its purpose was, what method was used, whether its goal could be attained by this method, and whether it was, in fact, attained.

(a) Method Relating to the Natural Sciences (Experimental-psychological)

There is a purely scientific method of dealing with woman's unique nature. This is the procedure of anatomy and physiology which describe and explain experientially the structure and functions of the feminine body. So also does that branch of psychology called scientific or experimental psychology: with the help of observation and experiment, it examines psychic data pertaining to the largest possible number of cases; and it seeks to derive universal laws of psychic characteristics from them. At the beginning of the twentieth century, sexual psychology also advanced in this manner. Individual psychic performances and their recognizable attributes of a number of persons from both sexes were investigated, such as the acuteness of the senses, the capacity to learn and to retain learning, the aptitude for different disciplines, the kinds of tendencies manifested (for instance, in such things as favorite games and activities), peculiarities of imagination, emotion, and will, etc.

All of these scientific investigations assume the differences between the sexes as a universal fact; they strive to establish as exactly as possible the details of the differences. They describe the uniqueness of each through *traits* which are present *on average* or whose frequency, perhaps also whose degree of occurrence, can be quantified. However, they do not succeed in giving an overall picture of uniqueness; and, moreover, they are unable to determine whether woman is to be considered as a variable type or as a fixed species.

(b) Method Relating to the Liberal Arts

Psychology underwent a great change by the turn of the century: behavioristic psychology was repressed more and more in favor of other kinds known as *cognitive, structural,* and also *humanistic* psychology. Here several lines of thought would need to be differentiated. Common to them all is the *psychic* life conceived as a *uniform whole* which can neither be separated into its component parts nor reassembled into them. (In the beginning of scientific psychology, one was apt to hear of "psychology without the soul"; at the least, it was left undecided whether or not an authentic unity existed among individual, psychic facts. This skepticism regarding the existence of the soul has yet in no way been surmounted in humanistic psychology.)

This new method has been established in answer to the needs of the humanities (history, literature, etc.) and for the diagnosis and therapy of psychic abnormalities. In both instances, it is a matter of grasping definite individual personalities; hence, the description of the entire individual psychic context plays an important role in this new method. Its material is supplied by personal experiences, educational and psychiatric practice, diaries, and memoirs. However, such analysis could not be satisfied with simply the description of the individual. First, every description of an individual must also deal with the concept of his type because the individual as such cannot be understood abstractly. Secondly, definite types are brought into relief by the evidence under study; the structural context is neither simply universal (the same with all beings, without any differentiation) nor simply individual (singular to each one, without being common to all). Third, the types are of practical importance for the methods used in education and medicine; hence the feminine type or a diversity of feminine types is respectively encountered here.

The psychology of the individual cannot be content with making one momentary cross-section at a time through the psychic life but must rather strive for the most attainable grasp of its total progress within a given time; hence it also escapes the danger of taking the types as it finds them in each case to be something inflexible and permanent. The changing behavior of the type according to the change of outer circumstances is most evident. Moreover, the outlook which views personality as a totality is impelled to accept the psyche in its psychosomatic oneness. Since the human being is always a being in the world and since his psychic characteristics are always defined by it, it is necessary that psychology embrace anthropological, sociological, and cosmological considerations. . . .

(c) Philosophical Method

Problems of philosophy begin where the work of positive sciences leave off. For philosophy the "X" of an unknowable *natural predisposition* could not suffice. I would like to affirm that philosophy is able to make a threefold analysis of this "X" (separable only by abstraction, not in reality): the "species" of humanity, the species of woman, and individuality.

We are now faced with the important questions of *philosophical method*. Within our context it is impossible to develop this method in its entire scope and to derive a method based on the primary causes. I can only specify the ways which could lead, according to my conviction, to the solution of the problems raised.

With the phenomenological school, i.e., the school of Edmund Husserl, I share the view that the philosophical method differs in principle from that of the positive sciences: it commands its own function of cognition, and it is exactly this function which makes possible the foundation necessary for the other sciences; this foundation, which the various sciences are not able to achieve themselves, delimits the scope of their subject-matter and shows the means and method suitable for each of them. Phenomenology has designated this peculiar function of cognition as intuition or *Wesensanschauung*. Terms such as this one have given rise to many misunderstandings because their meanings bear the charge of history. By this function of cognition, I mean the perceptual achievement which confers on a concrete subject its universal structure; for instance, it enables us to say what a material thing is in its entirety—a plant, an animal, a person—or what the meaning of these terms is. What I am calling *intuition* here relates very closely to what traditional philosophy signifies as *abstraction*. A thorough phenomenological analysis of intuition and abstraction could perhaps demonstrate that there is really no sense in arguing about which of the two is the true philosophical method.

This is obviously related to the formulation of our question. It is possible to present the meaning of the terms "essence of woman" or "species of woman" only if a function of cognition exists capable of grasping such a universal slant. On the whole, most of the writers on these questions began their work without considering the question of method inasmuch as they were not confined within the framework of a positive science. They wrote out of *feeling* or *instinct*. That is not to say that this entire literature may be worthless. It has the value of all disciplines formed by prescientific experience and hypotheses: the value of material which must be critically processed. To be sure, everyone knows women from experience and believes he knows what a woman is from that experience. But should he generalize on the basis of that experience, we could not be certain whether it is a true generalization or whether what may be actually observed in this or that case may in no way be true of others. But even beyond that, a criticism of the individual experience is necessary. Has even the individual woman been rightly understood? All experiences are prone to the dangers of error and delusion which are perhaps more numerous and more serious here than elsewhere. What guarantee do we have that such hazards have been avoided? Or it may be that an ideal image of woman is being presented to us by which particular women are to be measured as authentic women. Then again, we must inquire into the origin of this ideal image and of what value it is as a contribution to understanding.

In any case, there is one significant factor which must be singled out from all these considerations: the self-evident *claim* of being able to make universal statements. Without justifying it to himself, a person takes it for granted that he is grasping something of a universal nature through his own experiences. From this arises the philosopher's task of identifying this universal function of cognition which is operative in experience, or organizing it into a system, and by this means raising it to the rank of a scientific method.

(d) Theological Method

With this we now come to the remaining method for discussion concerning the treatment of our question, the *theological* method. It is of fundamental importance to us to know what Catholic doctrine affirms regarding the essence or nature of woman. To be informed we will first of all refer to doctrine in the narrowest sense: that which we are obligated to believe; i.e., to definitions of dogma. We will not gain very much here. We shall then extend the area of inquiry to interpretation of doctrine, i.e., we will cite the writings of the Doctors and Fathers of the Church as well as contemporary statements concerning dogma. Of course, in the latter we shall find more plentiful material; however, this material possibly invites criticism.

For instance, when St. Thomas says *Vir est principium mulieris et finis* ("Man is the source and end of woman"),[1] we must ask what meaning this sentence has and from what source it was taken. In this instance, it is not difficult to specify the source. It is the Bible and, indeed, it is the account of creation; some passages from the *Epistles* of St. Paul come to mind as well. To determine the meaning of this sentence from St. Thomas, it would first be necessary to know from the context of the Thomistic world of thought what he means by designating one thing as the principle and end of another. It would then be necessary to refer to all scriptural passages from which a definition of the end of woman could be drawn (and likewise anything concerning her *subordination* to man); and what appears here as principle and end would have to be compared to that sentence of St. Thomas. Should there be a conformity, one would have to ask what inference might be drawn concerning the *nature* of woman from the definition of woman's end and the relationship of order between her and man. For it is clear that, if woman were created for a predestined purpose, her nature must needs be suited to that purpose. The types which we are familiar with from experience could be compared to the concept of nature yielded by this indirect method of cognition. If deviations were found, we should have to ask how such a falling-off from nature is possible and how this is to be explained. But moreover, should we attain a concept of woman's *essence* entirely by philosophy, we would have to compare this directly perceived essence to the concept of nature made accessible by theological considerations. Should there prove to be inconsistencies, this would be due to error in either perspective. However, it may also be that the terms *nature* and *essence* are not completely identical in meaning. This is an ontological problem which we will not investigate at this time.

Finally, with the discussion of theological didactic concepts, we are faced with still another method of theological analysis, one to which dogma refers, namely, ascertaining what the Bible itself says. . . .

■ ■ ■

Potential of the Individual Methods for an Understanding of the Content of Women's Education

We have now established a whole range of different methods which have attempted or could attempt to discover woman's unique nature. It would now be feasible to summarize once more the potential contribution of each method to our problem according to the means of cognition utilized.

To expound on the *species* is proper to the cognitive function of *philosophy* which alone can achieve a valid explanation. To even begin to explain how I think this problem can be solved, I must integrate it as I see it into the totality of philosophic problems.

As I have already stated in a previous passage, I regard Ontology, i.e., a science of the basic forms of Being *(Sein)* and of beings *(Seienden),* as the fundamental discipline. It is able to demonstrate that there is a radical division within being: *pure Being* holds nothing of non-being in itself, has neither beginning nor end, and holds in itself all which can be; *finite being* has as its allocation both beginning and end. We call the one uncreated Being, the other created being; the Creator corresponds to the former and creatures to the latter. (These terms are borrowed from the language of theology, but the reality thus signified can be shown by purely philosophical methods.)

Creatures are arranged into grades depending on how they more or less approximate pure Being, for all created being is an analogy to divine Being. However, the *analogia entis* [analogy of being] is different for each grade; each one corresponds to another kind of being and a different basic form of being: material, organic, animal, and rational being.

Inasmuch as all lower grades are contained in man's structure of being, he occupies a place peculiar to him in this graded structure. His body is a *material body,* but not *only* that. Rather, at the same time, it is an *organism with a soul* which, in the sensitive manner peculiar to him, is open to himself and his environment. And, finally, he is a *spiritual* being who is consciously cognizant of himself and others and can act freely to develop himself and others. All this belongs to the *human species,* and whatever does not evidence this structure of being cannot be termed a *human being.* However, this species appears differentiated in individuals: notwithstanding his specific human nature, every person has his own unrepeatable singularity. Philosophy can also demonstrate that *individuality,* in the sense of uniqueness, is proper to the human species. To comprehend respective individuals is not the concern of philosophy; rather, we utilize a specific experiential function in our daily contact with people. Another, simple differentiation cuts across this differentiation of humanity into a limitless multiplicity of individuals: *sexual* differentiation.

I would now like to point out several significant questions regarding the education of girls. Does the difference between man and woman involve the whole structure of the person or only the body and those psychic functions necessarily related to physical organs? Can the mind be considered unaffected by this difference? This view is upheld not only by women but also by many theologians. Should this latter view be valid, education would then strive towards development of the intellect without consideration of sexual difference. If, on the other hand, the difference does involve the person's entire structure, then educational work must consider the specific structure of the masculine and feminine mind. Furthermore, if the nature of each individual contains both masculine and feminine elements and if only one of these elements is predominant in each person, would not individuals of both *species* then be needed to represent perfectly the human species as a whole? Could it not be fully represented by one individual? This question is also of practical significance because, depending on the answer, education must be geared to either overcoming limitations of the specifically masculine and feminine natures or to developing their potential strengths.

In order to answer this question, we would need to refer to the entire context of *genetic* problems; this has hardly been done so far. It would be feasible to examine at some time the specific existential mode exclusive to the human being: the species does not come about in ready-made form at the beginning of existence; rather, the individual develops progressively in a process dependent on time. This process is not unequivocally predetermined but depends rather on several variable factors, among others, on man's freedom which enables him to work towards his own formation and that of others. The possibility of a diversity of types is rooted in this human characteristic which encourages the formation of the species in changing circumstances. There are also further questions to be considered: the generation of new individuals; the transmission of the species through successive generations; and their modification in a variety of types as sexual evolution advances. In considering these questions, philosophy is not concerned with specific changes either in a particular individual's existence or in the factual course of history but rather with their potentiality for change. The connection of genetic problems to that of the development of the species can be expressed in a further question: Is the concrete development of the species as a whole perhaps possible only in the entire succession of generations in their sexual and individual differentiation?

The concern of philosophy is to investigate the necessary and potential characteristics of being through its specific function of cognition. *Theology* seeks to establish woman's unique nature according to divine revelation. Its direct concern is not to investigate the problem itself but rather to assemble and explain historical records. Generally, Scripture does not deal with natural necessities and potentialities but rather reveals facts and gives practical instructions. For instance, philosophy asks whether the world was created in time or whether we may consider it as existing through eternity. But the account of creation tells us that it did begin in time and how it began. The Scriptures do not ask whether the sexual differentiation is necessary or accidental but say: "God created man according to His image. He created them as man and woman." Here we find the expression of the facts of oneness and differentiation. However this is a terse statement which requires explanation. What is meant by God's image in man? We find the answer in the complete history and doctrine of salvation, and it is summarized briefly in the words of Our Lord: "Be ye perfect as your heavenly Father is perfect." I will not at this time discuss the nature of this ideal of perfection. I would simply suggest that in the words "Be ye" the image of God is established as a duty, vocation, or destiny of mankind—i.e., of man and of woman. . . .

I cannot delve any further into this explanation of what can be learned from the theological perspective, especially from the Bible, on the problem of the sexes. Revelation does not, by any means, provide us with all the knowledge that we can and would like to assimilate; rather, it leaves us much latitude for rational inquiry. Yet we find here positive facts and norms resting on a firm foundation, and many errors in theory and practice could be averted if this scriptural source were thoroughly utilized. Rightly understood and employed, the theological and philosophical approaches are not in competition; rather, they complete and influence each other ("I believe that I may understand"; "Faith seeking understanding"). The philosophizing mind is challenged to make the realities of faith as intelligible as possible. On the other hand, these realities protect the mind from error, and they answer certain questions concerning matters of faith which reason must leave undecided. . . .

■ ■ ■

A Sketch of the Subjects to Be Educated

. . . I am convinced that the species *humanity* embraces the double species *man* and *woman*; that the essence of the complete *human* being is characterized by this duality; and that the entire structure of the essence demonstrates the specific character. There is a difference, not only in body structure and in particular physiological functions, but also in the entire corporeal life. The relationship of soul and body is different in man and woman; the relationship of soul to body differs in their psychic life, as does that of the spiritual faculties to each other. The feminine species expresses a unity and wholeness of the total psychosomatic personality and a harmonious development of faculties. The masculine species strives to enhance individual abilities in order that they may attain their highest achievements. . . .

The species humanity, as well as the species femininity, is revealed differently in different individuals. First of all, they represent the species more or less perfectly; then, they illustrate more or less one or another of its characteristics. Man and woman have the same basic human traits, although this or that trait predominates not only in the sexes but also in individuals. Therefore, women may closely approximate the masculine type, and conversely. This may be connected to their individual vocation. If, on the whole, marriage and motherhood are the primary vocations for the feminine sex, it is not necessarily true for each individual. Women may be called to singular cultural achievements, and their talents may be adapted to these achievements.

This brings us to *feminine types* classed *according to their natural abilities.* Given the finiteness of human nature, the impulse to cultural creativity expresses itself in a multiplicity of vocations. And since human nature is finite, man constantly longs for perfection, to which all human beings are called. . . . The species *humanity* is realized perfectly only in the course of world history in which the great individual, humanity, becomes concrete. And the species *man* and *woman* are also fully realized only in the total course of historical development. Whoever is active in educational work is given the human material which he must help form in order that it may become part of the species to which it is called.

Extracted from "Problems of Women's Education," in *Essays on Woman,* translated by Freda Mary Oben, in *The Collected Works of Edith Stein,* vol. 2 (Washington, D.C., 1987), 161–81.

■ ■ ■

Note

1. *Summa Theologiae,* 1.92.1.

COMMENTARY

■ ■ ■

Analysis of the Selection

It is important to begin an analysis of Edith Stein's philosophy with a consideration of her methodology. In the passage on women's education selected for this chapter, four different methods of approach to the question of woman's identity are distinguished: (1) experimental-psychological, (2) humanistic-psychological, (3) philosophical, and (4) theological. Each method, she argues, brings forth a different aspect of truth about woman, and each is limited when applied alone to the object of study. It is important to point out, however, that Stein does set the third method apart from the other three as being the most useful approach to the study of woman's identity. In short, the first method focuses on generalizations about woman's behavior; the second on individuals and types of women, with a therapeutic goal in mind; and the fourth on interpretation of guidelines about women in Scripture and through the illumination of faith. Though useful, none of these three methods, argues Stein, can replace the particular focus of philosophy, which is to grasp by an intuition the essence of the object being studied.

When Edith Stein describes the philosophical method, she is thinking of the phenomenological method as first developed by Edmund Husserl. This method, which was proposed as a scientific approach to reality, begins with sense perceptions of real objects, which are then submitted to a rigorous critical analysis by the exercise of reason. The goal of this phenomenological analysis is to reach an intuition of the essence of the object being studied. It seeks to grasp what is real, and for this reason Stein refers to its ontological basis. Stein believes that 'being' is intelligible to the mind of the philosopher who comes into contact with the essence of something through this scientific application of the method of phenomenology.

In this way the philosophical method of phenomenology reaches a different kind of truth than the generalizations of empirical psychology, the particular insights of humanistic psychology, or revelations of faith, because it limits itself to the combined working of the reason and the senses to lead to a philosophical intuition of the essence of a particular real object. In the case of the present study, the object sought is "woman" in specific relation to the question of education.

Stein concludes that the proper place for this particular study is in "philosophical anthropology." She lists three different ways in which this can be approached: through the species "human," through the species "woman," and through the individual. Her introduction of the middle category, the species "woman," is unusual in philosophy, although it has a precedent in the theory of Duns Scotus (1266–1308) that individuals are differentiated through their nature or form rather than through their matter.[1] She argues that a species depends upon an inner form that does not change. She contrasts this unchanging inner *form* with changing *types*. A young girl can become a woman, a wife become a widow, and so forth. In these situations the woman, while retaining the same form, changes from one type to another.

The crucial part of Stein's argument focuses on the question of the relation of soul and body. In Thomistic thought, which she generally accepts, the soul is understood to be the form of the body. So the question is whether bodily differences between men and women are simply the result of matter, and therefore accidental to the essence of men and women, or whether they are essential differences found in the soul itself. Edith Stein defends this latter view, as she makes the claim that the soul of a woman is a different species of soul than that of a man. However, she says, women and men also *share the same human soul* and equally belong to the human species. So Stein is maintaining that men and women are at the same time members of the same species "human" and members of different species, "man" or "woman."

In addition, the argument is made that individuals represent a species only more or less perfectly; so it would follow that an individual could be more or less fully a woman or a man, and more or less fully human. It is in this context that education becomes so important, for its goal is to encourage the fullest possible development of the individual. The teacher seeks to encourage the most perfect unfolding of the inner form of the student, to help remove blocks in that development, and to foster the fullest development of the individual personality of the woman or man.

There is a further aspect to Stein's thought that opens up the meaning of individuality as a "unique and unrepeatable singularity." Stein emphasizes that, in order for a man or woman to achieve the fullest development of his or her inner form as a human being and person, education through a dynamic continuous interaction with other human beings is essential. It demands a commitment in the teacher to become a well-ordered and developed human being himself or herself, and to be willing to educate other human beings to their full potential. This orientation toward cooperative interactive dynamics between women and men has implications for her philosophy of the differences of the sexes.

In her attempt to articulate what some essential differences between man and woman as species might be, the philosopher suggests that women tend to aim more toward a holistic expression of personality, while men tend to aim toward the perfecting of individual abilities. In her other works, Stein seeks to elaborate other essential differences that flow from this fundamental difference. She argues, for example, that women have a natural tendency toward empathy in that they seek to grasp the other person as a whole being. Emphasizing the role of feelings as motive forces for action, she argues that one of the central goals of education is to help the individual achieve a harmonious balance of intellect, will, and emotions. Given a woman's different affectivity, Stein argues that her education will take a different approach toward this integrative education than with male students.

At the same time that Dr. Stein sought to articulate essential differences between the inner forms of the two sexes, the species "man" and "woman," through the phenomenological method, she also recognized that individuals vary and that some women could be more masculine than feminine. Her approach is not bound by stereotypes, but is flexible at the same time, as it seeks fundamental truths about human, sexual, and individual identity.

Finally, in the selection of her writing included in this chapter, the question of the relation of philosophy to theology is ever present. Stein directly raises the issue of what it means to say that men and women are created "in the image of God." She understands philosophy and theology to be complementary ways of seeking truth, the one using reason and the observation of the senses, the other using revelation and faith. Ultimately she holds that the two paths must be compatible so that a woman's and man's vocation can be solidly situated in a real knowledge of their human and sexual nature.

In conclusion, all of the above themes that have been briefly introduced—namely, philosophical methodology, the soul/body relation, essence and nature, the theory of types, the uniqueness of human individuality, the complementarity of men and women, and the complementarity of philosophy and theology—are elaborated in much greater detail in Stein's other essays. In the short selection chosen for this chapter we find, however, the core components of her theory of human identity.

■ ■ ■

Philosophical Critique

Edith Stein's focus on the philosophical study of woman is very significant. Her work pre-dates by nineteen years that of Simone de Beauvoir, who is often identified as the contemporary foundress of women's studies. In addition to being the first contemporary philosopher of woman's identity, Edith Stein also offered original arguments about woman's identity that avoided both the extremes of an emerging militant feminism on the one hand, and a rigid stereotypical post-Enlightenment theory of an eternal feminine on the other. In this critique I will try to evaluate the significance of Edith Stein's contributions to the philosophy of sex identity by placing her work in the evolving historical context of this area of philosophical anthropology.

The pre-Socratics were the first to reflect on the fact that the philosophy of man demanded reflection on the philosophy of woman. They asked whether male and female were opposite or the same, what the philosophical significance of the contribution of the mother and father to generation was, whether men and women were wise in the same or different ways, and whether men and women were good in the same or different ways. To summarize, the pre-Socratics delineated four fundamental categories of the philosophy of sex identity, which can be called opposition, generation, wisdom, and virtue. These categories fall into the traditional philosophical fields of metaphysics (or ontology, as Stein calls it), the philosophy of science, the theory of knowledge, and ethics and politics.

Plato then argued that men and women were essentially the same if they had the same kind of soul (e.g., a physician's soul, or a carpenter's soul). This sexless soul could be reincarnated in the body of a man, a woman, or even an animal. By devaluing the body, Plato argued that human identity was essentially an identity in soul. Plato's theory, which can be called sex unity (or unisex), denies that a significant differentiation between men and women exists, while it affirms an equality, sameness, or oneness.[2]

Aristotle followed with an argument that men and women were significantly different. This theory advocated what can be called "sex polarity." Aristotle appealed to the difference in body between the male and female to explain his theory that the female was an imperfect representation of the human species. He believed that females were generated because the form that was contained in the seed of the father met imperfectly with the material that was supplied by the mother. As a consequence, he called the female an "imperfect or deformed" male.[3]

A third theory of sex identity (sex complementarity, which argues for the simultaneous differentiation and equality of man and woman) was first suggested by Saint Augustine in response to the polarity argument. Augustine stated that if woman is an imperfect man, then after the resurrection of the body, when all imperfections cease, a woman should be turned into a man. Saint Augustine rejected this view, and concluded that there was no imperfection in being a woman.[4] Hildegard of Bingen further defended sex complementarity in the eleventh century by developing an elaborate typology of the differentiation and oneness of man and woman.[5]

It is now possible to reflect on the significance of Edith Stein's contribution, as her views support this third view of sex complementarity. Stein argues that there are philosophically significant differences between man and woman, and at the same time she claims that they have a "oneness." This similarity she identifies as their participation in the same human species. Aristotle also would have agreed that men and women have the same form, that of the human species, but, as mentioned previously, he argued that the woman had embodied it imperfectly. Stein, on the other hand, rejected this unbalanced view of the natural superiority of the male over the female.

Stein's original contribution to the study of sex identity was to ask the question whether there might also be a "species" of man and a "species" of woman. For many, who identify species, essence, and form strictly with the category of humanness, Stein's question seems odd. How could woman be a species, given that the traditional definition of species involves the capacity of self-reproduction, and obviously woman cannot reproduce herself by herself, nor can man. In other words, man and woman together form a species because only together can they reproduce. Therefore, it is important to realize that Edith Stein is offering a slightly different interpretation of species. She claims that it involves a "constancy of form" in contrast with a type, which can change. Therefore, she is asking whether what woman is and what man is might be better identified through the notion of a constant rather than a variable category.

Another way of asking this question is to reflect on whether there is something unchanging about a woman's identity and about a man's identity. If one gives an affirmative answer to this, then the next step is to consider whether this identity can be explained through a theory of a different kind of form for woman than for man. What is the philosophical basis for the differentiation of the sexes? For Aristotle it was a qualitative differentiation so that a female was qualitatively inferior in relation to the form of the human species. For Stein, differentiation between the sexes is not a question of quality but rather of kind. Women simply have a different kind of form than men. Companion to these considerations is the deeper issue of whether philosophy, and particularly phenomenology, is able to identify what characteristics these constants might have.

In the excerpt being studied in this chapter, Edith Stein hints at what might be constant, but it is not developed here in detail. It is on this issue that criticism is often leveled at her views. When it is specified that women aim more toward a holistic expression of personality and men toward the perfecting of individual abilities, some philosophers object that this is perhaps better explained by sociological and psychological factors than by an appeal to a difference in species. At the same time, however, it is worth reflecting on the deeper claim that Stein is making, namely that the differences are so significant between women and men that they cannot be explained simply by a difference in body. She believes that there must be a difference in mind and soul as well.

It may very well be that Edith Stein was moving toward a new theory of sex complementarity, but that the adequate philosophical foundation for such a theory had not yet been developed at the time of her writing. Therefore, she knew that the previous explanations fell short of the truth of the subject, but she was not yet able to defend her own views adequately.

To be more specific, Stein's explanation lacks an adequate differentiation between four different categories of sex identity; namely, male and female, masculine and feminine, man and woman as individuals, and man and woman as persons. In the history of philosophy, focus on the first category, male and female, was dominant from approximately 600 B.C. to A.D. 1400. Then the category of masculine and feminine was introduced, primarily by Renaissance humanist philosophers, and it was frequently considered during the period 1400–1800.

Next, during the nineteenth century the existentialist philosophers advanced the view of man and woman as self-defining individuals. Finally, in the twentieth century, through the writings on personalism and existential personalism, the further distinction between individual and person has been made. The individual defines himself or herself as unique in relation to the human species, while the person develops his or her potential to the fullest by entering into relations of self-gift to other persons in community. The elaboration of this philosophy of existential personalism for the philosophy of woman and man is just now beginning to be made.

In reading the work of Edith Stein it can be seen that she was reaching toward a philosophy of sex complementarity that aimed at this fullness of expression of man as person and woman as person. However, her analysis fell short of this goal. She reached what could be called a theory of "fractional sex complementarity," in which man and woman together make up a single whole, each supplying what is lacking in the other. In "integral sex complementarity," on the other hand, man and woman are complete wholes in their own respective identities, but they are complementary wholes, and therefore they can enter into relationships that generate more than what they began with.[6]

I would like to suggest that a contemporary theory of integral sex complementarity needs to include reference to the male and female as a starting point. This means that a man needs to consider his maleness, which springs from his genetic, hormonal, and anatomical identity; and a woman needs to consider her femaleness, which springs from her genetic, hormonal, and anatomical identity. The specifics of these factors are being explored in the science of biology, and they apply to all male and all female human beings; so a philosopher must reflect on the facts that these scientists uncover.

Next, a man needs to reflect on how he expresses the characteristics that are identified as masculine and feminine in his own culture; and similarly, a woman needs to reflect on how she expresses characteristics that are identified as feminine and masculine in her culture. These characteristics often vary from culture to culture, and yet a philosopher can consider whether any seem more closely related to the maleness and femaleness identified in the first category as transcultural. It is primarily this step that Edith Stein considered in the essay under consideration here.

Thirdly, a man and woman need to enter into the activity of self-definition. This introduces the notion of a psychic depth of individuality. A man will define himself in relation to his maleness, his masculinity, and his femininity, while a woman will define herself in relation to her femaleness, her femininity, and her masculinity. Stein mentioned this aspect when she said that a woman might choose to follow a vocation other than biological motherhood. Following self-definition, individual men and women make choices about what kind of man or what kind of woman they want to be.

Finally, a man and a woman can enter into the fuller development of their personality by choosing to interact with one another in communities of persons, bound together by the gift of self in the practice of virtuous love. Edith Stein hinted at this possibility when she reflected on the fact that some individuals are more fully human than others. However, the vocabulary and philosophy of the person had not yet been articulated fully when she wrote her text, so she did not develop this theory as fully as many contemporary thinkers would like.

On the other hand, it should be mentioned that Stein realized the importance of education in developing a mature basis from which a man or a woman can begin to define and develop his or her identity. Stein constantly raised the question of whether there should be a difference in education in some respects for girls and boys. It would seem that there are important areas to consider here. For example, in order for a woman to define herself, she would need to know how her body functions, and how these functions are different from those of the male. In addition, she would need to know something of her inherited past, which would include her relation to her own language, culture, history, and even archetypes. The same applies to the man. Next, it would be important for the woman to know facts related to her own sex identity from her recent past, from the time of her birth. This could include insights gleaned from psychological study of the stages of development of sex identity, the sociological study of sex roles within her own culture, the economic study of options for professional development, and so forth. Again, a similar study for a man would be important. Therefore, education is an important area of consideration for a philosophy of sex identity.

In this brief critique of Edith Stein's philosophy of man and woman, it has been shown that she raised the fundamental questions of sex identity, questions that have been reflected on historically by significant philosophers. However, in some respects her theory needs to be developed further to provide a solid basis for a philosophy of integral sex complementarity today. In particular, there needs to be a sharper differentiation of male and female from masculine and feminine, and a sharper differentiation of individual and person. Further, the question of whether it is appropriate to consider man and woman as "separate species" needs to be reconsidered, given traditional views about the meaning of "species."

Finally, although I would praise Edith Stein for struggling to defend sex complementarity (in contrast with sex unity or sex polarity), I believe that her views need to be developed further than the more limited "fractional sex complementarity" into a philosophy of "integral sex complementarity," in which man and woman are viewed as complete and integral wholes capable of complementary relationships through being alike and different at the same time.

■ ■ ■

Religious Critique

It should be mentioned at the outset that Edith Stein is very clear on the different ways in which philosophers and theologians approach a subject. The former consider things through the exercise of reason and the observation of the senses, while the latter appeal to revelation or faith and the study of the Scriptures. Ultimately these two paths to truth are compatible, and she argues that "they complete and influence each other."

Once again, it is important to recognize that Edith Stein's emphasis here reveals a shift or new development in Christian thought. Saint Augustine had argued that a woman by herself cannot reflect the image of God, whereas a man by himself could. This followed from an emphasis on God as one, and the belief that man was able in himself to reflect this singularity of identity.[7] Saint Thomas qualified Saint Augustine's views somewhat to argue that woman was in the image of God in herself, but that her nature reflected it less perfectly than man's. He also followed the Augustinian emphasis on the significance of God as one, and man's special relation to Him.[8]

By placing an emphasis on our obligation to reflect the image of God as a Trinity of Persons, Edith Stein has opened the way to a contemporary unfolding of the philosophy of community. Differentiation of persons can occur in sacramental marriage and in Christian communities. One particular application of this notion is found in Roman Catholicism's post–Vatican II consideration of the complementary interaction of three complementary kinds of vocation in the Church: to sacramental priesthood, to religious life, and to the lay state. In this way, "whenever two or three are gathered together" in Christ's name there is the potential for an imaging of the trinitarian God.

It is of particular interest to Catholics that Pope John Paul II has recently written several works in which this view of the significance of the trinitarian model of imaging the Trinity is emphasized. In his recent *Homilies on the Book of Genesis*, he argues that man more perfectly images God "in the moment of communion of persons" than he does as a solitary individual.[9] Even more significant for the philosophy of sex identity is the pope's recent *Apostolic Letter on the Dignity and Vocation of Woman*. Here he states that women and men are called to mirror the communion of love that is manifest in the Three Persons of the Trinity, and that this goes beyond their being simply rational and free individuals who image God in a single identity.[10] This new emphasis on communities of persons, therefore, moves forward in a direction that Edith Stein established in her writing nearly fifty years ago. Her emphasis on the importance of education for personal development is crucial. We come to know who we are as woman and as man in interpersonal relationships, and the more we know who we are, the more we are able to give ourselves to others in building up Christian community.

Therefore, it would seem as though Edith Stein's philosophy of man and woman has important religious implications for a Christian theology of vocation as a call to "image the Trinity."

It establishes a philosophical foundation to understand sex complementarity as a unique way in which the Trinity is imaged through the interaction of two or more persons who are at the same time significantly different and alike. Man and woman can be seen as a paradigm for this trinitarian model.

Following this line of thinking, it would seem that the challenge for contemporary Christians would be to avoid sliding into a sex-unity interpretation in which differentiation is lost, or into a sex-polarity interpretation in which likeness, equality, or oneness is lost. With sex unity there is a blurring of distinctions that leads to a sterility of interaction, while in sex polarity there is a rigidity of distinctions that leads to an imbalance of contributions in communitarian interaction. Therefore, what Edith Stein challenges us to think about is how a philosophy of sex complementarity can provide a solid educational basis from which to develop oneself as man or as woman, and to enter into integral relationships with one another through a "gift of self to the other," in vocations to the lay state, the sacramental priesthood, or consecrated religious life. With her claim that the call to image the Trinity is a vocation and duty, we have set before us a path for the twenty-first century that may open up to the Church dynamic new possibilities of the complementary interaction of men and women.[11]

■ ■ ■

Summary

We have considered many aspects of Edith Stein's life and work. She was a brilliant student of philosophy who converted from Judaism to Catholicism, gave public lectures on women, lost her job as part of the persecution of the Jewish people, entered a contemplative Carmelite monastery, and was arrested and sent to her death in Auschwitz because she was Jewish.

Her philosophical method focused on seeking an intuition of the essence of the object being studied. In her study of woman, she identified a permanence of form that she called the "species" of woman. Her development of a theory of sex and gender identity has been described as moving toward a theory of sex complementarity.

Stein held that the goal of education must be to promote the fullest possible development of the individual personality of a woman or man. In this context, sex and gender differences led to a consideration of different ways of educating boys and girls. Finally, Stein considered some religious implications of her philosophy of woman. It has been suggested that her theory introduces a way of understanding what it means to "image the Trinity" as a community of persons composed of women and men.

■ ■ ■

Notes

1. The traditional view, as developed by Aristotle in his *Metaphysics*, book 10, claims that woman and man do not constitute different species because they have the same form. Instead, the female is the contrary of the male, in that she is a weaker or deformed version of the species. For Aristotle and Saint Thomas, individuals are differentiated by matter, and not, as Scotus held, by form. For a more detailed study of ancient and medieval philosophies of woman, see Sister Prudence Allen, *The Concept of Woman: The Aristotelian Revolution (750 B.C.–A.D. 1250)* (Montreal and London, 1985).
2. Plato, *Republic*, 5.455e–456a.
3. Aristotle, *The Generation of Animals*, 728a–775b.
4. Saint Augustine, *The City of God* (Cambridge, Mass., 1966), 12.17.
5. Hildegard of Bingen, *Heilkunde: Causae et curae* (Salzburg, 1972).
6. This idea may be symbolized in the following way: fractional sex complementarity implies that ½ plus ½ makes 1, while integral sex complementarity implies that 1 plus 1 makes 3!
7. St. Augustine, *The Trinity* (Washington, D.C., 1963), 12.7.351. Even though Augustine argued that woman was not by herself "in the image of God" he did not conclude that she was imperfect, but rather that this was the perfection that God had planned for her. Her perfection consisted in being a "helpmate" to man.
8. Thomas Aquinas, *Summa Theologiae*, 1.28.4.
9. Pope John Paul II, *Original Unity of Man and Woman: Catechises on the Book of Genesis* (Boston, 1981), 73–74.

10. Pope John Paul II, *On the Dignity and Vocation of Woman* (Boston, 1988), #7, p. 28.
11. Research for this chapter has been supported by funds from the Social Sciences and Humanities Research Council of Canada.

■ ■ ■

Further Reading

W. Herbstrith, *Edith Stein: A Biography* (San Francisco, 1992).

E. Stein, *Life in a Jewish Family: 1881–1916,* in *The Collected Works of Edith Stein,* vol. 1 (Washington, D.C., 1986).

E. Stein, *On the Problem of Empathy,* in *The Collected Works of Edith Stein,* vol. 3 (Washington, D.C., 1989).

13

LUDWIG WITTGENSTEIN

• • •

THE HUMAN PERSON
AS LINGUISTIC ANIMAL

Introduction and Commentary by John J. Haldane

INTRODUCTION

As the end of the twentieth century approaches, it is natural to find oneself reviewing the achievements and failings of the last one hundred years, comparing them to those of preceding centuries, and speculating on what products of the present period will endure as contributions to civilization. Assessment and prediction are, of course, liable to error, but sometimes matters seem to be clear. Thus, in connection with Western philosophy it is inconceivable that informed opinion could ever doubt that Ludwig Wittgenstein was one of the major thinkers of the twentieth century, and I believe he will be judged its greatest philosopher. Placed in the wider context of the history of the subject from Socrates onwards, Wittgenstein stands higher than Kierkegaard, Nietzsche, and Sartre, and is probably on a level with Descartes and Hume. Thus, no one who wants to understand the continuing course of Western philosophy can afford to neglect Wittgenstein's work, and this is especially so in connection with the perennial question: What is the nature of the human person?

■ ■ ■

Wittgenstein's Life and Works

Wittgenstein was born in Vienna in 1889, the youngest of eight children. On his father's side the family was of Jewish descent but his paternal grandfather had converted to Protestantism and his mother was Roman Catholic. Ludwig was baptized in the Catholic Church and received instruction in the faith. At an early age, however, he abandoned Christianity and seems to have become an agnostic who nonetheless remained sympathetic to religious belief and was convinced of its importance as an expression of the profundities of human experience. This outlook is associated with the intense seriousness of Wittgenstein's character, and it also helps to explain the meaning of his statement, "I am not a religious man but I cannot help seeing every problem from a religious point of view."[1]

The Wittgenstein family was wealthy as well as intellectually and artistically gifted. Ludwig's father was a major industrialist, and the home was a place of high culture. The composer Brahms was a family friend, and Ludwig inherited from his parents a musical sensibility and an admiration for creative talent. On his father's death in 1912 Ludwig inherited a considerable fortune, part of which he donated as a fund for writers and the remainder of which he later gave away.

Ludwig received his early education at home. At the age of fourteen he entered an Austrian school and three years later advanced to a technical institute in Berlin. There he studied engineering, which took him in 1908 to England. Working on various aeronautical designs, Ludwig became interested in pure mathematics and this led him to ask deep philosophical questions. In pursuit of answers to these questions, he made contact with the two greatest logicians of the period: Gottlob Frege in Germany and Bertrand Russell in Cambridge. Immediately Wittgenstein abandoned his research in engineering and was admitted to Trinity College, Cambridge, in 1912 where he studied with Russell.

Wittgenstein's academic career was both brilliant and intermittent. He was quickly recognized as a genius, and in the years prior to World War I he began to develop a system of philosophy on which he continued to work while serving in the Austrian army. This system was published in 1921 as the *Tractatus Logico-Philosophicus* (referred to simply as the *Tractatus*). After the war Wittgenstein spent some years in Austria, first as an elementary school teacher and then as a gardener in a monastery. He also designed a house for his sister in Vienna. During this period, however, he began to doubt his earlier philosophy and started to develop a new approach. In 1929 he returned to Cambridge where he was made a Fellow of Trinity and began teaching.

In 1939 Wittgenstein was appointed Professor, but the war led him away from academic life into service as a medical orderly in hospitals in England, and it was not until 1945 that he actually became a Professor at Cambridge. Two years later he resigned because he did not like university positions. Ludwig spent the following year in Ireland, where he completed the major statement of his new philosophy—posthumously published as the *Philosophical Investigations*. In 1949 he was diagnosed as having cancer and the last two years of his life were spent back in Cambridge where he died on 29 April 1951. His last words to Mrs. Bevan, the wife of his Cambridge doctor in whose house he died, were, "Tell them I've had a wonderful life."

During his lifetime Wittgenstein published only one book (the *Tractatus*) and one article ("Some Remarks on Logical Form," 1929), but since his death many volumes of writings have appeared. Most of these writings are difficult to understand and some are not yet understood even by professional philosophers. The best place to begin reading Wittgenstein is the work dictated to students between 1933 and 1935, which appeared as *The Blue and Brown Books*. This book contains early statements of the ideas more fully developed in the two works from which the selections for this chapter have been extracted: *Philosophical Investigations* and *Remarks on the Philosophy of Psychology*. For short and very readable accounts of Wittgenstein's life and character see *Ludwig Wittgenstein: A Memoir* by Norman Malcolm, with a *Biographical Sketch* by G. H. von Wright.

■ ■ ■

How to Read Wittgenstein

The texts of Wittgenstein that follow belong to the later, post–*Tractatus* philosophy. Their style is somewhat unusual but it is not as difficult as is sometimes supposed. It represents an imagined discussion in which Wittgenstein tackles a philosophical question, for example, about the nature of thinking—from different angles. He proposes certain ideas and then entertains the sorts of objections someone might make in reply. Each point and discussion (where there is one) is numbered consecutively. The easiest and most effective way to follow the "investigation" is by reading the passages aloud and trying to catch the puzzled, questioning tone of the imagined objector and the gently instructive tone of Wittgenstein himself. Interestingly, Wittgenstein made the following observation in a notebook: "Sometimes a sentence can be understood only if it is read at the right tempo. My sentences are all supposed to be read slowly. Consider, for example, *Investigations* I, 244:

> "How do words refer to sensations?—There doesn't seem to be any problem here; don't we talk about sensations every day, and give them names? But how is the connection between the name and the thing set up? . . . Here is one possibility: words are connected with the primitive, the natural, expressions of the sensation and used in their place. . . . 'So you are saying that the word *pain* really means crying?'—On the contrary: the verbal expression of pain replaces crying and does not describe it."

The question under investigation is the relationship between words like *ache, tingle, sore,* and so on, and certain conditions that a human subject may experience. It may seem obvious that the English term *ache* refers to a kind of sensation—an ache—in the way that the word *table* refers to the kind of object I am sitting at as I write this sentence. By his emphasis on the word *refer*, Wittgenstein is warning us that matters may not be so simple. He follows this observation with the sentence, "There doesn't seem to be any problem here," which then introduces the name/object account (as in *table*/table). This is ironic; saying "There isn't a problem" signifies a mistaken assumption. What follows is an initial rough statement of Wittgenstein's own account of the word/sensation relationship: "Here is one possibility: words are connected with the primitive, the natural, expressions of the sensation and used in their place." The suggestion is that when a child, say, comes to use the word *sore*, as in "My knee is sore," the term functions not as a name or description of a sensation but as a linguistic way of expressing the condition the child is experiencing. Saying "My knee is sore," perhaps immediately after scraping it on the ground, is not a report of a state but an expression of it, like saying, "My knee, ouch!" As soon as Wittgenstein introduces this account he imagines someone voicing an objection: "So you are saying that the word *pain* really means crying?" He then goes on to respond by clarifying his view: "On the contrary: the verbal expression of pain replaces crying and does not describe it." As we might put it, saying "That's sore" is the linguistic counterpart of crying. It is not a description of a state that is *in* the speaker, as an object may be in a container; rather, it is an expression of the speaker's being *in* a certain state, as a liquid may be in a boiling state.

According to Wittgenstein, then, sensations are natural states or conditions of living human beings that they initially express through such behaviour as crying, jumping about, giggling, and so on, but which they later learn to voice through language. Sensation terms may have other uses, but the expressive one is primary. This style of presenting ideas is unusual but it is very effective once one gets the hang of it; and as I indicated, the easiest way of doing so is by reading the passages aloud. As one does this, it becomes clear that in one sense, at least, Wittgenstein's method is very traditional. What he gives us is a kind of dialogue with commentary, which is certainly no harder to read than the Platonic dialogues and which has the merit of presenting objections we might ourselves want to raise.

■ ■ ■

What to Look For in the Selections

So much, then, for Wittgenstein's style. What exactly is going on in these texts? In essence Wittgenstein is dismantling a theory of human persons that he believes to be misconceived and that he detects as lying behind a number of recurrent philosophical mistakes. His method is to show how the assumptions of that theory lead to difficulties and also how they arise from misapprehensions of common phenomena. In other words, he tries to demonstrate that the theory is incoherent and that it lacks any solid basis. The theory in question is an amalgam of ideas developed by two seventeenth-century philosophers, Descartes and Locke. However, since Locke is generally regarded as accepting the same basic assumptions as Descartes, who preceded him, it is now common to refer to the general view as Cartesianism.

What Cartesianism amounts to is a series of dualisms: of mind and body, of subject and object, of volition and behavior, and of thought and utterance. The Cartesian regards human persons as combinations of conscious selves and material organisms, the former being *located in* and operating the latter. The general notion of mind/body dualism is familiar enough but the other aspects of Cartesianism may not be apparent, and therefore it is easy to find oneself agreeing with them, even though one might not accept dualism as such. It is a major part of Wittgenstein's enterprise to alert us to the less obvious tendencies toward Cartesianism and to show how and why they should be resisted.

The principal technique Wittgenstein employs is one that he sometimes called "grammatical reminders." This can sound rather trivial, as if he were just making observations about language. Nothing could be further from the truth. When Wittgenstein speaks of "grammar" he is talking about things themselves as they are represented in our understanding of them. Earlier, I mentioned that Wittgenstein developed two philosophies—one set out in the *Tractatus* and one in the *Investigations*. Much of the latter is concerned with rejecting aspects of the earlier view, in particular those aspects that marked his own unquestioning acceptance of Cartesianism.

I shall return to this matter, but for now I want to focus on a point of continuity in Wittgenstein's philosophy.

In the notebooks where he set down his thoughts during World War I, Wittgenstein writes: "Philosophy teaches us the logical form of propositions; that is its fundamental task."[2] What this means is that the aim of philosophy should be to reveal how things are by fully displaying the structure of our understanding of them and by showing the implications of this structure. In the *Tractatus* this aim was pursued by analyzing the structure of thoughts (propositions) as they are expressed in indicative sentences of the form "Such and such is the case"; for example, "My pen is in the drawer of the desk." At that time Wittgenstein believed that language was the material expression or embodiment of thoughts (this was one of the subtler forms of dualism: thoughts animating utterances, as, more generally, minds animate bodies), and that thoughts were psychic pictures of the states of affairs they describe. So, the sentence about the pen will be true if (and only if) the thought it expresses is an accurate picture of the situation; if it has elements corresponding to the pen, the drawer, and the desk; and if these stand to one another in the same relation as do the things themselves.

This structure of mental elements in the mind of the thinker is what Wittgenstein first took to be "the logical form of a proposition." By stages, however, he came to see that this "picture theory" could not cope with all meaningful propositions, and, worse still, that it was dangerously misleading in many important cases. As regards the first point, Wittgenstein saw that many uses of language or types of thought have nothing to do with representing situations. Think, for example, of commands, warnings, endearments, petitions, and expressions of hope or fear. "Let me be free of unnecessary worries" is an intelligible petition but it does not describe or represent anything. With respect to the second point, consider what happens if one applies the picture theory to another proposition that has the same indicative structure as the pen case, for example, "My mind is in a bit of a fog." According to the theory, this statement will be true if (and only if) there is a correspondence between the elements of the proposition and those of the situation it describes. But this account suggests that there is an object I possess, a mind, and another object or part of one, a bit of a fog, and that the first object is inside the second. Clearly, however, this is nonsense. There are no "bits of fog" with "minds" inside them. The proposition is a metaphorical way of announcing one's confusion, of indicating that one cannot think clearly.

By the time of the later work represented here, *Philosophical Investigations* and *Remarks on the Philosophy of Psychology*, Wittgenstein had rejected the idea of propositions as mental pictures converted into verbal form as they are expressed in utterances. Both aspects of this view seemed to be mistaken. First, propositions are not always representations, and even when they are descriptive they should not always be interpreted literally. And secondly, propositions are not something mysterious inhabiting an occult interior realm like unseen forces. Rather, they are the meanings of what are generally public performances, that is, utterances. Just as the meaning of a welcoming gesture is not something unseen lying behind it, but rather the public purpose of the gesture itself, so the meaning of an uttered sentence is what the speaker and hearer have learned to understand by it.

■ ■ ■

Notes

1. Quoted by M. Drury in R. Rees, ed., *Recollections of Wittgenstein* (Oxford, 1984).
2. L. Wittgenstein, *Notebooks, 1914–1916,* G. H. von Wright, and G. E. M. Anscombe, eds. (Oxford, 1961).

SELECTIONS FROM WITTGENSTEIN

■ ■ ■

Philosophical Investigations, Part I

243. A human being can encourage himself, give himself orders, obey, blame, and punish himself; he can ask himself a question and answer it. We could even imagine human beings who spoke only in monologue; who accompanied their activities by talking to themselves.—An explorer who watched them and listened to their talk might succeed in translating their language into ours. (This would enable him to predict these people's actions correctly, for he also hears them making resolutions and decisions.)

But could we also imagine a language in which a person could write down or give vocal expression to his inner experiences—his feelings, moods, and the rest—for his private use?—Well, can't we do so in our ordinary language?—But that is not what I mean. The individual words of this language are to refer to what can be known only to the person speaking; to his immediate private sensations. So another person cannot understand the language.

244. How do words *refer* to sensations?—There doesn't seem to be any problem here; don't we talk about sensations every day, and give them names? But how is the connection between the name and the thing named set up? This question is the same as: how does a human being learn the meaning of the names of sensations?—of the word "pain," for example? Here is one possibility: words are connected with the primitive, the natural, expressions of the sensation and used in their place. A child has hurt himself and he cries; and then adults talk to him and teach him exclamations and, later, sentences. They teach the child new pain-behaviour.

"So you are saying that the word 'pain' really means crying?"—On the contrary: the verbal expression of pain replaces crying and does not describe it.

249. Are we perhaps over-hasty in our assumption that the smile of an unweaned infant is not a pretence?—And on what experience is our assumption based?

(Lying is a language-game that needs to be learned like any other one.)

250. Why can't a dog simulate pain? Is he too honest? Could one teach a dog to simulate pain? Perhaps it is possible to teach him to howl on particular occasions as if he were in pain, even when he is not. But the surroundings which are necessary for this behaviour to be real simulation are missing.

255. The philosopher's treatment of a question is like the treatment of an illness.

256. Now, what about the language which describes my inner experiences and which only I myself can understand? How do I use words to stand for my sensations?—As we ordinarily do? Then are my words for sensations tied up with my natural expressions of sensation? In that case my language is not a "private" one. Someone else might understand it as well as I.—But suppose I didn't have any natural expression for the sensation, but only had the sensation? And now I simply *associate* names with sensations and use these names in descriptions.

257. "What would it be like if human beings showed no outward signs of pain (did not groan, grimace, etc.)? Then it would be impossible to teach a child the use of the word 'tooth-ache.'"—Well, let's assume the child is a genius and itself invents a name for the sensation!—But then, of course,

he couldn't make himself understood when he used the word.—So does he understand the name, without being able to explain its meaning to anyone?—But what does it mean to say that he has "named his pain?"—How has he done this naming of pain?! And whatever he did, what was its purpose?—When one says "He gave a name to his sensation" one forgets that a great deal of stagesetting in the language is presupposed if the mere act of naming is to make sense. And when we speak of someone's having given a name to pain, what is presupposed is the existence of the grammar of the word "pain"; it shows the post where the new word is stationed.

269. Let us remember that there are certain criteria in a man's behaviour for the fact that he does not understand a word: that it means nothing to him, that he can do nothing with it. And criteria for his "thinking he understands," attaching some meaning to the word, but not the right one. And, lastly, criteria for his understanding the word right. In the second case one might speak of a subjective understanding. And sounds which no one else understands but which I *"appear to understand"* might be called a "private language."

271. "Imagine a person whose memory could not retain *what* the word 'pain' meant—so that he constantly called different things by that name—but nevertheless used the word in a way fitting in with the usual symptoms and presuppositions of pain"—in short he uses it as we all do. Here I should like to say: a wheel that can be turned though nothing else moves with it, is not part of the mechanism.

281. "But doesn't what you say come to this: that there is no pain, for example, without *pain-behaviour?*"—It comes to this: only of a living human being and what resembles (behaves like) a living human being can one say: it has sensations; it sees; is blind; hears; is deaf; is conscious or unconscious.

283. What gives us *so much as the idea* that living beings, things, can feel? Is it that my education has led me to it by drawing my attention to feelings in myself, and now I transfer the idea to objects outside myself? That I recognize that there is something there (in me) which I can call "pain" without getting into conflict with the way other people use this word?—I do not transfer my idea to stones, plants, etc.

Couldn't I imagine having frightful pains and turning to stone while they lasted? Well, how do I know, if I shut my eyes, whether I have not turned into a stone? And if that has happened, in what sense will *the stone* have the pains? In what sense will they be ascribable to the stone? And why need the pain have a bearer at all here?!

And can one say of the stone that it has a soul and that is what has the pain? What has a soul, or pain, to do with a stone?

Only of what behaves like a human being can one say that it has pains.

For one has to say it of a body, or, if you like, of a soul which some body *has*. And how can a body *have* a soul?

284. Look at a stone and imagine it having sensations.— One says to oneself: How could one so much as get the idea of ascribing a *sensation* to a *thing*? One might as well ascribe it to a number.—And now look at a wriggling fly and at once these difficulties vanish and pain seems able to get a foothold here, where before everything was, so to speak, too smooth for it.

And so, too, a corpse seems to us quite inaccessible to pain.—Our attitude to what is alive and to what is dead, is not the same. All our reactions are different.—If anyone says "That cannot simply come from the fact that a living thing moves about in such-and-such a way and a dead one not," then I want to intimate to him that this is a case of transition "from quantity to quality."

285. Think of the recognition of *facial expressions*. Or of the description of facial expressions—which does not consist in giving the measurements of the face! Think, too, how one can imitate a man's face without seeing one's own in a mirror.

286. But isn't it absurd to say of a *body* that it has pain?— And why does one feel an absurdity in that? In what sense is it true that my hand does not feel pain, but I in my hand?

What sort of issue is: Is it the *body* that feels pain?—How is it to be decided? What makes it plausible to say that it is *not* the body?—Well, something like this: if someone has a pain in his hand, then the hand does not say so (unless it writes it) and one does not comfort the hand, but the sufferer: one looks into his face.

302. If one has to imagine someone else's pain on the model of one's own, this is none too easy a thing to do: for I have to

imagine pain which *I do not feel* on the model of the pain which *I do feel*. That is, what I have to do is not simply to make a transition in imagination from one place of pain to another. As from pain in the hand to pain in the arm. For I am not to imagine that I feel pain in some region of his body. (Which would also be possible.)

Pain-behaviour can point to a painful place—but the subject of pain is the person who gives it expression.

304. "But you will surely admit that there is a difference between pain-behaviour accompanied by pain and pain-behaviour without any pain?"—Admit it? What greater difference could there be?—"And yet you again and again reach the conclusion that the sensation itself is a *nothing*?" Not at all. It is not a something, but not a nothing either! The conclusion was only that a *nothing* would serve just as well as a *something* about which *nothing* could be said. We have only rejected the grammar which tries to force itself on us here.

The paradox disappears only if we make a radical break with the idea that language always functions in one way, always serves the same purpose: to convey thoughts—which may be about houses, pains, good and evil, or anything else you please.

308. How does the philosophical problem about mental processes and states and about behaviourism arise?—The first step is the one that altogether escapes notice. We talk of processes and states and leave their nature undecided. Sometime perhaps we shall know more about them—we think. But that is just what commits us to a particular way of looking at the matter. For we have a definite concept of what it means to learn to know a process better. (The decisive movement in the conjuring trick has been made, and it was the very one that we thought quite innocent.)—And now the analogy which was to make us understand our thoughts falls to pieces. So we have to deny the yet uncomprehended process in the yet unexplored medium. And now it looks as if we had denied mental processes. And naturally we don't want to deny them.

309. What is your aim in philosophy?—To show the fly the way out of the fly-bottle.

415. What we are supplying are really remarks on the natural history of human beings; we are not contributing curiosities

however, but observations which no one has doubted, but which have escaped remark only because they are always before our eyes.

416. "Human beings agree in saying that they see, hear, feel, and so on (even though some are blind and some are deaf). So they are their own witnesses that they have *consciousness*." But how strange this is! Whom do I really inform, if I say "I have consciousness"? What is the purpose of saying this to myself, and how can another person understand me?—Now, expressions like "I see," "I hear," "I am conscious," really have their uses. I tell a doctor "Now I am hearing with this ear again," or I tell someone who believes I am in a faint "I am conscious again," and so on.

420. But can't I imagine that the people around me are automata, lack consciousness, even though they behave in the same way as usual?—If I imagine it now—alone in my room— I see people with fixed looks (as in a trance) going about their business—the idea is perhaps a little uncanny. But just try to keep hold of this idea in the midst of your ordinary intercourse with others, in the street, say! Say to yourself, for example: "The children over there are mere automata; all their liveliness is mere automatism." And you will either find these words becoming quite meaningless or you will produce in yourself some kind of uncanny feeling, or something of the sort.

Seeing a living human being as an automaton is analogous to seeing one figure as a limiting case or variant of another; the cross-pieces of a window as a swastika, for example.

421. It seems paradoxical to us that we should make such a medley, mixing physical states and states of consciousness up together in a single report: "He suffered great torments and tossed and tossed about restlessly." It is quite usual; so why do we find it paradoxical? Because we want to say that the sentence deals with both tangibles and intangibles at once.—But does it worry you if I say "These three struts give the building stability"? Are three and stability tangible?—Look at the sentence as an instrument, and at its sense as its employment.

427. "While I was speaking to him I did not know what was going on in his head." In saying this, one is not thinking of brain-processes, but of thought-processes. The picture should be taken seriously. We should really like to see into his head.

And yet we only mean what elsewhere we should mean by saying: we should like to know what he is thinking. I want to say: we have this vivid picture—and that use, apparently contradicting the picture, which expresses the psychical.

428. "This queer thing, thought"—but it does not strike us as queer when we are thinking. Thought does not strike us as mysterious while we are thinking, but only when we say, as it were retrospectively: "How was that possible?" How was it possible for thought to deal with the very object *itself*? We feel as if by means of it we had caught reality in our net.

432. Every sign *by itself* seems dead. *What* gives it life?—In use it is *alive*. Is life breathed into it there?—Or is the *use* its life?

435. If it is asked, "How do sentences manage to represent?," the answer might be: "Don't you know? You certainly see it, when you use them." For nothing is concealed.

How do sentences do it?—Don't you know? For nothing is hidden.

But given this answer, "But you know how sentences do it, for nothing is concealed," one would like to retort, "Yes, but it all goes by so quick, and I should like to see it as it were laid open to view."

436. Here it is easy to get into that dead-end in philosophy, where one believes that the difficulty of the task consists in our having to describe phenomena that are hard to get hold of, the present experience that slips quickly by, or something of the kind. Where we find ordinary language too crude, and it looks as if we were having to do, not with the phenomena of everyday, but with ones that "easily elude us, and, in their coming to be and passing away, produce those others as an average effect."

577. We say "I am expecting him" when we believe that he will come, though his coming does not *occupy our thoughts*. (Here "I am expecting him" would mean "I should be surprised if he didn't come," and that will not be called the description of a state of mind.) But we also say "I am expecting him" when it is supposed to mean: I am eagerly awaiting him. We could imagine a language in which different verbs were consistently used in these cases. And similarly more than one verb where we speak of "believing," "hoping," and so on. Perhaps the concepts of such a language would be more

suitable for understanding psychology than the concepts of our language.

580. An "inner process" stands in need of outward criteria.

581. An expectation is imbedded in a situation, from which it arises. The expectation of an explosion may, for example, arise from a situation in which an explosion *is to be expected*.

585. When someone says "I hope he'll come"—is this a *report* about his state of mind, or a *manifestation* of his hope?— I can, for example, say it to myself. And surely I am not giving myself a report. It may be a sigh; but it need not. If I tell someone "I can't keep my mind on my work today; I keep on thinking of his coming"—*this* will be called a description of my state of mind.

592. "But when you say 'I intend to go away,' you surely mean it! Here again it just is the mental act of meaning that gives the sentence life. If you merely repeat the sentence after someone else, say in order to mock his way of speaking, then you say it without this act of meaning."—When we are doing philosophy it can sometimes look like that. But let us really think out various *different* situations and conversations, and the ways in which that sentence will be uttered in them.—"I always discover a mental undertone; perhaps not always the same one." And was there no undertone there when you repeated the sentence after someone else? And how is the "undertone" to be separated from the rest of the experience of speaking?

593. A main cause of philosophical disease—a one-sided diet: one nourishes one's thinking with only one kind of example.

■ ■ ■

Philosophical Investigations, Volume II, Section 4

"I believe that he is suffering."—Do I also *believe* that he isn't an automaton?

It would go against the grain to use the word in both connexions.

(Or is it like this: I believe that he is suffering, but am certain that he is not an automaton? Nonsense!)

Suppose I say of a friend: "He isn't an automaton."—What information is conveyed by this, and to whom would it be information? To a *human being* who meets him in ordinary circumstances? What information *could* it give him? (At the very most that this man always behaves like a human being, and not occasionally like a machine.)

"I believe that he is not an automaton," just like that, so far makes no sense.

My attitude towards him is an attitude towards a soul. I am not of the *opinion* that he has a soul.

Religion teaches that the soul can exist when the body has disintegrated. Now do I understand this teaching?—Of course I understand it—I can imagine plenty of things in connexion with it. And haven't pictures of these been painted? And why should such a picture be only an imperfect rendering of the spoken doctrine? Why should it not do the same service as the words? And it is the service which is the point.

If the picture of thought in the head can force itself upon us, then why not much more of thought in the soul?

The human body is the best picture of the human soul.

And how about such an expression as: "In my heart I understood when you said that," pointing to one's heart? Does one, perhaps, not *mean* this gesture? Of course one means it. Or is one conscious of using a *mere* figure? Indeed not.—It is not a figure that we choose, not a simile, yet it is a figurative expression.

■ ■ ■

Philosophical Investigations, Volume II, Section 5

Then psychology treats of behaviour, not of the mind?

What do psychologists record?—What do they observe? Isn't it the behaviour of human beings, in particular their utterances? But *these* are not about behaviour.

"I noticed that he was out of humour." Is this a report about his behaviour or his state of mind? ("The sky looks threatening": is this about the present or the future?) Both; not side-by-side, however, but about the one *via* the other.

A doctor asks: "How is he feeling?" The nurse says, "He is groaning." A report on his behaviour. But need there be any question for them whether the groaning is really genuine, is really the expression of anything? Might they not, for example, draw the conclusion, "If he groans, we must give him more analgesic"—without suppressing a middle term? Isn't the point the service to which they put the description of behaviour?

■ ■ ■

Philosophical Investigations, Part II, Section 11

Is there such a thing as "expert judgment" about the genuineness of expressions of feeling?—Even here, there are those whose judgment is "better" and those whose judgment is "worse."

Correcter prognoses will generally issue from the judgments of those with better knowledge of mankind.

Can one learn this knowledge? Yes; some can. Not, however, by taking a course in it, but through *"experience."*—Can someone else be a man's teacher in this? Certainly. From time to time he gives him the right tip.—This is what "learning" and "teaching" are like here.—What one acquires here is not a technique; one learns correct judgments. There are also rules, but they do not form a system, and only experienced people can apply them right. Unlike calculating-rules.

What is most difficult here is to put this indefiniteness, correctly and unfalsified, into words.

■ ■ ■

Remarks on the Philosophy of Psychology, Volume I

267. The expression of soul in a face. One really needs to remember that a face with a soulful expression can be *painted*, in order to believe that it is merely shapes and colours that make this impression. It isn't to be believed that it is merely the *eyes*—eyeball, lids, eyelashes etc.—of a human being that one can be lost in the gaze of, into which one can look with

astonishment and delight. And yet human eyes just do affect one like this. "From which you may see. . . ."

268. Do I *believe* in a soul in someone else, when I look into his eyes with astonishment and delight?

277. "The sentence 'If only he would come' may be laden with our longing."—What was it laden with there? It is as if a weight were loaded on to it from our spirit. I should indeed like to say all of that. And doesn't it matter that I want to say that?

278. Doesn't it matter that I want to say that? Isn't it important? Is it not important that for me hope lives in the *breast?* Isn't this a picture of one or another important bit of human behaviour? Why does a human being believe a thought comes into his head? Or, more correctly, he does not *believe* it; he lives it. For he clutches at his head; he shuts his eyes in order to be alone with himself in his head. He tilts his head back and makes a movement as a sign that nothing should disturb the process in the head.—Now are these not important kinds of behaviour?

279. And if the picture of the thought in the head can force itself upon us, why not, much more, that of thought in the soul?

280. What better picture of believing could there be than the human being who, with the expression of belief, says "I believe . . ."?

281. The human being is the best picture of the human soul.

312. The confusing picture is this: that we observe a substance—its changes, states, motions; like someone observing the changes and motions in a blast furnace. Whereas we observe and compare the attitudes and behaviour of human beings.

314. Forms of behaviour may be incommensurable. And the word "behaviour," as I am using it, is altogether misleading, for it includes in its meaning the external circumstances—of the behaviour in a narrower sense.

629. When we talk to ourselves in thought: "Something happens: that's for sure." But the usefulness of these words is in reality as unclear as that of the special psychological propositions that we are trying to explain.

630. Instead of the unanalysable, specific, indefinable: the fact that we act in such-and-such ways, e.g., *punish* certain actions, *establish* the state of affairs thus and so, *give orders*, render accounts, describe colours, take an interest in others'

feelings. What has to be accepted, the given—it might be said—are facts of living.

■ ■ ■

Remarks on the Philosophy of Psychology, Part II

15. Someone says: "Man hopes." How should this phenomenon of natural history be described?—One might observe a child and wait until one day he manifests hope; and then one could say "Today he hoped for the first time." But surely that sounds queer! Although it would be quite natural to say "Today he said 'I hope' for the first time." And why queer? One does not say that a suckling hopes that . . . , but one does say it of a grown-up.—Well, bit by bit daily life becomes such that there is a place for hope in it.

16. In this case I have used the term "embedded," have said that hope, belief, etc., were embedded in human life, in all of the situations and reactions which constitute human life. The crocodile doesn't hope, man does. Or: one can't say of a crocodile that it hopes, but of man one can.

But how would a human being have to act for us to say of him: he never hopes? The first answer is: I don't know. It would be easier for me to say how a human being would have to act who never yearns for anything, who is never happy about anything, or who is never startled or afraid of anything.

20. Where do we get the concept "thinking" from, which we now want to consider here? From everyday language. What first fixes the direction of our attention is the word "thinking." But the use of this word is tangled. Nor can we expect anything else. And that can of course be said of all psychological verbs. Their employment is not so clear or so easy to get a synoptic view of, as that of terms in mechanics, for example.

21. Psychological words are similar to those which pass over from everyday language into medical language ("shock").

240. If you want to find out how many different things "thought" means, you have only to compare a thought in pure mathematics with a non-mathematical one. Only think how many things are called "sentences"!

Ludwig Wittgenstein

Extracted from *Philosophical Investigations* (New York, 1953), 88–92, 94–95, 97–98, 101–3, 125–29, 152–53, 155, 178–79, and 227, and *Remarks on the Philosophy of Psychology* (Oxford, 1980), vol. 1, pp. 54, 56, and 115–16, and vol. 2, pp. 4–5, and 46.

COMMENTARY

We have said that there was a radical shift in Wittgenstein's thinking. But it did not put an end to the idea that the aim of philosophy is to show the logical form of propositions. Rather, it gave rise to a new and important way of understanding that idea. Philosophy can save us from confusion and error by showing the true nature of what we find reason to think and say. By offering "grammatical reminders," indications of the real meaning of our words, it preserves us from false theories of the world and of ourselves. This theme recurs again and again in Wittgenstein's later writings, both as a methodological claim about philosophy and in connection with particular failures to understand the true meaning of what we say about psychological phenomena. Consider, for example, *Investigations* I, 255: "The philosopher's treatment of a question is like the treatment of an illness"; 304: "We have only rejected the grammar [of name and object] which tries to force itself on us here. The paradox disappears only if we make a radical break with the idea that language always functions in one way"; and 308: "How does the philosophical problem about mental processes and states . . . arise?—The first step is the one that altogether escapes notice—We talk of processes and states. . . ."

Wittgenstein's central warning is that of all the things we are likely to be misled about, we are in greatest danger of misunderstanding ourselves; and, when made, this error will darken and destroy our understanding of other things as well. That consequence is no accident, for if we make a radical mistake about what it is to be a thinking, acting person, then we will also go wrong in our judgments about what we are thinking and doing and thus about what we should think and do. So great was Wittgenstein's commitment to freeing himself and others from errors threatening self-understanding, and so intense was his struggle against what he sometimes described as the bewitchment of language, that one may speak of his philosophy as a kind of spiritual-cum-pastoral vocation.

■ ■ ■

Wittgenstein's Anti-Cartesianism

As was noted in the introduction, Wittgenstein mainly opposed Cartesianism because it embodied the development into a theory of those misunderstandings about ourselves that arise from common ways of speaking about thoughts, feelings, intentions, and sensations. The attempt to do away with Cartesianism proceeds slowly and subtly. In the first part of the selection we see Wittgenstein raising questions about sensations and how one might speak of them. His target is the idea that sensations are inner objects located in an essentially private sphere residing within the living human organism. This picture would allow that a child might give names to his or her sensations in a private language that only he or she could possibly understand. Wittgenstein argues that this theory makes no sense. The very prospect of correct and incorrect uses of a language depends on the possibility of these applications being checked against rules of correct usage, and that implies objective, publicly confirmable validation. This fact also emerges when one considers how it is possible to teach a child terms for psychological phenomena. One could never instruct people in the use of such expressions as *think, fear, intend, ache,* and so on, unless they sometimes showed themselves to be thinking, fearing, intending, and aching. As Wittgenstein puts the point in *Investigations* I, 283: "What gives us so much as the idea that living beings think, can feel? . . . Only of what *behaves* [my emphasis] like a human being can one say that it has pains"; and later at 580: "An *inner process* stands in need of outward criteria."

In the second set of *Philosophical Investigations* and in the *Remarks on the Philosophy of Psychology,* Wittgenstein is more direct. Having developed detailed analyses of the "logical form" of psychological propositions, he considers the subjects of them, that is, human beings. Here he begins to use the term *soul* but in ways that are quite different from the dualist's employment of it. Two pairs of sentences are crucial for any attempt to understand Wittgenstein's mature view. In *Investigations* II, *iv,* he writes: "My attitude towards him [a human being] is an attitude towards a soul. I am not of the opinion that he has a soul"; and "The human body is the best picture of the human soul." In the *Remarks* these views are paralleled as follows: "Do I believe in a soul in someone else, when I look into his eyes with astonishment and delight?" (268); and "The human being is the best picture of the human soul" (281).

According to the Cartesian account, the mind or soul is an unseen and undetectable inhabitant of the human body. How then do I know that there are any minds or souls other than my own? This is the philosophical problem of solipsism, the theory that one is oneself the sole existing person, or even the sole existing thing. If all I encounter are bodies, how can I know whether they contain selves or are mere mindless automata? At best the Cartesian can offer an argument from analogy. I behave like this when I have such and such a feeling; that body is behaving like this; so, I am justified in holding the view that there is a self "inside" that body that is having experiences of the sort I have had. In opposition to this, Wittgenstein emphasizes the absurdity of supposing that our dealings with those around us—our family, friends, associates, and so on—are based upon opinions or judgments that there are unseen souls inside and animating the bodies we see and are familiar with. "Do I believe in a soul in someone else?" No, "I am not of the opinion that he has a soul," my attitude is "an attitude towards a soul." The person is not something whose existence I infer, it is something I am already dealing with in face-to-face exchanges.

Similarly, and following from this, Wittgenstein's use of the term *soul* ties it to the observable life of a human being. If we are to have any conviction in saying that someone has a soul, then what we say must be linked to what we can see; and that is, and can only be, the intelligent initiating and responsive behavior of a boy or girl, man or woman: "The human body is the best picture of the human soul" (*Investigations* I, 178).

■ ■ ■

Philosophical Critique

Clearly, Wittgenstein is dealing with issues of the utmost philosophical, moral, and, indeed, spiritual importance. He is trying to undo the tangled lines of our thinking that have become knotted into a theory (Cartesianism) that regards the human as, in fact, something other than human—a dimensionless mental entity manipulating a lump of flesh and bones. It is natural to ask for Wittgenstein's alternative theory, but that is at odds with the spirit of his work. Having untangled the lines, he sees no need to weave them together into another pattern, and indeed he thinks that any attempt to do so will result only in the recreation of the old confusions or the construction of new ones. An instance of the latter consequence is the theory of philosophical behaviorism. This theory rejects the Cartesian account of the meaning of psychological claims as descriptions of events and objects in an inner realm and instead treats them as abbreviated descriptions of bodily movements or tendencies to movement under certain environmental conditions. For example, whereas the Cartesian regards the sentence "John is in pain" as a report of an event or a state in John's mind, the behaviorist treats it as a shorthand description of the movements of John's body—for example, facial contortions, muscle spasms, and so on—in response to some bodily stimulation such as the skin's being cut.

The problem with behaviorism is the contrary to that of Cartesianism. For whereas the latter lost sight of the fact that we are organic creatures, the former seems to neglect our nature as conscious, reflective subjects. Wittgenstein believed that in the modern and recent periods the greatest threat to self-understanding has come from the side of Cartesianism, and so he labored to pull us away from it. But in doing so he recognized that it might seem as if he was moving us toward behaviorism. He anticipates this response throughout the later work represented above. For example, in *Investigations* I, 281, he writes (on behalf of an objector): "But doesn't what you say come to this: that there is no pain, for example, without pain-behaviour?" And at 304 he continues the objection: "But you will surely admit that there is a difference between pain-behaviour accompanied by pain and pain-behaviour without any pain?" And again, in *Investigations* II, 4: "Then psychology treats of behavior, not of the mind?" In each place the suspicion of behaviorism is responded to, not by the presentation of a new theory, but by reminders of what we are right to say about thoughts and experiences and by the implied advice that we should not try to go beyond this. Here an important and distinctive feature of Wittgenstein's general philosophy reveals itself. He is against theorizing because he thinks it is not necessary for true understanding and that, in fact, it destroys true understanding. What supports this opposition is a certain view of theories that sees them as arising out of modern science. This view has taught us to explain phenomena in terms of underlying elements and forces interacting with one another to produce observable effects. So when a question arises about the nature of something, we look for an account of its causes and then are quickly drawn away from the phenomenon itself toward a theory of what is supposed to underlie it. This process is what leads, in the effort to understand ourselves, to such theories as Cartesianism and behaviorism, which move away from the manifestations of conscious intelligence, such as meaningful speech or purposeful action, toward something else—namely, the bodiless soul and the soulless body, respectively.

Wittgenstein wants us to deal with the phenomena themselves and to learn to be content with accurate and illuminating descriptions of them. In that respect one might see him as an advocate of common sense in opposition to philosophical theory. This view can seem odd, however, given his reputation for obscure and complex thought; but I believe the best chance of understanding and learning from his work is by viewing it as a continuous reminder of the observable facts. Indeed, this is Wittgenstein's own account of what he is trying to do. In *Investigations* I, 309, he answers an imagined question: "What is your aim in philosophy?—To show the fly the way out of the fly-bottle." And at 415 he gives an explicit account of how this liberation may be achieved in connection with understanding our own nature: "What we are supplying are really remarks on the natural history of human beings; we are not contributing curiosities however, but observations which no one has doubted, but which have escaped remark only because they are always before our eyes."

While taking to heart the warnings against theorizing, we can, I think, give a more general account of the positive view that arises from Wittgenstein's very effective challenges to Cartesianism. This account even begins to emerge in the selected passages from the second set of *Investigations* and from the *Remarks*, where the expressions *soul* and *human being* are repeated several times. The rejection of the tradition of Descartes and Locke introduces a view in many respects similar to those of Aristotle and Aquinas. The subjects of experience, the authors of thoughts and deeds, are rational animals. Human beings are living entities possessed of a range of vital powers including perceptual and intellectual abilities. Like trees we are in a close relationship with the natural environment, and like brute animals we move around, and reproduce by mating. But unlike mere vegetable and sentient life our nature includes the capacity for thought and deliberate action. In terms of the scholastic vocabulary of Aquinas, our souls are rational as opposed to merely vegetative or sentient, as are the souls of plants and animals, respectively.

There is, however, an element in Wittgenstein's view that is wholly or perhaps largely absent (or underdeveloped) in the philosophical anthropologies of Aristotle and Aquinas. This is the social dimension of human existence. Certainly these other writers speak of humans as "social animals," but neither considers to what extent our very existence as persons depends upon our membership in human communities. That a social context is necessary is perhaps the central thesis of Wittgenstein's philosophy. It is expressed in terms of the idea that the background to what we say and do is our having been introduced from infancy onwards into shared forms of life. Earlier we saw how the possibility of meaningful propositions was taken to depend upon publicly regulated language; and the status of language as the carrier of socially embodied rationality is continuously, if sometimes indirectly, emphasized throughout the post-*Tractatus* writings. These two ideas, of shared life and of a common language, are brought together in a remark from an earlier part of the *Investigations* (I, 19): "To imagine a language means to imagine a form of life."

■ ■ ■

Religious Critique

When Wittgenstein wrote that he could not help seeing every problem from a religious point of view, he did not mean that for him every idea or issue had to be assessed in the light of a commitment to certain theological doctrines—as, for example, a Roman Catholic might consider sexual relations in the light of church teaching on human procreation and the sacrament of marriage. I have indicated already that the "religious viewpoint" was an outlook of intense seriousness about the importance and mystery of human existence. But if his view was not credal, it was nonetheless spiritual, and this raises the large and important question of how Wittgenstein's philosophy might be related to a theological outlook. It is an interesting fact that among his closest students several were religious believers. One such former student is Elizabeth Anscombe, a convert to Roman Catholicism who succeeded to the Professorship once held by Wittgenstein and who is one of his literary executors and an editor of many of his posthumously published writings. She reports a remark that Wittgenstein made about his later work: "Its advantage is that if you believe, say, Spinoza or Kant, this interferes with what you believe in religion; but if you believe me, nothing of the sort."

One way of understanding Wittgenstein's observation is in terms of the antitheoretical character of his philosophy. If he is describing the phenomena of human existence without trying to get behind or beyond them, then nothing he says will be incompatible with, for example, a theological account of the origin and purpose of life. But, in fact, much of what he argues in connection with human nature does have implications for religious beliefs, or, more precisely, for certain interpretations of them. I will end with two examples: the "interior" life of the soul and the prospect of future existence.

The injunction to attend to the spiritual condition of one's soul is a recurrent element in religious teaching. In the modern period, that is, during the last three centuries, it has been given a quasi-Cartesian interpretation, as if it meant that one should attend to the well-being of something private that is never in contact with others. If we follow Wittgenstein, however, such an interpretation will be seen as a serious error that threatens to corrupt spirituality rather than to promote it. In a work entitled *Zettel* (published in 1967 after Wittgenstein's death) he writes: "Only God sees the most secret thoughts. But why should these be all that important? And need all human beings count them as important?" For the religious believer these ideas may serve as a reminder that what truly matters is the spiritual quality of one's life, and that is something spread across its private and its public aspects without one aspect having priority over another—"By their fruits you shall know them!" (Mt 7:16).

It is common among Christians to believe that one's spiritual condition is relevant to the question of whether (and how) one may live again. The final article of the Creed speaks of "the life of the world to come," and Cartesianism has had a marked influence on modern Christian ways of thinking about the possibility of an afterlife. It is common to find believers speaking of the souls of the deceased as having departed their bodies and ascended or descended to other, non-material, realms. Wittgenstein's view might allow a place for this as a religious way of speaking, but his anti-Cartesianism would rule it out as a literal description of a process of relocation of objects. This, however, does not imply that his account of human beings as linguistic animals is incompatible with a literal interpretation of the Christian hope for future life. What it suggests, however, is that any such hope must depend upon the restoration of truly human existence. But that is very much in accord with the traditional Christian belief in the resurrection of the dead, following the pattern of the bodily resurrection of Jesus Christ. Earlier, I mentioned a resemblance between Wittgenstein's view of persons and that advanced by Aristotle and Aquinas. I conclude then with an interpretation of the prospects for future life presented by Aquinas in his *Commentary on I Corinthians,* and with the suggestion that what he says might as easily have been written by Wittgenstein: "Even if my soul were to find salvation in some other world, neither I nor any man would do so."

■ ■ ■

Conclusion

Though Wittgenstein's style of writing seems difficult at first, a little practice at reading it makes it quite understandable. Wittgenstein wished to expose what he regarded as Descartes' principal error, namely the idea that a human person is composed of a mind and a body, being two things rather than one. He wished to oppose Descartes, however, without falling into the opposite "error" of behaviorism. And he did not want to establish an alternative theory, but simply to practice "therapy" on the others.

Wittgenstein also stressed the dependence of human beings on society for their formation. We are thoroughly social beings, and to a considerable extent dependent upon our society for our formation, as is evident in our participation in a common language.

For Wittgenstein, too, our external actions are as much an indication of who we are as are our private thoughts, and our body is essential to us as complete human beings.[1]

■ ■ ■

Note

1. This commentary was written during the period of a Visiting Fellowship at the Institute for Advanced Studies, University of Edinburgh, in 1991.

I am grateful to the Director (Professor Peter Jones) and staff of the Institute for providing such a congenial working environment, and to the Carnegie Trust for the Universities of Scotland for providing financial support.

■ ■ ■

Further Reading

A. J. Ayer, *Wittgenstein* (London, 1987).

A. Kenny, *Wittgenstein* (Harmondsworth, 1973).

F. Kerr, *Theology after Wittgenstein* (Oxford, 1986).

N. Malcolm, *Ludwig Wittgenstein: A Memoir, with a Biographical Sketch by G. H. von Wright* (Oxford, 1962).

■ ■ ■

A Short Bibliography of Writings by Wittgenstein

The Blue and Brown Books (Oxford, 1958).

Culture and Value (Oxford, 1980).

Philosophical Investigations (Oxford, 1958).

Remarks on the Philosophy of Psychology, vols. 1 and 2 (Oxford, 1980).

"Some Remarks on Logical Form," *Proceedings of the Aristotelian Society,* 1929.

Tractatus Logico-Philosophicus (London, 1922).

Zettel (Oxford, 1967).

14

B. F. SKINNER

...

THE HUMAN PERSON
AS NECESSITATED

Introduction and Commentary by Celia Wolf-Devine

INTRODUCTION

. . .

Skinner's Life and Works

Burrhus Frederic Skinner, like Sigmund Freud, was a psychologist interested in explaining human behavior scientifically, yet for several reasons his work requires philosophical examination. First, Behaviorism, the school of psychology that he helped found, has been very influential and now dominates many academic psychology departments. Second, the techniques for behavior modification that he developed are in widespread use today, especially by those who work with prisoners, the retarded, and the mentally ill. Third, and most important, Skinner goes beyond his own experimental data to make sweeping claims about human nature, dealing with problems properly the preserve of philosophers: whether we have free will, whether we have moral responsibility, what counts as an adequate explanation of human behavior, and whether the mind is distinct from the body. His outspoken attack on such important traditional notions as freedom, dignity, and moral responsibility has earned him many enemies.

Skinner was born in 1904 in Susquehanna, Pennsylvania. He studied literature at Hamilton College, Clinton, New York, and, after a brief but unsuccessful foray into writing fiction, attended Harvard, where he received a Ph.D. in psychology. Drawn to the work of J. B. Watson (1878–1958), the founder of Behaviorism, Skinner focused on strictly experimental psychology. Like Watson and other behaviorists, Skinner believed that we ought to attempt to explain human and animal behavior by reference only to variables that can be observed in a laboratory rather than in terms of the inner states (mental or physiological) of the organism, and he worked to develop techniques for shaping that behavior.

B. F. Skinner was a dynamic lecturer and popular writer, as well as a respected experimental psychologist. He gained national fame with his controversial utopian novel *Walden Two* (1948), which offered his prescription for how society should be designed. Skinner served as Peirce Professor of Psychology at Harvard until his retirement. Other books include *The Behavior of Organisms* (1938), *Science and Human Behavior* (1953), *Verbal Behavior* (1957), *Contingencies of Reinforcement* (1969), and *Beyond Freedom and Dignity* (1971). He died in 1990.

■ ■ ■

What to Look For in the Selections

What interests the philosopher most about Skinner is not the details of his work in experimental psychology but his denial of human freedom. He holds a view called determinism, according to which human beings never have free will. To hold that humans do have free will is to hold that they are at least sometimes capable of making choices different from the ones they actually do make. For example, a believer in free will would hold that even if everything in your life up to this moment remained the same, you could have chosen not to be reading this book now. A determinist would deny this possibility.

In the following selections from Skinner, it is important to be able to identify his reasons for denying human freedom. To pinpoint his reasons you must try to determine what model of science he offers, how he understands scientific method, and why he believes that scientific explanations of human behavior leave no room for freedom. Ask yourself the following questions:

1. Is Skinner's argument persuasive?
2. Why or why not?
3. Given that Skinner wants to eliminate all references to purposes, goals, and intentions, do you think that human behavior can be adequately explained or even described without reference to these?
4. Finally, do you think that a society of the sort described in *Walden Two* is either possible or desirable?
5. Why or why not?

SELECTIONS FROM SKINNER

■ ■ ■

The Need for a Technology of Behavior

In trying to solve the terrifying problems that face us in the world today, we naturally turn to the things we do best. We play from strength, and our strength is science and technology. To contain a population explosion we look for better methods of birth control. . . . We try to stave off world famine with new foods and better ways of growing them. . . . The application of the physical and biological sciences alone will not solve our problems because the solutions lie in another field. Better contraceptives will control population only if people use them. . . . New methods of agriculture and medicine will not help if they are not practiced. . . . In short, we need to make vast changes in human behavior, and we cannot make them with the help of nothing more than physics or biology, no matter how hard we try. . . . What we need is a technology of behavior. . . .

It is easy to conclude that there must be something about human behavior which makes a scientific analysis, and hence an effective technology, impossible, but we have not by any means exhausted the possibilities. There is a sense in which it

473

can be said that the methods of science have scarcely yet been applied to human behavior. . . . Something essential to scientific practice is missing in almost all current discussions of human behavior. It has to do with our treatment of the causes of behavior. . . .

Man's first experience with causes probably came from his own behavior: things moved because he moved them. If other things moved it was because someone else was moving them, and if the mover could not be seen it was because he was invisible. . . . Physics and biology soon abandoned explanations of this sort and turned to more useful kinds of causes, but the step has not been decisively taken in the field of human behavior. . . .

Unable to understand how or why the person we see behaves as he does, we attribute his behavior to a person we cannot see. . . . The function of the inner man is to provide an explanation which will not be explained in turn. Explanation stops with him. He is not a mediator between past history and current behavior, he is a *center* from which behavior emanates. He initiates, originates, and creates, and in so doing he remains, as he was for the Greeks, divine. We say that he is autonomous—and, so far as a science of behavior is concerned, that means miraculous.

The position is, of course, vulnerable. Autonomous man serves to explain only the things we are not yet able to explain in other ways. His existence depends upon our ignorance, and he naturally loses status as we come to know more about behavior. The task of a scientific analysis is to explain how the behavior of a person as a physical system is related to the conditions under which the human species evolved and to the conditions under which the individual lives.[1]

■ ■ ■

Shaping Behavior by Operant Conditioning

We select a relatively simple bit of behavior which may be freely and rapidly repeated, and which is easily observed and recorded. If our experimental subject is a pigeon, for example, the behavior of raising the head above a given height is convenient. This may be observed by sighting across the pigeon's head at a scale pinned on the far wall of the box. We first study the height at which the head is normally held and select some line on the scale which is reached only infrequently. Keeping our eye on the scale, we then begin to open the food tray very quickly whenever the head rises above the line. If the experiment is conducted according to specifications, the result is invariable: we observe an immediate change in the frequency with which the head crosses the line. . . . In the pigeon experiment, then, food is the "reinforcer," and presenting food when a response is emitted is the "reinforcement." The "operant" is defined by the property upon which the reinforcement is contingent—the height to which the head must be raised. The change in frequency with which the head is lifted to this height is the process of "operant conditioning." . . .

The only way to tell whether or not a given event is reinforcing to a given organism is to make a direct test. We observe the frequency of a selected response, then make an event contingent upon it, and observe any change in frequency. If there is a change, we classify the event as reinforcing to the organism under existing conditions. . . . A survey of the events which reinforce a given individual is often required in the practical application of operant conditioning. . . . We cannot dispense with this survey simply by asking a man what reinforces him. His reply may be of some value, but it is by no means necessarily reliable. A reinforcing connection need not be obvious to the individual reinforced. . . .

Operant conditioning shapes behavior as a sculptor shapes a lump of clay. Although at some point the sculptor seems to have produced an entirely novel object, we can always follow the process back to the original undifferentiated lump, and we can make the successive stages by which we return to this condition as small as we wish. At no point does anything emerge which is very different from what preceded it. The final product seems to have a special unity or integrity of design, but we cannot find a point at which this suddenly appears. In the same sense, an operant is not something which appears full grown in the behavior of the organism. It is the result of a continuous shaping process. The pigeon experiment demonstrates this clearly. . . .[2]

■ ■ ■

The External Causes of Behavior

Consider the act of drinking a glass of water. . . . Suppose now we bring someone into a room and place a glass of water before him. Will he drink? . . . We have a causal chain consisting of 3 links: (1) an operation performed upon the organism from without—for example, water deprivation; (2) an inner condition—for example, physiological or psychic thirst; and (3) a kind of behavior—for example, drinking. Independent information about the second link would obviously permit us to predict the third without recourse to the first. It would be a preferred type of variable because it would be nonhistoric; the first link may lie in the past history of the organism, but the second is a current condition. Direct information about the second link is, however, seldom, if ever, available. Sometimes we infer the second link from the third; an animal is judged to be thirsty if it drinks. In that case the explanation is spurious. Sometimes we infer the second link from the first; an animal is said to be thirsty if it has not drunk for a long time. In that case, we obviously cannot dispense with the prior history.

The second link is useless in the control of behavior unless we can manipulate it. At the moment, we have no way of directly altering neural processes at appropriate moments in the life of a behaving organism. . . .

The objection to inner states is not that they do not exist, but that they are not relevant in a functional analysis. We cannot account for the behavior of any system while staying wholly inside it; eventually we must turn to forces operating upon the organism from without. Unless there is a weak spot in our causal chain so that the second link is not lawfully determined by the first, or the third by the second, then the first and third links must be lawfully related. If we must always go back beyond the second link for prediction and control, we may avoid many tiresome and exhausting digressions by examining the third link as a function of the first. . . .

The external variables of which behavior is a function provide for what may be called a causal or functional analysis. We undertake to predict and control the behavior of the individual organism. This is our "dependent variable"—the effect for which we are to find the cause. Our "independent variables"—the causes of behavior—are the external conditions of which behavior is a function. Relations between the two—the "cause-and-effect relationships" in behavior—are the laws of a science. A synthesis of these laws expressed in quantitative terms yields a comprehensive picture of the organism as a behaving system.

This must be done within the bounds of a natural science. We cannot assume that behavior has any peculiar properties which require unique methods or special kinds of knowledge. It is often argued that an act is not so important as the "intent" which lies behind it, or that it can be described only in terms of what it "means" to the behaving individual or to others whom it may affect. If statements of this sort are useful for scientific purposes, they must be based upon observable events, and we may confine ourselves to such events exclusively in a functional analysis. . . .

The independent variables must also be described in physical terms. . . . The events affecting an organism must be capable of description in the language of physical science. It is sometimes argued that certain "social forces" or the "influences" of culture or tradition are exceptions. But we cannot appeal to entities of this sort without explaining how they can affect both the scientist and the individual under observation. The physical events which must then be appealed to in such an explanation will supply us with alternative material suitable for a physical analysis.

By confining ourselves to these observable events, we gain a considerable advantage, not only in theory but in practice. A "social force" is no more useful in manipulating behavior than an inner state of hunger, anxiety, or skepticism. Just as we must trace these inner events to the manipulable variables of which they are said to be functions before we may put them to practical use, so we must identify the physical events through which a "social force" is said to affect the organism before we can manipulate it for purposes of control. In dealing with the directly observable data we need not refer to either the inner state or the outer force. . . .[3]

■ ■ ■

Doing without Final Causes

It is not correct to say that operant reinforcement "strengthens the response which precedes it." The response has already occurred and cannot be changed. What is changed is the future probability of responses in the same class. It is the operant as a class of behavior, rather than the response as a particular instance, which is conditioned. There is, therefore, no violation of the fundamental principle of science which rules out "final causes." But this principle is violated when it is asserted that behavior is under the control of an "incentive" or "goal" which the organism has not yet achieved or a "purpose" which it has not yet fulfilled. Statements which use such words as "incentive" or "purpose" are usually reducible to statements about operant conditioning, and only a slight change is required to bring them within the framework of a natural science. Instead of saying that a man behaves because of the consequences which are to follow his behavior, we simply say that he behaves because of the consequences which have followed similar behavior in the past. This is, of course, the Law of Effect or operant conditioning.

It is sometimes argued that a response is not fully described until its purpose is referred to as a current property. But what is meant by "describe"? If we observe someone walking down the street, we may report this event in the language of physical science. If we then add that "his purpose is to mail a letter," have we said anything which was not included in our first report? Evidently so, since a man may walk down the street "for many purposes" and in the same physical way in each case. But the distinction which needs to be made is not between instances of behavior; it is between the variables of which behavior is a function. Purpose is not a property of the behavior itself; it is a way of referring to controlling variables. If we make our report after we have seen our subject mail his letter and turn back, we attribute "purpose" to him from the event which brought the behavior of walking down the street to an end. This event "gives meaning" to his performance, not by amplifying a description of the behavior as such, but by indicating an independent variable of which it may have been a function. We cannot see his "purpose" before seeing that he mails a letter, unless we have observed similar behavior and similar consequences before. Where we have done this, we use the term simply to predict that he will mail a letter upon this occasion.

Nor can our subject see his own purpose without reference to similar events. If we ask him why he is going down the street or what his purpose is and he says, "I am going to mail a letter," we have not learned anything new about his behavior but only about some of its possible causes. The subject himself, of course, may be in an advantageous position in describing these variables because he has had an extended contact with his own behavior for many years. But his statement is not therefore in a different class from similar statements made by others who have observed his behavior upon fewer occasions. . . . Moreover, he may be wrong. He may report that he is "going to mail a letter," and he may indeed carry an unmailed letter in his hand and may mail it at the end of the street, but we may still be able to show that his behavior is primarily determined by the fact that upon past occasions he has encountered someone who is important to him upon just such a walk. He may not be "aware of this purpose" in the sense of being able to say that his behavior is strong for this reason.

The fact that operant behavior seems to be "directed toward the future" is misleading. Consider, for example, the case of "looking for something." In what sense is the "something" which has not yet been found relevant to the behavior? Suppose we condition a pigeon to peck a spot on the wall of a box and then, when the operant is well established, remove the spot. The bird now goes to the usual place along the wall. It raises its head, cocks its eye in the usual direction, and may even emit a weak peck in the usual place. Before extinction is very far advanced, it returns to the same place again and again in a similar behavior. Must we say that the pigeon is "looking for the spot?" . . .

It is not not difficult to interpret this example in terms of operant reinforcement. Since visual stimulation from the spot has usually preceded the receipt of food, the spot has become a conditioned reinforcer. It strengthens the behavior of looking in given directions from different positions. Although we have undertaken to condition only the pecking response, we have in fact strengthened many different kinds of precurrent behavior which bring the bird into positions from which it sees the spot and pecks it. These responses continue to appear, even though we have removed the spot, until extinction occurs. The spot which is being "looked for" is the spot which has occurred in the past as the immediate reinforcement of the behavior of looking. In general, looking for something consists of emitting responses which in the past have produced "something" as a consequence.

The same interpretation applies to human behavior. When we see a man moving about a room opening drawers, looking under magazines, and so on, we may describe his behavior in fully objective terms: "Now he is in a certain part of the room; he has grasped a book between the thumb and forefinger of his right hand; he is lifting the book and bending his head so that any object under the book can be seen." We may also "interpret" his behavior or "read a meaning into it" by saying that "he is looking for something," or, more specifically, that "he is looking for his glasses." What we have added is not a further description of his behavior but an inference about some of the variables responsible for it. There is no current goal, incentive, purpose or meaning to be taken into account. This is so even if we ask him what he is doing and he says "I am looking for my glasses." This is not a further description of his behavior but of the variables of which his behavior is a function; it is equivalent to "I have lost my glasses," "I shall stop what I am doing when I find my glasses," or "When I have done this in the past, I have found my glasses." These translations may seem unnecessarily roundabout, but only because expressions involving goals and purposes are abbreviations.

Very often we attribute purpose to behavior as another way of describing its biological adaptability. . . . In both operant conditioning and the evolutionary selection of behavioral characteristics, consequences alter future probability. Reflexes and other innate patterns of behavior evolve because they increase the chances of survival of the species. Operants grow strong because they are followed by important consequences in the life of the individual. Both processes raise the question of purpose for the same reason, and, in both, the appeal to a final cause may be rejected in the same way. A spider does not possess the elaborate behavioral repertoire with which it constructs a web because that web will enable it to capture the food it needs to survive. It possesses this behavior because similar behavior on the part of spiders in the past has enabled them to capture the food they needed to survive. A series of events have been relevant to the behavior of web-making in its earlier evolutionary history. We are wrong in saying that we observe the "purpose" of the web when we observe similar events in the life of the individual.[4]

■ ■ ■

Eliminating Mentalistic Language

The text will often seem inconsistent. English, like all languages, is full of prescientific terms which usually suffice for purposes of casual discourse. No one looks askance at the astronomer when he says that the sun rises or that the stars come out at night, for it would be ridiculous to insist that he should always say that the sun appears over the horizon as the earth turns or that the stars become visible as the atmosphere ceases to refract sunlight. All that we ask is that he can give a more precise translation if one is needed. The English language contains many more expressions referring to human behavior than to other aspects of the world, and technical alternatives are much less familiar. The use of casual expressions is therefore much more likely to be challenged. It may seem inconsistent to ask the reader to "keep a point in mind" when he has been told that mind is an explanatory fiction, or to "consider the idea of freedom" if an idea is simply an imagined precursor of behavior, or to speak of "reassuring those who fear a science of behavior" when all that is meant is changing their behavior with respect to such a science. The book could have been written for a technical reader without expressions of that sort, but the issues are important to the nonspecialist and need to be discussed in a nontechnical fashion. No doubt many of the mentalistic expressions imbedded in the English language cannot be as rigorously translated as "sunrise," but acceptable translations are not out of reach.[5]

■ ■ ■

Practical Applications: Designing a Culture

A child is born a member of the human species, with a genetic endowment showing many idiosyncratic features, and he begins at once to acquire a repertoire of behavior under the contingencies of reinforcement to which he is exposed as an individual. Most of these contingencies are arranged by other people. They are, in fact, what is called a culture. . . . The social environment . . . shapes and maintains the behavior of those who live in it. A given culture evolves as new practices arise. . . . A culture which for any reason induces its members to work for its survival is more likely to survive. It is a matter of the good of the culture, not of the individual. Explicit design promotes that good by accelerating the evolutionary process. . . . Survival is the only value according to which a culture is eventually to be judged. . . .

The outlines of a technology are already clear. An assignment is stated as behavior to be produced or modified, and relevant contingencies are then arranged. A programmed sequence of contingencies may be needed. The technology has been most successful where behavior can be fairly easily specified and where appropriate contingencies can be constructed—for example, in child care, school, and the management of retardates and institutionalized psychotics. . . .[6]

■ ■ ■

Values

The forces which shape ethical behavior to group standards are powerful. The group steps in to suppress lying, stealing, physical assault, and so on, because of immediate consequences to its members. Its behavior in so doing is eventually a function of certain characteristic features of the "good" and "bad" behavior of the controlled individual. Among these is lack of conformity to the general behavior of the group. There is thus a frequent association of aversive properties of behavior with the property of nonconformance to a standard. Nonconforming behavior is not always aversive, but aversive behavior is always nonconforming. If these properties are paired often enough, the property of nonconformance becomes aversive. "Right" and "wrong" eventually have the force of "conforming" and "nonconforming."[7]

"Should" and "ought" begin to raise more difficult questions when we turn to the contingencies under which a person is induced to behave for the good of others. "You should (you ought to) tell the truth" is a value judgment to the extent that it refers to reinforcing contingencies. We might translate it as follows: "If you are reinforced by the approval of your fellow men, you will be reinforced when you tell the truth." The value is to be found in the social contingencies maintained for the purposes of control. It is an ethical or moral judgment in the sense that ethos and mores refer to the customary practices of a group.[8]

■ ■ ■

Walden Two

The Designer of Walden Two: A Pot Marred in the Making

Frazier [the designer of Walden Two]: "You think I'm conceited, aggressive, tactless, selfish. . . . My motives are ulterior and devious, my emotions warped. In a word—of all the people you've seen in the past four days, you're sure that I'm one, at least, who couldn't possibly be a genuine member of any community."

Skinner: I still found nothing to say. It was as if Frazier were snatching the words away as I reached for them. He accepted my silence as assent.

"Well, you're perfectly right," he said quietly. Then he stood up, drew back his arm, and sent the tile shattering into the fireplace. "But God damn it, Burris!" he cried, timing the "damn" to coincide with the crash of the tile. "Can't you see? I'm not a product of Walden Two! . . . Isn't it enough that I've made other men likable and happy and productive? Why expect me to resemble them? Must I possess the virtues which I've proved to be best suited to a well-ordered society? . . .

After all, emulation isn't the only principle in education—all the saints to the contrary. Must the doctor share the health of his patient?" . . .

"We expect the physician to heal himself, I suppose," I said.

"I know of no remedy, and I'd be in no position to administer it if I did. . . . There's never a complete rebirth. There's never a total conversion. The final social structure we're working toward must wait for those who've had a full Walden Two heritage. They will come, never fear, and the rest of us will pass on to a well-deserved oblivion—the pots that were marred in the making."

But in Possession of a Powerful Technology of Behavior

"Mr. Castle [a philosopher]," said Frazier very earnestly, "let me ask you a question. I warn you, it will be the most terrifying question of your life. *What would you do if you found yourself in possession of an effective science of behavior?* Suppose you suddenly found it possible to control the behavior of men as you wished. What would you do?" . . .

"What would I do?" said Castle thoughtfully. "I think I would dump your science of behavior in the ocean."

"And deny men all the help they would otherwise lose forever?"

"And give them the freedom they would otherwise lose forever."

"How could you give them their freedom?"

"By refusing to control them."

"But you would only be leaving the control in other hands."

"Whose?"

"The charlatan, the demagogue, the salesman, the ward heeler, the bully, the cheat, the educator, the priest—all who are now in possession of the techniques of behavioral engineering. . . .

"No, Mr. Castle, when a science of behavior has once been achieved, there's no alternative to a planned society. We can't leave mankind to accidental or biased control. But by using the principle of positive reinforcement—carefully avoiding force or the threat of force—we can preserve a personal sense of freedom."

The Power of the Scientist

"I'll let you in on a secret," Frazier continued, lowering his voice dramatically. "You have just described the *only* side of Walden Two that really interests me. To make men happy, yes. To make them productive in order to assure the continuation of that happiness, yes. But what else? Why, *to make possible a genuine science of human behavior!*

"These things aren't for the laboratory, Burris. . . . They concern our very lives! We can study them only in a living culture, and yet a culture which is under experimental control. Nothing short of Walden Two will suffice. . . .

"What remains to be done?" he said, his eyes flashing. "Well, what do you say to the design of personalities? Would that interest you? The control of temperament? Give me the specifications, and I'll give you the man. What do you say to the control of motivation, building the interests which will make men most productive and most successful? Does that seem to you fantastic? Yet some of the techniques are available, and more can be worked out experimentally. Think of the possibilities! A society in which there is no failure, no boredom, no duplication of effort!

"And what about the cultivation of special abilities? Do we know anything about the circumstances in the life of the child which give him a mathematical mind? Or make him musical? Almost nothing at all. These things are left to accident or blamed on heredity. I take a more optimistic view: we can analyze effective behavior and design experiments to discover how to generate it in our youth. . . . There's no virtue in accident. Let us control the lives of our children and see what we can make of them."

Jesus

Frazier: "Now, early forms of government are naturally based on punishment. It is the obvious technique when the physically strong control the weak. . . . That's why I insist that Jesus, who was apparently the first to discover the power of refusing to punish, must have hit upon the principle by accident. He certainly had none of the experimental evidence which is available to us today. . . . Jesus discovered one principle because it had immediate consequences, and he got another thrown in for good measure."

Skinner: I began to see light. "You mean the principle of 'love your enemies?'" I said.

Frazier: "Exactly. To 'do good to those who despitefully use you' has two unrelated consequences. You gain the peace of mind we talked about the other day. Let the stronger man push you around—at least you avoid the torture of your own rage. That's the immediate consequence. What an astonishing discovery it must have been to find that in the long run you could control the stronger man in the same way!"

Frazier as God?

"We call this ledge the 'Throne,'" Frazier said, as he put the glass to his eye. "Practically all of Walden Two can be seen from it. I come up occasionally to keep in touch with things. Right now, I'm looking at the foundation of the new shop just north of the garage. They seem to be pouring the last of the concrete this morning. And there's Morrison at the piggery again. More inoculations, I presume. And over here—a load of early kale going into the poultry house. . . . The cattle are far up in the pasture today. I wonder why? . . . And there's the mailman nudging his old Ford over the hill. Our boy ought to be—yes, there he is—emptying the box into the basket on his bike. . . . The corn looks good. I wish we could irrigate over that way. . . . There's old Mrs. Ackerman out for a walk again. And that must be Esther with her."

This had begun as an account for my benefit, but it fell away into the merest mumble. Frazier had apparently forgotten me. He finally took the glass from his eye, collapsed it, and restored it to his pocket. I shifted my position to attract his attention, and I thought I saw him start. He laughed nervously. "Not a sparrow falleth," he said, patting the glass in his pocket. . . .

"It must be a great satisfaction," I said finally. "A world of your own making."

"Yes," he said. "I look upon my work, and, behold, it is good."

. . . with a shock, I saw that he had assumed the position of crucifixion. . . .

"Just so you don't think you're God," I said hesitantly, hoping to bring matters out into the open. . . .

"There's a curious similarity," he said.

I suffered a moment of panic.

"Rather considerably less control in your case, I should imagine," I said, attempting to adopt a casual tone.

"Not at all," he said, looking up. "At least if we can believe the theologians. On the contrary, it's the other way round. You may remember that God's children are always disappointing Him. . . .

"The parallel is quite fascinating. Our friend Castle is worried about the conflict between long-range dictatorship and freedom. Doesn't he know he's merely raising the old question of predestination and free will? All that happens is contained in an original plan, yet at every stage the individual seems to be making choices and determining the outcome. The same is true of Walden Two. Our members are practically always doing what they want to do—what they 'choose' to do—but we see to it that they will want to do precisely the things which are best for themselves and the community. Their behavior is determined, yet they're free." . . .

"To use a term I professionally dislike, you have a sizeable God complex."

"Of course I'm not indifferent to power!" Frazier said hotly. "And I like to play God! Who wouldn't, under the circumstances? After all, man, even Jesus Christ thought he was God!"

He stared at me in silence, as if to see whether I had caught the full significance of his remark. He was not challenging me, and there was no hint of blasphemy. His tone had been almost devout. He spoke as if Jesus were an honored colleague whose technical discoveries he held in the highest esteem. . . .

"There's another point of similarity," he said at last when he saw that I was not going to speak. "I don't know know whether you'll understand this, Burris. . . ." He dropped the telescope and hesitated for a moment. Then he flung his hands loosely in a sweeping gesture which embraced all of Walden Two. "These are my children, Burris," he said, almost in a whisper. "I *love* them. . . ."

"What is love," he said, with a shrug, "except another name for the use of positive reinforcement?"

"Or vice versa," I said.[9]

Extracted from the titles listed in the following notes.

1. B. F. Skinner, *Beyond Freedom and Dignity* (New York, 1971), 5–14.
2. B. F. Skinner, *Science and Human Behavior* (New York, 1981), 63–66, 72–75, 91.
3. Ibid., 31–36.
4. Ibid., 87–90.
5. *Beyond Freedom and Dignity*, 23–24.
6. Ibid., 149–50.
7. *Science and Human Behavior*, 418.
8. *Beyond Freedom and Dignity*, 112–13.
9. B. F. Skinner, *Walden Two* (New York, 1976), 207–8, 217–20, 242–43, 245–50.

COMMENTARY

■ ■ ■

Skinner the Scientist and Popularizer of Science

Two facts must be kept in mind in order to understand why Skinner thinks as he does. First, he greatly admires science and regards himself as a scientist, applying the methods of science to the study of human behavior. Second, his main interest is in solving the problems of the world by developing ways to predict and control human behavior.

Science, Skinner notes, has made enormous progress through the centuries, while our understanding of human behavior has not. He attributes the success of science to its adopting the correct method and proposes to apply the same method to studying people. Scientists, he believes, confine themselves to publicly observable events and perform experiments that can be repeated by others. The results of these experiments can be quantified. Scientists eliminated notions such as goals and purposes (final causes) from their explanations of nature and sought to discover general laws of the "Whenever A, then B" variety. For example, whenever certain atmospheric conditions prevail (such as the meeting of a warm front and a cold front), hail will form. If we understand enough of these laws, we can predict the weather, and perhaps, someday, even (to the extent that we can generate these conditions) control it. We should, Skinner believes, approach human behavior in the same way, rather than focusing on inner states, such as emotions, thoughts, or intentions, or invoking inner forces, such as the ego, the id, and the superego, as the Freudians do. Nothing that is not publicly observable can be included in a scientific explanation of human behavior.

Science, as Skinner understands it, leaves no room for freedom. He believes that human behavior is strictly determined by causal laws in the same way that the behavior of animals, the growth of plants, and the motion of the stars are. The causes of human behavior are, he believes, environmental, although genetics plays a role in accounting for why we are reinforced by certain things—individuals who were strongly reinforced by these things survived and passed on their genes. We have failed to apply scientific method to human behavior until now partly because we do not want to admit that our behavior is not free; we cling to the myth of "autonomous man." Another reason for this failure is an inability to understand the way in which the environment shapes our behavior. Earlier psychologists focused on reflex actions and ways in which they could be conditioned (*respondent conditioning*). For example, Pavlov's dog salivated at the ringing of a bell because the sound of the bell had been associated with being fed. Skinner, by contrast, developed methods for what he called *operant conditioning.*

Operant behavior is behavior that operates on the environment to generate consequences. Some of these consequences are reinforcing; they increase the probability of the organism repeating the behavior. If a pigeon is fed immediately when it stretches its neck, the probability that it will do so again increases, and the more the reinforcement (food) is made contingent upon the operant (stretching its neck), the higher the probability of the pigeon repeating this behavior (when hungry). The environment thus *selects for* certain behaviors by reinforcing them when they occur. By using operant conditioning techniques, Skinner was able to condition animals to perform complex behaviors; for example, getting pigeons to play ping-pong.

Reinforcements are of two types: positive reinforcement (presenting a stimulus such as food) and negative reinforcement (removing a stimulus such as a loud noise). There are also conditioned reinforcers that acquire their ability to reinforce by being regularly paired with a primary reinforcer such as food. Thus if we feed a pigeon each time a red light is lit, then that light itself comes to serve as a reinforcer. There are also generalized reinforcers, attention, affection, or money, which are paired with more than one of the primary reinforcers. The primary reinforcers, according to Skinner, are basically biological in origin: food, drink, sexual contact, warmth in winter, and so on. All other reinforcers acquire their power to reinforce only by being associated with the primary reinforcers. This biologistic view of human nature has something in common with Freud, who said that "hunger and [sexual] love move the world."

Reinforcement is not the only way to control behavior. We can also use punishment or what Skinner calls "aversive control." In punishment one presents a stimulus (an electric shock, for example) or removes a stimulus (by taking away a naughty child's dessert). Skinner strongly advocates the use of reinforcement rather than punishment, because reinforcement works better, is more humane (because it does not cause discomfort), and allows the person who is being controlled to feel free (although, of course, that is not the case).

Operant conditioning as we have just described it may seem rather commonsensical and not particularly novel. True, parents and educators may be more effective if they understand the importance of reinforcing the child who is behaving well, and of not unwittingly reinforcing bad behavior, but if that were all there were to Skinner's theory of operant conditioning it would not be nearly so controversial. But Skinner claims that all behavior (human as well as animal) is determined by the ways in which the environment (social and physical) has reinforced or punished previous behaviors of the organism. Since our behavior is determined by the contingencies of reinforcement that have occurred in our past, moral responsibility for our actions disappears. It is the environment that is to blame, not the individual.

491

Skinner identifies three links in the causal chain involved in behavior: (1) the action of the environment on the organism (such as when a dog is deprived of water), (2) the inner physiological or psychological state of the organism (changes in the dog's blood chemistry or feelings of thirst), and (3) the behavior of the organism (the dog drinks). We rarely have adequate information about (2) to enable us to act directly on it in order to control behavior, and for the purposes of a "functional analysis," Skinner believes that we can omit it. For if (3) is determined by (2) and (2) is determined by (1), we should be able to establish a connection between (1) and (3). Whether inner states of a psychological sort (that is, feelings or beliefs) exist does not really matter; either they do not exist or they can be disregarded.

At this point we can see why Skinner's interest in prediction and control is so important to understanding him, and why his work so often annoys philosophers whose business it is to clarify such issues as the nature of the mind and its relation to the body. It is clear that Skinner rejects dualism (Descartes' theory), but it is rather unclear what his own view is. He waffles between central state materialism, which equates the mind with the brain and central nervous system, and epiphenomenalism, the view that mental states do exist but are merely by-products of brain activity with no independent causal power of their own. On the one hand, he says that what we discover by introspection is our own body—that part of the universe contained within our skin—but he also says that this inner world is private, while our brains are clearly not private, since a neurophysiologist could observe them. Clarifying these kinds of questions is not important to Skinner as a hands-on behavioral technologist. Like many modern materialists, he simply assumes that science will eventually understand neurophysiology well enough to be able to explain how the effects of the environment on the organism cause its behavior. This assumption, however, is merely a (highly speculative) promissory note on the far distant future of science.

In the meantime, Skinner believes that we must use the techniques of operant conditioning which we already possess in order to solve social problems such as overpopulation, pollution, and crime. This would not be taking away people's freedom, after all, since, according to Skinner, they are not free now. It would only be substituting more effective and consistent conditioning instead of the haphazard variety now prevalent. A child growing up in a ghetto, for example, is actually positively reinforced for criminal behavior. A high degree of control of an environment is required, of course, in order to be able to control what Skinner calls the "contingencies of reinforcement." For example, if my receiving food can be made contingent upon my performing some particular behavior, then my behavior can be reliably controlled. However, we seldom have such a high degree of control over other people's social environment, which is why Skinner's methods have mainly been successful in institutional settings such as prisons or mental hospital wards.

■ ■ ■

Skinner the Utopian Social Theorist

Skinner offered *Walden Two* as a model for constructing an ideal society, a society in which the planners (presumably scientists familiar with the techniques of behavioral engineering) possess a high degree of social control. People are carefully conditioned from birth to be fitted for life in community. Being far more pessimistic than Marx, Skinner assumes that people's interests naturally conflict with each other, so that they can live together successfully only with the help of extensive "behavioral engineering." Babies sleep in air-conditioned cubicles, live constantly in a group setting, and are cared for by scientifically trained childcare workers. They are gradually trained to develop "self-control" by introducing small doses of frustration and adversity. Behavioral engineers eliminate negative emotions, such as jealousy, which would be divisive of the community. Individuals are not singled out for any sort of recognition of their accomplishments (so as not to generate competitiveness or envy). Nor are they blamed; those who fail to perform adequately at their jobs (they work only four hours a day) are sent to the psychologist for correction. Leaders are not elected and seek no recognition. The crematory "disposes of our ashes as it sees fit."

In addition to shaping behavior at Walden Two, the designer of Walden Two hopes eventually to move toward "experimental breeding," which would be made possible by the weakening of family ties. Already the "unfit" are "discouraged" from having children.

■ ■ ■

Philosophical and Religious Critique

Skinner, like Freud, was strongly hostile to religion, and did not ever take its claims to truth sufficiently seriously to argue against them. In other words, he simply assumed that it was false. Skinner's understanding of religion was shallower than Freud's or Marx's, and he could see nothing in it except an institution formed to control people's behavior. If Skinner's view of human nature could be demonstrated to be correct, of course, this would have serious implications for the Judeo-Christian tradition, which holds that we are free, and morally responsible for our actions.

It would also necessitate a radical revision of our social institutions and our ordinary ways of thinking and talking. We do, in fact, praise and blame people for their actions, which if Skinner were right, we ought not to do. Our criminal justice system is built largely on the assumption that human beings are responsible for their acts. Skinner, however, would have us treat criminals simply as sick and as the victims of bad conditioning—and argue that they need to be somehow reconditioned until their behavior is socially acceptable. There is certainly something to the idea that many criminals could use therapy, but moving completely to the therapy model has dangers. For one thing, subjecting someone to therapy is alarmingly open-ended; he or she will not be released until the authorities determine that his or her behavior conforms to acceptable social norms. Punishment, by contrast, respects the individual's status as a free moral agent. Consequently, punishments are intended to reflect the seriousness of the crime—once the sentence is served, the prisoner is set free.

Another feature of our ordinary ways of thinking that would have to be changed is our deeply engrained habit of understanding people's behavior in terms of their "beliefs," "desires," and "purposes"; for example, John is rummaging around on his desk because he is looking for his glasses (his purpose). Skinner rejects these sorts of explanations as unscientific; you can't experimentally observe a purpose or a desire. Thus John's behavior cannot be under the control of some as-yet-unattained purpose. Instead Skinner would say that it is caused by reinforcing consequences that have followed in the past after his performance of these sorts of behaviors. Essentially, then, Skinner is claiming that explanations of people's behavior in terms of their intentions is incorrect because it is unscientific. This claim has the interesting implication that a person's own description of what he is doing is in no way privileged. If I say I am going to mail a letter, my evidence for this is no different in kind from anyone else's. (Hence the old joke about the two behaviorists who meet walking down the street. One of them says, "You're fine; how am I?") Skinner's elimination of intentions in explaining human behavior is, however, open to some serious objections.

First, Skinner makes a number of simplistic and controversial assumptions about the nature of explanation, such as that the "scientific" explanation is the only correct one. He also, in common with most modern materialists, assumes that explanations in terms of physics are primary. In the case of human beings, of course, materialists look to neurophysiology to provide the ultimate explanation of behavior, but they understand neurophysiology in wholly mechanistic terms.

A simple example illustrates why explanations in terms of physics are not necessarily primary or ultimate.[1] Suppose you have a metal sphere and a metal ring, and you want to explain why the sphere will not go through the ring. An explanation that provided a complete description of the location and motion of each particle in each of the objects (1) would be impossible in principle, as Heisenberg's uncertainty principle has shown, and (2) would not provide an explanation even if it could be given. Telling us that the diameter of the sphere is larger than that of the ring, by contrast, does provide an appropriate explanation. The idea that the true explanation will always be the one stated in terms of the basic particles of physics is simply a prejudice in favor of physics.

What counts as an explanation is in part a function of our purposes. For example, we might explain Mary's eating by saying: (1) she feels hungry (a psychological matter), (2) it is dinnertime (a matter of social customs), or (3) her body requires food (a biological matter). All three may be true, and we may choose which one to employ depending on our purpose in asking the question "Why is she eating?" Skinner's purpose in seeking explanations of behavior is prediction and especially control, and so he selects explanations that facilitate this. But surely there are many other legitimate purposes we might have in mind in asking why a person performs a particular action. We might be interested in getting to know the person, for example, or in applying the maxim "to understand is to forgive," and for these purposes Skinner's type of explanation would be of no use.

Secondly, Skinner holds that explaining human behavior in terms of the purposes of the agents is unscientific. Why? One reason he offers is that purposes are not observable. But even physicists often postulate unobservable entities, and this is regarded as completely acceptable just so long as they can be connected in some regular way with things we can observe. So we can't rule out purposes just because they are not directly observable. The other reason he gives is that they are "final causes," and physics, he tells us, has dispensed with final causes. But even supposing that physics has eliminated final causes, it does not follow that biology must do so also (unless we presuppose the primacy of physics, which has been criticized above). In addition, Skinner completely misunderstands the notion of a final cause by assuming that final causes involve causation backward through time, that is, the goal not yet attained causes the behavior. But this interpretation is incorrect. A tadpole has a built-in tendency toward becoming a frog, but this does not mean that the future frog is acting backward through time on the tadpole. Nor is the event of my finding my glasses acting backward through time to cause my behavior in looking for them. To suppose it must do so, is to wrongly treat final causes as efficient causes. (An efficient cause is something that makes or produces its effect—for example, the author of a book or the parents of a human being.)

A third problem with Skinner's proposed elimination of all teleology (purposiveness) in explaining human behavior is that his rejection of "desires" and "purposes" makes him unable to say what a reinforcer is and to explain why it reinforces in terms of its satisfying the desires of the organism. Instead, Skinner defines a reinforcer in terms of its power to increase the frequency of a behavior upon which the reinforcer has been made contingent. That certain things reinforce behavior is just an unexplained fact. Therefore, when he says that an organism performs a behavior because of reinforcements that have followed previous behaviors of this sort, he is simply saying that it is behaving in that way because it has been acted on in the past in ways that have increased the probability of this sort of behavior. Hardly a very illuminating explanation.

Fourth, purging our language of terms like *desires, beliefs,* and *intentions* (what philosophers call *intentional language*), is harder than Skinner would have us believe. Whether or not such language is eliminable in principle from our language is, perhaps, one of the hottest issues in philosophy of language and philosophy of mind today. Many of the best contemporary philosophers (Hilary Putnam at Harvard, for example) have argued persuasively against the possibility of this purging. Certainly Skinner himself has not succeeded in eliminating intentional language. He does not even claim to have done so anywhere but in his most technical work. Indeed it is hard to see how he could. The problem for Skinner here is both theoretical and practical. On a theoretical level, what he is conditioning the pigeon, for example, to perform is an "operant" that is defined as a "set of acts defined by the property of the height to which the head is to be raised." An operant is thus a class of behaviors or acts. It may be possible to specify the operant in simple quantitative terms in the pigeon experiment, but the moment we go outside the laboratory and begin to work with people, serious problems arise with specifying the operant or, in other words, the behavior to be produced or modified.

One such problem is determining what counts as one "act" or "behavior." Is there a neutral way of describing human behavior that does not presuppose purposiveness? Skinner thinks that there is and that the behavior of a man looking for his glasses can be described in "scientific" language; for example, "He grasped a book between the thumb and forefinger of his right hand." But even when he tries to describe his behavior in this way, he illegitimately sneaks in the notion of purpose when he says "so that any object under the book can be seen." If he were to describe an action wholly in terms such as "Now he is lifting his left foot six inches from the floor and putting it down on a spot nine inches ahead of his right foot and two inches to the left of it, while simultaneously moving his right arm behind him with the palm turned forward, and the angle his arm makes with his body at time t^1 is 30 degrees, at time t^2 is 35 degrees, at time t^3 is 40 degrees, etc." (the description would, of course, be endlessly complex, since the body position changes constantly), it would simply not be intelligible as a human action. "He is throwing a ball" would describe an action, but it has a built-in purposiveness (being undertaken because it is pleasant, or to practice one's pitching, or because it is part of a game, or even just to get the ball from one place to another). What action or behavior a person is performing cannot be specified in neutral "scientific" terms. The very *concept* of an "action" or "behavior" already has a sort of built-in teleology. For example, we do not say that a person thrashing about in an epileptic fit is performing an action.

This problem has practical implications. Consider, for example, one of Skinner's plans, namely using operant conditioning to solve the problem of environmental pollution. Even if you have limitless power to make certain important reinforcements for the people in your society contingent upon their disposing safely of toxic wastes, you need to specify precisely and scientifically the operant or type of behavior you intend to reinforce. And this simply cannot be done in what Skinner would consider properly scientific terms, because there is an infinite multiplicity of physical motions of our bodies, involving a dizzying variety of substances, which constitute safe disposal of toxic wastes. The people you are controlling can be conditioned only if they have an understanding of the concept of a "toxic waste," for a start, and the notion of toxicity is parasitic on the idea of human health or flourishing, which is clearly a teleological notion.

One area of Skinner's thought that is of particular interest to philosophers is the way he sees human beings as related to animals. Essentially he does not see them as different. He treats them as continuous and believes that the same techniques that he used to shape animal behavior can be used on people, the only difference being that people's behaviors are more complex. He points out, correctly, that we cannot simply assume that animals and humans are radically different. On the other hand, he cannot simply assume that they are essentially the same and that results obtained with animals can be projected onto human beings.

Traditionally, philosophers have often claimed that one way in which human beings differ from animals is in their use of language (see, for example, Descartes' arguments on this point). It is interesting, therefore, that one area in which Skinner's work has come under attack scientifically is his account of language learning. Noam Chomsky, who teaches linguistics at the Massachusetts Institute of Technology, claims that operant conditioning simply cannot explain how a child learns his or her native language. Chomsky argues for the necessity of supposing some innate structures that enable a child to grasp the grammatical rules of language on the basis of a very limited sample of sentences, to understand unfamiliar sentences, and to generate new ones. Skinner's attempt to explain it in terms of reinforcement, Chomsky argues, led him to stretch the notion of reinforcement to the point where it became too vague to be of any scientific value. If Chomsky is right, then he has come up with a conclusive argument against Skinner's claim to be able to account for all human behavior by operant conditioning.

Skinner's expertise is in the field of experimental psychology and when he goes outside this field, he has no particular authority. But his most philosophically controversial claims are in fact precisely those that go outside the area of experimental psychology. If he is to be scientific, he ought to accept only those beliefs that can be scientifically proven, that is, those that can be demonstrated experimentally in a laboratory. But science does not prove experimentally that all human behavior is determined by causal laws. Scientists may look for such laws in whatever they study, but cannot claim to have proven that all human behavior is causally determined, and certainly not that it is causally determined by the environment. Such claims are not falsifiable by any sort of experiments. Another basic assumption made by Skinner is the truth of "scientism." This, too, cannot be proven scientifically. Scientism (not to be confused with respect for science) is the belief that (1) science can tell us the truth about every sort of thing there is, and (2) science can tell us the complete truth about every thing it treats. These claims are certainly not self-evident. There may be some kinds of things the truth of which cannot be ascertained by science, or science may give us only partial truth about some of the things it studies. One cannot prove scientifically that science is the only way to truth.

In addition, it can be argued that determinism is self-refuting. Notice that there is a tension between Skinner's philosophy and his own practice. On the one hand he wishes to persuade us that determinism is true and that we have no freedom, but on the other hand the attempt to persuade us presupposes that we have the freedom to choose, on rational grounds, to accept the truth of determinism and to change our ways of behaving and speaking—something that we cannot have if his version of determinism is true. Thus the attempt to persuade us of determinism presupposes freedom.[2]

If we turn finally to Skinner's more popular writing, namely his prescription for the "ideal society," *Walden Two* can be criticized from a number of directions. First, since it is a work of fiction, it cannot prove that it is possible to create such a society. Skinner can easily say that children in Walden Two are happy, secure, creative, and so on; that his techniques have been able to successfully eliminate negative behaviors; and that all the possible bad effects of these techniques have been carefully monitored and corrected for scientifically, but the only way to show that it is possible is to do it, and several attempts to set up communities modeled on Walden Two have not been successful.

Skinner assumes that human nature is totally adaptable. People can be conditioned to virtually any pattern of behavior, he thinks, including not treating their own children any differently from other people's children and allowing the crematorium to "dispose of" the ashes of their loved ones as it sees fit. All the historical evidence flies in the face of this project. Indeed, one of the main ways in which anthropologists tell whether fossils they uncover are homo sapiens is by looking for evidence of ritual burial of the dead. Human behavior in these areas clearly springs from some of the most deeply rooted urges in our nature, and thus any attempt to eliminate these behaviors is unlikely to succeed.

One particularly interesting objection from a philosophical point of view is that Skinner has destroyed any basis for values except the way in which the individual has been conditioned in the past. So how are the planners to determine what is a "good" society? When pushed, all they can do is to fall back on "survival." A good society is one that survives. The behaviors we ought to condition people to perform are those that are conducive to the survival of the society. But no rational basis can be provided within his system for any choice of value, even survival.

Finally, since Frazier (the designer of Walden Two) is, by his own admission, a "pot marred in the making," there is no reason to suppose that his warped emotions and his ulterior and devious motives will not in turn be reflected in the society he has designed. The techniques of operant conditioning, although discovered by science, are employed by human beings who are themselves marred in the making or, as the believer would put it, who suffer from the effects of original sin.

■ ■ ■

Summary and Conclusion

Skinner, in contrast with the many philosophers who have emphasized the possibilities for transcendence and freedom inherent in our nature as self-conscious and rational beings, views human beings simply as biological organisms differing from other animals only in the greater complexity of the behaviors we can form. Our behavior, like theirs, is simply a result of the way in which we have been reinforced and punished in the past, and if we had sufficiently detailed information about a person's history, we could, in principle, predict his or her behavior. If Skinner were right, this would imply that people are not morally responsible for their actions, since it would have been impossible for them to act differently.

Skinner's radical rejection of human freedom and moral responsibility stands in conflict not only with religious tradition but also with beliefs and assumptions that underlie both our laws (which hold people accountable for their actions) and the way we treat each other daily in our personal lives. While most people are willing to grant that human beings *sometimes* suffer from diminished moral responsibility, we nonetheless do continue to praise and blame people—things that we ought not to do if Skinner is right. Our very experience of deliberating about what we should do indicates that we spontaneously experience ourselves as free (at least sometimes). Acceptance of Skinner's view of human nature would require radical changes, then, in the way we treat people, the way we understand ourselves, and even in the way we speak, since we understand and speak about human actions in terms of the beliefs, intentions, and purposes of the persons involved.

In light of the degree to which notions like freedom, dignity, moral responsibility, and intentionality are deeply embedded in our experience, language, and shared way of life, it is appropriate to put the burden of proof on Skinner to show that he is right—in other words, we are entitled to take ourselves to be free until the contrary is proven. Has Skinner in fact provided a convincing argument against the existence of human freedom?

Certainly neither Skinner nor anybody else has succeeded in predicting human behavior with anything more than the roughest probability. Why, then, should we believe that it is in principle predictable? At this point Skinner falls back on science. Science for him is the only way to truth, and science leaves no room for freedom; so even though we do not now know enough about the neurophysiology of the brain to be able to predict behavior accurately, science will eventually enable us to do so. But this is only a promissory note on future science, and one which there is no reason to believe that science will be able to pay.

As has been argued above, Skinner's appeal to science fails to establish that human behavior is strictly necessitated. He cannot prove scientifically that science is the only way to truth; his rather simple-minded conception of scientific method does not in fact accurately reflect the actual practice of scientists; his claim that all human behavior can be explained by operant conditioning has been disputed on scientific grounds (for example, by Chomsky); and contemporary scientists in the wake of quantum theory, Heisenberg's uncertainty principle, and the theory of chaos, no longer hold that even the behavior of the objects of physics (let alone that of people) is predictable even in principle. It would be claiming too much to say that science has *proved* the existence of free will—indeed it is arguably not the province of science to answer these sorts of questions at all—but it is fair to say that science can no longer be understood in a way that lends support to determinism in anything akin to the way Skinner thinks it does.

Thus, in arguing against Skinner, it is unnecessary for the believer to have recourse to revelation. The claims about human nature that he makes go far beyond his area of professional competence as an experimental psychologist; they are not adequately supported by his appeal to science; and his theory is in any case fraught with serious internal difficulties.

Ultimately, Skinner is less interested in reflecting deeply about what it is to be human than he is in attempting to solve the problems of the world by developing techniques for controlling human behavior. Variables that cannot be controlled presently are therefore put aside in favor of those that can be manipulated, and as a result he pays little attention to developing a sophisticated or consistent position on important philosophical issues that are raised by his work: the mind/body problem, or the nature or freedom, or how we should understand causality.

While many of his techniques are no doubt valuable, particularly for use with animals, prerational children, retarded people, and the mentally deranged (where reasoning is of limited use), there is no evidence that they give one the degree of control that Skinner supposes they do, since he has not disproved the existence of human freedom. Nor is it desirable that behavioral technologists be put in charge of society, since they themselves are not exempt from the imperfection and perversity of human nature. Emphasis on controlling other human beings (as opposed to seeking their rational consent) is politically as well as morally dangerous. Exclusive emphasis on the control of physically observable behavior also leads one to think of people mechanistically in terms merely of input and output (behavior) and thus to overlook much that is distinctive about human beings: our ability to grow in understanding of ourselves, others, and the world; our experience of moral obligation; and our capacity to know and love God.

■ ■ ■

Notes

1. I am indebted to Hilary Putnam for this example.
2. This sort of self-referential argument in favor of free will has recently been developed more rigorously in J. Boyle, G. Grisez, and O. Tollafsen, *Free Choice.* Some other valuable criticisms of Skinner, to which I am in part indebted, are found in L. Stevenson, *Seven Theories of Human Nature,* and C. S. Evans, *Preserving the Person.*

■ ■ ■

Further Reading

C. S. Evans, *Preserving the Person: A Look at the Human Sciences* (Downers Grove, Ill., 1977) (an integration of faith and psychology).

C. S. Evans, *Wisdom and Humanness in Psychology: Prospects for a Christian Approach* (Grand Rapids, Mich., 1989) (contains an excellent bibliography).

B. F. Skinner, *Beyond Freedom and Dignity* (New York, 1971).

B. F. Skinner, *Science and Human Behavior* (New York, 1981).

15

JEAN-PAUL SARTRE

...

THE HUMAN PERSON AS FREEDOM

Introduction and Commentary by Leonard A. Kennedy

INTRODUCTION

■ ■ ■

Sartre's Life and Works

Jean-Paul Sartre was born in 1905 in Paris, where he lived most of his life. After college he attended the prestigious École Normale Superieure. After finishing his studies in 1929, Sartre taught philosophy, with the exception of the two years (1933–35) he spent studying philosophy in Germany, until the Second World War began in 1939. Sartre then joined the French army in 1939 and was captured by the Germans in 1940. After the war ended in 1945, Sartre stopped teaching and devoted his life to writing. He edited *Les Tempes Modernes*, a political and literary journal; wrote novels, plays, and short stories; and continued with his philosophical works. He was a radical socialist, and favored Communism until the quelling of the Hungarian uprising in 1956. He was concerned for the poor, and took part in several political movements on their behalf. He died in 1980.

His best-known works are *Nausea* (1938), *Being and Nothingness* (1943), *Existentialism* (1946), and *The Critique of Dialectical Materialism* (1960). The text under consideration here is *Existentialism*. Though Sartre later changed his mind on some of the opinions expressed in this work, we will deal with the text in its original form and with regard to its original intent.

Sartre has been known as an *existentialist*. The term itself is difficult to define because it seems to mean slightly different things to each of the writers who profess to be existentialists. Therefore, to avoid confusion, we will understand *existentialism* as Sartre uses it throughout his philosophical writings.

Sartre's thesis in this work is that his philosophy, existentialism, is a humanism; that is, he views existentialism as a philosophy that has value to mankind. The thesis is a difficult one to defend, however, because of Sartre's own definition of existentialism. He states that existentialism is the logical consequence of atheism. Because atheism denies the existence of God, it seems simultaneously to deny that there is any such thing as an objective morality. Consequently, if there is no such thing as objective morality under Sartre's brand of existentialism, it would seem that human beings are either free to do whatever they wish or at least free to do whatever they can get away with. With such boundless freedom as the consequence, mankind would be reduced to living the law of the jungle, which would obviously be of no value to mankind as a whole.

Let us, then, read Sartre's work in order to see how he defends his philosophy and to assess the success or failure of his defense.

■ ■ ■

What to Look For in the Selection

As you read Sartre's work to see how he defends his philosophy and to assess the success or failure of his defense, ask yourself the following questions.

1. Should atheism produce anguish, forlornness, and despair?
2. If there is no God, how significant a purpose can we give ourselves?
3. Does freedom necessitate responsibility?

4. Does Sartre successfully answer the four charges brought against existentialism?
5. How can Sartre pass judgment on others if there are no given moral values?

SELECTION FROM SARTRE

■ ■ ■

Existentialism

I should like on this occasion to defend existentialism against some charges which have been brought against it.

First, it has been charged with inviting people to remain in a kind of desperate quietism because, since no solutions are possible, we should have to consider action in this world as quite impossible. . . . The Communists in particular have made these charges.

On the other hand, we have been charged with dwelling on human degradation, with pointing up everywhere the sordid, shady, and slimy, and neglecting the gracious and beautiful, the bright side of human nature; for example, according to Mlle. Mercier, a Catholic critic, with forgetting the smile of the child.

Both sides charge us with having ignored human solidarity, with considering man as an isolated being. The Communists say that the main reason for this is that we take pure subjectivity, the *Cartesian* "I think," as our starting point; in other words, the moment in which man becomes fully aware of what it means to him to be an isolated being; as a result, we are unable to return to a state of solidarity with the men who are not ourselves, a state which we can never reach in the *cog-ito* ["I think"].

From the Christian standpoint, we are charged with denying the reality and seriousness of human undertakings, since, if we reject God's commandments and the eternal verities, there no longer remains anything but pure caprice, with everyone permitted to do as he pleases and incapable, from his own point of view, of condemning the points of view and acts of others.

I shall try today to answer these different charges. . . .

What can be said from the very beginning is that by existentialism we mean a doctrine which makes human life possible. . . . As is generally known, the basic charge against us is that we put the emphasis on the dark side of human life. Someone recently told me of a lady who, when she let slip a vulgar word in a moment of irritation, excused herself by saying, "I guess I'm becoming an existentialist." Consequently, existentialism is regarded as something ugly. . . . Can it be that what really scares them in the doctrine I shall try to present here is that it leaves to man a possibility of choice? To answer this question, we must re-examine it on a strictly philosophical plane. What is meant by the term *existentialism?*

Most people who use the word would be rather embarrassed if they had to explain it since, now that the word is all the rage, even the work of a musician or painter is being called existentialist. A gossip columnist in *Clartés* signs himself *The Existentialist,* so that by this time the word has been so stretched, and has taken on so broad a meaning, that it no longer means anything at all. . . .

Let us consider some object that is manufactured; for example, a book or a paper-cutter: here is an object which has been made by an artisan whose inspiration came from a concept. He referred to the concept of what a paper-cutter is and likewise to a known method of production, which is part of the concept, something which is, by and large, a routine. Thus, the paper-cutter is at once an object produced in a certain way and, on the other hand, one having a specific use; and one can not postulate a man who produces a paper-cutter but does not know what it is used for. Therefore, let us say that, for the paper-cutter, essence—that is, the ensemble of both the production routines and the properties which enable it to be both produced and defined—precedes existence. Thus, the presence of the paper-cutter or book in front of me is determined. Therefore, we have here a technical view of the world whereby it can be said that production precedes existence.

When we conceive God as the Creator, He is generally thought of as a superior sort of artisan. Whatever doctrine we may be considering, whether one like that of Descartes or that of Leibnitz, we always grant that will more or less follows understanding or, at the very least, accompanies it, and that when God creates He knows exactly what He is creating. Thus, the concept of man in the mind of God is comparable to the concept of paper-cutter in the mind of the manufacturer, and, following certain techniques and a conception, God produces man, just as the artisan, following a definition and a technique, makes a paper-cutter. Thus, the individual man is the realization of a certain concept in the divine intelligence.

In the eighteenth century, the atheism of the *philosophes* discarded the idea of God, but not so much for the notion that essence precedes existence. To a certain extent, this idea is found everywhere; we find it in Diderot, in Voltaire, and even in Kant. Man has a human nature; this human nature, which is the concept of the human, is found in all men, which means that each man is a particular example of a universal concept, man. . . .

Atheistic existentialism, which I represent, is more coherent. It states that, if God does not exist, there is at least one being in whom existence precedes essence, a being who exists before he can be defined by any concept, and that this being is man, or, as Heidegger says, human reality. What is meant here by saying that existence precedes essence? It means that, first of all, man exists, turns up, appears on the scene, and, only afterwards, defines himself. If man, as the existentialist conceives him, is indefinable, it is because at first he is nothing. Only afterward will he be something, and he himself will have made what he will be. Thus, there is no human nature, since there is no God to conceive it. Not only is man what he conceives himself to be, but he is also only what he wills himself to be after this thrust toward existence.

Man is nothing else but what he makes of himself. Such is the first principle of existentialism. It is also what is called subjectivity, the name we are labeled with when charges are brought against us. But what do we mean by this, if not that man has a greater dignity than a stone or table? For we mean that man first exists, that is, that man first of all is the being who hurls himself toward a future and who is conscious of imagining himself as being in the future. Man is at the start a plan which is aware of itself, rather than a patch of moss, a piece of garbage, or a cauliflower; nothing exists prior to this plan; there is nothing in heaven; man will be what he will have planned to be. Not what he will want to be. Because by the word "will" we generally mean a conscious decision, which is subsequent to what we have already made of ourselves. I may want to belong to a political party, write a book, get married; but all that is only a manifestation of an earlier, more spontaneous choice that is called "will." But if existence really does precede essence, man is responsible for what he is. Thus, existentialism's first move is to make every man aware of what he is and to make the full responsibility of his existence rest on him. And when we say that a man is responsible for himself, we do not only mean that he is responsible for his own individuality, but that he is responsible for all men. . . .

When we say that man chooses his own self, we mean that every one of us does likewise; but we also mean by that that in making this choice he also chooses all men. In fact, in creating the man that we want to be, there is not a single one of our acts which does not at the same time create an image of man as we think he ought to be. To choose to be this or that is to affirm at the same time the value of what we choose, because we can never choose evil. We always choose the good, and nothing can be good for us without being good for all.

If, on the other hand, existence precedes essence, and if we grant that we exist and fashion our image at one and the same time, the image is valid for everybody and for our whole age. Thus, our responsibility is much greater than we might have supposed, because it involves all mankind. If I am a workingman and choose to join a Christian trade-union rather than be a Communist, and if by being a member I want to show that the best thing for man is resignation, that the kingdom of man is not of this world, I am not only involving my own case—I want to be resigned for everyone. As a result, my action has involved all humanity. To take a more individual matter, if I want to marry, to have children, even if this marriage depends solely on my own circumstances or passion or wish, I am involving all humanity in monogamy and not merely myself. Therefore, I am responsible for myself and for everyone else. I am creating a certain image of man of my own choosing. In choosing myself, I choose man.

This helps us understand what the actual content is of such rather grandiloquent words as anguish, forlornness, despair. As you will see, it's all quite simple.

First, what is meant by anguish? The existentialists say at once that man is anguish. What that means is this: the man who involves himself and who realizes that he is not only the person he chooses to be, but also a lawmaker who is, at the same time, choosing all mankind as well as himself, can not help escape the feeling of his total and deep responsibility. Of course, there are many people who are not anxious; but we claim that they are hiding their anxiety, that they are fleeing from it.

For every man, everything happens as if all mankind had its eyes fixed on him and were guiding itself by what he does. And every man ought to say to himself, "Am I really the kind of man who has the right to act in such a way that humanity might guide itself by my actions?" And if he does not say that to himself, he is masking his anguish. . . .

When we speak of forlornness, a term Heidegger was fond of, we mean only that God does not exist and that we have to face all the consequences of this. The existentialist is strongly opposed to a certain kind of secular ethics which would like to abolish God with the least possible expense. About 1880, some French teachers tried to set up a secular ethics which went something like this: God is a useless and costly hypothesis; we are discarding it; but, meanwhile, in order for there to be an ethics, a society, a civilization, it is essential that certain values be taken seriously and that they be considered as having an *a priori* existence. It must be obligatory, *a priori* [prior to experience], to be honest, not to lie, not to beat your wife, to have children, etc., etc. So we're going to try a little device which will make it possible to show that values exist all the same, inscribed in a heaven of ideas, though otherwise God does not exist. In other words—and this, I believe, is the tendency of everything called reformism in France—nothing will be changed if God does not exist. We shall find ourselves with the same norms of honesty, progress, and humanism, and we shall have made of God an outdated hypothesis which will peacefully die off by itself.

The existentialist, on the contrary, thinks it very distressing that God does not exist, because all possibility of finding values in a heaven of ideas disappears along with Him; there can no longer be an *a priori* Good, since there is no infinite and perfect consciousness to think it. Nowhere is it written that the Good exists, that we must be honest, that we must not lie; because the fact is we are on a plane where there are only men. Dostoyevsky said, "If God didn't exist, everything would be possible." That is the very starting point of existentialism. Indeed, everything is permissible if God does not exist; and as a result man is forlorn, because neither within him nor without does he find anything to cling to. He can't start making excuses for himself.

If existence really does precede essence, there is no explaining things away by reference to a fixed and given human nature. In other words, there is no determinism, man is free, man is freedom. On the other hand, if God does not exist, we find no values or commands to turn to which legitimize our conduct. So, in the bright realm of values, we have no excuse behind us, nor justification before us. We are alone, with no excuses.

That is the idea I shall try to convey when I say that man is condemned to be free. Condemned, because he did not create himself, yet in other respects is free; because, once thrown into the world, he is responsible for everything he does. The existentialist does not believe in the power of passion. He will never agree that a sweeping passion is a ravaging torrent which fatally leads a man to certain acts and is therefore an excuse. He thinks that man is responsible for his passion. . . .

As for despair, the term has a very simple meaning. It means that we shall confine ourselves to reckoning only with what depends upon our will, or on the ensemble of probabilities which make our action possible. When we want something, we always have to reckon with probabilities. I may be counting on the arrival of a friend. The friend is coming by rail or street-car; this supposes that the train will arrive on schedule, or that the street-car will not jump the track. I am left in the realm of possibility; but possibilities are to be reckoned with only to the point where my action comports with the ensemble of these possibilities, and no further. The moment the possibilities I am considering are not rigorously involved by my action, I ought to disengage myself from them, because no God, no scheme, can adapt the world and its possibilities to my will. When Descartes said, "Conquer yourself rather than the world," he meant essentially the same thing. . . .

When all is said and done, what we are accused of, at bottom, is not our pessimism, but an optimistic toughness. If people throw up to us our works of fiction in which we write about people who are soft, weak, cowardly, and sometimes even downright bad, it's not because these people are soft, weak, cowardly, or bad; because, if we were to say, as Zola did, that they are that way because of heredity, the workings of environment, society, because of biological or psychological determinism, people would be reassured. They would say, "Well, that's what we're like, no one can do anything about it." But when the existentialist writes about a coward, he says that this coward is responsible for his cowardice. He's not like that because he has a cowardly heart or lung or brain; he's not like that on account of his physiological make-up; but he's like that because he has made himself a coward by his acts. There's no such thing as a cowardly constitution; there are nervous constitutions; there is poor blood, as the common people say, or strong constitutions. But the man whose blood is poor is not a coward on that account, for what makes cowardice is the act of renouncing or yielding. A constitution is not an act; the coward is defined on the basis of the acts he performs. People feel, in a vague sort of way, that this coward we're talking about is guilty of being a coward, and the thought frightens them. What people would like is that a coward or a hero be born that way. . . .

What the existentialist says is that the coward makes himself cowardly, that the hero makes himself heroic. There's always a possibility for the coward not to be cowardly any more and for the hero to stop being heroic. What counts is total involvement; some one particular action or set of circumstances is not total involvement.

Thus, I think we have answered a number of the charges concerning existentialism. You see that it can not be taken for a philosophy of quietism, since it defines man in terms of action; nor for a pessimistic description of man—there is no doctrine more optimistic, since man's destiny is within himself; nor for an attempt to discourage man from acting, since it tells him that the only hope is in his acting and that action is the only thing that enables a man to live. Consequently, we are dealing here with an ethics of action and involvement. . . .

This theory is the only one which gives man dignity, the only one which does not reduce him to an object. The effect of all materialism is to treat all men, including the one philosophizing, as objects, that is, as an ensemble of determined reactions in no way distinguished from the ensemble of qualities and phenomena which constitute a table or a chair or a stone. We definitely wish to establish the human realm as an ensemble of values distinct from the material realm. But the subjectivity that we have thus arrived at, and which we have claimed to be truth, is not a strictly individual subjectivity, for we have demonstrated that one discovers in the *cogito* not only himself, but others as well.

The philosophies of Descartes and Kant to the contrary, through the *I think* we reach our own self in the presence of others, and the others are just as real to us as our own self. Thus, the man who becomes aware of himself through the *cogito* also perceives all others, and he perceives them as the condition of his own existence. He realizes that he can not be anything (in the sense that we say that someone is witty or nasty or jealous) unless others recognize it as such. In order to get any truth about myself, I must have contact with another person. The other is indispensable to my own existence, as well as to my knowledge about myself. This being so, in discovering my inner being I discover the other person at the same time, like a freedom placed in front of me which thinks and wills only for or against me. Hence, let us at once announce the discovery of a world which we shall call intersubjectivity; this is the world in which man decides what he is and what others are.

Besides, if it is impossible to find in every man some universal essence which would be human nature, yet there does exist a universal human condition. It's not by chance that today's thinkers speak more readily of man's condition than of his nature. By condition they mean, more or less definitely, the *a priori* limits which outline man's fundamental situation in the universe. Historical situations vary; a man may be born a slave in a pagan society or a feudal lord or a proletarian. What does not vary is the necessity for him to exist in the world, to be at work there, to be there in the midst of other people, and to be mortal there. . . .

This does not entirely settle the objection to subjectivism. In fact, the objection still takes several forms. First, there is the following: we are told, "So you're able to do anything, no matter what!" This is expressed in various ways. First we are accused of anarchy; then they say, "You're unable to pass judgment on others, because there's no reason to prefer one . . . [way of life] to another"; finally they tell us, "Everything is arbitrary in this choosing of yours. You take something from one pocket and pretend you're putting it into the other."

These three objections aren't very serious. Take the first objection. "You're able to do anything, no matter what" is not to the point. In one sense choice is possible, but what is not possible is not to choose. I can always choose, but I ought to know that, if I do not choose, I am still choosing. Though this may seem purely formal, it is highly important for keeping fantasy and caprice within bounds. If it is true that in facing a situation, for example, one in which, as a person capable of having sexual relations, of having children, I am obliged to choose an attitude, and if I in any way assume responsibility for a choice which, in involving myself, also involves all mankind, this has nothing to do with caprice, even if no *a priori* value determines my choice. . . .

Man is in an organized situation in which he himself is involved. Through his choice, he involves all mankind, and he can not avoid making a choice: either he will remain chaste, or he will marry without having children, or he will marry and have children; anyhow, whatever he may do, it is impossible for him not to take full responsibility for the way he handles this problem. Doubtless, he chooses without referring to preestablished values, but it is unfair to accuse him of caprice.

. . . [And] one can still pass judgment, for, as I have said, one makes a choice in relationship to others. First, one can judge (and this is perhaps not a judgment of value, but a logical judgment) that certain choices are based on error and others on truth. If we have defined man's situation as a free choice, with no excuses and no recourse, every man who takes refuge behind the excuse of his passions, every man who sets up a determinism, is a dishonest man.

The objection may be raised, "But why mayn't he choose himself dishonestly?" I reply that I am not obliged to pass moral judgment on him, but that I do define his dishonesty as an error. One can not help considering the truth of the matter. Dishonesty is obviously a falsehood because it belies the complete freedom of involvement. On the same grounds, I maintain that there is also dishonesty if I choose to state that certain values exist prior to me; it is self-contradictory for me to want them and at the same time state that they are imposed on me. Suppose someone says to me, "What if I want to be dishonest?" I'll answer, "There's no reason for you not to be, but I'm saying that that's what you are, and that the strictly coherent attitude is that of honesty."

Besides, I can bring moral judgment to bear. When I declare that freedom in every concrete circumstance can have no other aim than to want itself, if man has once become aware that in his forlornness he imposes values, he can no longer want but one thing, and that is freedom, as the basis of all values. That doesn't mean that he wants it in the abstract. It means simply that the ultimate meaning of the acts of honest men is the quest for freedom as such. A man who belongs to a Communist or revolutionary union wants concrete goals; these goals imply an abstract desire for freedom; but this freedom is wanted in something concrete. We want freedom for freedom's sake and in every particular circumstance. And in wanting freedom we discover that it depends entirely on the freedom of others, and that the freedom of others depends on ours. Of course, freedom as the definition of man does not depend on others, but, as soon as there is involvement, I am obliged to want others to have freedom at the same time that I want my own freedom. I can take freedom as my goal only if I take that of others as a goal as well. Consequently, when, in all honesty, I've recognized that man is a being in whom existence precedes essence, that he is a free being who, in various circumstances, can want only his freedom, I have at the same time recognized that I can want only the freedom of others.

Therefore, in the name of this will for freedom, which freedom itself implies, I may pass judgment on those who seek to hide from themselves the complete arbitrariness and the complete freedom of their existence. Those who hide their complete freedom from themselves out of a spirit of seriousness or by means of deterministic excuses, I shall call cowards; those who try to show that their existence was necessary, when it is the very contingency of man's appearance on earth, I shall call stinkers. But cowards or stinkers can be judged only from a strictly unbiased point of view. . . .

The third objection is the following: "You take something from one pocket and put it into the other. That is, fundamentally, values aren't serious, since you choose them." My answer to this is that I'm quite vexed that that's the way it is; but if I've discarded God the Father, there has to be someone to invent values. You've got to take things as they are. Moreover, to say that we invent values means nothing else but this: life has no meaning *a priori*. Before you come alive, life is nothing; it's up to you to give it a meaning, and value is nothing else but the meaning that you choose. In that way, you see, there is a possibility of creating a human community. . . .

From these few reflections it is evident that nothing is more unjust than the objections that have been raised against us. Existentialism is nothing else than an attempt to draw all the consequences of a coherent atheistic position. It isn't trying to plunge man into despair at all. . . .

Extracted from *Existentialism* (New York, 1957).

COMMENTARY

■ ■ ■

Analysis of the Selection

Sartre begins his defense of his brand of existentialism by listing four charges commonly brought against it. According to its opponents, existentialism (1) leads to inaction, (2) takes a pessimistic viewpoint, (3) leads to individualism and thus absolves humans from social responsibility, and (4) allows human beings to do whatever they want.

Sartre acknowledges and addresses the serious repercussions created by his denial of God's existence. If there is no God, he says, there is no *a priori* morality, that is, no *given* morality. Whereas theists see that the morality they accept is based on the purpose of their lives, a purpose given to them by the Creator in planning them and bringing them into existence, atheists remove God and therefore remove the objective purpose of human beings. Sartre expresses this fundamental difference between existentialism and theism by saying "our existence precedes our essence." In other words, we find ourselves in existence and realize that we have no given purpose.

Sartre realizes that it is possible to accept atheism without facing up to all its consequences, to think that roughly the same objective moral order remains even if God goes, a moral order founded on a common human nature. But he thinks that such an atheism is illogical, that it does not follow through to its ultimate conclusions. For Sartre, an atheist should squarely confront the products of atheism: anguish, forlornness, and despair.

Atheism produces anguish because we are free. Sartre is emphatic in teaching that humans are free; one might say that for him freedom is our essence. And, because we are free, we are responsible for our actions. And to be responsible and yet have no guide for action is to experience anguish, dread. It is possible, he knows, to run away from the real situation in order to escape or lessen the anguish, but he says that this is not good philosophy.

The absence of God also produces forlornness, the feeling of being abandoned. We have no Heavenly Father to watch over us. Moreover, we have no Heavenly Father to give our life a purpose, to tell us how to live. We are free but do not know what to do with our freedom. Freedom calls out for guidance, and there is none. We are, Sartre says, *condemned* to be free. This freedom, which is our essence, which so many people consider to be a great good, is seen by Sartre as a burden, even a prison. Thus our forlornness is one with our anguish.

Finally, the absence of God produces despair. It does so because we must admit that we are alone in the universe, with no help possible from above. We realize that what we become depends entirely on us. If we are to make something of ourselves, we must do it entirely on our own. We must take personal responsibility for all our failures. Again, the despair we feel is one with our forlornness and our anguish.

Having faced these apparent consequences of atheism, Sartre tries to show that things are not really as bad as they seem. He has three arguments to show that his existentialism does not lead to the law of the jungle; on the contrary, it makes people responsible not only for themselves but for everyone else.

(a) He says that, since we have no *given* purpose, it is up to us to choose how to live, to give ourselves a purpose. Since we do this freely, we are responsible for our choice. "And," he says, "when we say that a man is responsible for himself, we do not mean only that he is responsible for his own individuality, but that he is responsible for all men." We are thus not as free as it seemed. We may not do whatever we want; indeed, "there is not a single one of our acts which does not at the same time create an image of man as we think he ought to be."

(b) Since there are no objective moral values it is impossible for us to do what is wrong; everything we choose is good. It becomes good by the very fact that we choose it. "To choose to be this or that is to affirm at the same time the value of what we choose, because we can never choose evil." Moreover, what is good for us must be good for everyone. "We always choose the good, and nothing can be good for us without being good for all." Thus, again, we are responsible for ourselves and also for everyone else.

(c) We are free. And freedom is such a great good that, in exercising itself, it must have itself as its goal. The purpose of freedom is to preserve freedom. It would be incorrect to say that we are free to pursue values. What should be said is that freedom is the *only* value; freedom exists for freedom's sake. Now, we realize that the exercise of our freedom is tied in with the exercise of the freedom of others. Accordingly, "I am obliged to want others to have freedom at the same time that I want my own freedom." Thus we come to the same conclusion: I am responsible for others as well as for myself.

With these three arguments purporting to show that human beings are responsible for all other human beings, Sartre considers that he has established his thesis, has shown that his philosophy leads not to the law of the jungle but to a human life in which each person is responsible for every other person.

He can thus claim that he has satisfactorily answered the four complaints against existentialism mentioned earlier:

1. It does not lead to inaction; it is not paralyzed by the lack of a given purpose, since human beings find purposes of their own, and their freely chosen purposes respect the right of others to freely choose their purposes.
2. It is not pessimistic. Sartre says that "there is no doctrine more optimistic," for the reason that "man's destiny is within himself." It seemed to be pessimistic because man

was in the universe without God, without a purpose, and filled with anguish, forlornness, despair. But then it was shown that he had the resources within himself to give himself a purpose, and a purpose that did not war with the purposes of other human beings.

3. Existentialism does not lead to individualism and absolve us from social responsibility. Some philosophers have claimed that the philosopher Descartes, in discovering his own existence in his *I think, therefore I am*, leads us to a concern with our own existence to the exclusion of the existence of others. But, for Sartre, this discovery of ourselves shows us at the same time the existence of others and our profound connections with them. We are individuals but we are also social. We share our human nature with all other human beings. When Sartre says that "existence precedes essence," he does not really mean that there is no human nature; what he really means is that our existence precedes our purpose. He is quite willing to restore human nature (though under the title "a universal human condition"). By our nature we are distinguished from all other objects in the universe, and Sartre claims that his philosophy is the only materialism that respects human dignity, since humans are on a higher plane than all other material things, especially because of their freedom. And, when we realize that only human beings are free and that we are human beings, we see that we must use our freedom not just as individuals but as members of society.

4. Existentialism does not allow us to do whatever we want. It seemed at first that there were no given guidelines for us, but Sartre has shown that there are strict guidelines since, when we choose for ourselves a purpose in life, we must choose one suitable for all human beings and one that respects the freedom of all other human beings.

An objection is raised by Sartre, however, to his answer to the fourth objection to existentialism. He raises the objection that, if things are as he claims, we cannot pass judgment on the choices others make. If other persons deny their freedom and blame their passions for their wrong actions, how can we question their free decision to do so? What is wrong with their being dishonest in this matter, since there are no *given* moral values? Is it not a contradiction to find fault with dishonesty unless we admit that honesty is a given moral value?

It is clear that this objection is a serious one for Sartre, though he claims it isn't. He calls *dishonest* and *cowards* those who say that they are not completely free, and *stinkers* those who say that their existence is not radically contingent, that is, that there is no necessary reason why they exist or why they have the nature that they have. Now, such terms are terms of moral reprobation, but Sartre has to claim that in using them he is not passing a "judgment of value" but a "judgment of logic." They are used, he says, simply to indicate that the people being judged are in error. For Sartre there *is* actually a *given* value in ethics: one *must* admit that existence is contingent and freedom complete.

To the further objection that the other values found in existentialist ethics are not "serious" since they are arbitrarily chosen, Sartre seems to concede the point ("I'm quite vexed that that's the way it is," he says here), but yet adds that "there is a possibility of creating a human community," that is, a community that can live together in peace.

We must examine now, however, whether what Sartre says is consistent; whether, indeed, granting for the sake of argument that God does not exist, it is possible, according to Sartre's reasoning, to create a human community. Or, as Sartre puts it, is he simply taking something from one pocket and putting it into the other?

Let us first restate quite clearly what Sartre's position is. He says that there are no *given* moral values because there is no God to give them. He denies that human nature (or "the human condition") is able to prescribe moral values. No doubt he realizes that a certain way of life is *in accordance with* human nature, that is, such that it maximizes the happiness of human beings, but he claims that, if there is no God, such a way of life cannot of itself be imposed on human beings since there is no planner of human life and no authority to impose such a way of life. Yet Sartre does manage to require such a way of life by stating that, in choosing my own way of life, I must choose a way of life suitable for everyone; that, in saying what is good, I must choose what is good for everyone; that, in exercising my freedom, I must respect everyone else's freedom.

■ ■ ■

Philosophical Critique

One can well ask why such consequences follow. If there are no given moral values, why must I, in choosing for myself a way of life, choose a way of life suitable for everyone? To claim that I must worry about others is to say, implicitly, that worrying about others is a given moral requirement. If there are no given moral values, why must I, in choosing what I will establish as good, choose what will be good for everyone? To claim that I must choose what is good for everyone is to say, implicitly, that being responsible for others is a given moral requirement. If there are no moral values, why must I, in exercising my freedom, respect the freedom of others? To claim that I must exercise my freedom so as not to interfere with others' freedom is to say, implicitly, that to respect others' freedom is a given moral requirement. Sartre *is*, then, giving with one hand what he has taken away with the other. He is sneaking in given moral values after he has thrown them out. Refusing to ground these moral values on God, Sartre has grounded them on fallacious reasoning.

If, as Sartre says, I am completely free, and there are no given moral values except that I must admit that I am radically contingent and completely free, why may I not do whatever I want, not caring at all about others? Why must I assume responsibility for them? Why must I respect their freedom? The answer is that there is no reason at all.

When Sartre says that we can never choose evil, the truth in his claim is that, since for him there is no given moral good or evil, there is no evil to choose. And, when he says that we always choose the good, all that he can mean is that we choose what we want to choose; he cannot justifiably mean that what we choose becomes a moral good. Yet he proceeds as if such were the case.

And, when he says that we are responsible in a world devoid of given moral values, what truth can there be in such a claim?

If there are no moral values, how can there be responsibility? If I give you a worthless object, say a stone, and tell you that you may do whatever you want with it but that you are responsible for what you do, how much responsibility do you have? None. If I tell you that there are no moral values, that you may do whatever you want, but that you are responsible for what you do, how much responsibility do you have? None.

Sartre is therefore wrong to think that one should experience anguish, forlorness, and despair as a result of having a sense of responsibility in a universe devoid of moral values. Responsibility is valid only when there are moral values to which one is bound. Responsibility cannot generate moral values; it is a consequence of them. A condition for experiencing anguish, forlornness, and despair is that we, explicitly or implicitly, know that there are moral values.

Sartre's thesis, then, that existentialism is a humanism, is quite unproven.

■ ■ ■

The Problem of Freedom

Perhaps the greatest lesson we can learn from Sartre's work has to do with freedom. Sartre has canonized one understanding of freedom, one kind of freedom. We might call it freedom of choice. It is the ability to choose something or not choose it, or to choose one thing and not another. It is, of course, a real freedom. But, for Sartre, it is the only kind of freedom.

Before showing that there is another type of freedom, however, let us examine freedom of choice. According to Sartre, it is its own end; that is, the purpose of freedom of choice is directed solely to its own preservation. He realizes that freedom of choice cannot simply choose itself; it already has itself, as it were. But it "chooses itself" by choosing other things simply for the sake of exercising itself. What it chooses is not important; the important thing is that it choose freely.

Here, then, we have a freedom that is not directed to an end outside itself. Human beings need not use their freedom to go anywhere, but simply to stay where they are.

One problem with this theory is that it is impossible to stay where we are. Whenever we use our freedom, we tend to lose it because we are creatures of habit. If we use it to have a gin and tonic before dinner each evening, such behavior tends to become habitual, and we are less free in regard to it; it is harder for us to stop it. And this is true of any free decision we make, at least if we perform certain actions regularly. If we decide to get up every morning at seven o'clock, we use our freedom to do so but then we lose our freedom to get up at some other time. To hang onto our freedom of choice, we should get up at a different time each day, a time freely decided the night before.

But the major decisions of our life do not lend themselves to such rapid changes. For example, if we decide to be become a lawyer, and it takes, say, three years in law school, our decision is meaningless unless we keep it for three years. So, during those three years, we lose our freedom of choice. We are not free not to be a lawyer. And, even after the three years, to decide to not practice law simply in order to keep our freedom of choice might well impose on us intolerable hardship. And, if we decide to marry someone and have children and then decide to get out of family life, life will be very complicated indeed. And these considerations apply to a host of major decisions we are constantly forced to make. If we decide to live in a certain city, we lose our freedom of choice to live elsewhere unless we are willing to keep moving from city to city.

But there is a problem even here. If we develop a particular lifestyle (for example, being sober, rising early, being married, being a lawyer, living in a certain city, watching certain TV programs we like) and want to retain freedom of choice by changing (for example, becoming a drunkard, sleeping in all morning, leaving our family, giving up our profession, moving to another city, watching TV programs we don't like), we are not really exercising freedom of choice. What we are doing is being changeable persons, and to be changeable persons is to be in a fixed way of life just as much as if we adopted any definite lifestyle.

It is impossible, then, to keep our freedom of choice. And for Sartre this is a tragedy. He thinks that the greatest thing humans can hope for is to hang onto this freedom, even though it doesn't lead anywhere. But it would be a tragedy if Sartre were right. We would, at best, be like Sisyphus in Greek mythology. He was a cruel king of Corinth who was condemned forever to roll a huge stone up a hill, and have it roll down again on nearing the top. That is the real meaning of Sartre's claim that we are "condemned" to be free.

Fortunately, however, Sartre is wrong. There is another kind of freedom. Let us call it the freedom of willingness. It is the freedom to do what we want to do. This is a true freedom because, if we are doing what we want to do, we are doing it freely. And this is true even if we cannot help doing it, that is, even if we do not have freedom of choice.

Moreover, this kind of freedom is a *higher* kind of freedom. Freedom of choice is ordained to it. We have freedom of choice so that we can live in a certain way. Now, certain ways of living make us happy and others do not. And we know that, since we have to live some kind of life, we will use our freedom of choice in one way or the other; we will train ourselves to live in a way that makes us happy or we will allow ourselves to live in a way that makes unhappy. (Of course it is possible to live in an in-between manner, but we will neglect that since our point can be made without going into it.) Whether we use our freedom of choice to make us happy or unhappy we will lose it (or greatly reduce it) in either case. Since we are creatures of habit, to use our freedom of choice to develop ourselves in either direction is to decrease our freedom of choice. If, for example, we become drunkards, it is extremely difficult for us to become sober. If we use our freedom of choice to enter into a happy married life, it is difficult for us to give up this life. Freedom of choice, then, leads to either happiness or unhappiness (or a mixture of the two), but in any case it uses itself up in the process.

We might regret losing our freedom of choice since it seems to be such a great good. But we should realize that it is a means to happiness. If we can achieve happiness, much of our freedom of choice is no longer necessary, like a ladder once we have reached the top of the wall we are climbing. Moreover, we should also realize that, in losing freedom of choice, we are not losing freedom. We are losing one kind of freedom but gaining another kind, a higher kind, and a freedom which can be gained only by "spending" the lower kind. If we had a large number of pennies and could turn them in for the same number of hundred dollar bills we would not regret losing them. Similarly, we should not regret spending our freedom of choice to receive the higher kind of freedom.

What we must ensure, in spending our freedom of choice, which we must do, is that we do indeed get the higher kind of freedom, which accompanies happiness, rather than no freedom of all, which accompanies unhappiness.

In heaven we shall have complete freedom of willingness, since we shall be perfectly happy, but no freedom of choice to do evil, since we will be joined to God, the infinite good, necessarily. In hell there is no freedom of willingness, since there is only unhappiness, and no freedom of choice, since escape is impossible.

Comparable to these two situations is life on earth. Those who are striving for eternal happiness experience the joy of a good conscience and the hope of heavenly bliss. They thus have the freedom of willingness that can be found in this life, and still some freedom of choice to do evil, since they are not confirmed in their present state. Those who are not on their way to heaven, who know that they are going the wrong way, have the pangs of a guilty conscience and the fear of eternal unhappiness. They have no freedom of willingness but still have some freedom of choice, since there is the possibility of reform.

We should thus consider the paradox pointed out by Saint Augustine: we can willingly bring ourselves to a place where we do not will to be. We can do it willingly because it can be done with freedom of choice. We can also not will it because it makes us unhappy, it is against our freedom of willingness. When we tell ourselves, then, that we are free to do whatever we want, we should realize that this has two meanings. We are free to do anything, but something we do with this freedom of choice may make us unhappy, be against our freedom of willingness, and thus be something we don't want to do. We should make sure that what we do (with our freedom of choice) is something we *really* want to do (with our freedom of willingness).

■ ■ ■

Religious Critique

It is Sartre's idea of freedom that has led to the present-day fear of commitment. If we are to hang onto our freedom of choice as much as we can, we have to continually "keep our options open," and committing ourselves involves closing some options. If we commit ourselves to marry a certain person, both the single life and marriage to someone else must be ruled out. If we commit ourselves to being a medical doctor, all other professions are ruled out. If we commit ourselves to serve God in a religious commitment as a priest or a religious, another type of work, and married life, are ruled out. If we commit ourselves as parents we rule out lots of activities incompatible with this, and it is obvious that we also rule out opting out of our commitment.

What encourages this lack of commitment is a lack of faith in what really constitutes happiness. People are not really convinced that our nature is fulfilled in only certain ways, and that we are wasting our time looking for happiness elsewhere. They fear that they will lose out by complete dedication to anything. Though they must realize that their choices dwindle as they age, they are not convinced that *anything* is so connected with happiness that they should pursue it wholeheartedly.

To try to hang onto freedom of choice and not "spend it" on certain choices is to be like a miser who hoards his money and never spends it on anything. We consider misers to be foolish because they have the means to make themselves and others happy and yet they prefer the means to the end. Uncommitted persons are the same: they prefer the means to happiness over happiness itself.

Such a position is understandable in Sartre. In denying God's existence he has ruled out the purpose of human life, the goal of human beings, that which makes them happy. And, in ruling out the purpose of human life, he has ruled out any fully satisfying object of human striving. It thus makes some sense for him to glorify freedom of choice. But this makes no sense for those who know that freedom of choice is of its very nature ordained to freedom of willingness, that we are free so that we can be happy. Some people wonder what it means to say that the truth will make us free, since we are already free (with freedom of choice). What it means is that the truth will lead us to freedom of willingness, true freedom. Sartre is right in claiming that we are contingent. But this does not mean that we are unplanned; it means simply that God freely willed us to exist. Thus we are not radically contingent, in the sense that everything about us is contingent. Our existence is contingent, but our nature and its purpose are not; they are necessary once our existence is posited. Our freedom also is necessary once our existence is posited. We make ourselves not in the sense that we give ourselves our purpose but in the sense that we freely decide to work for it (or not to work for it). Only in this sense do we "make ourselves." And we have seen that, if we had to "make ourselves" in the sense intended by Sartre, we could not even give a rationale for a half-decent life here on earth, not to mention a fully satisfying life in eternity.

■ ■ ■

Conclusion

We have seen Sartre's answers to four objections to his philosophy and his reasons for claiming that this philosophy can be the basis for an ethics other than the law of the jungle. And we have seen that these reasons are faulty because they unjustifiably bring into Sartre's philosophy what he has initially thrown out.

We have also seen that Sartre's notion of freedom is such that his followers have no reason to commit themselves to a stable way of life, since no lasting happiness is foreseen, but that a different notion of freedom *can* give a solid basis for a life committed to a socially beneficial ethics and a personally satisfying life.

■ ■ ■

Further Reading

T. M. King, *Sartre and the Sacred* (Chicago, 1974).

R. Marill-Albérès, *Philosopher without Faith* (New York, 1961).

16

SIMONE DE BEAUVOIR

. . .

THE HUMAN PERSON
AS CO-EXISTENT

Introduction and Commentary by Janine D. Langan

INTRODUCTION

■ ■ ■

De Beauvoir's Life and Works

Simone de Beauvoir was born in January 1908 into a typical Parisian bourgeois family. She had a very happy childhood. Her mother, lively, feminine, and pious, sent her to a Catholic school: le Cours Désir. She was very intelligent and enjoyed her self-image as good little girl. As we will see from the selection that follows this introduction, de Beauvoir said of herself: "I do not know anyone as gifted as I have been for happiness. . . . I demanded it. I had begun with a childhood experience which had demonstrated, in a way, that this demand could be met." However, her father was not a believer. Her "intellectual life—incarnated by [her] father—and [her] spiritual life—directed by [her] mother—were totally separate domains." "To me," she says in the first book of her memoirs, "all things human—culture, politics, business, customs—had nothing to do with religion. Thus, God was relegated outside this world of ours, which eventually influenced in depth my evolution."

In 1918 de Beauvoir began an intense friendship with Zaza (Elizabeth Mabille). It lasted until Zaza's death at twenty-one, in 1929. Simone blamed this death on the bourgeois family conventions that impeded Zaza's love affair with a common friend, Merleau Ponty, who later became a famous philosopher. This tragedy partly inspired her decision to write *The Second Sex.*

At fourteen Simone had lost her faith: "I realized that nothing could make me give up the joys of this earth. 'I no longer believe in God,' thought I, not particularly surprised." At twenty-one, she passed brilliantly the *Agrégation de Philosophie,* a tough competitive exam that opens up the teaching career in France. Her family was upset: she would never be a charming young woman. She began to feel ostracized in her social milieu; the resulting sudden alienation from her father was a terrible shock.

By then (1929) she had left home and met Jean-Paul Sartre, a fellow student, "the main event of my existence," she will say later. The two young people struck a pact with one another: "We would never be strangers to one another, never would one call on the other for help without response, and nothing would ever come in the way of that covenant; but it must never degenerate into constraints or habits." Hence the second half of the pact: "Between us [said Sartre] there exists a necessary love; it is proper that we should also experience contingent loves." Complete frankness would make their relationship unique in the history of human behavior. They would begin it, however, with two years of exclusivity.

In 1931 Simone was named professor of philosophy in Marseille, five hundred miles away. She panicked at the thought of their separation. Sartre proposed marriage. She refused, and decided to begin to practice true independence. Every vacation, the two would go on trips to which Simone dedicated herself with passionate intensity. Sartre often kidded her about this "schizophrenic obstinacy towards happiness" that "subjugated fallaciously the universe to [her] plans." "Wandering around in this relaxed, obstinate fashion anchored my great optimistic delirium in reality; I was tasting the delights of the gods; I was, myself, the creator of the gifts by which I felt fulfilled." Sartre, who was doing research in Berlin, began making full use of their contract and had his first "serious" affair; so worried was she, she came to check.

One of de Beauvoir's students, Olga Kosakievicz who deeply admired Simone, fascinated both her and Sartre with her wild revolt against every stricture, including the needs to sleep and eat. In 1933 they decided to be inventive and to "adopt" Olga, transforming their couple into a trio. This experiment in creative human relations was catastrophic; it finally exploded in 1936. This experience provided Simone with the theme of her first published novel, *L'Invitée* (1943), in which Françoise, who plays Simone's role, murders the third party to recover her self-respect. In reality, Olga left the trio for one of Sartre's pupils, J. L. Bost, whom she eventually married, and whose lover Simone became the next year. Olga and Bost became the nucleus of a kind of court around de Beauvoir and Sartre—the "family," many members of which received financial assistance from the two successful authors.

Emotionally, de Beauvoir's relationship to Sartre was less than perfect, nor was it harmless to the numerous third parties involved. De Beauvoir, for example, entered into a very close relationship with the American novelist, Nelson Algren, in 1947. Algren brought the affair to an end with an ultimatum to choose in 1951.

However, Sartre and de Beauvoir lived an unusually fruitful intellectual symbiosis. He persuaded her to write *The Second Sex* (1949) and to dare to use her life experience as matter of her works, which launched her into her five-volume autobiography. She criticized his theories and drew him into dialogues that were later filmed or published. Both were frank and severe in their judgments of each other's works. Sartre commented on this relationship: "She was the perfect person . . . with whom to engage in dialogue. . . . It is a unique grace." And he gave one of the most moving testimonies to the quality of her friendship in a letter to her, later published in *Lettres au Castor:* "Your judgment is more precious to me than anything in the world. . . . You are not only my life but the only truthful and honest aspect of it." World War II forced the two young people to abandon their semi-anarchical, semi-surrealistic, individualistic revolt against all limits, and to face their political responsibility. In 1943, Camus recruited Sartre and Simone for *Combat,* a clandestine newspaper. Its editorial secretary, Jacqueline Bernard, was arrested by the Gestapo in the summer of 1944, and Sartre and Simone went into hiding until the liberation of Paris. De Beauvoir explored the ambiguity of her war experience in *Le Sang des autres* (1945), a novel that raises the issue of violence and "engagement." She was discovering "solidarity, my responsibilities, and the possibility that one should consent to death in order to save the meaning of life." Her optimistic individualism was crumbling under "that primordial malediction originating for each individual in the coexistence with all the others." For the first time, she saw her writing as a way of "creating fraternity with words."

In the meantime, the couple founded a new journal, *Les Temps Modernes*. Vocal disputes among its editorial board only added to their notoriety; Simone became referred to as "la Grande Sartreuse," or "Notre Dame de Sartre." Both began to take strong left-wing stands.

A four-month lecture trip to the United States in 1947 led to the publication of *L'Amérique au jour le jour* (1948) in which, with complete confidence in her judgment, de Beauvoir describes the States as hopelessly apolitical and exploitative. Despite close contact with Koestler, the Nazi-Soviet Pact of 1939, the Kravchenko affair, and revelations about the Soviet camps in 1949, she always refused to join in anti-Russian attacks. Simone and Jean-Paul had decided that they would "make the Soviet Union's fortunes [their] own" because, there, "man is being created." Over this decision, Camus broke with the pair; Pasternak and Solzhenitsyn refused to see them. In 1957 Simone wrote a long book similarly supporting what was happening in Communist China: *La longue marche*. Both participated in demonstrations against de Gaulle's return to power during the Forces de la Libération Nationale (FLN) terrorist crisis. Their lives were threatened, and they felt isolated from their compatriots.

During the May 1968 student revolt, de Beauvoir and Sartre backed two Maoist papers. This led to further isolation from public opinion. Deeply depressed by the international scene, shocked by Sartre's offer of marriage to his eighteen-year-old mistress, Arlette El-Kaim, watching herself getting old, de Beauvoir turned her pen to exploration of the problem of aging. In 1964 she had already published a description of her reactions to her mother's death, in *Une Mort très douce*, with

Dylan Thomas's "Do not go gentle into that good night" as epigraph. Two years later she wrote three short stories, *La Femme rompue* (1968), to describe the bitter disappointment that assails older women abandoned by their men. Her dissatisfaction with these tales led her to begin a new sociologico-cultural enquiry into old age, "symmetrical to *The Second Sex*": *La Vieillesse* (1970). It was intended to give the old a voice and to blast modern societies' inadequate response to their condition. Finally, in response to a call from critics and readers, she published the fourth tome of her memoirs, *Tout compte fait*, in 1972. She describes herself as fundamentally unchanged, not resigned but at peace. Her last autobiographical work, *La Cérémonie des adieux*, is a stroke-by-stroke report on the slow disintegration of Sartre's health to the day of his burial. The book begins: "You are in your little box; you will never get out of it, and I will not rejoin you there," and concludes with "My death will not reunite us. So it is. It was already a wonderful thing that our lives managed to remain so long in unison."

Most of her life, Simone de Beauvoir had rejected specific feminine action. She felt that the differences between the sexes were created by society, and could be improved only by its radical transformation. But by 1972 she decided that she must begin "struggling for specifically feminine claims at the same time as carrying on the class-war"; and she declared herself a feminist. She joined the *Mouvement de Libération des Femmes*; she had already signed for them the famous *Manifeste des 343*, a manifesto signed by 343 women who admitted to having had abortions. In June 1972, she helped found the pressure group *Choisir*, dedicated to political implementation of free contraception and abortion for all. In 1974 she became president of the *Ligue des Droits des Femmes*. No longer waiting for the revolution, she now campaigned for the old, mentally sick, delinquents, prisoners, and so on. Her main preoccupation remained, however, writing for "what is really important, to change relationships between people," as she told Caroline Moorehead, in an interview for *The Times*, 16 May 1974. However opposed she had declared herself to participating in the political process, she voted for Mitterand in 1981; she even accepted a seat on a committee for women and culture, but declined to be decorated with the *Légion d'honneur*. She died in 1986.

■ ■ ■

De Beauvoir as Philosopher

There is a reason for giving a long biography of de Beauvoir: the bulk of her published work is more or less autobiographical. This is no accident. As the "Texts on Writing" excerpts given below demonstrate, de Beauvoir saw her major contribution as "philosopher" not as theoretical but as "existential." Descartes had founded the most universal of philosophies on the experience of being an I, an Ego. Hegel had developed the insight that the Idea was to be realized through the "concrete universal," the individual. Marx had warned against idealizing such an insight; he instead stressed the social and economic underpinnings of human thought, and the link between it and practice. Armed with the categories of such predecessors, Simone de Beauvoir spent her life attempting to live it as a fully human endeavor. She explored the "peculiar taste" of that life to reveal to others what is most "general" about each individual existence: the experience of being a human existent, paradoxically both free and limited, responsible for "making sense." Her life was in a sense her laboratory. She experimented with her theories on herself. Hence the interest of her life for us. Its ambiguities, successes, and failures grounded her philosophy of life as free enterprise. She saw her work as the essential aspect of her life: "Writing remained the central business of my life."

The Second Sex is indeed rooted in personal experience; above all, in her reaction to the conditions under which her mother had lived: "Every day, lunch, dinner; every day, dishes; these hours repeated ad infinitum, which go nowhere: would I live like that? No, I told myself while putting away a pile of dishes in the cupboard; my life will lead somewhere."

This demand that every moment in life be part of a personal project and make sense remained the fuel of her philosophy. Experience shook, but never fully shattered, that idealism. She wrote at fifty-five: "I can still see this hedge of filberts, shaken by the wind; and the promises with which I would drive my heart wild as I contemplated this gold mine at my feet, a whole life to live. They were fulfilled. However, when I look

with incredulity at my adolescent self, I measure with stupe-
faction how badly I have been swindled."

That last sentence, as she told the interviewer F. Jeanson,
sums up her "whole vision of existence. . . . Existence is a vain
search for Being. . . . We want the absolute yet we never reach
anything but relativity. . . . The promises [of my youth] have
been kept, but a promise kept is never what one had promised
oneself, since one always aims at Being, at the Absolute, and
one only ever has a relative existence. . . . When I was young,
I thought I had a life ahead; but life is neither behind nor
ahead, it is not something one has, it is something that passes.
. . . One undergoes life even if one creates it (even if one wills
it, constructs it). . . ."[1]

Simone de Beauvoir never considered herself an original
philosopher. She contributed to philosophy through her close
intellectual partnership with Sartre. She argued with his positions until she could truly state on almost any topic: "We think
that. . . ." Where she differs from Sartre is precisely in her focus
on life rather than on ideas. Her contribution is mainly ethical
and sociological, rather than dealing with basic philosophy.

■ ■ ■

What to Look For in the Selections

In reading the following selections, ask yourself the following
questions:

1. *The Second Sex*
   What is wrong with being perceived as an "object"? What
   is involved in being a "subject"?

2. **How can the present condition of women be explained?**
   What is wrong with being "natural"?

3. **The key problem of male-female relations: Bad Faith**
   "Bad Faith" is the unpardonable sin. It is a false response to
   the fundamental problem in our human makeup. What is
   that problem?

4. The present "Feminine Fact" is a cultural construct
Women are not fundamentally "different" by nature. "Only the intervention of someone else (i.e., a cultural event) can establish an individual as other." What does de Beauvoir mean? Is what she says true?

5. The formation of women in our society
Why does de Beauvoir consider aggressivity as essential to the truly human self?

6. Results of such an education: Contemporary forms of Bad Faith in our Society
Women are described here as passive-aggressive, wallowing in sacrilege. This is the feminine form of human "bad faith," i.e., failure at true selfhood. What is at the root of this kind of bad faith? Is this a good explanation of passive-aggressivity?

7. Conclusion
What is the key to positive co-existence between men and women?

8. Texts on writing
How can literature replace religion?

■ ■ ■

Note

1. F. Jeanson, "Entretiens avec Simone de Beauvoir," in *Simone de Beauvoir ou l'entreprise de vivre* (Paris, 1966), 272–73.

SELECTIONS FROM DE BEAUVOIR

■ ■ ■

1. *The Second Sex*

Those who are condemned to stagnation are often pronounced happy on the pretext that happiness consists in being at rest. This notion we reject, for our perspective is that of existentialist ethics. Every subject concretizes itself as transcendence through projects; it achieves its own freedom only through overtaking itself again and again by reaching for other freedoms. Present existence can only be justified by its expansion towards an indefinitely open future. Every time transcendence falls back into immanence, existence is degraded into an *en soi* [*in itself*], and freedom into facticity. This downfall represents a moral fault if the subject consents to it; if it is inflicted upon the subject, it spells frustration and oppression. In either case, it is an absolute evil. Every individual concerned to justify his or her existence experiences it as an undefined urge to transcend himself or herself. Now, what is peculiar to the situation of woman is that she—a free and autonomous being like all humans—nevertheless finds herself and chooses herself within a world where men compel her to assume the status of the Other. They propose to freeze her into an object and to doom her to immanence since her transcendence is to be forever transcended by another consciousness, itself essential and sovereign. This is woman's drama: a conflict between the fundamental demand of any subjectivity—to affirm itself as essential—and the exacting requirements of her situation, a situation in which she is constituted as the inessential. How can a human being in woman's position attain fulfilment? . . . What circumstances limit woman's liberty, and how can they be overcome? These are the fundamental questions on which I wish to throw some light. . . . We will begin by discussing the views of women held by biology, psychoanalysis, and Marxism. We will then show positively how "the feminine fact" was created, why woman was defined as "Other," and the impact of this from men's standpoint. We will then describe women's point of view on the world thus proposed to them; and we will be able to understand what difficulties they encounter when they attempt to escape from the sphere up to now assigned to them, in order to participate in the human *Mitsein* [co-existence].

■ ■ ■

2. How can the present condition of women be explained?

(a) Biologically.

It is worth notice that, the more separate the female individual, the more imperiously does the continuity of life assert itself against her separateness. . . . The female mammal is her offspring's prey, more so than the fish or the bird, who expel the virgin ovule or the egg. Not that the female mammal lacks individual qualities; on the contrary; . . . but she does not claim this individuality: the female abdicates herself for the good of the species which demands this abdication.

(b) Historically.

When sub-species of humans are brought together, each aspires to impose its sovereignty upon the other. If both are able to resist this imposition, there is created between them a reciprocal relation, sometimes in enmity, sometimes in amity, but always in a state of tension. It is therefore understandable that man would wish to dominate woman; but what advantage has enabled him to carry out his will?

The reason is that mankind is not simply a natural species: it is not intent on maintaining itself as species; its project is not stagnation, but self-transcendence. . . .

Birth and suckling are not activities, they are natural functions; no project is involved; and that is why woman found in them no reason for a lofty affirmation of her existence—she submitted passively to her biological fate. The domestic labors that fell to her lot because they were reconcilable with the cares of maternity imprisoned her in repetition and immanence; they were repeated from day to day in identical form, which was perpetuated almost without change from century to century; they produced nothing.

Man's case was radically different; he provides for the group, not in the manner of worker bees by a simple vital process, through biological behavior, but by means of acts that transcend his animal nature. *Homo faber [man the maker]* has from the beginning of time been an inventor. . . . To get at the riches of the world, he annexed the world itself. By acting, he put his power to the test; he set up goals and opened up roads toward them; in brief, he found self-realization as an existent. To maintain, he created; he burst out of the present; he opened a future. This is the reason why fishing and hunting expeditions had a sacred character. When celebrating their success with festivals and triumphs, man was giving recognition to his humanness. . . . He had not merely worked at conserving the world as given; he had burst its limits; he had laid down the foundations of a new future.

Early man's activity had another dimension that gave it supreme dignity: it was often dangerous. . . . The warrior risked his life to augment the prestige of the horde, of the clan to which he belonged. In so doing, he clearly demonstrated that life is not the supreme value for humans, but on the contrary that it should be made to serve ends more important than itself. The worst curse laid upon woman is that she is excluded from these warlike forays. For it is not through giving life but through risking it that we rise above the animal;

which is why humanity has granted superiority not to the sex that gives birth but to that which kills.

Here we have the key to the whole mystery. Biologically speaking, a species, in order to maintain itself, must create itself anew. That creation, however, is but repetition of the same life in different forms. Humans, by contrast, insure the repetition of life by transcending Life through Existence. Overstepping life's boundaries, they create values that deprive pure repetition of all value. . . .

While serving the species, the human male changes the face of the earth, he creates new instruments, he invents, he forges a future. When he so establishes his own sovereignty, he finds in woman an accomplice: for she, too, is an existent; she, too, feels the urge to transcendence; and her project is not mere repetition but surpassing it towards a different future. In her heart of hearts, she finds confirmation of the male's pretensions. She joins man in celebrating his successes and victories. . . . Her misfortune is to have been biologically destined for the repetition of Life, when even in her own eyes Life does not carry within itself its reasons for being, while those reasons are more important than life itself. . . .

The female is, to a greater extent than the male, prey to the species; and the human race has always attempted to escape its specific destiny. The support of life became, for man, action, a project, through the invention of the tool; in maternity, woman remained closely bound to her body like an animal. It is because humanity puts its own Being in question—in other words because it values reasons for living above mere life—that, when he confronted woman, man assumed mastery.

(c) Institutionally and symbolically.
Should we regret matriarchy?

Little by little, man succeeded in mediating existence. Both in symbolic representations and in practical life, the male principle triumphed. Spirit prevailed over Life, transcendence over immanence, technology over magic, and reason over superstition. The devaluation of woman represents a necessary stage in the history of humanity: for her prestige originated not from her own positive worth, but from man's weakness. She incarnated the disturbing mysteries of nature. Man escapes her control when he liberates himself from nature. . . .

The reign of woman was bound to the reign of agriculture, . . . of irreducible duration, of contingency, of chance, of waiting, of mystery; the reign of *homo faber* is the reign of time manageable as space, of necessary consequences, of the project, of action, of reason. . . . Agriculture enslaved humanity to chance: to the hazards of soil, germination, seasons. The peasant is passive, he prays and waits; . . . the worker by contrast shapes his tool after his own design: confronting inert nature, he overcomes its resistance, and asserts himself as sovereign will. . . . He learns by making objects his own responsibility. . . . His success depends, not on the favor of the gods, but upon himself. . . . Through the relation of his creative hand to the fabricated thing, he experiences causality. The world of tools can be embraced within clear concepts: rational thought, logic, and mathematics can then be born. . . . Those peoples who remained under the thumb of the Mother Goddess, those who perpetuated matriarchy, remained at a primitive stage of civilization. For woman was venerated only in so far as man made himself the slave of his own fears, a party to his own impotence: he worshipped her in terror and not in love. To become himself, he had first to dethrone her.

(d) Ontologically: woman posited as other.

Man never thinks "Self" without thinking "Other"; he views the world under the sign of duality, a polarity which is not at first sexual in character. But, being different from man, who sets himself up as self, it is naturally to the category of the other that woman is consigned; the Other includes Woman. . . . In truth, the Golden Age of Woman is only a myth. To say that woman was the Other is to say that there did not exist between the sexes a reciprocal relation. Earth, Mother, Goddess—she was no fellow creature in man's eyes, it was beyond the human realm that her power was affirmed. . . . For the male it is always another male who is the fellow being, the Other who is also the same, with whom reciprocal relations are established.

. . . To the precise degree to which woman is regarded as the absolute other—that is, as the inessential—it is to that degree impossible to consider her as another subject. Engels gave only an incomplete explanation for her degradation: it is not enough to say that the invention of bronze and iron profoundly disturbed the equilibrium of the forces of production, thus bringing about the inferior position of woman; this inferiority is not sufficient in itself to explain the oppression that woman has suffered. What was devastating was that, failing to become a fellow workman, she was excluded from the human *Mitsein*. Woman's weakness and inferior productive capacity would not suffice to explain this exclusion; it is because she did not share his way of working and thinking, because she remained in bondage to life's mysterious processes, that the male failed to recognize in her a being like unto himself. Since he did not adopt her, since she kept in his eyes the stamp of Otherness, he could not but be her oppressor. The male will to power and expansion turned woman's incapacity into a curse.

■ ■ ■

3. The key problem of
male-female relations: Bad Faith

(a) The human situation as the source of Bad Faith.

When a subject attempts to assert itself, the Other who limits it and denies its autonomy is paradoxically necessary to it: it can only reach selfhood through this reality which it is not. Hence life for humans can never be fulfilment and rest; it is lack and movement, it is struggle. Man encounters nature, facing him; . . . he attempts to appropriate it, but it is unable to fulfill him. . . . To be encountered as presence, the other must be present to itself. The only true other is a consciousness separated from mine, but identical to it. Only the existence of other humans can extract each individual from immanence and allow him or her to accomplish himself or herself in truth, as transcendence, as escape towards an object, as project. But the foreign freedom which confirms my own freedom at the very same time conflicts with it; such is the tragedy of the unhappy consciousness: each consciousness attempts to posit itself as lone sovereign subject; each attempts to reduce the other to slavery. . . . It is possible to rise above this conflict if each individual freely recognizes the other, both reciprocally positing simultaneously both self and other as at once object and subject. But friendship and generosity, which are the concrete manifestations of such reciprocal recognition of free beings, are not facile virtues; they certainly represent man's highest achievement, and through that achievement alone can he fulfill his own truth. But this truth is struggle; . . . it requires that humans outdo themselves at every moment. In other words, humans attain an authentically moral attitude when they renounce mere Being to assume Existence; it is a conversion, through which they renounce all possessions, for possession is one way of seeking mere being; but conversion to true wisdom is never done with, it must be ceaselessly repeated; it calls for constant tension. Incapable of true self-fulfilment in solitude, the human being who relates with other human beings is in perpetual danger; his or her life is a difficult enterprise, the success of which is never certain. . . .

But man does not like difficulty; he is afraid of danger. He aspires in contradictory fashion both to life and to rest, to existence and to mere being; he knows full well that "trouble of spirit" is the price of development . . . but he dreams of quiet in disquiet and of an opaque plenitude that nevertheless would be endowed with consciousness. The incarnation of this dream is precisely woman; she is the wished-for intermediary between nature, a stranger to humans, and the fellow being who is too closely identical. She opposes to him neither the hostile silence of nature nor the hard requirements of a reciprocal relation; through a unique privilege, she is a conscious being and yet it seems possible to possess her in the flesh. Thanks to her there is a means for escaping that implacable dialectic of master and slave which has its source in the reciprocity that exists between free beings. . . . Therein lies the wondrous hope that man has often put in woman: he hopes to fulfill himself as a being by carnally possessing a being, while at the same time confirming his sense of freedom through the docility of a free person. . . . Appearing as the Other, woman appears at the same time as an abundance of being in contrast to that existence the nothingness of which man senses in himself. The Other, being the object from the subject's standpoint, is regarded as *en soi*; therefore as a real being. Man has his roots deep in Nature; like the animals and plants, he has been engendered; he well knows that he exists only in so far as he lives. . . . But life wears in his eyes a double aspect: it is consciousness, will, transcendence, it is the spirit; and it is matter, passivity, immanence; it is the flesh. . . . Man may dream of losing himself anew in the maternal shadows, to find there again the true sources of his being. . . . But more often he tends to revolt against his carnal state; he sees himself as a fallen god. . . . He wishes to be inevitable, like a pure Idea, like the One, the All, the absolute Spirit; and he finds himself shut up in a body of limited powers, in a place and time he never chose, where he was not called for, useless, cumbersome, absurd. The contingency of all flesh is his own to suffer in his abandonment, in his unjustifiable needlessness. This quivering jelly which is elaborated in the womb (the womb, secret and sealed like a tomb) evokes too clearly the soft viscosity of carrion for him not to turn shuddering away; . . . the slimy embryo begins the cycle that is completed in the putrefaction of death. Because he is horrified by needlessness and death, man feels horror at having been engendered; he would fain deny his animal ties; but through the fact of his birth, murderous Nature has a hold upon him.

(b) The peculiar problem with Bad Faith for women.

In the domain of feelings, discrimination between the imaginary and the real can be made only through behavior. . . . A woman has hardly any means for sounding her own heart; according to her moods, she will view her own feelings in different lights, and, as she submits to them passively, one interpretation will be no truer than another. . . . For a great many women, the roads to transcendence are blocked: because they do nothing, they fail to make anything of themselves. They wonder indefinitely what they could have become, which gets them wondering what they are. It is a vain question. . . . the feminine mystery is immediately implied in the mythology of the absolute Other. If it were admitted that the inessential conscious being, too, is a clear subjectivity, capable of performing the *Cogito [I think]*, then it would have to be also admitted that this being is in truth sovereign and it would again have to be recognized as essential; for all reciprocity to appear quite impossible, it is necessary for the Other to be *for itself* an other; its very subjectivity must be affected by its otherness; but this demands that such a consciousness be alienated as consciousness. Its pure immanent presence would then evidently be Mystery. It would be Mystery *in itself* from the fact that it would be Mystery *for itself*; it would be absolute Mystery.

■ ■ ■

4. The present "Feminine Fact" is a cultural construct

One is not born, but rather becomes, a woman. No biological, psychological, or economic fate determines the figure that the human female presents in society; it is civilization as a whole that produces this creature, an intermediate between male and eunuch, which we describe as feminine. Only the intervention of someone else can establish an individual as an Other. In so far as it exists in and for itself, the child would hardly be able to think of itself as sexually differentiated.

■ ■ ■

5. The formation of women in our society

(a) The impact of childhood education.

Passivity is indeed the essential characteristic of the "feminine" woman. But it is not a biological datum; it is a destiny imposed upon her in her earliest years by her teachers and by society. . . . The real advantage enjoyed by the boy is that his mode of existence in relation to others leads him to assert his subjective freedom. His apprenticeship in life consists in free movement toward the outside world; he competes in hardihood and independence with other boys, he scorns girls. . . .

There is no fundamental opposition between his concern for that objective figure which is his and his will to self-realization in concrete projects. It is by doing that he creates his existence, both of them by one and the same act.

In woman, on the contrary, there is from the beginning a conflict between her autonomous existence and her objective self, her "being the other"; she is taught that, to succeed, she must try to please, that she must make herself object; that she should therefore renounce her autonomy.

(b) The teenage years.

Just as the penis derives its privileged evaluation from the social context, so it is the social context that makes menstruation a curse. The one symbolizes manhood, the other femininity; and it is because femininity signifies otherness and inferiority that its manifestation is met with shame. . . . [The teenage girl] would retain her pride in her bleeding body if she did not lose her pride in being human. . . . If the young girl at about this stage frequently develops a neurotic condition, it is because she feels defenseless before a dull fatality which condemns her to unimaginable trials; her femininity means in her eyes sickness, suffering, and death, and she is obsessed with this fate. The sexual life of the young girl has always been secret; . . . it is not active; it is a state from which, even in imagination, she cannot find relief by any decision of her own. She does not dream of taking, shaping, violating: her part is to await, to want; she feels dependent; she scents danger in her alienated flesh.

In their early teens, boys go through a real apprenticeship in violence, when are developed their aggressiveness, their will to power, their love for competition; at that very time, girls give up rough games. . . . Against any insult, any attempt to reduce him to the status of object, the male has recourse to his fists. . . . He does not let himself be transcended by others, he is himself at the heart of his subjectivity. Violence is the authentic proof of each human being's loyalty to himself, to his passions, to his own will; radically to deny this will is to deny oneself any objective truth, it is to wall oneself up in an abstract subjectivity; anger or revolt that does not get into the muscles remains a figment of the imagination. It is a profound frustration not to be able to register one's feelings upon the face of the world.

For the young woman, there is a contradiction between her status as a real human being and her vocation as a female. . . . This is why adolescence is for a woman so difficult and decisive. . . . Up to this time she has been an autonomous individual: now she must renounce her sovereignty. . . . A conflict breaks out between on the one hand her original claim to be a subject, active, free, and on the other hand her erotic urges and the social pressure to accept herself as passive object. . . . In the adolescent girl, there is opposition between [narcissistic] love of herself and the erotic urge that urges her towards becoming an object to be possessed. . . . In a complex impulse she aspires to the glorification of her body through the homage of the males to whom this body is destined; and it would be an oversimplification to say either that she wants to be beautiful in order to charm, or that she seeks to charm in order to gain assurance of her beauty. . . . She does not distinguish the desire of the man from the love of her own ego.

■ ■ ■

6. Results of such an education: Contemporary forms of Bad Faith in our society

It is remarkable that through her behavior the young girl does not seek to transcend the natural and social order, she does not aim to extend the limits of the possible nor to work a transvaluation of values; she is content to display her revolt within a well-established world, the borders and laws of which are preserved. That is the attitude often defined as "demoniac"; it is, fundamentally, cheating: the good is recognized in order to be flouted, the rule is set in order to be broken, the sacred is respected to make sacrilege possible. The attitude of the young girl is to be defined essentially by the fact that, in the anguished shadows of bad faith, she denies, while accepting them, the world and her own destiny.

It is clear that all these faults flow simply from the adolescent girl's situation. What an unfortunate condition to be in, aware of one's passivity and dependency at the age of hope and ambition. . . . At just this conquering age, woman learns that . . . her future depends on man's good pleasure. Socially and sexually, new aspirations awake in her, only to be condemned to frustration. All her eagerness for action, whether physical or spiritual, is instantly thwarted.

[Woman's] anxiety is the expression of her distrust of the world as given; . . . she is unhappy in it. . . . She is not resigned to being resigned; she knows very well that she suffers as she does against her will: she is a woman without having been consulted in the matter. She dares not revolt; she submits unwillingly; her attitude is one of constant reproach. A free individual blames only himself for his failures, he assumes responsibility for them; but everything happens to women through the agency of others, and therefore these others are held responsible for her woes.

■ ■ ■

7. Conclusion

We have seen why men enslaved women in the first place; the devaluation of femininity has been a necessary step in human evolution. But it might have led to collaboration between the two sexes: oppression is to be explained by the tendency of the existent to flee from itself by means of identification with the other, whom it oppresses to that end. In each individual man that tendency exists today; and the vast majority yield to it. . . . It must be admitted that the males find in woman more complicity than the oppressor usually finds in the oppressed. And in bad faith they take authorization from this fact to declare that woman has desired the destiny they have imposed on her. We have seen that all the main features of her training combine to bar her from the roads of revolt and adventure. . . . The innumerable conflicts that set men and women against one another come from the fact that neither is prepared to assume all the consequences of this situation, which the one proposed and the other accepted.

Woman is not the victim of any mysterious fatality. The peculiarities that specify her as woman get their importance from the signification placed upon them; as soon as they are grasped from new perspectives, they can be overcome; . . . erotically, for example, woman experiences—and often resents—male domination; it would be a mistake to conclude from this fact that her ovaries condemn her to live forever on her knees. Virile aggressivity seems to be lordly privilege only when perceived within a whole system conspiring to assert masculine sovereignty; woman feels so deeply passive in the act of love only because she already thinks of herself as passive. While laying claim to their human dignity, many modern women still envisage their erotic life from the standpoint of a tradition of enslavement: hence, they consider it humiliating to lie under their man, to be penetrated by him; and they tense up into frigidity; but were the social reality different, the symbolic meaning of amorous gestures and postures would also be different. A woman who finances, who dominates, her lover can, for example, be proud of her superb idleness and consider as a service to her the male's active exertion. And here and there, there are many sexually well-balanced couples for whom the notions of victory and defeat are giving place to the idea of exchange.

As a matter of fact, man is, like woman, flesh, therefore passivity; he, too, is the plaything of his hormones and of the species, the restless prey of his desires. And she, like him, in the very midst of the carnal fever, is a consenting, voluntary gift, an active force. Each lives in his or her own way the strange ambiguity of existence made flesh. In what they perceive as a fight where each is confronting the other, both are really struggling against themselves, while projecting onto the partner that part of self each rejects; instead of living out his or her ambiguous condition, each attempts to lay its abject aspects on the other, while retaining the glory of it for himself or herself. Should, however, both assume this condition with that clear-sighted modesty which is correlative to authentic pride, they would be able to recognize in each other kindred beings, and they could live out as friends the erotic drama.

The fact of being humans is infinitely more important than any of the peculiarities which distinguish human beings from one another. What is given is never what confers superiority: "virtue," as the ancients called it, is defined by what depends on us. In both sexes is played out the drama of flesh and spirit, of finitude and transcendence; both are worn away by time, stalked by death. Each has an equally essential need of the other. Both can use their freedom to achieve the same glory; if they knew how to appreciate it, they would no longer be drawn into arguments over fallacious privileges, and true fraternity could flower between them. . . .

One might argue that this is utopian fancy: for woman to be made over, society would have to have granted her full equality with men. In similar circumstances, conservatives never fail to refer to that vicious circle. However, history does not go in circles. Obviously, a caste kept in a state of inferiority will no doubt remain inferior. But freedom can break that circle; let blacks vote, they become worthy of the right to vote. Give women responsibilities, they assume them. One cannot, indeed, expect from oppressors gratuitous gestures of generosity; but either the revolt of the oppressed, or the very evolution of the privileged caste, eventually creates new situations. Thus, men have been led, in their own interest, to partially emancipate women. All that women need to do now is continue their ascent; it seems almost certain that they will sooner or later reach total economic and social equality, which will bring about an inner metamorphosis.

It is for humans to establish the reign of liberty in the midst of the world of the given. To gain the supreme victory, it is necessary, for one thing, that by and through their natural differentiation men and women unequivocally affirm their brotherhood.

■ ■ ■

8. Texts on Writing

Literature took the place in my life that had once been occupied by religion: it absorbed me entirely, and transfigured my life.

I understood that what was bothering me was the problem of the other, the relationship to another person's consciousness. I attempted to render the lived experience of "being-in-the-world," as Sartre puts it. I wish to offer to perusal my own experience, a concrete universal, much more interesting than a fake documentary. . . . One of the irreplaceable and essential tasks of literature is this: to help us communicate one with the other in what is most solitary about us, which is also what ties us most intimately to one another.

Extracted from *The Second Sex* (Toronto, 1980), xxix (1), 20–21 (2a), 56–60 (2b), 69–70 (2c), 63, 65, 72 (2d), 129–31, 135 (3a), 243 (3b), 249 (4), 261–62 (5a), 295–96, 300, 308–9, 314, 316–17 (5b), 334, 337, 570–71 (6), 677–79, 686, 689 (7); and from *Memoirs of a Dutiful Daughter* (New York, 1958), 187, and "Mon expérience d'écrivain," in *Les écrits de Simone de Beauvoir* (Paris, 1979), 457, translated by J. D. Langan (8).

COMMENTARY

■ ■ ■

Analysis of *The Second Sex*

De Beauvoir's main claim to fame is *The Second Sex*, the publication of which in 1949 was an intellectual event. It moved the women's issue from the literary and political arena to the philosophical. Later, de Beauvoir even thought that she had overdone it: she should have provided "a materialistic, not an idealistic, theoretical foundation for the opposition between the Same and the Other." In any case, the book became "the classic manifesto of the liberated woman," as the cover of its Vintage edition proclaims. Since 1953, nearly a million paperback copies have been sold. The first North American feminist best-seller, Betty Friedan's *The Feminine Mystique* (1970), owes much to her encounter with de Beauvoir.

Basic principles.

The conclusion of *The Second Sex* sums up the essential aspects of Simone de Beauvoir's feminist philosophy.

1. Women are humans first, females second. Everything fundamental about themselves, they share with the males of the species. To understand their present predicament, which is a bio-economico-sociological problem, reinforced by the bad faith of individuals, it is essential to understand first what a human being is, and how this "essence" is frustrated by the present situation.

2. The human race is unique in nature, because its members alone *exist*, that is, instead of merely being.

    (i) Humans alone are true *subjects:* free, active centers of meaning. They are *transcendent,* that is, not stuck in the *situation* out of which they operate. To *ex-ist* implies "getting out." They alone can *appropriate* and transform through action the world in which they find themselves. This demands a constant struggle to avoid assimilating oneself to one's given, passive, *object*-like reality: one's *en soi,* or mere being-dumped-there. We must refuse to be superfluous *unessential* additions to an already overwhelming quantity of worthless objects. To be truly human, we must constantly *transcend* being-what-we-happen-to-be. We must interpret our situation, and project a future; this transforms the world and our life into meaningful creations, no longer given, but willed by us.

    Our greatest risk is thus the temptation of "rest"; Sabbath delight and self-satisfied contemplation are out. Transcendence demands constant action and change. The unpardonable sin is falling into *immanence,* that is, getting stuck in *being,* in what already is.

    (ii) Spontaneously, true subjects will their own absolute *necessity:* they want to become world-centers, linchpins of a meaningful, comprehended, and comprehensive universe. The existence of other subjects, reaching for the same centering *universality,* is thus a threat. Hence our tendency to reduce other humans to the position of *others,* that is, to beings understandable and meaningful only by reference to our self. I am the pattern, whom you imitate. I am the center, giving the world order and meaning, and you appear in its periphery, accidentally, as support, decoration, or enemy. There is nothing more threatening to our drive for universality, necessity, and creative freedom than the ironic eye of the Other. As Sartre put it in *Huis Clos:* hell often seems to be other people. However, in fact, we depend on other subjectivities to discover our own, through the encounter and recognition of other selves.

(*iii*) Human *authenticity* consists in affirming one's own *autonomy* and that of all others. Each self is "sovereign," self-creating, value-projecting, responsible. By contrast, *bad faith* consists in accusing "destiny" of determining us, or in demeaning others to the role of objects in order to avoid the difficult process of human co-existing. There is no human destiny, there are only situations. Limiting circumstances, uncriticized world perceptions, and solitude can always be transcended, once consciousness is raised.

The special case of women.

Since women are human beings, they are, like men, born free; they are not fated to any biological "nature." "Femininity" is a mere *singularity*, that is, a superficial peculiarity; what is essential is the incarnate freedom that defines our human condition.

This freedom, however, is not abstract; like all humans, women are conditioned by their society and by their physique. The peculiarities of the present feminine situation originate from various pressures:

1. Biological pressure of the species.
   Female mammals are in a specially difficult relation to procreation: they are more enslaved than most animals to their offspring.
2. Psycho-sociological pressure from male society.
   The spontaneous tendency of every self to reduce the other to the "inessential," that is, to a mere appendage or slave, has pushed men to persuade women of their

"Otherness" and to create institutions that define them as such.
3. Economic pressure, combining the other two pressures, which originated in the development of the work processes.

Men got the creative, conquering, future-projecting jobs, while women raised babies. Thus women for centuries could only participate in the truly human experiment second-hand.

However, these pressures are not determining limits of women's activity, but their original conditions. Human reality is fundamentally dynamic. Humanity moves ever onwards towards more freedom and more consciousness: either through class struggle or through the logic of economics. The social situation is evolving, and all woman needs to find her authentic self is to participate in this evolution through work. This will give her a chance to actualize her freedom, instead of dreaming about it. She will discover her true, glorious self as she creates meaning out of today's givens, and as she encounters in the public arena other consciousnesses that will affirm that discovery and recognize her freedom. She will then know once and for all that she is not a thing, an *en soi*, but indeed a true subject co-existing with other subjects, who confirm her autonomy.

Proposals for a new ethics.

A *transvaluation of values* is needed. A new ethics must be founded on the recognition of both poles of the paradox of existence: freedom and situation, spirit grounded in nature. *Authenticity* calls for assuming fully, joyously, and consciously this paradoxical human condition.

Nothing is more destructive to women's humanization than the exaltation of her "naturalness." Women are no closer to nature than men. Both are based in a biological species; both are influenced by hormones. Both however are fundamentally oriented to transcendence, being "spiritual" entities. Nature is humanity's natural opponent. Adulation of nature is capitulation of the human spirit to mere being, to necessity, force, destiny. Women, like men, discover their full humanity when conquering nature through work, as Hegel and Marx made clear.

We must live in the realm of biosocial reality to exist at all. But the *value* of natural life is to serve as a springboard for transcendence. *Value creation* is what saves us from that natural repetition that dehumanizes. Constantly bursting out of the present into a new future, humanized life is creativity, work, risk. Such an attitude towards life is difficult:

1. It demands rejection of one's very own mere present being: a constant break with the past; a distrust of all institutions; disentanglement from all "having," so that one may do and make. The true existent is detached from anything already possessed, for the sake of future projection.
2. It implies demythologizing: clear-eyed recognition of the vacuum in which freedom operates. Creativity arises ever again from "nothing."

   We are never saved, never done. There can be no paradise. Idolatrous satisfaction with any *status quo* is "copping out."

   No outside help can be expected and no excuse is relevant. The givens are not what matter, but what each person does with such givens. Neither our situation, nor our objective results, but the "virtue" demonstrated in the struggle against immanence, is what makes the difference between a true human and a failure: this is precisely the etymological sense of virtue (*vir* is *man* in Latin).

   Hence the key human virtue, the other face of authenticity, is courage.
3. The new ethics must also deal with another major paradox: *Mitsein, co-existence*. Human selves are plural. Each of them tends towards absolute transcendence and necessity, and therefore spontaneously threatens the autonomy of all others. If women usually fail by giving in to nature's pull towards immanence, men tend to fail by giving in to the spirit's tendency towards self-universalization: a totalitarian self-affirmation which denies autonomy to other selves. As human co-existents, we need to find confirmation of our own sovereign subjectivity through respectful

recognition by other free subjects. No thing or animal can do this for us. The easiest shortcut to this is forcing another subject to give up its own autonomy to affirm ours. Participating as pure *transcendent* self in the *immanence* of a beloved female is a typical male cop-out from the paradoxes of existence in common.

4. *Bad faith* is thus essentially a flight from the two major human juggling acts: the struggle with nature for transcendent Ex-istence, and the challenge of *Mitsein*, i.e., of co-existence with other autonomous subjects. No wonder that we often succumb to it, since our fundamental drive is doomed to ultimate frustration. We strive for (1) freedom, (2) meaning, (3) being "essential," (4) universality. But our body involves us in (1) limit, (2) the chaos of "facticity," (3) contingency, and (4) "singularity." However, existence finds its sense not through success, but through the effort to shape history, to conquer nature and stamp meaning onto it, to live the miracle of an autonomous life.

The transvaluation of values is the test of our success. In a truly human society, each individual would have the chance to demonstrate new "reasons for living," for others to recognize and share. "Lovers would experience themselves both as selves and other; neither would abdicate transcendence; neither would be mutilated. Both would reveal together in this world values and ends. For both, love would be self-revelation and enriching of the universe." Should both men and women shoulder their responsibility, sex would find its full meaning, as both partners experienced, in flesh and spirit, the joy of shared human freedom, not as an ideal, but as fleshed-out reality. True "brotherhood" would replace the battle of the sexes; "fraternity" is the last word of *The Second Sex*.

■ ■ ■

Summary

To be human is to exist. This means being free to create ever new situations, to escape the present state of affairs through ever new projects into ever new futures. Our "nature" is precisely to transcend what we are, to be the kind of animal that always goes beyond itself, as active subject of an expanding world.

The "woman problem" is merely a sociohistorical problem. Women and men are born equally "existent" and free. But the human race, in order to reach our state of development, has had to specialize. Women, biologically more involved in the reproductive process through childbearing, were given all the "caring" roles. They insured the bodily viability of the race, stabilizing a base for action in the present. Men, by contrast, took on the conquering role, accepting its risks, freeing themselves from natural constraints through action and invention, revolt, and adventure.

It is now time, however, for woman to join the truly human race. She must learn that life exists for a higher end: the exercise of personal freedom. She must demand recognition as a free subject, like man; she must stop thinking of herself as a mere object, that is, as an appendage of another subject, whose identity depends on his recognition of her.

Should she succeed in this endeavor, men themselves would profit from it. For treating women as objects is "bad faith"; it is mere escapism, originating in the male's own deep denial of the true human situation. We all, male or female, are both subjects and objects: we are free, but founded in a bodily situation. We are paradoxically flesh and spirit, finite and transcendent. This struggle is our glory, and we can help one another live it out through fraternal recognition of our common human identity. We can indeed inspire one another by communicating to each other in words the experience of autonomous solitude, that is, of freedom, that essentially human experience which links us so intimately to one another.

■ ■ ■

Philosophical Critique

The Second Sex had a definite impact on the development of feminist thought, though de Beauvoir's relationship with feminism remained stormy. She long refused to be called a feminist herself, because she detested both what she called the

American aggressive, anti-male approach, and the way other neofeminists celebrated their femaleness instead of their humanity. Reciprocally, many feminists attacked her.

Betty Friedan was taken aback by her mentor's extremist, anarchist approach to politics. De Beauvoir saw no point in partial improvements in women's position, thinking that only a total reorganization of society, abolishing all elitism, ambition, and competitiveness, could bring about the necessary "transvaluation of values." This intractable attitude explains partly why de Beauvoir had relatively little direct impact on the feminist movement proper.

Generally, however, feminists have tended to reject her as a "phallic woman." To many, "her emancipated woman sounds just like that familiar nineteenth-century character, the self-made man."[1] They dislike her total disinterest in maternity; her advocacy of male values. Some question her relationship with Sartre as a kind of abdication to patriarchal exploitation; others lambaste her for having served the literary establishment as a "token woman"; many object to her refusal to use inclusive language.

In other words, they resent her adamant refusal to recognize any form of sexual "separatism." She told Jeanson that *The Second Sex* was "radically feminist: one never betrays my thought when it is pulled towards . . . absolute feminism." What she meant by this is that the heart of the work is the famous sentence that opens Book II: "One is not born, but rather becomes, a woman." As she put it in *All Said and Done,* "I utterly revolt at the idea of shutting up women in a feminine ghetto." She always disliked what she saw as a typically American female attitude of "challenge" to men (e.g., the attitude of SCUM, the Society for Cutting Up Men). She found it absurd to treat human males as enemies when they are our peers; in fact, she found them more interesting work and sex coexistents than most contemporary women.

Today's feminist literary establishment tends to complain about de Beauvoir's lack of interest in psychoanalysis or about her ambiguous relationship to Marxism. Some, however, like Toril Moi, fully agree with her rejection of biological femaleness and cultural femininity. They see her most important legacy to feminism to be her affirmation that no human person passively suffers any fate; that we are perpetually creative; that, as a corollary, no human person can ever become complete, closed; that the self is a fundamentally open entity.

■ ■ ■

Religious Critique

1. On July 13, 1956, *The Second Sex* and *The Mandarins* were put on the *Index of Prohibited Books*. Simone de Beauvoir is indeed fundamentally an atheist.

   (*i*) Her philosophy is based on our full responsibility for projecting values and meaning on existence. She denies any objective "natural law"; we have no creator or law-giver except ourselves. To her, any given, even something physical, is of interest only when transformed by us into a cultural reality. She rejects any "objective" definition of sexual morality, except for the universal moral requirement of authenticity.

   (*ii*) She also rejects, in post-Nietzschean fashion, any purposive vision of history: the human experiment has no "end." The future cannot possibly even be imagined, since it is wide open to human creativity. There can thus be no question of looking forward to any final "New Jerusalem," or "Kingdom on Earth."

   (*iii*) She sees no forgiveness nor help available anywhere for the human existent, except the support of other similar freedoms. Recourse to a *transcendent* source, either in the form of revelation or of grace, is mere mythological escapism in her eyes.

   (*iv*) Because of her detestation of sheer "presence," she has no sense of sacrament. She was never at ease even with her own incarnation; she rejected with horror the notion of owing gratitude for a gift received; and she hated repetition and permanence. Ritual, and full participation in a community that subordinates the individual to the Body of Christ, could only revolt her.

   (*v*) For all her stress on reality and brotherhood, she is strongly influenced by Cartesian individualism. Her adolescent revolt against her family's "efforts to transform [her] into a monster" left her traumatized: "The existence of other consciousnesses remained for me a danger, . . . a scandal of the same order as death, equally unacceptable." Since, for de Beauvoir, all meaning and value originate and end in the "ego's" autonomy, fraternity is primarily the reciprocal respect for, and recognition of, isolated freedoms. Cooperation is necessary, because consciousnesses coexist in the same world. Successful social intercourse is essentially recognition of our participation in the same kind of lonely consciousness—of our primordial *Mitsein*. Total commitment to anything or anyone is thus out of the question; it would be "alienation" of the fundamental freedom which is the very basis of any friendship. She is therefore opposed to marriage, and strongly supports contraception and abortion. She also never joined a party, but involved herself in short-term activism, with specific goals. She rejects all responsibility to family, country, or institutions.

2. Interestingly enough, however, critics have all noted how marked she remained by her childhood Catholicism.

   (*i*) To begin with, that is where she learned that she was fundamentally equal to all males, being human first, and woman second: "I always thought of myself as 'a soul'. At the soul level, the problems [of male vs. female] do not get raised at all. God loved me as much as if I had been a man; there was no difference between male and female saints; the whole domain was completely a-sexual. . . . [Thus, from childhood on,] a kind of moral spiritual equality, as human being, was granted me—by the very importance that my religious education had for me, in spite of all."

   (*ii*) Secondly, through close spiritual direction, she developed early a strong sense of personal responsibility. She always expressed an almost puritan desire for moral perfection. Jeanson sees her writing enterprise as an effort to "save," "redeem," the present, the world, herself. This is the attitude with which, for example, she tackled university: "I no longer wondered: 'What is there to do?' Everything needed to be done; everything I had long ago wished I could do: fight error, find truth, say it, enlighten the world, maybe even help change it." However blind her readers may think her to be at times, one cannot help admiring her tireless effort to reach lucidity about her own motivations. She relentlessly worked at authenticity: that her life and beliefs should match without any compromise.

(*iii*) She also shares with Christian thinkers like Pascal an intense awareness of the paradoxical nature of human existence, our "self-will." "Man is a fallen king," Pascal kept repeating. Much in the same vein—but without intimating an original fall, of course—de Beauvoir always stressed both the sovereignty of our free consciousness and its involvement in biological and sociological reality. As Pascal put it, whoever attempts to play the angel, ends up acting as a beast. Her focus is always on incarnate meaning: making sense out of history, expressing the inner self in the flesh. To her, life is the practical resolution of this paradox through perpetual action.

(*iv*) She was committed to the human community as a whole. Her work is indeed often, as Elaine Mark complains, "oracular: solemn, concerned, humorless, optimistic," and therefore aesthetically unpleasant. But if she often sounds moralistic, it is because she did wish to help save us all. This attitude is certainly in line with her childhood education: the Catholic revival of the 1900s was intent on mission, conversion, on reclaiming the world for Christ the King, on lay action. De Beauvoir dedicated a similar missionary spirit to left-wing ideology, for she rejected all divine interference in human responsibility. She saw religion as the opium of the people. And she stuck to her allegiance to Socialism to the very end. It alone could bring respectable freedom to humanity; this faith withstood Socialism's worst failures, including the revelation of Stalin's concentration camps. Her own politics were fundamentally anarchist. She devoted her action to attacks on the establishment. As she puts it in *The Prime of Life,* "We were hostile to all institutions, because freedom is alienated there." Hence her detestation of the Church as public reality.

(*v*) Her mother's "piety" may have influenced de Beauvoir's natural tendency to mystical intensity. Her travelmania seems to have originated in a call to contemplation, strangely projected onto tourism. "It seemed to me vaguely that, from the moment when an object became integrated to my life story, it acquired privileged illumination. A country was virgin land until I saw it with my very own eyes. . . . Therefore, it was urgent, both for the universe and for myself, that I should know everything about it. Enjoyment was secondary to this perpetual mandate; I accepted pleasure with enthusiasm, but did not look for it."

This form of contemplation, however, was antagonistic to the sentimentality fostered by her religious educators: she had, for example, been promised ecstasies at the time of her First Communion. She deftly faked them, and later recognized them for the illusion they had been. As she later put it, "I enjoyed losing myself at the foot of the Cross, while vaguely fantasizing about the bowl of chocolate awaiting me at home." She and her friends were "totally disgusted by what is called 'interior life'; these gardens where fine souls cultivate exquisite secrets stank in our eyes like swamps; there are silently struck all the dirty deals of bad faith, there are sipped the fetid delights of narcissism. In order to dissipate these shadows and miasmas, we always exhibited to daylight our lives, thoughts, and feelings." Personal spirituality, for de Beauvoir, was always outer-oriented, toward honest interpretation of the situation, action, and communication. She was totally antipathetic to dreaming, which she saw, with Hegel, as a most dangerous capitulation to immanence.

Many critics of the early '60s point out what a loss she represents to Christianity. Henry, for example, lambastes the kind of Catholicism she encountered for failing to attract that powerful a personality. He attacks its sentimental pietism: why was she given the *Imitation of Christ* to read, rather than the Gospels? He deplores its dogmatism, its fear of intellectual challenge. He blames above all the separation of public from private life that gave much of bourgeois French Catholicism of the time its "hypocritical" flavor; it should have faced Christianity's incompatibility with certain aspects of bourgeois culture: nationalism, legalism, exaggerated emphasis on good manners, shying from social responsibility, a mistrust of the flesh and the world. Though, at Ste. Marie, Simone later encountered a vital kind of modern Catholicism, it was too late. Earlier experiences had given her the excuses she needed to reject the Church as a whole. Given her exacerbated independence, and her incapacity to compromise, this was to be expected.[2]

■ ■ ■

Conclusion

The dangers of a vision of the self like the one presented in *The Second Sex* are obvious. It was specifically intended to undermine the "metaphysical" vision of man as image of God found in *Genesis:* a created being, made to become God's fuller likeness, in cooperation with grace. It also wished to explode an illusory hope of eternal life.

On the other hand, Christians also hold that our personhood is not just participation in a general "nature" but also a call, "by name," to a unique vocation; and that we are free to respond or not. Christians also hold that this vocation contributes to Christ's continuing incarnation in his people, in this world, and is therefore practice-oriented. Finally, Christians hold that God is infinite, and "still at work always," so that the effort to "image" him is endless. These are aspects of human reality de Beauvoir always stressed.

Christians do not see human freedom as depending on the denial of a *transcendent* God and of his will. They see it rather as an ability to cooperate with God, to participate in his overflowing life. Once this is kept firmly in mind to counter-balance her voluntarism, many of Simone de Beauvoir's insights can become of use. Her relentless attack on cultural presuppositions may help Christians review their perception of what it means to be "God's image." Should their concept of imaging God imply exclusive, authoritarian, insensitive, self-satisfied egotism, de Beauvoir's unforgiving irony may help them eradicate dangerous misconceptions.

Certain aspects of de Beauvoir's thought, however, can obviously never be reconciled with a Christian point of view: her strong support for free abortion on demand, for example, is no accident. It flows logically from her individual-centered voluntaristic morality. "A living being is nothing else but what it does; . . . essence does not precede existence: in its pure sub-jectivity, the human being is nothing." Such a vision of self and others cannot coexist with the vision of our 'being' as divine gift, worthy of infinite respect. De Beauvoir would pre-cisely avoid 'being' as totally as possible. She downplays the splendor of life's givens, to enhance the brilliance of our inter-pretation, or the success of our work. As a young woman, her detestation of all received reality was so great that, she tells us, "I recognized a certain metaphysical dignity to madness: I could see in it a rejection and a transcending of the human condition."

Sadly, de Beauvoir's tremendous thirst for life trapped her early into what Saint Augustine would have termed cupidity of the eyes: a restless need to experience all and anything, which kept her from listening to the still small voice at the heart of Christian existence.

As a result, she failed to perceive the spiritual richness of the feminine condition. She rejected as narcissism women's instinctive delight in merely being, instead of seeing in this self-acceptance a way of "giving grace" to the creator; she questioned their spontaneous joy in serving and self-giving as potentially sadomasochist; she opposed total commitment as self-alienating. She knew nothing of the ecstatic experience of becoming an instrument of cocreation, which childbirth so often reveals, finding it disgusting instead.

Simone is right, however, to point out the danger of per-version inherent in "feminine" experience. Too often, hidden resentment, evasion of responsibility, passive-aggressive revolt, do deform many women's existence. Reconciling individual autonomy with generosity and receptivity is no easy task. Much can be learned from her advocacy of what never ceased being her main message: "a certain courage to live, both intellectual and practical."[3]

What de Beauvoir refused to accept is recourse to the Source of All Energy that makes such courage possible and fruitful. As a result, there is a tragic dimension to her attempts at full life and human communication: as there is to one lost in the desert, attempting to drink one's own blood. Simone de Beauvoir's uneasy relation to femininity is certainly linked to a flight from "authenticity"; to a personal fear of the body as limit on personal freedom. But her work is a challenge that Christians cannot merely sweep under the rug. For, after all, participation in God's life, through true freedom transcending the Law, was, first, Christ's call.

■ ■ ■

Notes

1. Margaret Walters, "The Rights and Wrongs of Women," in A. Oakley and J. Mitchell, eds., *The Rights and Wrongs of Women* (Harmondsworth, 1976), 357.
2. A.-M. Henry, *Simone de Beauvoir, ou l'échec d'une Chrétienne* (Paris, 1961).
3. F. Jeanson, "Entretiens avec Simone de Beauvoir," in *Simone de Beauvoir ou l'entreprise de vivre* (Paris, 1966), 298.

■ ■ ■

Further Reading

E. Mark, *Simone de Beauvoir: Encounter with Death* (New Brunswick, N.J., 1973).
M. E. Tavistock, *Simone de Beauvoir, Feminist Mandarin* (London, 1985).

17

MIGUEL DE UNAMUNO AND ERNEST BECKER

...

THE HUMAN PERSON AS MORTAL

Introduction and Commentary by John D. Morgan

INTRODUCTION

From Plato to the present, the long tradition of answers to the question Who am I? is rooted in an analysis of human nature's powers of thinking. *Images of the Human* presents several examples of such orientations. With few exceptions, the authors represented in this collection answer the question Who am I? by examining the question What is a human? In other words, the individual person is understood to be primarily an isolated example of the human species. While the distinction between an individual (one member of the species) and a person (an individual substance of a rational nature) is as old as Boethius (c. A.D. 600), the full implications of that distinction have been emphasized only in the twentieth century.

It is precisely in one's confrontation with death that one becomes aware of uniqueness. The syllogism "All persons are mortal; Socrates is a person; Socrates is mortal" states a universal but trivial truth. It becomes personally significant only when the syllogism reads "All persons are mortal; *I am a person; I am mortal.*" It is the purpose of this chapter to examine the person's confrontation with death and draw from that confrontation an analysis of what a person is.

Several recent authors have stressed the importance of our recognizing our own mortality. Best known among these authors are the philosophers Kierkegaard, Heidegger, and Sartre. Two lesser-known but still highly influential authors are Miguel de Unamuno y Jugo and the anthropologist Ernest Becker. We will consider selections from Unamuno and Becker. These authors are among the several who have provided the theoretical foundation of the contemporary death awareness movement, also called the hospice movement. In order to understand the implications of death for a philosophy of the person, we will examine the attitudes toward death prevalent in North America in the last years of the twentieth century, comparing them with attitudes of other times. We will also look at what pain control, care of the bereaved, and some findings about clinical death have taught us about being a person. Finally, we will look at the roots of violence, the quest for spirituality in the face of death, and the meaning of the heroic in human experience.

■ ■ ■

Unamuno's Life and Works

Miguel de Unamuno y Jugo was born in Bilbao, Spain, on September 19, 1864. He received his primary and secondary education at Bilbao. A precocious child, he studied Kant and Hegel at the age of ten. Unamuno completed his studies at the Central University of Madrid and in 1884 returned to Bilbao where he married and served as a private tutor. He worked prodigiously, producing over four thousand articles. Unamuno was appointed rector of the University of Salamanca in 1901. Because of political difficulties, he went into voluntary exile in 1924, but returned to Spain in 1930. He died in 1936.

The characters of Unamuno's novels have many interests, but one passionate determination. So it was in his own life. Unamuno was passionately involved in the question of the immortality of the person. Although he said, "As from the plague, I flee being classified," he is thought of as a "Catholic philosopher," because he wrote from within the dominant tradition of Spain. Unamuno's Catholicism in spirit did not, however, stop him from anticlericalism, an attitude for which he was excommunicated from the Church; and *The Tragic Sense of Life*, from which our selection is taken, was placed on *The Index of Forbidden Books*. Unamuno was reconciled with the Church before his death.

■ ■ ■

What to Look For in the Unamuno Selection

In the following selection, pay attention to the way in which Unamuno focuses on fundamental philosophical questions. These questions about ultimate matters and the theory of knowledge are not simply abstract questions about the existence of God or the ability of the human mind to ascertain truth. For Unamuno, these questions are lived experiences about the meaning of life in the face of death. "Philosophy is a product of the humanity of each philosopher, and each philosopher is a man of flesh and bone who addresses himself to other men of flesh and bone like himself." God is not an answer primarily to the question Where did the world come from? but an answer to the question Where am I going?

■ ■ ■

Becker's Life and Works

The second selection dealing with the role that death plays in our lives is from the anthropologist, Ernest Becker. Becker was born in Springfield, Massachusetts, on September 27, 1924. He died in Vancouver, Canada, March 6, 1974. His book *The Denial of Death*, from which the selection comes, was praised by both the academic community and the general public. In spite of its scholarly nature, the book received a Pulitzer Prize and was on the *New York Times* best-seller list for several weeks. In addition, Becker has written *The Structure of Evil*, *The Birth and Death of Meaning*, and *Escape from Evil*. Becker described *The Denial of Death*, written only one year before he died, as his first mature work.

Becker was a professor of anthropology at the University of California during the student rebellions of the 1960s. He was an engaging speaker, and in spite of the criticism of professors common at the time, his classes were well received. He did not wish to continue teaching in the atmosphere of Berkeley in the sixties, and took a position at Simon Fraser University in Vancouver, Canada, where he was employed at the time of his death at the age of forty-nine.

His goal in all his intellectual work was to merge science and religion. For him, the human person is a creature whose nature is to deny its creatureliness and, in the ensuing frustration caused by this impossible task, to create violent evil.

Becker argues that the solution to overcome the urge to create violent evil is to learn to accept the human reality of death. The way to find meaning in life is to be a hero, that is, to leave behind something that heightens life, and, by so doing, to tie oneself to the will of God. The realization that this is God's world, and that everything is in his hands, is a hard wisdom by which to live, but for Becker it is the only wisdom that makes life possible in the face of death.

■ ■ ■

What to Look For in the Becker Selection

In the following selection from Becker's *The Denial of Death*, pay attention to William James's distinction between the healthy-minded and the morbidly-minded, and Becker's position concerning this distinction. Our psychological make-up is a consequence of the fear of death. Look at the way Becker has taken some of the common notions of psychoanalysis (anal fixation, the castration complex, and the Oedipus complex) and shown how Freud misunderstood them to be related solely to sex. For Becker, they are related to sex only because sex is nature's way of compensating for death.

SELECTION FROM UNAMUNO

■ ■ ■

The Tragic Sense of Life

Man has debated at length and will continue to debate at length—the world having been assigned as a theatre for his debates—concerning the origin of knowledge; but, apart from the question as to what the real truth about this origin may be, . . . it is a certainly ascertained fact that in the apparential order of things, in the life of beings who are endowed with a certain more or less cloudy faculty of knowing and perceiving, or who at any rate appear to act as if they were so endowed, knowledge is exhibited to us as bound up with the necessity of living and of procuring the wherewithal to maintain life. It is a consequence of that very essence of being, which, according to Spinoza [1632–77], consists in the effort to persist indefinitely in its own being. . . .

Knowledge, then, is primarily at the service of the instinct of self-preservation that makes perceptible for us the reality and the truth of the world; for it is this instinct that cuts out and separates that which exists for us from the unfathomable and illimitable region of the possible. In effect, that which has existence for us is precisely that which, in one way or another, we need to know in order to exist ourselves; objective existence, as we know it, is dependent on our own personal existence. And nobody can deny that there may exist, and perhaps do exist, aspects of reality unknown to us, today at any rate, and perhaps unknowable, because they are in no way necessary to us for the preservation of our own actual existence. . . .

And now, why does man philosophize? That is to say, why does he investigate the first causes and ultimate ends of things? Why does he seek the disinterested truth? For to say that all men have a natural tendency to know is true; but wherefore?

Philosophers seek a theoretic or ideal starting-point for their human work, the work of philosophizing; but they are not usually concerned to seek the practical and real starting-point, the purpose. What is the object in doing philosophy, in thinking it, and then expounding it to one's fellows? What does the philosopher seek in it and with it? The truth for the truth's own sake? The truth, in order that we may subject our conduct to it and determine our spiritual attitude towards life and the universe comformably with it?

Philosophy is a product of the humanity of each philosopher, and each philosopher is a man of flesh and bone who addresses himself to other men of flesh and bone like himself. And, let him do what he will, he philosophizes not with the reason only, but with the will, with the feelings, with the flesh and with the bones, with the whole soul and the whole body. It is the man that philosophizes. . . .

Knowledge for the sake of knowledge! Truth for truth's sake! This is inhuman. And if we say that theoretical philosophy addresses itself to practical philosophy, truth to goodness, science to ethics, I will ask: And to what end is goodness? Is it perhaps an end in itself? Good is simply that which contributes to the preservation, perpetuation, and enrichment of consciousness. Goodness addresses itself to man, to the maintenance and perfection of human society which is composed of men. And to what end is this? "So act that your action may be a pattern to all men," Kant tells us. That is well, but wherefore? We must needs seek for a wherefore.

In the starting-point of all philosophy, in the real starting-point, the practical not the theoretical, there is a wherefore. The philosopher philosophizes for something more than for the sake of philosophizing. *Primum vivere, deinde philosophari* [You have to live before you can philosophize], says the old Latin adage; and as the philosopher is a man before he is a philosopher, he must needs live before he can philosophize, and, in fact, he philosophizes in order to live. And usually he philosophizes either in order to resign himself to life, or to seek some finality in it, or to distract himself and forget his griefs, or for pastime and amusement. . . .

Take the man Spinoza, that Portuguese Jew exiled in Holland; read his *Ethic* as a despairing elegiac poem, which in fact it is, and tell me if you do not hear, beneath the disemburdened and seemingly serene propositions *more geometrico* [in a geometric method], the lugubrious echo of the prophetic psalms. It is not the philosophy of resignation but of despair. And when he wrote that the free man thinks of nothing less than of death, that his wisdom consists in meditating not on death but on life—*homo liber de nulla re minus quam de morte cogitat et eius sapientia non mortis, sed vitae, meditatio est* [The free person thinks of nothing less than of death, and his wisdom is a meditation not on death but on life]—when he wrote that, he felt, as we all feel, that we are slaves, and he did in fact think about death, and he wrote it in a vain endeavour to free himself from this thought. Nor in writing that "happiness is not the reward of virtue but virtue itself" did he feel, one may be sure, what he wrote. For this is usually the reason why men philosophize—in order to convince themselves, even though they fail in the attempt. And this desire of convincing oneself—that is to say, this desire of doing violence to one's own human nature—is the real starting-point of not a few philosophies.

Whence do I come and whence comes the world in which and by which I live? Whither do I go and whither goes everything that environs me? What does it all mean? Such are the questions that man asks as soon as he frees himself from the brutalizing necessity of labouring for his material sustenance. And, if we look closely, we shall see that beneath these questions lies the wish to know not so much the "why" as the "wherefore," not the cause but the end. Cicero's definition of philosophy is well known—"the knowledge of things divine and human, and of the causes in which these things are contained," *rerum divinarum et humanarum, causarumque in quibus hae res continentur;* but in reality these causes are, for us, ends. And what is the Supreme Cause, God, but the Supreme End? The "why" interests us only in view of the "wherefore." We wish to know whence we came only in order the better to be able to ascertain whither we are going. . . .

Why do I wish to know whence I come and whither I go, whence comes and whither goes everything that environs me, and what is the meaning of it all? For I do not wish to die utterly, and I wish to know whether I am to die or not definitely. If I do not die, what is my destiny? And, if I die, then nothing has any meaning for me. And there are three solutions: (a) I know that I shall die utterly, and the irremediable despair, or (b) I know that I shall not die utterly, and then resignation, or (c) I cannot know either one or the other, and then resignation in despair or despair in resignation, a desperate resignation or a resigned despair, and hence conflict. . . .

For the present let us remain keenly suspecting that the longing not to die, the hunger for personal immortality, the effort whereby we tend to persist indefinitely in our own being, which is, according to the tragic Jew [Spinoza], our very essence, that this is the affective basis of all knowledge and the personal inward starting-point of all human philosophy, wrought by a man and for men. And we shall see how the solution of this inward affective problem, a solution which may be but the despairing renunciation of the attempt at a solution, is that which colors all the rest of philosophy. Underlying even the so-called problem of knowledge there is simply this human feeling, just as underlying the enquiry into the "why," the cause, there is simply the search for the "wherefore," the end. All the rest is either to deceive oneself or to wish to deceive others; and to wish to deceive others in order to deceive oneself.

And this personal and affective starting-point of all philosophy and all religion is the tragic sense of life.

Extracted from *The Tragic Sense of Life,* translated by J. E. C. Flitch (London, 1921), 21–22, 24, 28–29, 31–33, 36–37.

SELECTION FROM BECKER

■ ■ ■

The Denial of Death

Here we introduce one of the great rediscoveries of modern thought: that of all things that move man, one of the principal ones is his terror of death. After Darwin, the problem of death came to the fore as an evolutionary problem, and many thinkers immediately saw that it was a major psychological problem for man. They also very quickly saw what real heroism was about, as Shaler wrote just at the turn of the century: Heroism is first and foremost a reflex of the terror of death. We admire most the courage to face death; we give such valour our highest and most constant adoration; it moves us deeply in our hearts because we have doubts about how brave we ourselves would be. When we see a man bravely facing his own extinction we rehearse the greatest victory we can imagine. And so the hero has been the center of human honor and acclaim since probably the beginning of specifically human evolution. . . .

The "Healthy-Minded" Argument

There are "healthy-minded" persons who maintain that fear of death is not a natural thing for man, that we are not born with it. An increasing number of careful studies on how the actual fear of death develops in the child agree fairly well that the child has no knowledge of death until about the age of three to five. How could he? It is too abstract an idea, too removed from his experience. He lives in a world that is full of living, acting things, responding to him, amusing him, feeding him. He doesn't know what it means for life to disappear forever, nor theorize where it would go. Only gradually does he recognize that there is a thing called death that takes some people away forever; very reluctantly he comes to admit that it sooner or later takes everyone away, but this gradual realization of the inevitability of death can take up until the ninth or tenth year. . . .

The child who has good maternal experiences will develop a sense of basic security and will not be subject to morbid fears of losing support, of being annihilated, or the like. As he grows up to understand death rationally by the age of nine or ten, he will accept it as part of his world view, but the idea will not poison his self-confident attitude toward life. The psychiatrist Rheingold says categorically that annihilation anxiety is not part of the child's natural experience but is engendered in him by bad experiences with a depriving mother. This theory puts the whole burden of anxiety onto the child's nurture and not his nature. . . .

The "Morbidly-Minded" Argument

The "healthy-minded" argument just discussed is one side of the picture of the accumulated research and opinion on the problem of the fear of death, but there is another side. A large body of people would agree with these observations on early experience and would admit that experiences may heighten natural anxieties and later fears, but these people would also claim very strongly that nevertheless the fear of death is natural and is present in everyone, that it is the basic fear that influences all others, a fear from which no one is immune, no matter how disguised it may be. William James spoke very early for this school, and with his usual colourful realism he called death "the worm at the core" of man's pretensions to happiness. No less a student of human nature than Max Scheler thought that all men must have some kind of certain intuition of this "worm at the core," whether they admitted it or not. . . .

I frankly side with the second school—in fact, this whole book [*The Denial of Death*] is a network of arguments based on the universality of the fear of death, or "terror" as I prefer to call it, in order to convey how all-consuming it is when we look it full in the face. . . .

Zilboorg says that most people think death-fear is absent because it rarely shows its true face; but he argues that, underneath all appearances, fear of death is universally present:

> For behind the sense of insecurity in the face of danger, behind the sense of discouragement and depression, there always lurks the basic fear of death, a fear which undergoes most complex elaborations and manifests itself in many indirect ways. . . . No one is free of the fear of death. . . . The anxiety neuroses, the various phobic states, even a considerable number of depressive suicidal states and many schizophrenias, amply demonstrate the ever-present fear of death which becomes woven into the major conflicts of the given psychopathological conditions. . . . We may take for granted that the fear of death is always present in our mental functioning.

Zilboorg points out that this fear is actually an expression of the instinct of self-preservation, which functions as a constant drive to maintain life and to master the dangers that threaten life:

> Such constant expenditure of psychological energy on the business of preserving life would be impossible if the fear of death were not as constant. The very term "self-preservation" implies an effort against some force of disintegration; the affective aspect of this is fear, fear of death.

In other words, the fear of death must be present behind all our normal functioning, in order for the organism to be armed for self-preservation. But the fear of death cannot be present constantly in one's mental functioning, else the organism could not function. Zilboorg continues:

> If this fear were as constantly conscious, we should be unable to function normally. It must be properly repressed to keep us living with any modicum of comfort. We know very well that to repress means more than to put away, and to forget that which was put away, and the place where we put it. It means also to maintain a constant psychological effort to keep the lid on and inwardly never relax our watchfulness.

And so we can understand what seems like an impossible paradox: the ever-present fear of death in the normal biological functioning of our instinct of self-preservation, and our utter obliviousness to this fear in our conscious life.

Therefore in normal times we move about actually without ever believing in our own death, as if we fully believed in our own corporeal immortality. We are intent on mastering death .... A man will say, of course, that he knows he will die some day, but he does not really care. He is having a good time with living, and he does not think about death and does not care to bother about it—but this is a purely intellectual, verbal admission. The effect of fear is repressed. . . .

The "Disappearance" of the Fear of Death

Its disappearance doesn't mean that the fear was never there. The argument of those who believe in the universality of the innate terror of death rests its case mostly on what we know about how effective repression is. . . . For one thing, there is a growing body of research trying to get at the consciousness of death, denied by repression, by using psychological tests such as measuring galvanic skin responses; it strongly suggests that underneath the most bland exterior lurks the universal anxiety, the "worm at the core."

For another thing, there is nothing like shocks in the real world to jar repressions loose. Recently psychiatrists reported an increase in anxiety neuroses in children as a result of the earth tremors in Southern California. For these children the discovery that life really includes cataclysmic danger was too much for their still-imperfect denial systems—hence there were open outbursts of anxiety. With adults we see this manifestation of anxiety in the face of impending catastrophe where it takes the form of panic. Recently several people suffered broken limbs and other injuries after forcing open their airplane's safety door during take-off and jumping from the wing to the ground; the incident was triggered by the backfire of an engine. Obviously underneath these harmless noises other things are rumbling in the creature. . . .

I think we have reconciled our two divergent positions on the fear of death. The "environmental" and the "innate" positions are both part of the same picture; they merge naturally into one another; it all depends from which angle you approach the picture: from the side of the disguises and transmutations of the fear of death or from the side of its apparent absence. . . . On the one hand, we see a human animal who is partly dead to the world, who is most "dignified" when he shows a certain obliviousness of his fate, when he allows himself to be driven through life; who is most "free" when he lives in secure dependence on powers around him, when he is least in possession of himself. On the other hand, we get an image of a human animal who is overly sensitive to the world, who cannot shut it out, who is thrown back on his own meagre powers, and who seems least free to move and act, least in possession of himself, and most undignified. Whichever image we choose to identify with depends in large part upon ourselves.

* * * * *

Why exactly is the world so terrible for the human animal? Why do people have such trouble digging up the resources to face that terror openly and bravely? To talk about these things takes us right into the heart of psychoanalytic theory and what is now the existential rebirth in psychology; it lays bare the nature of man with a clarity and comprehensiveness that are truly amazing.

Man's Existential Dilemma

We always knew that there was something peculiar about man, something deep down that characterized him and set him apart from the other animals. It was something that had to go right to his core, something that made him suffer his peculiar fate, that made it impossible to escape. For ages, when philosophers talked about the core of man they referred to it as his "essence," something fixed in his nature, deep down, some special quality or substance. But nothing like it was ever found; man's peculiarity still remained a dilemma. The reason it was never found, as Erich Fromm put it in an excellent discussion, was that there was no essence, that the essence of man is really his *paradoxical* nature, the fact that he is half animal and half symbolic. . . .

We might call this existential paradox the condition of *individuality within finitude*. Man has a symbolic identity that brings him sharply out of nature. He is a symbolic self, a creature with a name, a life history. He is a creator with a mind that soars out to speculate about atoms and infinity, who can place himself imaginatively at a point in space and contemplate bemusedly his own planet. This immense expansion, this dexterity, this ethereality, this self-consciousness, gives to man literally the status of a small god in nature, as the Renaissance thinkers knew.

Yet, at the same time, as the Eastern sages also knew, man is a worm, and food for worms. This is the paradox: he is out of nature and hopelessly in it; he is dual, up in the stars and yet housed in a heart-pumping, breath-gasping body that once belonged to a fish and still carries the gill-marks to prove it. His body is a material fleshy casing that is alien to him in many ways—the strangest and most repugnant way being that it aches and bleeds and will decay and die. Man is literally split in two: he has an awareness of his own splendid uniqueness in that he sticks out of nature with a towering majesty, and yet he goes back into the ground a few feet in order blindly and dumbly to rot and disappear forever. It is a terrifying dilemma to be in and to have to live with. The lower animals are, of course, spared this painful contradiction, as they lack a symbolic identity and the self-consciousness that goes with it. They merely act and move reflexively as they are driven by their instincts. If they pause at all, it is only a physical pause; inside they are anonymous, and even their faces have no name. They live in a world without time, pulsating, as it were, in a state of dumb being. This is what has made it so simple to shoot down whole herds of buffalo or elephants. The animals don't know that death is happening, and continue grazing placidly while others drop alongside them. The knowledge of death is reflective and conceptual, and animals are spared it. They live and they disappear with the same thoughtlessness: a few minutes of fear, a few seconds of anguish, and it is over. But to live a whole lifetime with the fate of death haunting one's dreams and even the most sun-filled days—that's something else.

It is only if you let the full weight of this paradox sink down on your mind and feelings that you can realize what an impossible situation it is for an animal to be in. I believe that those who speculate that a full apprehension of man's condition would drive him insane are right, quite literally right. . . . I think such events illustrate the meaning of the chilling reflection of Pascal [1623–62]: "Men are so necessarily mad that not to be mad would amount to another form of madness." *Necessarily* because the existential dualism makes an impossible situation, an excruciating dilemma. *Mad* because, as we shall see, everything that man does in his symbolic world is an attempt to deny and overcome his grotesque fate. He literally drives himself into a blind obliviousness with social games, psychological tricks, personal preoccupations so far removed from the reality of his situation that they are forms of madness—agreed madness, shared madness, disguised and dignified madness, but madness all the same. . . . Eric Fromm wondered why most people did not become insane in the face of the existential contradiction between a symbolic self, that seems to give man infinite worth in a timeless scheme of things, and a body that is worth about 98¢. How to reconcile the two? . . . We realize directly and poignantly that what we call the child's character is a *modus vivendi* [a way of living] achieved after the most unequal struggle any animal has to go through; a struggle that the child can never really understand because he doesn't know what is happening to him, why he is responding as he does, or what is really at stake in the battle. The victory in this kind of battle is truly Pyrrhic: character is a face that one sets to the world, but it hides an inner defeat. The child emerges with a name, a family, a play-world in a neighborhood, all clearly cut out for him. But his insides are full of nightmarish memories of impossible battles, terrifying desires, sensations of unspeakable beauty, majesty, awe, mystery, and fantasies and hallucinations of mixtures between the two, the impossible attempt to compromise between bodies and symbols. . . . To grow up at all is to conceal the mass of internal scar tissue that throbs in our dreams.

So we see that two dimensions of human existence—the body and the self—can never be reconciled seamlessly, which explains the second half of Pascal's reflection: "Not to be mad would amount to another form of madness." Here Pascal proves that great students of human nature could see behind the masks of men long before scientific psychoanalysis. They lacked clinical documentation but they saw that the coolest repression, the most convincing equanimity, or the warmest self-satisfaction were accomplished lies both to the world and to oneself. With the clinical documentation of psychoanalytic thought, we got a fairly comprehensive picture of human character styles—what we can now call "styles of madness," after Pascal. We might say that psychoanalysis revealed to us the complex penalties of denying the truth of man's condition, what we might call *the costs of pretending not to be mad*. If we had to offer the briefest explanation of all the evil that men have wreaked upon themselves and upon their world since the beginning of time right up until tomorrow, it would be not in terms of man's animal heredity, his instincts and his evolution: it would be simply *the toll that his pretence of sanity takes*, as he tries to deny his true condition. . . .

Sexuality is inseparable from our existential paradox, the dualism of human nature. The person is both a self and a body, and from the beginning there is the confusion about where "he" really "is"—in the symbolic inner self or in the physical body. Each phenomenological realm is different. The inner self represents freedom of thought, imagination, and the infinite reach of symbolism. The body represents determinism and boundedness. The child gradually learns that his freedom as a unique being is dragged back by the body and its appendages, which dictate "what" he is. For this reason sexuality is as much a problem for the adult as for the child: the physical solution to the problem of who we are and why we have emerged on this planet is no help—in fact, it is a terrible threat. It doesn't tell the person what he is deep down inside, what kind of distinctive gift he is to work upon the world. This is why it is so difficult to have sex without guilt: guilt is there because the body casts a shadow on the person's inner freedom, his "real self" that—through the act of sex—is being forced into a standardized, mechanical, biological role. Even worse, the inner self is not even being called into consideration at all; the body takes over completely for the total person, and this kind of guilt makes the inner self shrink and threaten to disappear.

This is why a woman asks for assurance that the man want "me" and not "only my body"; she is painfully conscious that her own distinctive inner personality can be dispensed with in the sexual act. It is dispensed with, it doesn't count. The fact is that the man usually does want only the body, and the woman's total personality is reduced to a mere animal role. The existential paradox vanishes, and one has no distinctive humanity to protest. One creative way of coping with this is, of course, to allow it to happen and to go with it: what the psychoanalysts call "regression in the service of the ego." The person becomes, for a time, merely his physical self and so absolves the painfulness of the existential paradox and the guilt that goes with sex. Love is one great key to this kind of animal dimension without fear and guilt, but instead with trust and assurance that his distinctive inner freedom will not be negated by an animal surrender.

Extracted from *The Denial of Death* (New York, 1973), 11–17, 20–21, 24–30, 41–42. The quotations from Gregory Zilboorg are from his "Fear of Death," *Psychoanalytic Quarterly* 12 (1943): 465–71.

COMMENTARY

In the preceding selections you have seen two presentations of the role of death in our consciousness. The Trappist Monks of Utah have a saying that "you don't have your feet on the ground until you have put somebody into it." This seemingly gruesome statement means that until we take the limitations of life seriously, we do not really have the equipment to live life completely. We accept the reality of the limits of our energy or our finances, but we act as though we can always reach into our pocket or purse and "pull out" another year or two of life. How different would our relationships be if we really believed that when we said good-bye to someone, it might be for the last time! Yet that is the reality of our lives. In what follows, we will look at some of the ways we have of understanding death and loss, and ways we have developed to cope with them.

■ ■ ■

The Meaning of Death in Our Lives

William James has said that the word *good* fundamentally means "destined to survive." To say that something is good is implicitly to affirm that the thing ought to exist. To say that something is bad is implicitly to hold that it ought not to exist. Becker and Unamuno deal with the consequent enigma: I am; I am good; yet I shall die. Individuals are aware of their uniqueness, their own intrinsic goodness; therefore they believe that they ought to continue to exist. Yet the knowledge of inevitable death, not only for themselves but for all their loved ones, is constantly present. This awareness is, in the words of William James, "the worm at the core of our pretensions to happiness"; "it makes routine, automatic, secure, self-confident activity impossible. It makes thoughtless living . . . an impossibility." According to both Unamuno and Becker, all human activities, including abstract philosophizing, are reactions to our knowledge of the impending death of ourselves or those we love.

Only the human animal is conscious of death. Other animals are given instincts to protect them from what would do them harm, but we learn to cope with impending death without the protection of built-in defenses. According to Becker, knowing we will die the entire time we are alive is "the most unequal struggle any animal has to go through." Perhaps the human situation is best summarized in the lines Becker quotes from André Malraux: "It takes sixty years of incredible suffering and effort to make such an individual; then he is good only for dying." One learns the rules of social living in a family and in a society. One goes to school, develops a career with all its strife, marries and raises a family with all its tensions. For what? So that one can die! Statistically there is a longer life expectancy today than there was even fifty years ago. Because of clean drinking water, better food storage and distribution, and advanced medicine, the diseases that carried off most of our ancestors no longer exist as most people live to, and even beyond, the biblical three score years and ten. But the most important reality has not changed. Death is still one per customer and one for every customer.

■ ■ ■

What Are Death, Dying, and Bereavement?

We assume that the experiences of death, dying, and bereavement are understood by all in the same way. Death, the irreversible cessation of biological functions, is a fact, but even death is defined with difficulty. While death is something that happens to us, dying and grieving are primarily activities. With the possible exception of those who die suddenly and without warning, dying and grieving are projects to be done, not things that happen. The term *death system* was coined by Robert Kastenbaum to describe the manner in which we understand and engage in dying and related activities. The term refers to our whole "orientation toward death." It is "the total range of thought, feeling, and behavior that is directly or indirectly related to death. This includes conceptions of death, attitudes toward dying persons, funerary practices. . . ."[1] What we have received from our culture about the ways we understand death and bereavement, and how to act on that understanding, constitutes our death system. The death system includes ideas (such as health, sickness, dependence, independence, life, death, bereavement, and dying); persons (such as the patient, family members, physicians, clergy, funeral directors, cemetery personnel); and places (such as hospitals, hospices, morgues, funeral homes, churches). In sum, the death system is the totality of the ways we think, speak, feel, and act in regard to death, dying, and bereavement.

How we understand death is shaped by four elements: (1) life expectancy, (2) exposure to death, (3) the conception of the person, and (4) the individual's perception of having control over the forces of nature.[2]

(1) Most of us in North America will probably live into our late seventies. This is a new development in the history of the human race. In Plato's day, average life expectancy was twenty years; it was thirty-three years at the time of Anselm and Aquinas. When William James lived, at the beginning of this century, average life expectancy was no more than forty years. Plato, Aristotle, Anselm, Aquinas, and James understood, and thus experienced, death and

bereavement differently from the way we do, precisely because their expectations about the length of life was considerably different from our own.

(2) Exposure to death is a second element in our understanding of death. A child born in Vietnam, Mexico, Pakistan, or the former Yugoslavia, would have considerably more exposure to death than the average North American. Someone living in the inner city of a major North American city has a different understanding of the presence of death than does someone living in suburbia. The family members of a funeral director or an emergency room physician would have a different understanding of death than does the child of a tax accountant.

(3) On a more theoretical level, our attitudes toward death are shaped by our philosophy, specifically by our understanding of the person, and by our view of the physical universe. In a culture such as ours, which puts emphasis on the uniqueness of the individual, persons will have a different orientation toward death than in a culture that perceives each individual as having meaning primarily as a part of the whole, whether that whole is religious (as in the case of Aquinas) or political (as in the case of Marx). This uniqueness of the person—the realization that this person has never before existed in the history of the human race and will never exist again—causes what Becker calls "the ache of cosmic specialness."

(4) Our view of the physical universe is also important in the development of our death attitudes. If we believe that we are impotently subject to the laws of nature, then our death attitudes will differ from those whose view is that we have significant control over the forces of nature. In North America we build domed stadia and malls to protect us from the elements, we send astronauts into space, we expect to control disease. It is an easy leap to the assumption that we have total control over nature.

Since we have "professionalized" death, that is, turned over to professionals the care of the dying, the dead, and the bereaved, we have little day-to-day contact with death and bereavement. The historian Philippe Ariès has characterized our age as "death-denying."

As a result of his study of the literature of different periods, Ariès has postulated that previous to our age there have been three basic kinds of death. He has titled these: "Tamed Death," "The Death of the Self," and "The Death of the Other."[3] Ariès, as a historian, understood these kinds of death in terms of their temporal progression. We may wish to understand them as evidencing attitudinal trends that can still be found today.

Ariès called tamed death "unchronicled death throughout the long ages of the most ancient history." It was dominant until the late middle ages; it involves familiarity with death. Since life was, as Thomas Hobbes (1588–1679) summarized it, "solitary, poor, nasty, brutish, and short," one was constantly exposed to death. Death was a familiar, even if not always welcome, neighbor. The dying person first of all was thought to be the best judge of his impending death, who, having said his farewells, calmly commended his soul to God. Sudden death, which did not give one the opportunity to put temporal and spiritual affairs in order, was considered a curse. The Litany of the Saints has an invocation "to preserve us from a sudden death." This prayer seems less attractive to us when we are exposed to the chronic debilitative diseases of the closing days of the twentieth century, but to those whose life span was already short, the prospect of a sudden death was more terrifying.

Whereas the first period put emphasis on familiarity with death, Ariès' second period placed an emphasis on loss of personal identity—one's own death. From the twelfth to the fifteenth century, individuals became increasingly more conscious of themselves outside the group. As a consequence, death was perceived as the last act of a unique, personal drama. It was the duty of dying persons to be master over their own deaths and to organize an appropriate exit. Wills, especially those that arranged for prayers for the deceased as they met God, became common. Consciousness of one's sinfulness had the twofold effect of fear of hell (the Latin poem *Dies Irae—Day of Wrath*—dates to this period) and emphasis on good works—even if these good works were carried out after one's death. Death was no longer quite the welcomed friend it was in the earlier period.

The nineteenth century saw the emphasis change from death as a usual and common destiny (tamed death), and death as a personal and specific act (one's own death), to death as an emphasis on the loss of a relationship—the death of the other. Death was the last act of an intimate relationship. Privacy became important because it was the ingredient necessary for a relationship to develop. Few wills were written at the time, as though it would be bad faith to have a will when one had loved ones to carry out one's wishes.

What conclusion can we draw from this brief history of the structure of our ideas of death and bereavement? An integrated death system should enable individuals "to think, feel, and behave with respect to death in ways that they might consider to be effective and appropriate." A valuable death system is one that contributes to psychological growth and that alleviates fears of death and bereavement so that one can get on with life. Do our traditional ways of relating to our final end contribute to our personal happiness? Do we, in the words of the Harvard psychiatrist Avery Weisman, die an appropriate death?

> [The dying person] should be relatively pain-free, his suffering reduced, and emotional and social impoverishments kept to a minimum. Within the limits of disability, he should operate on as high a level as possible, even though only tokens of former fulfilments can be offered. He should also recognize and resolve residual conflicts, and satisfy whatever remaining wishes are consistent within his present plight and his own ego ideal. Finally, among his choices, he should be able to yield control to others in whom he has confidence. He also has the option of seeking or relinquishing significant key people.[4]

In many ways, as a consequence of our death system, we cannot consciously *live* our dying. Because we ignore the reality of death, we do not adequately prepare for it. How different our lives would be if we took seriously the possibility that, when we say good-bye to a loved one, it could be a final good-bye. Also, once we are seriously ill, the decisions about the remaining aspects of our lives, and the decisions concerning the arrangements after our deaths, are made by others. Personal, creative dying is denied to us. Except for those who decide to terminate their own lives, dying remains beyond their control.

■ ■ ■

Care of the Dying and the Bereaved

The death awareness movement has been one of the great inspirations for better pain and symptom control. We have discovered that, in 95 percent of the cases, adequate pain control is available when the available medications are used effectively. One of the most important studies about pain, the Melzak-Wall "gate control" theory of pain, gives scientific evidence for what we all know intuitively: that pain is never merely physical. Pain includes psychological, spiritual, and relational elements, which control the amount of pain a person has. If the suffering person experiences emotional turmoil for interpersonal, psychological, economic, or spiritual reasons, pain medication will not work effectively. Dr. Cecily Saunders, the founder of Saint Christopher's Hospice in Britain, uses the concept "total pain" in reference to the dying. One reason the hospice movement has insisted that the unit of care is the whole family, not only the patient, is that the patient is more than a diseased body.[5] The person has a unique history of relationships. We have discovered that the person, in order to have adequate pain control, must have emotional and spiritual calm.

Perhaps this whole-person orientation is best illustrated in bereavement literature. Lindemann's classic study of bereavement indicates five common elements of grief: bodily distress, psychological preoccupation with the deceased person, feelings of guilt, loss of the ability to feel anything emotionally, and disorientation. Our culture believes that one should "get over" a bereavement in a matter of a few weeks; normally employees are given three days to grieve. If our culture is correct then we must assume that the relationship of the deceased to the bereaved person is merely accidental, such as the relationship between people and their clothing or glasses. There would be no reason for the symptoms that Lindemann mentions to occur at all, much less to last for even more than two years. But the evidence is otherwise. Bereaved persons have *literally* lost a part of themselves. *This is not mere metaphor.* Persons are composed not only of bodily parts but also of history and relationships. The bereaved person is wounded as truly as if blood were dripping from torn flesh.

The reader will find several authors in *Images of the Human* who deal with the question of immortality. Here we will limit our discussion to what has been called "clinical" immortality. Clinical manifestations of immortality, or near-death experiences, refer to the experiences of those who have been resuscitated after they have died clinically, that is, after their heartbeats and breathing have stopped, electroencephalograph readings are flat, and evidence of sensation has ceased. When these persons were resuscitated they began to tell stories of what they had perceived during this period of clinical death.

The stories have several common links. For the most part the persons heard themselves pronounced dead and could see their own bodies at a distance; they were aware of feelings of peace and quiet, although also aware of a buzzing sound; they perceived that they floated through a dark tunnel. Often they met friends and relatives whom they knew had already died; and they were in the presence of "a being of light." They had a review of their past lives, and after resuscitation had a changed view of life and death. Finally, they were conscious of some sort of border and knew that if they went over it they would not be able to come back; they were reluctant to come back; and they found themselves unable to communicate the experience to others.[6]

It must be borne in mind that these experiences are not daily occurrences. Some researchers have been unable to find any patients who have undergone these experiences. Other researchers have found patients who have negative feelings about this experience. The literature today, for the most part, reflects the positive experiences. Much of the data can be explained naturally. We have seen enough television shows to be able to imagine what goes on in an emergency room situation even though we might never have been there ourselves. Meeting someone from the past, hearing beautiful music, and seeing God (a being of light), could be explained as wish-fulfillment. In those last moments of consciousness, we might desire an experience that is safe and meaningful.

There is, however, one part of the evidence that has implications for a philosophy of the person. Sometimes the "dead" persons have been able to describe intricate details of what went on while they were clinically dead. One of the usual tests to see if a person has truly died is to prick the skin to see if there is any sensory response; a flat electroencephalogram seems to indicate that the senses have ceased functioning. Thus, if there is evidence that the persons have actually gained knowledge when their bodies were clinically dead, there is evidence that they knew in some way other than by normal sensation.

■ ■ ■

Violence

Why do rational creatures act violently? It is impossible to listen to the news or pick up the newspaper without being confronted with a "nightmare spectacular taking place on a planet that has been soaked for hundreds of years in the blood of all its creatures." Violence exists in spite of the fact that for millennia the great religions have taught that we are responsible for each other, and the fact that some of them teach that we are to see the Creator in the least of our neighbors. Even apart from religion, philosophical systems have agreed with Immanuel Kant that one ought never to use another person as a means.

One must ask if there is something intrinsically violent in the human person. Perhaps the most famous answer to that question comes from Thomas Hobbes, who believed that the very nature of the person is violent and self-seeking; each person acts solely for self-interest; in theory, all persons are equal in that the weakness in one characteristic (e.g., physical strength) is compensated for in another (e.g., cunning); in practice, because some will always be stronger than others, one is on guard all the time.

Not everyone agrees that the nature of the person is fundamentally violent. Jean-Jacques Rousseau (1712–78) believed that all individuals are intrinsically good, "born free," but that society or government enchains people by interfering with their best instincts. One enters society with the belief that a few rights guaranteed by the sovereign are better than an infinite number of unguaranteed ones, but violence occurs, according to Rousseau, because someone steps outside the social contract and acts solely for self-interest at the expense of another.

In each of these two versions of a "social contract" theory, society is perceived as based on an unnatural construct, a necessary evil, by which individuals surrender their rights for the sake of mutual protection. One effect of such a theory is that when people see the limits that exist in all political systems, they may believe they have given up too much to protect the rights of the few, who do not always include themselves. There is another view that for centuries has been called the natural law theory. This theory holds that society is a natural organization, and individuals have obligations to society because they cannot be fully human outside of society. According to this view, one gives up nothing in entering society because one never had the unlimited rights viewed by either Hobbes or Rousseau. Ernest Becker takes a different view of violence from either the social contract theory or the natural law theory. The root of violence, in Becker's thesis, is the fact that humans are terrified of death. When they recognize the normal flaws in their lives, they either have to accept responsibility for their lives or find someone else to blame. And it is easy to blame others for one's basic dissatisfaction with the world. For Becker, violence is "a symbolic solution of a biological limitation." Taking action against another who is seen as the root of their frustration gives people a sense of being in charge of their destinies. It is easy to believe that they are masters of their own lives when they hold someone else's fate in their hands.

Becker's position is perhaps most easily seen in the violence that results from prejudice. Prejudice occurs when a person is evaluated as a member of a group rather than as a unique person. Thinking of persons simply as women, blacks, Indians, homosexuals, or Jews ignores their unique characteristics. Hatred of such groups leads to a violence whose purpose is "to cleanse the earth of tainted ones." In order to feel more in control of one's own fate, one takes action against those who are viewed as a threat. Mastery over death can be found in mastery over those identified in a person's mind with death. "All the intolerable sufferings of mankind result from man's attempt to make the whole world of nature reflect his reality."

Violence does not have to be rooted in what is perceived as an immediate physical threat. The revolutionary movements of the twentieth century such as those in Russia, China, Iran, Yugoslavia, Iraq, and Ireland are based more on religious and philosophical differences about the meaning of human existence than on the desire for political or economic liberation. The history of wars from the Crusades to the present gives witness to violence caused by ideological or philosophical differences. Those who are insecure about their place in the world will perceive a different world view as a physical threat. "No wonder men go into a rage over fine points of belief: if your adversary wins the argument about truth, you die." "My view is safe; yours is dangerous." The evil that troubles persons most is their vulnerability; they feel impotent to guarantee the absolute meaning of their lives.

■ ■ ■

Spirituality

The death awareness movement has shown that the human quest is a quest for meaning. Spirituality is seen in the answer to the question How can you make sense out of a world that does not seem to be intrinsically reasonable? We use the term *spirit* in many ways, referring to the vitality of a high school team, to the chemical content of beverages, or to a conscious being who is not bodied. The term fundamentally means independence from matter: that there is something about the human person that cannot be fully explained by bodily functions. Because the language of Greek philosophy was a convenient tool for presenting their message, early Christians adopted the doctrine of a spiritual soul, a notion not found in quite the same way in either Judaism or non-Western philosophies. As a consequence, we who live in Western culture, shaped by the language both of Greek intellectual experience and Christian religious experience, identify the idea of spirituality with religion. But the spiritual nature of the person is not just a religious matter.

Those human pursuits that exist primarily at the abstract level of thinking and willing indicate a person's spiritual awareness. The meaning that one finds in music, art, and literature, while dependent on the physical characteristics of tones, rhythm, paint, canvas, and words, is not identifiable with these tools of expression. The arts enable people to find meaning in their lives, "to overcome fragmentation in their lives." Art, as Jacques Maritain has said, is "the expression of the inexpressible." It is the awareness of a value that is not found directly in the material make-up of the work of art. Our culture—"the ideas by which we live"—exists for us not as a group of physical facts, but as human constructs, as interpretations of fact, and thus is part of our spiritual heritage.

The ability of persons to determine their lives is perhaps the most fundamental example of their spiritual nature. We must make sense out of our lives by our decisions and our actions. Jean-Paul Sartre has told us that we are the only animals that can fail. We are, in his words, "condemned to be free." We alone must decide, moment by moment, if we will be, what we will be, and whether we will be the kind of persons that we know we could be. Our spirituality is expressed through our decision making, establishing values, and communicating them to others. Spirituality consists in taking seriously the fact that things do not just happen, that each of us has a responsibility to strive for ideals.

The concept of the spiritual nature of the person encompasses the idea that each of us is part of a larger whole. We not only find meaning in our lives in that larger whole but also have some obligation to it. This is what is meant by religion. In this sense, the term *religious* applies not only to Western or Eastern religions, but also to philosophies and other movements through which persons find meaning in their lives. Each person must ask what it is that gives meaning to life, and whether whatever is chosen will be a defense against the bad times, such as death and bereavement, that come into each life.

■ ■ ■

Heroism

Becker outlines three possible responses to the fact of death: (1) to pretend that there is no problem, the titular theme of *The Denial of Death;* (2) to live life as a hero, to live out one's possibilities in a creative way; (3) to enter into religion or cosmic heroism, to unite one's fate with the divine, something beyond oneself.

(1) Becker points out that there is a thin line between the way "normal" persons block out reality and the way those suffering from mental illness do. In order for normal persons to manage to live their day-to-day experiences, they must develop what Becker calls the "vital lie." This is the denial of creatureliness, the attempt to ignore the fact that death awaits all. Childhood's task is to learn the skills necessary to survive in the world, one of which is to repress consciousness of death. "If the child were to give in to the overpowering character of reality and experience, he would not be able to act with the kind of equanimity we need in our non-instinctive world." Normality is the refusal to be conscious of the precariousness of reality. Character is a *modus vivendi* (a way of living), a "controlled obsession" that "hides an inner defeat."

(2) The second response to death is heroism. Heroes are those who make a contribution with their transitoriness. All people realize that they have a unique set of talents and human possibilities. What Becker calls heroism is the actualization of these possibilities: existentialist philosophers call this "authentic existence." Becker cites Kierkegaard's idea that "good" is "opening toward new possibility and choice, the ability to face . . . anxiety." The hero is the one who realizes the possibilities of creating a greater level of human achievement, who leaves behind "something that heightens life and testifies to the worthwhileness of life." This may be great deeds recorded in history or simply a commitment to one's family, community, or profession.

To be a hero involves taking risks. Mediocrity is the safe route. What motivates the hero is coming to grips with the fact that we all die. There is no reason not to fulfill one's possibilities because the threats, real or imagined, from those who would interfere with one's goals can do no more than nature itself has done: shorten one's life. Because death always wins, individuals might as well die with the kind of fulfillment they know is possible. Rather than having a passivity based on frustration, heroes fulfill possibilities because they have already accepted the ultimate threat.

(3) Religion for Becker is the highest form of heroism. For most people, the urge to immortality is a simple reflex of anxiety about death, but for the religious person it is "a reaching out by way of one's whole being toward life" both for oneself and for the universe. In its ideal form, religion satisfies both of the individual's fundamental needs. It provides affirmation of one's uniqueness, since God knows and loves individuals in their uniqueness; and it provides consolation for death in the promise of an eternal life. For Becker, religion is the highest form of creativity, an "outgrowth of genuine life-longing, a reaching out for a plenitude of meaning" allowing one to be "open, generous, courageous; to touch others' lives and enrich them and open to them in return." The function of religion in the world has been to free individuals from the complete control of the powerful. The most remarkable achievement of the great religions has been that persons of all social or economic classes, "slaves, cripples, imbeciles, the simple, and the mighty," could become heroes. The world may be "a vale of tears, of horrid sufferings, of incommensurateness, of tortuous and humiliating daily pettiness, of sickness and death, a place . . . where man could expect nothing, achieve nothing for himself. Little did it matter, because it served God and so would serve the servant of God."

Life is a gift from God that places on the individual the obligation to return the gift lovingly by the acceptance of death. *Death ultimately is the proof that no matter what powers we as humans have or develop, we still are not God.* As indicated above, the meaning of "is good" is "ought to exist." Death reminds us that we are good, but not absolutely so. Death does not mean that life is without meaning; indeed death gives meaning to our lives because it is that by which we understand the importance of what we do and that by which we render homage to God, the task for which we were born.

■ ■ ■

Summary and Conclusion

The North American death system is shaped by the assumption that each of us is unique and that we have control over the forces of nature; and is shaped also by our limited exposure to death. Consequently, we live in a culture that easily ignores death. The great American dream is that everything is subject to our manipulation—give us enough money and we can solve any problem—yet death is a slap in the face of that dream. Our brief analysis of the death system teaches us that even if we block it from consciousness we live with and are shaped by the reality of death—the knowledge that death is the destruction of personal identity as we know it, and important relationships as they are presently lived.

We have learned from care of the dying and the bereaved that a person is not simply an independent entity. The person is a network of relationships that are as real and as important as the relationship one has to one's own body. The (still debatable) experience of clinical immortality is consistent with the teachings of the great philosophers from Plato to the present about the immateriality of the human person and the ability of the human person to transcend the limits of material existence.

Becker has shown us that violence is rooted in the loss of meaning in life; persons insecure about death, without faith or any other reason to feel confident in the world, will act violently in the hope that, by proving control over their neighbors, they will have proved that they have power over their own lives. Becker's understanding of heroism underlines the fact that our destiny is not a merely physical one. Persons are capable of doing something within their limits and leaving the world a better place than it was.

The death-awareness movement that began in the 1950s has put great emphasis on the fact that persons are unique, that they are interrelated, and that material things will not give meaning to life. In forty years the death-awareness movement has become an established part of our culture. The fact that it has been a success indicates that the movement is consistent with basic human understanding. While the movement is broader than Christianity, most of the key figures have been deeply religious persons, if not when they began work with the dying and the bereaved, then as a consequence. The movement has proven again that the human quest is a quest for meaning. It is consistent with the *fides quaerens intellectum* (faith seeking understanding) of Saint Anselm and with the lament of Saint Augustine that our hearts are restless until they rest in God.

■ ■ ■

Notes

1. R. Kastenbaum and R. Aisenberg, *The Psychology of Death* (New York, 1972), 191–92.
2. Ibid., 193.
3. P. Ariès, *The Hour of Our Death* (New York, 1981).
4. A.Weisman, "An Appropriate Death," in R. Fulton et al., eds., *Death and Dying: Challenge and Change* (Reading, 1978).
5. D. A. E. Shephard, "Principles and Practice in Palliative Care," in M. A. and J. D. Morgan, eds., *Thanatology: A Liberal Arts Approach* (London, Canada, 1977).
6. R. A. Moody, *Life After Life* (New York, 1976).

■ ■ ■

Further Reading

P. Ariès, *Western Attitudes Toward Death: From the Middle Ages to the Present* (Baltimore, 1974).

C. A. and D. M. Corr, *Hospice Care: Principles and Practice* (New York, 1983).

K. Doka and J. D. Morgan, eds., *Death and Spirituality* (Amityville, 1992).

J. D. Morgan, ed., *Personal Care in an Impersonal World* (Amityville, 1993).

C. M. Parkes and R. S. Weiss, *Recovery from Bereavement* (New York, 1983).

INDEX

A

Abraham's life, Kierkegaard's view of, 219, 229–30
Adeodatus, son of Saint Augustine, 91
  baptism of, 92
  death of, 92
Aesthetic stage of reality, Kierkegaard's, 224–27, 239–42
Algren, Nelson, relationship of Simone de Beauvoir and, 539
Allen, Prudence, analysis of Edith Stein by, 399–404, 419–32
Ambrose as influence on Saint Augustine, 91
America, impact for Marx of discovery of, 263–64
Anscombe, Elizabeth, Wittgenstein's view of religion described by, 463
Apology for Raimond of Sebonde (Montaigne), 172, 177

Apostolic Letter on the Dignity and Vocation of Woman (John Paul II), 429
Aquinas, Thomas, 47, 119–46
  agent intellect in the soul for, 87
  birth of, 121
  body as essential for, 129
  contrast of views of Plato, Aristotle, Democritus, and Augustine and, 130–31, 143–44
  corporeal phantasms for, 127–28
  education of, 121–22
  faith and truth for, 134, 144–45
  individuals differentiated by matter, not form, for, 431n.1
  intellect for, 126–27, 130, 132–34, 136–38, 141, 145–46, 178
  knowledge for, 127–29, 134, 138–40, 145–46
  knowledge of objects outside the mind for, 132–33, 141–42

religious critique of, 144–45, 327

self-knowledge for, 142–43

senses for, 130–31, 139–41

sensible forms for, 130–31

similarities and differences in views of Wittgenstein and, 462–63

species for, 132–33, 138, 141–42, 406

Stein's work in integrating thought of Husserl with, 400

synthesis of previous philosophers' teachings by, 135, 143

teaching positions of, 122

view of mind of, 142–43

view of soul of, 125–29, 135–38, 143, 145, 420–21

women as imperfectly reflecting image of God for, 411–12, 429

works of, 122–23, 125–34, 143

Arabic numeral system, revival and impact of, 169

Ariès, Philippe, our age characterized as "death-denying" by, 600–601

Aristotle, 46, 49–87

accident category for, 70, 108

action category for, 70

actual, potential, and intellectual knowledge for, 66–67, 76, 81–84, 132, 139–40

birth of, 51

categories of, 69–70, 72

causes for, 60, 71–74, 81–82

comparison of views of Augustine and, 108

comparison of views of Plato and, 86

contrast of views of Thomas Aquinas and, 131–32, 143

Copernican Revolution's impact on reputation of, 168–69

death of, 51

as first great scientist, 52

form of men and women for, 431n.1

forms of sense for, 59–63, 65–66, 71–72, 74–75, 78–80, 82, 131–32, 140

habit category for, 70

influence of, 85–87

natural bodies for, 57, 74–75, 141

organs for, 57–58

ousia (being-ness) category for, 69

parts of a body for, 58–60

passion category for, 70

phantasms for, 137

in Plato's Academy, 51

positioning category for, 70

power of self-nutrition for, 59

predicables (genus, species, difference, property, accident) for, 70–72, 74–75, 140

principles for, 60

quantity versus quality category for, 70

relations category for, 70

sensation for, 59–60, 77–81, 84

similarities and differences in views of Wittgenstein and, 462–63

spirituality of the tablet for, 82–83

substance category for, 69

theory of "sex polarity" of, 423, 425

view of mind of, 65–67, 75, 81–82

view of soul of, 52–60, 63–65, 67, 69, 73–77, 135, 137

works of, 55–67

Asclepius (god of healing),
  Socrates' debt to, 27, 45
Augustine, 89–117
  agent intellect as separate
    spiritual being for, 87
  autobiographical writings of,
    110–11
  baptism of, 91–92
  birth of, 91
  as bishop of Hippo, 92
  cause of evil for, 103–6, 113
  comparison of views of
    Aristotle and, 108
  contrast of views of Thomas
    Aquinas and, 143
  death of, 92
  education of, 91
  free will for, 98–99, 104–6,
    111–16
  human person as relational
    being in I-Thou relation-
    ships for, 109–10
  as Manichee, 91
  miracle causing conversion of,
    102–3, 112
  mistresses and sexual sins of,
    91, 92, 97–103, 111–12
  nature of the human mind for,
    108
  personality according to, 110,
    113
  relationship of God the
    Father, Son, and Holy Spirit
    for, 95–96, 108
  substance and accident of
    Aristotle for, 108
  theory of sex complementar-
    ity of, 424, 428, 431n.7
  view of mind of, 100–101
  view of soul of, 96
  works of, 92, 95–106

B
Becker, Ernest, 581–82, 587–613
  anxiety about death for,
    590–91
  birth of, 581
  death of, 582
  distinction of humans from
    animals for, 591–93
  heroism for, 587, 609–11
  human existential dilemma
    for, 591–95
  individuality within finitude
    for, 592
  religion for, 610–11
  responses to fact of death for,
    587–91, 609–11
  sexuality for, 594–95
  view of violence of, 606
  violence for, 605–7, 611
  "vital lie" for, 609
  works of, 581, 587–95
Beeckman, Isaac, applications of
  mathematics discussed by
  Descartes and, 150
Behavior of Organisms, The
  (Skinner), 470
Behaviorism
  founded by J. B. Watson and
    B. F. Skinner, 469
  uses of, 503
Being and Nothingness (Sartre),
  507
Bentham, Jeremy, as utilitarian,
  371
Bereavement literature, 603–4
Bergson, Henri, methodological
  principles of, 210
Berkeley, George
  as bishop, 186
  empiricist method of, 187, 188
Beyond Freedom and Dignity
  (Skinner), 470
  selections from, 473–74, 481,
    483

Beyond the Pleasure Principle (Freud), 369

Birth and Death of Meaning, The (Becker), 581

Bloom, Anthony, relationship of personal identity with others of, 209

Blue and Brown Books, The (Wittgenstein), 437

Bost, J. L., relationship of Simone de Beauvoir and, 539

Bourgeoisie
battles with proletariat and foreign bourgeoisies of, 272–73
class division between proletariat and, 284
continued existence of, 265–66, 275–76
defined, 284
developed from feudal society, 263–64
as generating proletariat, 268–69, 292
impact on nationalism of products, cities, and populations of, 265–67

Bourke, V. J., view of free choice described by Saint Augustine for, 110–11

Brown, Hunter
analysis of David Hume by, 185–90, 203–11
analysis of William James by, 297–303, 319–30

Buber, Martin, relationship of personal identity with others of, 209

C

Camus, Albert, relationship with Sartre and de Beauvoir of, 539–40

Capital (Marx), 255–56
commentary on, 280–81
selection from, 260–61

Capitalism
evolution from feudalism of, 284–85
evolution of communism from, 285–86
Marx's critique of, 255, 284–86, 289

Cartesianism
impact on modern view of afterlife of, 464
Wittgenstein's dismantling of, 440, 458–62, 465

Cebes, dialogue with Socrates of, 11–12, 15–18, 19–26, 38–39, 43–44

Cérémonie des adieux, La (de Beauvoir), 541

Chomsky, Noam, language acquisition not explained by operant conditioning according to, 499, 503

Christian philosophers, challenges to today's, 326

Christianity
coming to the conflicted self, 234
Kierkegaard's drive to restore stature among intellectuals of, 216, 221, 248
Nietzsche's concept of the anti-life force of, 359–61, 362

Christina, Queen of Sweden, as student of Descartes, 152–53

Cities and concentrated populations created by the bourgeoisie for Marx, 267

City of God, The (Augustine), 92
selection from, 103–6

Civilization and Its Discontents (Freud), 369, 370–71
commentary on, 385–95

questions about, 373
selection from, 375–83
Clark, M. T., lack of under-
standing of freedom by
Greeks according to, 115
Climacus, Johannes
(Kierkegaard), 238, 242–43,
244–45
"Clinical" immortality, 604–5
Cogito, ergo sum (I think, there-
fore I am) as starting point,
553
for Descartes, 156–57, 172–73
for existentialists, 511, 518
Commentary on I Corinthians
(Thomas Aquinas), 465
Communism, evolution from
capitalism of, 285
Communist Manifesto, The
(Marx), 255–56
commentary on, 280, 283–89
selection from, 262–76
Complete Treatise on Theology, A
(Summa Theologiae) (Thomas
Aquinas), 122, 125–34, 143
Concluding Unscientific Postscript
to the Philosophical Fragments
(Kierkegaard),
selection from, 222
Confessions, The (Augustine), 92
commentary on, 110–11
selection from, 97–103
Contingencies of Reinforcement
(Skinner), 470
Copernican Revolution, 167–71
Copernicus, Nicholas, theory of
Sun at center of heavens by,
168
Critique of Dialectical
Materialism, The (Sartre), 507
Crito at death of Socrates, 26–28

D
Darwin, Charles, Freud's theories reflecting evolutionary
theory of, 370
De Beauvoir, Simone, 535–75
authenticity for, 563–65, 569,
575
Bad Faith for, 550–53, 555–56,
562, 563, 566
birth of, 537
death of, 541
education of, 537–38
as foundress of women's
studies, 422, 561
freedom for, 563
humans as subjects for, 562
impact of education on
women for, 553–56
Mitsein (co-existence with
subjects) for, 546, 565–66,
570
personal responsibility for,
570–71
as philosopher, 542–43,
561–66
philosophical critique of,
567–69
politics of, 539–41, 571–72
present feminine situation for,
545–50, 563–64, 567, 574–75
proposals for a new ethics of,
564–66
relationship with feminism of,
567–69
relationship with Sartre of,
538–39, 540–41, 543
religious critique of, 569–73
subjective freedom expressed
by boys for, 553–54
transvaluation of values
called for by, 555, 564, 568
view of soul of, 570
women treated as objects
(Others) for, 548–53

works of, 538–42, 545–59, 572
Death
  cultural orientation toward,
    599–600
  defining, 599
  exposure to, 599–600
  history of our ideas toward,
    601–2
  meaning in our lives of, 598
  philosophers' concern with,
    583–613
  as proof we are not God,
    610–11
Death-awareness movement,
  603, 612
Death system, 599, 602, 611
Democritus
  knowledge for, 131–32
  likenesses of things in the
    mind according to, 140–41
Denial of Death, The (Becker)
  Pulitzer Prize awarded to, 581
  selection from, 587–95
  theme of, 609
Descartes, René, 147–81
  army service of, 150
  assumption of a thinking
    "subject" by, 353
  background of philosophy of,
    167–74
  birth of, 149
  comparison of animals and
    man by, 163–64, 177
  death of, 153
  education of, 149–50
  existence of God for, 157–61,
    173–75
  foundation for science of, 152,
    207
  immortality for, 173
  independence from tradition
    in philosophical reflection
    of, 206–7

knowledge of objects outside
    the mind for, 141–42
  mind independence from
    body (mind/body problem)
    for, 162–63, 177–78
  nature of God for, 160–61, 175
  philosophical and religious
    critique of, 180–83
  robots anticipated by, 162–63,
    176–77
  skepticism refuted by, 151,
    176
  theological considerations of,
    186
  truth for, 156–57
  universal methodological
    doubt at beginning of sys-
    tem of, 155–57, 171–72
  view of soul of, 164–65, 173,
    177–78
  Wittgenstein's dismantling of
    dualisms of, 440, 458–62,
    465
  works of, 150–52, 155–67
Dialogues of Plato, Socratic, 4
Dialogues on Natural Religion
  (Hume), 185
Discourse on Method (Descartes),
  151
  commentary on, 167–78
  selection from, 155–65
  steps of philosophy in, 178–79
"Don Juanism," 242
Dupré, Louis, critique of
  Communist Manifesto by, 280

E
Echecrates, questions about
  delay in Socrates' death by,
  5, 9
*Economic and Philosophical
  Manuscripts, The* (Marx), 255
Economics as a practical sci-
  ence, 52

Ego and the Id, The (Freud), 369
Eighteenth Brumaire of Louis Bonaparte, The (Marx), 255
Either/Or (Kierkegaard), 219
  selection from, 224–29
El–Kaim, Arlette, Sartre's proposal to, 540
Elizabeth, Princess of Bohemia, as Descartes' student, 152, 178
Empathy, Stein's view of women's tendency toward, 421
Empiricist method
  of Berkeley and Locke, 187
  of Freud, 370
  of Hume, 187, 188–89
Engels, Frederick
  friendship of Karl Marx and, 254
  scientific socialism of, 253
  on side of proletariat, 286
Enquiry Concerning Human Understanding, An (Hume), 185
Epicurus, free choice confused with spontaneity by, 115
Escape from Evil (Becker), 581
Essays Moral and Political (Hume), 185
Ethical stage of reality, Kierkegaard's, 227–29, 239, 242–44
Ethics as a practical science, 52
"Ethos of Women's Vocations, The" (Stein), 400
Existentialism
  charges brought against, 511–12, 518, 523–26
  definition of, 508, 512
  difference between theism and, 523
  starting point of, 516
  view of man and woman as self-defining individuals in, 426
Existentialism (Sartre), 507
  commentary on, 523–32
  questions about, 508–9
  selection from, 511–21

F
Fallibilism of James, 301
[Fear and Trembling and] *The Sickness unto Death* (Kierkegaard), 242
  selection from, 223–24
Feminine Mystique, The (Friedan), 561
Feudalism, evolution of capitalist society from, 262–68, 284–85
Feuerbach, Ludwig, projectionist critique of religion by, 392
Fideism, 170
Finite and Eternal Being (Stein), 401
FitzGerald, Desmond J., analysis of René Descartes by, 149–54, 167–81
Forms of Socrates, 34, 36
  as first principles versus causes, 42
Francis of Assisi, Nietzsche's opinion of, 249
Freedom
  for de Beauvoir, 563
  denial of, by Skinner, 470
  downplayed by Marx, 291–92
  Greek's lack of understanding of, 115
  philosophers' view of humans', *xviii*
  Sartre's view of human being as, 505–36
  as underived for James, 325

of willingness, 531–34

Frege, Gottlob, Wittgenstein's contacts with, 436

Freud, Sigmund, 367–95
beauty for, 382
birth of, 369
death of, 369
displacements of libido for, 379–81
drive of the libido for, 370, 385–88
dualism of body and soul for, 389
influences on theories of, 370–71
Kierkegaard's anticipation of concept of the unconscious of, 248
love for, 381–82
as moralist, 372, 388
philosophical and religious critique of, 393–95
reality principle of, 389–90
religion for, 375, 386, 389, 391–92, 494
repression of memories for, 370
tripartite theory of personality (id, ego, and superego) of, 370, 390
view of happiness (pleasure principle) of, 376–78, 380–83, 385–89, 393
works of, 369, 375–83

Friedan, Betty, influence of de Beauvoir on, 561, 568

Fromm, Eric, contradiction of worth of people's bodies and symbolic worth for, 593

"Function of Woman in National Life, The" (Stein), 400

Future of an Illusion, The (Freud), 369

G

Galileo, Descartes' concern about condemnation of, 151

Genesis
human form of creation singled out in, 328
vision of man as image of God in, 573

Geometry (Euclid) as model of scientific procedure, 170, 179

German Ideology, The (Marx), 255–56
commentary on, 280
selection from, 268

Gilson, Etienne, Descartes' argument for God analyzed by, 174, 180

Grundrisse (Marx), 255
commentary on, 278–79
selection from, 258–59

H

Haldane, John J., analysis of Ludwig Wittgenstein by, 435–42, 457–66

Harmony
according to Aristotle, 63, 79
according to Socrates, 17–19

Hedonism, 371, 393

Hegel, Georg
Divine without humanity for, 291
Marx's training in, 254, 292
understanding of reality through reason sought by, 217
view of state of, 278

Heisenberg's uncertainty principle, 495–96

Henry, P., Augustine as founder of study of the person for, 107

Heroism as response to fact of death, 609–11

Hildegard of Bingen, sex complementarity defended by, 424

Hobbes, Thomas
nature of person as violent and self-seeking for, 605
view of life of, 601

Homilies on the Book of Genesis (John Paul II), 429

Hospice movement, 603

Houser, R. E.
analysis of Aristotle by, 51–54, 69–87
analysis of Plato by, 3–8, 29–47

Hudecki, Dennis L., analysis of Søren Kierkegaard by, 215–20, 235–49

Hudson, Deal W., analysis of Sigmund Freud by, 369–75, 385–95

Human person, monistic and dualistic views of
scriptural portrayal of, 328
today, 326–29

Hume, David, 183–211
birth of, 185
causation for, 200
change for, 195–97
death of, 185
empiricist method of truth seeking of, 187, 203
identity and diversity for, 193, 204–5
James' critique of, 208–9
memory for, 199–201, 206, 209
objects as succession of parts for, 195–96, 201
philosophical critique of, 206–9
philosophical importance of, 186–91, 206–7

relationship of James' philosophy to, 321–22
religious critique of, 209–10
resemblance for, 199–200
skepticism of, 181
view of mind of, 193, 200
view of personal identity (selfhood) of, 186, 188–89, 191–93, 198–201, 204–7
view of soul of, 200, 322
works of, 185

Husserl, Edmund
phenomenological method of, 399, 410
Stein's work with, 400

I

Images of ourselves, *xviii*

Index of Prohibited Books
two of de Beauvoir's works on, 569
Unamuno's work on, 581

Industrial Revolution, 253, 279, 291

Intentional language, Skinner's call to eliminate, 497

Interpretation of Dreams, The (Freud), 369

Introductory Lectures on Psycho-Analysis (Freud), 369

Isocrates, view of philosophy of, 43–44

J

James, Henry, as brother of William James, 297

James, William, 295–330
abstractions blended with reality in philosophy for, 302–3, 309
birth of, 297
critique of Hume by, 208–9
death for, 588–59

death of, 299
education of, 298
Empirical Self for, 305
free will for, 314–15
freedom as underived for, 325
good for, 598
knowledge for, 301
marriage and family life of, 298
Material Self for, 306–7, 320
methodological principles of work of, 210
phenomenon of effort for, ethical importance of, 316–17
philosophical and religious critique of, 325–29
Pure Ego for, 306, 311, 320
religion for, 317
Social Self for, 306, 307–8, 320
Spiritual Self for, 306, 308–11, 321
Thought for, 313–14, 322–24
truth for, 300–302
view of personal identity of, 311–14
view of soul of, 310
works of, 298–99, 305–17
Jesus
Nietzsche's opinion of, 349
as refusing to punish, 485–86
Jewish Scriptures, condemnation of pursuit of self apart from relations with God and fellow creatures in, 209
John Paul II
agreement with much of Marx's view of labor of, 288–89
Benedicta of the Cross (Edith Stein) declared "Blessed" by, 402
trinitarian model of imaging the Trinity discussed by, 429

Journals of Kierkegaard, The (Kierkegaard), selections from, 221–22, 234

K
Kant, Immanuel
basis of morality for, 385
desire for happiness for, 387
evaluation of Descartes' metaphysical arguments by, 181
theological considerations of, 186
Kantian Philosophy, James' view of, 313
Kastenbaum, Robert, death system noted by, 599
Kennedy, Leonard A.
analysis of Jean-Paul Sartre by, 507–9, 523–34
analysis of Saint Augustine by, 91–93, 107–17
analysis of Saint Thomas Aquinas by, 121–23, 135–46
Kierkegaard, Søren, 213–49
anxiety for, 238–39
birth of, 215
boredom for, 224–26
depression of, 215
despair for, 223–24, 238–39
difference between ethics and religion for, 219–20, 229–31
engagement of, 215–16
Error and Sin for, 246–47
eternal versus infinite versus universal for, 236–37, 247
existence, aesthetic, ethical, and religiousness stages of human, 218, 222, 224–33, 237, 239–47
as existentialist, 243
friendship for, 226–27
goal as a writer of, 216–17
good for, 609

marriage for aesthete
described by, 227
paradox of faith for, 230–31
philosophical critique of,
247–48
religion for, 216–17, 231–33,
244–47
religious critique of, 248
remembering and forgetting
change for, 226
self for, 235–38, 248
Socrates an intellectual hero
for, 236
style of, 217–18
Truth for, 231–33
view of soul for, 237
Kosakievicz, Olga, relationship
with Sartre and de Beauvoir
of, 539

L
La longue marche (de Beauvoir),
540
La Mettrie, Julien, mind/body
problem addressed by, 178
La Vieillesse (de Beauvoir), 541
Laborem Exercens (John Paul II),
288–89
L'Amérique au jour le jour (de
Beauvoir), 540
Landulf of Aquino (father of
Saint Thomas Aquinas), 121
Langan, Janine D., analysis of
De Beauvoir by, 537–44,
561–75
Law of Effect, 478
Laws (Plato), 5
Lettres au Castor (de Beauvoir),
539
Life expectancies through the
ages, 599–600
L'Invitée (de Beauvoir), 539
Litany of the Saints, 601

*Literary Remains of the Late
Henry James, The* (James),
298
Locke, John
accountability for one's deeds
as issue of, 210
Cartesianism of, 440, 462
empiricist method of, 187–88
theological considerations of,
186
Logic as invented by Aristotle,
52
Lombard, Peter, textbook of theology by, 122
Luke, doctrine of absolute duty
toward God in, 229–30

M
Malraux, André, view of death
of, 598
Man, a Machine (La Mettrie), 180
Mandarins, The (de Beauvoir),
on *Index of Prohibited Books*,
569
Manifeste des 343, de Beauvoir's
signing of, 541
Marcuse, Herbert, liberation of
pleasure principle advo-
cated by, 372
Mark, Elaine, analysis of aesthetics of de Beauvoir's
works by, 571
Marx, Karl, 251–93
alienation for, 281–82, 285, 291
birth of, 253
bourgeois man for, 257–58,
284
capital as social issue for,
284–85
division of labor for, 283–84
education of, 254
fixed and relative drives for,
280
goal of history for, 258

human community for,
258–59, 278–79, 287–88
human freedom downplayed
by, 291–92
human person as worker for,
256, 260–61, 280–81, 288–91
marriage and family life of,
254
materialist conception of
human history for, 283–87
political power for, 276
religion for, 256, 261–62,
281–82, 285, 291, 392
strengths in position of,
287–79
surplus value as leading to
living labor serving dead
labor for, 284, 289
weaknesses in position of,
280–92
works of, 255, 257–76
Mathematicism, 180
Matriarchy for de Beauvoir,
548–49
Meaning of Truth, The (James),
299
Meditations on First Philosophy
(Descartes), 151, 175
Melzak-Wall "gate control" theory of pain, 603
Mersenne, Marin, publication of
Descartes' work arranged
by, 151
Merton, Thomas
relationship of personal identity with others of, 209
spirituality of, 300
Metaphysics (Aristotle), 52,
431n.1
Middle class, disappearance
into proletariat of, 270–71,
273

Mill, John Stuart
parallel between Freud and,
393–94
as utilitarian, 371
Mind
view of Aquinas of, 142–43
view of Aristotle of, 65–67, 75,
81–82
view of Augustine of, 100–101
view of Hume of, 193, 200
view of Socrates of, 20–22
Misologists (haters of arguments), 18
Monde, Le (The World)
(Descartes), 150–51
Montaigne, Michel de
skepticism of, 169–70
view of intelligence of animals of, 177
Morgan, John D., analysis of
Miguel de Unamuno y Jugo
and Ernest Becker by,
579–82, 597–613
Mortality, philosophers stress-
ing the importance of recognizing our, 580
Mother Goddess, 549

N
Nausea (Sartre), 507
Near-death experiences, 604–5
Neo-Scholaticism, Stein's development of, 400
Nicomachean Ethics (Aristotle),
52
Nietzsche, Friedrich, 331–65
birth of, 333
consciousness for, 339–40, 351,
353–55
death of, 334
education of, 333–34
friendship for, 361
human body for, 353
knowledge for, 337–39, 355

measurement of power for, 345, 357, 364

overman *(übermensch)* or superman of, 345–46, 357–58, 364, 365n.3

personal growth for, 356

perspectivism of, 338, 351, 361

philosophical and religious critique of, 361–65

physical reality for, 338–42, 352

religion for, 346–50 , 352, 358–63, 392

Schopenhauer's vision in writings of, 334

self-consciousness for, 355

will to power for, 352, 356, 362, 370–71

works of, 334, 337–50

O

Olsen, Regina, engagement of Kierkegaard to, 215–16

On Soul (Aristotle)
  commentary on, 69–84
  selection from, 55–67
  structure of, 52–53

On the Jewish Question (Marx), 255
  commentary on, 277–78
  selection from, 257–58

On the Trinity (Augustine), 92
  selection from, 95–97

Ontological argument for God's existence, 175

Ousia (being-ness), 69

P

Pain, theories of, 603

Pascal, Blaise, madness of man for, 593–94

Passions of the Soul (Descartes), 152

Paul
  Nietzsche's blame for counterfeits of true Christianity placed on, 346
  spiritual and fleshly forces noted by, 328

Pericles, use of philosophy by, 3

Phaedo (Plato), 4
  commentary on, 29–47
  introduction to, 5–7
  questions about, 7–8
  selection from, 9–28
  structure of, 6–7

Phenomenology
  integration of scholasticism with, 400
  reconciliation of Thomism with, 399
  Stein's ontological basis for, 410, 413, 420

Philosophers' views of the human person
  as a besouled body (Aristotle), 49–87
  as co-existent (De Beauvoir), 535–75
  as a collision of opposites (Kierkegaard), 213–49
  as a construct (Hume), 183–211
  as a dualism (Descartes), 147–81
  as elusive (James), 295–330
  as embodied spirit (Saint Thomas Aquinas), 119–46
  as freedom (Sartre), 505–36
  as linguistic animal (Wittgenstein), 433–66
  as male and female (Stein), 397–432
  as mortal (Unamuno and Becker), 577–613
  as necessitated (Skinner), 467–504

as relational and volitional (Saint Augustine), 89–117
as sexual (Freud), 367–95
as spirit (Plato), 1–48
as will to power (Nietzsche), 331–65
as worker (Marx), 251–93
Philosophical anthropology, Stein's, 407, 420
Philosophical behaviorism, 460–61, 465
Philosophical Fragments, or a Fragment of Philosophy (Kierkegaard), 245
selection from, 231–33
Philosophical Investigations (Wittgenstein), 437, 442
selection from, 443–52
Philosophy
decline of theological center of gravity for, 186
as defined by Cicero, 585–86
materialistic schools of, 85
as product of humanity of each philosopher, 584
source of term, 3
Physics (Aristotle), 52
Plato, 1–48, 115. *See also* Socrates
Academy (school) founded by, 4
achievements in the *Phaedo* of, 46
assumption of a thinking "subject" by, 353
comparison of views of Aristotle and, 86
contrast of views of Thomas Aquinas and, 130–31, 143
critique by Aristotle of, 52
knowledge of natures in physical world for, 130, 140–41
legacy to philosophy of, 47
theory of sex unity of, 423

two worlds of, 139–40
view of self of, 248
view of the soul-body relation of, 74, 135, 137, 237–38, 423
works of, 4–28
Plotinus, 115
assessment of Plato's arguments by, 46–47
revival of Aristotle's thought by, 85–86
Pluralistic Universe, A (James), 298
Politics (Aristotle), 52
Politics as a practical science, 52
Ponty, Merleau, Zaza's love affair with, 538
Poverty of Philosophy, The (Marx), 255
Pragmatism (James), 298
Pragmatism of James defined, 299
Pre-Socratics, philosophy of sex identity of, 423
Prejudice resulting in violence for Becker, 606–7
Prime of Life, The (de Beauvoir), 572
Principles of Philosophy (Descartes), 152
Principles of Psychology (James), 298, 299
selections from, 305–17
"Problems of Women's Education" (Stein), 400–401
commentary on, 419–31
questions about, 402–3
selection from, 405–17
Projectionist critique of religion, 392
Proletariat
class division between bourgeoisie and, 284
defined, 284

development and growth of, 275, 286

differences of age and sex lacking in work of, 270

as extension of machines, 269–70

future political supremacy of, 276

as generated by the bourgeoisie, 268–69, 273, 292

status of, 274

trade unions formed by, 272, 286

Przywara, Erich, work of Stein with, 400

Psychoanalysis, Freud as founder of school of psychiatry called, 369

Psychology: Briefer Course (James), 299

selections from, 305–17

Ptolemy, Claudius, Earth as center of the heavens for, 167–68

Purity of Heart (Kierkegaard), 242

Putnam, Hilary, advocacy of intentional language of, 497

R

Reincarnation myth described by Socrates, 16

Religion

for Becker, 610–11

for Freud, 375, 386, 389, 391–92, 494

for James, 317

for Kierkegaard, 216–17, 231–33, 244–47

for Marx, 256, 261–62, 281–82, 285, 291, 392

for Nietzsche, 346–50 , 352, 358–63, 392

for Skinner, 494

for Unamuno, 580–81

projectionist critique of, 392

Remarks on the Philosophy of Psychology (Wittgenstein), 437, 442

selection from, 452–55

Republic (Plato), 4

Rolland, Romain, objection to Freud's treatment of religion by, 389–91

Rousseau, Jean-Jacques, belief in person's intrinsic good by, 605–6

Russell, Bertrand, Wittgenstein's studies with, 436

Ryan, Michael T., analysis of Karl Marx by, 253–56, 277–93

S

Sages, Greeks regarded as, 3

Sang des autres, Le (de Beauvoir), 540

Sartre, Jean-Paul, 505–36, 608

atheism for, 508, 513, 523–24, 533

birth of, 507

de Beauvoir's relationship with, 538–39, 540–41, 543

death of, 507

education of, 507

essence as an atheist's freedom for, 516, 524–27, 529–32

fear of commitment stemming from idea of freedom of, 533

goodness of choices for, 520–21, 525–26

moral values not a given for, 523, 527–29

philosophical critique of, 528–29

religious critique of, 533–34

responsibility for choices for, 514–15, 524–25, 526, 529

works of, 507–8

Saunders, Cecily, "total pain" of the dying described by, 603

Scheler, Max

    intuition of death described by, 589

    Stein's study with, 400

Schopenhauer, Arthur

    Freud's theories reflecting pessimism of, 370

    Nietzsche's writings a reflection of vision of, 334

Science, advancement during early nineteenth century of, 216–17

Science and Human Behavior (Skinner), 470

    selections from, 474–81, 482–83

Science of the Cross, The (Stein), 401

Scientific socialism, 253, 287

Scotus, Duns, form of woman for, 420, 431n.1

Second Sex, The (de Beauvoir), 538, 539, 542

    commentary on, 561–67, 573

    on *Index of Prohibited Books*, 569

    selection from, 545–46

Serf, status of, 265, 275

Sex identity, theories of, 423–27

Sickness unto Death, The (Kierkegaard), selection from, 229–31

Simmias

    analysis of doctrine of recollection by, 12–15

    conception of the soul disputed by, 17, 25, 37–38

    Socrates' response to arguments of, 18–19, 39–40

Sisyphys, analogy between existential freedom and plight of, 530–31

Six Meditations (Descartes), 172

Skepticism

    Descartes' refutation of, 151, 176

    of Hume, 181

    of Montaigne, 169–70

    revival in Descartes' time of, 167

Skinner, B. F., 467–504

    animals as continuous with humans for, 499, 501

    birth of, 469

    causal chain of behavior for, 474, 476–83, 492, 495–98, 501

    contingencies of reinforcement for, 493

    death of, 470

    denial of human freedom by, 470

    designing a culture for, 482

    education of, 469–70

    elimination of intentional language advocated by, 481, 497

    "final causes" for, 496

    freedom required for determinism of, 500, 503

    language learning for, 499

    operant conditioning for, 474–75, 490–93, 498, 500

    philosophical and religious critique of, 494–501

    reinforcements (positive and negative) for, 487–88, 491, 495

    religion for, 494

    respondent conditioning for, 490

    revision of social institutions and modes of thought

required by system of, 494–95
school of Behaviorism founded by, 469
scientific method of, 485, 489, 492, 497, 502–3
as a utopian social theorist, 493–94
works of, 470, 473–88
Snyder, John J., analysis of Friedrich Nietzsche by, 333–35, 351–67
"Social contract" theory, 606
Socrates. *See also* Plato
called a philosopher by Isocrates, 3
children of, 26
cosmic myth by, 26, 44
counterarguments by Simmias and Cebes to, 17–19, 37–40
death of, in *Phaedo,* 5, 9–10, 26–28, 44–45
equality for, 13–15, 33–34
forms for, 34, 36, 42
knowledge as recollection for, 12–15, 32–35
proof of immortality of the soul by, 22–25
reincarnation myth for, 16, 37
speech about death of, 10–11, 30–31
trial of, 4
view of mind of, 20–22
view of self of, 248
view of the soul of, 11–12, 15–16, 24–25, 31–32, 35–37, 43–46, 223
wisdom defined by, 3–4
wonder (about doctrine of causality) of, 19–22, 40–42
Socratic principle, 233
Sophists, 3
rhetoric and, 52

Socrates' attack on, 4
Soul
of Metaphysics, 313
philosophers' view of human, *xvii–xviii*
view of Aristotle of, 52–60, 63–65, 67, 73–77, 135, 137
view of Augustine of, 96
view of de Beauvoir of, 570
view of Descartes of, 164–65, 173, 177–78
view of Hume of, 200, 322
view of James of, 310
view of Plato of, 74, 135, 137
view of Socrates of, 11–12, 15–16, 24–25, 31–32, 35–37, 43–46, 223
view of Stein of, 413, 420–21
view of Thomas Aquinas of, 125–29, 135–38, 143, 145
view of Wittgenstein of, 451–54, 459–60, 462
Spinoza, Benedict, philosophy of despair in, 585–86
Spirituality, quest for meaning in, 607–8
Stein, Edith (Teresa Benedicta of the Cross), 397–432
birth of, 399
conversion to Roman Catholicism of, 399, 400
death of, 399, 402
declared "Blessed" by John Paul II, 402
differences between men and women for, 421–22, 424, 426
education of, 399–400
experimental-psychological method relating to natural sciences of, 407–8
focus of philosophy of, 419
humanistic psychology relating to liberal arts method of, 408–9

imaging the Trinity for, 429–30

importance of education for, 405–7, 430–31

individuality for, 421

methodology of, 407–16, 419

as novitiate, 401

philosophical critique of, 422–28

philosophical importance of, 399

philosophical method of, 409–11, 415–16

relation of soul and body for, 420–21

religious critique of, 428–30

species for, 402, 406, 413–14, 416–17, 420, 422, 424

theological method of, 411–12, 415–16

view of soul of, 413, 416, 420–21

works of, 400–401, 405–17

Structure of Evil, The (Becker), 581

Substance underlying physical realities for empiricist method, 187–88

Summa Contra Gentiles (Thomas Aquinas), 122

Summa Theologiae (A Complete Treatise on Theology) (Thomas Aquinas), 122

commentary on, 135–43

selection from, 125–34

Symposium (Plato), 4

T

Taylor, Charles, Marx's philosophy as one of liberation according to, 281

Teleology in human behavior, Skinner's attempt to eliminate, 497–98

"Texts on Writing" (de Beauvoir), 542

selection from, 558–59

Theseus myth

analogy of Socrates' death with, 5–6, 9–10

analysis of, 29–30

Thus Spake Zarathustra (Nietzsche), 334, 358

Tout compte fait (de Beauvoir), 541

Toward a Critique of Hegel's Philosophy of Right (Marx), 256

commentary on, 281–82

selection from, 261–62

Tractatus Logico– Philosophicus (Wittgenstein), 437

Trade unions, 272, 286

Tragic Sense of Life, The (Unamuno) on *Index of Forbidden Books*, 581

selection from, 583–86

Transcendental Ego, 313, 324

Treatise of Human Nature, A (Hume), 185

commentary on, 203–9

questions about, 189–90

selection from, 191–201

Turing, Alan, response to Descartes' challenge to robots by, 177

Turing Test, 177

U

Unamuno y Jugo, Miguel de, 580–81, 583–86, 597–613

birth of, 580

death of, 580

education of, 580

goodness for, 584

knowledge for, 583–84

religion for, 580–81

works of, 581, 583–86

Une Mort très douce (de Beauvoir), 540–41

Utilitarianism, treatment of happiness in, 371

Utopianism, 371

V

Varieties of Religious Experience (James), 298

Verbal Behavior (Skinner), 470

View of the physical universe as influencing our view toward death, 599–600

Violence, reasons for existence of, 605–7

von Westphalen, Jenny, marriage of Karl Marx and, 254

W

Wagner, Richard, Nietzsche influenced by, 334, 358

Walden Two (Skinner), 470
  selection from, 483–88
  utopian social theory in, 493–94

Watson, J. B., Behaviorism founded by, 470

Wesensanschauung (cognition as intuition), 410

Wild, John, James' rejection of materialism noted by, 324

Will to Believe and Other Essays in Popular Philosophy, The (James), 298

Will to Power (Nietzsche), 334
  commentary on, 351–64
  questions about, 335
  selection from, 337–50

William, Judge (Kierkegaard), 242

Wittgenstein, Ludwig, 433–66
  anti-Cartesianism of, 440,
    458–62, 465
  birth of, 436
  death of, 437
  education of, 436
  "grammatical reminders" of, 440, 457
  language for, 441, 443–45, 447, 449–50
  philosophical critique of, 460–63
  philosophical importance of, 435
  propositions for, 441–42, 457, 459
  religious critique of, 463–65
  self-understanding for, 457–58
  sensations for, 439, 444
  shift in thought of, 442, 457
  thought for, 449, 454
  view of philosophical behaviorism of, 447–48, 451–52, 460–61, 465
  view of soul of, 446, 451–54, 459–60, 462
  way to read, 438–39
  works of, 437, 442, 443–57, 464

Wolf-Devine, Celia, analysis of B. F. Skinner by, 469–71, 489–504

Works of Love (Kierkegaard), 242

X

Xanthippe at death of Socrates, 10

Z

Zaza (Elizabeth Mabille), Simone de Beauvoir's friendship with, 537–38

Zettel (Wittgenstein), 464

Zilboorg, Gregory, death-fear described by, 589–90

CPSIA information can be obtained
at www.ICGtesting.com
Printed in the USA
FSHW021227180720
72242FS